Accidental Enlightenment

THE EXTRAORDINARY TRAVELS OF A MODERN-DAY GULLIVER

Stephen Banick

ONE MAN'S JOURNEY TO SELF-DISCOVERY

IN AN INTENSE, SHRINKING WORLD

ACCIDENTAL ENLIGHTENMENT:
THE EXTRAORDINARY TRAVELS OF A MODERN-DAY GULLIVER
PUBLISHED BY SYNERGY BOOKS
2100 KRAMER LANE, SUITE 300
AUSTIN, TEXAS 78758

For more information about our books, please write to us, call 512.478.2028, or visit our website at www.bookpros.com.

Publisher's Cataloging-in-Publication available upon request.

Library of Congress Control Number: 2006930116

ISBN-10: 1-933538-63-5
ISBN-13: 978-1-933538-63-1

Synergy Books

Preface

This book is about my travels – HOLD ON! DON'T GO AWAY! We're not talking about that ho-hum obligatory evening in the neighbors' family room where you get stuck viewing hours of home videos of themselves waving from the top deck of the Statue of Liberty, themselves posing in front of Honest Abe's Memorial, or themselves (and their grandchildren) eating ice cream at Baskin-Robbins in Bangkok. Rest assured the "stories" in this book are a tad more unusual…

What if you were my silent partner – traveling with me by foot, wing, rudder, and wheel, to all six of the world's inhabited continents (no offense to the penguins and research scientists of Antarctica)? What if we shared some of the weirdest and wildest adventures you or I could possibly imagine?

In recent years I consider myself lucky to have been able to wean myself away from Corporate America to "follow my bliss," in the words of mythologist Joseph Campbell. My academic disciplines (I was trained as an Industrial Engineer and also picked up a Master's Degree in Business Administration) are particularly slanted toward process-centric, rational, optimizing, strategic approaches. That's fair enough – those techniques grease the wheels of commerce and keep shareholders happy. They also put Bordeaux in the cooler and pay for some big time junkets. But for *me*, it was like rigging up a world-class sailboat and having no wind to blow me out of harbor.

Along the way, I've been laid off several times – never with a severance package – changed careers multiple times, changed "significant others," changed regional locations in the U.S., and (as a visitor) even changed countries for awhile.

Once it became evident that I was creating constant change in my life in order to keep it colorful and interesting, I realized I needed company – readers to travel with me to help sort out the messages or clues along the way…or even help me figure out what I'd learned from all of these experiences.

I also realized I'd reached the point where I had to make a decision: would I follow the piper's fife or heed the siren's call, even if it were to lead me into tar pits or piranha-infested waters? In other words, would I live *my* life, or someone else's? I wasn't born to be a nine-to-five guy, so why not finally admit it?

What I really wanted was to continue to enrich my life with diverse experiences of people, cultures, climate and topography, share these experiences through writing and speaking about them, and eventually structure programs that would entice and motivate others to dine at the table of "Trans-cultural Communication."

As I proceeded to collect all the notes from my travel journals in order to start writing this book, it occurred to me that I was, in fact, setting out for another journey that was leading me to equally "weird and wild" inner territories of self-discovery. I soon realized this was not a self-serving exercise but rather, an authentic plan for discovering why I was here, and what I wanted to give back to the world. It was my call to service.

Over the years, eight tenets or principles have gradually come to serve as my compass:

* Tread Lightly
* Travel Widely
* Think Deeply
* Listen Carefully
* Speak Truthfully
* Question Endlessly
* Laugh Heartily
* Love Fully

These guidelines are a personal mantra of sorts, and like Buddhism's noble eight-fold path, I've come to discover that only an ascetic with a loin cloth and halo could master them…and what fun would *that* be? Nevertheless, I've adopted this code if for no other reason than to navigate the shifting, sometimes arbitrary lines between "sense" and "non-sense."

I had concluded long ago that *True Travel* – exploration by foot, mind, heart, and soul/spirit – was the best way to create opportunities for understanding other people and cultures. If my beliefs and behaviors were truly correct or "superior" to someone else's, they would surely withstand the test of comparison. But if my travels were to expose a leaky foundation, what better way to shore it up?

I also discovered that the more we interact with others, the easier it is to shed those heavy layers of cultural sanitization and thus allow ourselves to respond to these people's deepest human needs...in the process, discovering similarities between those needs and our own.

It soon became apparent to me, however, that anyone who "skips the light Fandango" of immersed travel soon gets tangled in paradox: With so many colliding, intersecting and skewed cultural values, uh... who's "right?" Also, how does one stake a claim in the midst of the mêlée to say "I Am" this; or "I believe" that, and still be comfortable with The Great Unsettledness of it all?

The fact is, the more we reach out and "interact," *the more empowered we become.* So why hold back, when reaching out – growing, learning – is in our own self-interest? After all, what is at the core of cultural enmity but fear? Likewise, what is at the core of human and cultural similarities if not love? The more we appreciate and respect other cultures – even those radically different – the greater our opportunity for eradicating fear-based agendas and episodes such as nuclear annihilation, anarchy, genocide, militant fundamentalism, mass starvation, ratings-driven talk-show demagogues, archaic iron-fist agendas for "ruling the world," and other symptoms of separation.

Today, thanks to modern technology and the Internet, one needn't go *anywhere* to participate in Trans-cultural Communication, although physical travel surely adds a priceless dimension. All one has to do is simply open their mind and hearts and reach out. That is exactly what I am doing. Welcome aboard!

Acknowledgements

To Alexis Megeath, whose positive support has made it possible for her husband to pursue his passion.

To Carol Adler, whose editorial talents are exceeded only by her wisdom and patience.

To Patricia Pereira, who recognized my "callings" long before they were obvious to me, and for continually prodding me with the right words at the right times.

Introduction

Not all who wander are lost.
– J.R.R. Tolkien, *The Fellowship of the Ring*

The following stories actually happened as depicted. Here and there I've taken a few liberties in order to compensate for a forgotten tidbit or avoid having to go down the rabbit hole of lengthy, unnecessary explanation. One of my friends calls the process "faction" and that term seems to fit. The cast of characters is real, although to protect their identity (both the innocent and the guilty!), I've changed some of the names. None of the deviations from reality, however, significantly alter the stories or any "meaning" they may contain. In fact, the stranger and more bizarre the episode, the more likely my accounting to be faithfully accurate.

Although the stories follow an approximate chronology, there's no overriding argument for the order of presentation. There is, however, an evolving theme of "movement" in greater widening circles of geography, philosophy, and conclusions: observations, masquerading as "meaning." Transition has defined these ripples as they've fanned out.

Part I, "Up North by Out West," allowed me to see huge chunks of the U.S. and Canada – and myself – through my own eyes as well as those of several interesting characters. I had created the perfect opportunity for meeting individuals who had already made several life choices; thus showing me in advance the possible outcomes I could expect if I also decided to travel those paths. It was also a chance to examine my values and outlooks. How did they stack up; how *I* did stack up, compared to each of these highway hitchhikers? This made me realize that *travel was much more than seeing new places and meeting new people.* It became an important inner adventure where I would inevitably collide head-on with my dreams – and maybe even with my destiny as well.

Part II, "Mystics and Maniacs," is a journal of sorts from the early 1980s through the mid-1990s when I reluctantly followed the Western world's trajectory of career, trying to find meaning before learning that what I really wanted to do was *create* that meaning myself. These experiences reinforced the realization that it is through people that I learn the most about myself.

In Part III, "I Must Have Been Dreaming," the journey continues as I relate in "Sitiveni and the Kick-Boxers" (Chapter 19) the frustration and humor of being "trapped" in a Third World backwater Eden. This experience further accentuates the unanticipated challenges of both inner and outer journeys. As travelers in a strange land – and do we not arrive every day in a new and strange land? – we can choose to respond to incidents of deception and betrayal with anger or levity. If we pick the former, we can expect hostility; however, if we greet them as treasures whose value may still be hidden, we open the door to growth and deeper understanding of others as well as ourselves. We may also stumble upon another collectible to place on the altar of our hearts, as witnessed in the epilogue to this chapter.

"Dharma in a Delusional Age," Chapter 20, describes a key turning point in my life when my disillusion with many of society's sacred institutions compelled me to take a long philosophical look at the Western World's conundrum of "who I am versus what I do." I soon realized this was my invitation to greater self-awareness and a more fulfilling, heart-centered life.

"Because It Was There," Chapter 21, represents a personal triumph in daring to meet life head-on at its extreme. Were my wife Alexis and I crazy to decide to climb Mt. Kilimanjaro – on the wrong trail, in the wrong season – or were we just testing our limits so we could climb other physical and mental as well as emotional and spiritual "Kilimanjaros" with equal confidence and verve? One might object that it may not have been necessary to place ourselves in such extreme danger, but tell a marathon runner not to try to win the race, or a person with "terminal" cancer not to try to win that life-over-death contest for more time. We do what we have to do in order to resonate with our Highest Self – even if we seem like reckless, stubborn fools in the process...

The agony and ecstasy of overland-traveling through Africa in both "Because It Was There" and "Nyaminyami Throws a Tantrum," accentuate the paradoxical collision of cultures: highlighting humanity at its most beautiful and ugliest; eliciting gratitude for my circumstances with simultaneous disillusion for much of what my culture represents; observing that feelings of self-worth and self-loathing transcend cultural boundaries, wealth, class, creed, or education; recognizing that in the midst of despair there can still be hope; and in the cornucopia of plenty, unfortunately poverty and scarcity may still abide.

In Part IV, "Mindscapes and Soulscapes," life gives me an opportunity to view the inner landscape of loss and personal grieving. Chapter 23, "The Dragonfly Winks," drills home the temporal nature of incarnate life while titillating me with a miraculous glimpse of a playful immortality. Every journey has both a map that is created as we go, and a cosmic destination or destiny, where we eventually arrive. It seems to me that both are integrally linked to choices; our own, and those that have been cosmically "fixed" at the time of our birth by whoever or whatever we deem the Creator of Us All. As if we hadn't encountered enough paradoxes, the argument over free will and destiny surely gets the blue ribbon!

As I've come to appreciate and understand the many modalities of "True Travel," I'd be remiss to not delve into its more sublime elements. In Chapter 24, "Mucking About on the Ethereal Bridge," I wade into the realm of dreams, "out-of-body" journeys and "strange encounters," of which I've had many, and I describe how some of these memorable experiences have contributed to my personal growth. Also, for the first time, I grapple with the meaning of *commitment*. Real commitment – not just the textbook "being true to one's word" commitment.

At this point in the book, I pause to capture the metaphor of "The Marketplace" as representative of life itself. Part IV, Chapter 25, "The Grand Bizarre: Mayhem in the Market" is a play on words; although they sound the same, "bizarre" and "bazaar" have different meanings and roots, yet quixotically pair well together to deliver a colorful exposition of the ultimate power game between humans, nations and cultures.

It's a battle out there in The Market; and as such, The Market becomes a microcosm of our daily lives. The battle, however, is not with the carneys, touts, concessionaires or peddlers of wood from the True Cross; it is with *ourselves*, balancing between what we "want" versus what we "need;" what nurtures or heals us, versus what numbs the pain or inflicts it upon others.

I have come to believe that we meet our selves in the marketplace: our nobility, passions, discipline and temperament. If we lose our center, we risk becoming a schizophrenic in a hall of mirrors, succumbing to the temptation of acquiring stuff we don't like or won't use; or perhaps bringing people, situations and energies into our lives that cause conflict and challenge we hadn't bargained for. We also risk getting angry or greedy, the perfect environment for desperation's roller coaster as we tear up and down those slippery slopes through the amusement park of our egos.

In Part VI, my personal map starts to point toward a destination. Chapter 26 outlines "The Gulliver Project™: Creating Your Trans-Cultural Connection," the enterprise that was spawned from my travels and the writing of this book. An appendix, "What Can *You* Do?" follows this chapter as a candy box of ideas: my gift to you to help you set your own wheels rolling out from the familiar to the unknown: that larger world where you're bound to find, as I did, incredible adventures – and just as much fun.

There might be some who would consider some of the principles or observations I've expressed in this book as naïve or shortsighted, perhaps even recklessly foolish: It's a jungle out there, they rightfully exclaim, and chide me for hop-scotching over the landmines as if they weren't there. Let me assure the reader that I know first-hand that we live in a dangerous world. Coming out of the birth canal and taking that first gulp is risky enough. Certainly there are valid arguments about travel being "too dangerous" in many places. I do understand: I was an hour away from Mombassa, Kenya, in 2003 when it was shattered by a terrorist's bomb. In the 1980s, had I arrived at Machu Picchu's train station (in Agua Calientes, Peru) a week later, I would have been treated to an exploding platform, courtesy of the *Sendero Luminoso* ("Shining Path"), Marxist revolutionaries. I've been pickpocketed (Peru, again – another damn train station), horribly sick (Nepal), ostracized (by the spoiled sons and daughters of Her Majesty's far flung former dominions), ejected into Class V rapids (Africa), snubbed (Paris), hassled by border guards (Canada – but never in Third World countries!), sneered at (Greece…oh, and New Jersey), had a pack and clothing stolen (Australia), and was abandoned by a tour escort (Fiji). And these offenses don't even include having to watch American sitcoms, eat British cuisine, or observe Italian politics.

The irony is that life in any big U.S. city is just as dangerous as most of those threats. Sort of. So why sweat the small stuff?

I've also been treated like a king – and not just by those seeking a golden handshake. I've been given (loaned) the family car when a rental car didn't materialize. I've been quartered in the family's "master bedroom" while mama, papa and brood slept on reed thatch in the "family room." I've been force-fed the last tea and cakes of a poor fisherman. I'll never forget the guy in Izmir, Turkey, (wearing a Brooklyn Dodger's windbreaker!) picking up the suitcases of my sister and me and walking us around from hotel to hotel as we sought appropriate lodging (he also refused our proffered tip).

But if the hospitality, or just plain intrigue, of our brothers and sisters isn't impetus enough, there's always our Mother: the Earth herself. She's laid out a pretty magnificent playground. It's hard to imagine that with the exception of tele-babble from unmanned space missions or some meddlesome ET's beaming around in their comical saucers, everything we know (or *presume* to know), sense, think, and feel is confined to our twirling blue-green sphere. There's a reason why Earth is round – go far enough in any one direction and you're back where you started. As T.S. Eliot wrote, "We shall not cease from exploration, and the end of all our exploring will be to arrive where we started and know the place for the first time."

Some may wish to chasten me for purporting to have "no answers" while surreptitiously slipping an agenda of one-liners into your subconscious memory box…masking opinions as fact, in other words. They're right. I do have an agenda: to urge you to *s-t-r-e-t-c-h* yourself in as many ways as possible, through travel, questioning, reading, introspection, commerce, social exchange, correspondence, and whatever realm of experience expands your playing field. I want for you the very best – to "live an ordinary life in an extraordinary way" – and to step into your latent magnificence: bereft of fear, uncluttered by dogma, and dismissive of any snake-oil peddlers asking you to trade your power, money, or soul for their "answers" …unless your proclivities pull you that way, in which case, I honor your path. "Once more unto the breach!"

Most of all, I wish you happy hunting in your own quest to put meaning into Life. If the latter is indeed a gift from the Source, then surely your own actions are a gift back to it – and to me, and to all of creation.

"*To Live is to burn,*" wrote Fyodor Dostoevsky. And André Gide admonished: "*Listen to those who seek truth. Avoid those who find it.*" What better way to acknowledge the quest of our personal journey toward truth than to heed the words of those two literary masters…

Table of Contents

PART I
UP NORTH BY OUT WEST

Chapter One

Hitchhikers' Highway

"It's a great life, Steve, I wouldn't change a damn thing...well, I guess I *would* love to trade a few alimony payments for a Morgan 32 and hang out in the Bahamas for a while...but I've seen the world; I got no anchor or albatrosses 'round my neck..."

Charlie was on an extended leave from the Merchant Marines; I'd picked him up earlier that day in California heading north on Route 1, the Pacific Coast Highway. Forty-ish with short but wild, curly hair; traveling light, clothing and gear all blue and brown; he was a clean orderly guy almost too well-groomed for your ordinary hitchhiker. *"Easier to get rides,"* he'd grinned, climbing aboard and reading my thoughts. *"Appearances aren't everything but they're a nice door-opener."*

"...and I long ago got over my addiction to marriage," Charlie continued now, his voice tinged with bitterness. "Hell, loneliness is like virginity – it's curable – Ha! And I got 'cures' in every major seaport in the world, if ya know what I mean, heh-heh."

As he rambled on, it soon became evident that even if Charlie tried to give the outward appearance of having it all together, he was not only dealing with inner chaos and loneliness; he was also far from convinced that loneliness *was* curable. Maybe because I'd had my own trysts with relationship heartbreak and inner turbulence, I suddenly found myself reaching out to him.

It was September, 1981. I was almost 23, fresh out of college and driving all the way from Eastern Tennessee to Boise, Idaho where I'd accepted a position with Hewlett Packard. I'd decided to zigzag across the U.S. on a route that would eventually cover ten states, two

Canadian provinces, 7,000 miles, 30 rolls of film and a bag of cheap dope (for medicinal reasons: glaucoma runs in the family).

Hitchhiking was already a fading pastime in America, a relic of past generations like Burma Shave signs and smiling gas station attendants. Maybe it was the ubiquitous sterile "sameness" of America's vast interstate system, or maybe it was the rising rates of mischief. But people just didn't thumb as much anymore; either because they didn't need to, or because they were too scared of psychopathic drivers. Drivers in turn were increasingly afraid of psychopathic hitchhikers, and thus the cyclical paranoia made the experience a tad more problematic than in previous decades. Most places in the East had already prohibited hitchhiking on all but the back roads; the West was still holding on. Free spirits and losers still loitered around truck stops or lonely crossroads, silhouetted against the driving gray shadows of blizzards and swirling dust storms on forsaken roads.

For the first time since I'd picked up Charlie, suddenly he fell silent, both of us now intent on watching the sun ease into the Pacific. The spectacular sight deserved our full attention. We had just landed at Big Sur and after erecting a tent site on one of its vast and rugged beaches, we'd walked out to the Point to catch the sunset.

As soon as we touched the Pacific, instinctively I knew this adventure was far more than just another "flora & fauna" *Betters Homes and Gardens* whirl. I wasn't going back; at least, not any time soon.

I didn't know and didn't care what/who I would "become" or what glorious rainbows or treacherous pitfalls might lie ahead. *Wanderlust* was my piper; that it could come with a paycheck was an added bonus.

The HP-Boise employment choice hadn't been too difficult; my six other offers from a slew of Fortune 1000 stalwarts were in well-established and overrun places that could hardly compare to an area of the country that was apparently still a well-kept secret. Besides, I really wasn't excited about nuclear bombs, poison fertilizers or carbon drill bits as products; blizzards or swamps for climate and topography; or hootenannies for entertainment. Furthermore, any state with such a ludicrous claim as "Famous Potatoes" on its license tag figured to be hiding something good – and if that was the case, like B'rer Rabbit in the Briar Patch, by God I wanted in on the secret.

I soon learned that of all the states in the Lower 48, Idaho had the most miles of running and falling water (surprise, California!) and the most designated wilderness (whoddathunk it, Montana?). She also had the greatest number of peaks over 10,000 feet in the Northwest (gotcha, Oregon & Washington!)…and if the statistic means anything, the most millionaires per capita in the U.S., in land asset value, at least. That's a lotta 'taters.

On one of those classic swamp-choking summer days in Atlanta, I'd flown out to Boise to scope out the place. Stepping off the plane on that Midsummer's Eve jolted me in two ways: the sensation of feeling "cool" at 90 degrees, and the phenomenon of seeing the sun still in the sky at 9:00 p.m.

HP also impressed me with its softball fields, duck ponds and a catered coffee and donut tray that sauntered by your cubicle every morning. The town had relatively clean industry. You could look out across the valley at mountains, and the Boise River adorned downtown's pedestrian arcades with miles of receptive greenbelt. The HP plant's divisions were managed by bright people from Stanford and M.I.T. who also liked to ski, fish and throw hellacious beer-busts – on company time – whenever profitability justified, which, in the Golden Age of Silicon, was almost always. This was before the Golden Age of MADD – Mothers Against Drunk Driving – and the Golden Age of Outsourcing, described decades later in Tom Friedman's best-selling book, *The World is Flat*. All you had to do was show up, look interested, and some late-20-something (your boss) would pat you on the head and dispense raises two or three times yearly.

Rent? About a third of what I would have paid in Silicon Valley, on the same pay scale.

I had about five weeks to report to the job. I also had a brand new hatchback car, camping gear and a forward-paid travel reimbursement from HP (gotta love 'em) ostensibly for hotels and per diem expenses. The car, a Mazda GLC with a sunroof, was down-purchased with the ol' student loan sleight-of-hand trick. I was forced into the consumer market when my '66 Dodge Dart "Horace," named after a revered

Atlanta bartender, was stolen, followed by my Schwinn bike a week later. Six wheels in seven days! What could have been a disaster was quickly turned into an opportunity to learn how to manifest four new wheels from some lucky car dealer's lot. And now fate beckoned, and the Silver Bullet turned west.

My plan was to blast across Tennessee, Arkansas and Texas quickly; friends strategically located in Memphis and Dallas would make it easy. Tennessee passed by in a green blur, gradually receding from the mountainous east to the rolling middle hills followed by the western flatlands. I spent a night in Memphis with some former neighbors, just long enough for barbeque and a few drinks on historic Beale Street with all its famous nightclubs and shops.

Then it was lickety-split across the Mississippi River into Arkansas, where a youthful Bill Clinton was already donning Teflon and spouting platitudes. Somewhere in the haze to the north beyond Hot Springs lay the Ozarks, home of great canoeing and the hillbilly kindred spirits of my native Cumberlands. But they would have to wait for another day. I was Texas-bound, like another Tennessean, Davy Crockett: "Y'all can go to hell; I'm goin' to Texas."

Chapter Two

Ga-ga G.I.'s and Concrete Cowboys

Still a long way from California and Charlie, down near Louisiana about a mile from Texarkana, I picked up Ronnie at a rest stop. He said he was Army on leave and itching to go "somewhere west." A nice, friendly guy, but speaking of itching, the type that wears on you like an Irish Setter with fleas. Cheerful, bouncy, fidgety and prone to investigate or comment on whatever visceral stimuli appeared in his direct or peripheral vision, such as breasts (female), mag wheels, beer signs, road kill, or my glove compartment.

He: "Where you goin'?"

Me: "Idaho."

He: "Where's that?"

Me: "Canada."

He: "Oh…What for?"

Me: "Work."

He: "Can't you get no work in the U.S.?"

Me: "Yeah, but that's my best gig, and besides I like the name."

He: "Ya know, I dig Uncle Sam. I get three squares, I get to blow shit up legally, and they even pay me."

Me: "Reckon they might ship you off to Iran if things heat up?"

He: "Hey, that Ayatollah can kiss my Assaholah – Hah! You never know what them Dune-Coon's are gonna do. But I dunno. This ain't a bad job. Hey…what's this?"

Oops. In my glove compartment he'd uncovered my Jack Daniels: Tennessee Tranquilizer, Lynchburg Lemonade. Granny's rheumatism medicine.

Me: "Care for a swig?"

He: "Hell yes – you sure?"

Me: "Sure, pal, *mi casa es tu casa.*"

He: "Wha…?"

Me: "Bottoms up, bro. Help yourself."

He: "Why not? It's afternoon and I'm on R&R. *Slurp.* Yeee-aaah – that's righteous!"

As a responsible host, I couldn't let Ronnie drink alone. My parents had raised me better than that. Besides, I had several more days of Texas ahead of me. Might as well try to enjoy it. Sip-by-sip, mile-by-mile, we watched the hills roll by and the endless frontier of Tejas start to open up in front of us. We toasted the Alamo. We toasted Willy Nelson and Leon Russell and the hordes of Blues-TexMex-Country-Swing-Avantegarde-Funk musicians laboring anonymously down in Austin. We toasted barbeque. We toasted Comanches and desperados and conquistadors and carpetbaggers and politicians (is there any difference?). We got just plain toasted.

I liked Ronnie, possibly because he was an education. I'd met a few like him before at a distance, but inviting them into one's home or car is another thing. Yet…wasn't Ronnie one of the reasons why I'd started out on this cross-country journey? To feed myself with new experiences?

Possibly nineteen or twenty, short but powerful with frenetic darting eyes, Ronnie's world consisted of titties, beer, tanks, fishing rods, NASCAR, Black Sabbath and Louis L'Amour novels. I reckoned I'd want him in my foxhole. He was the guy who would charge up Iwo Jima or San Juan Hill for guts and glory. He was also the one who'd fire into a crowd at, say, a peaceful Kent State demonstration. "Orders," he'd say with a shrug.

Best to keep guys like Ronnie on your side and certain questions to yourself, such as: what if he was in the National Guard and his sister happened to have been among the Kent State protestors who'd gotten shot, or arrested by one of his buddies? Or, what if some titty-starved Army AWOL got drunk and raped his girlfriend?

On 635, the LBJ Freeway, Ronnie stood up on the seat and poked his upper torso through the sun roof (a posture not illustrated in the manual) while he "roped" trucks and cars like so many imaginary steers. Some laughed, some honked, others shot back with an Italian salute, and still others just stared in disbelief. A few, I'm sure, reached for their shooting irons just in case. Out of the layers of alcoholic effluvia it occurred to me that if I had to hit the brakes, he'd be launched halfway to Fort Worth like one of Reagan's MX missiles with a bad attitude. So, naturally I went faster. Rope 'em, cowboy!

My exit was coming up in a few miles. Don, a classmate from Georgia Tech, had just moved to Dallas with his wife, Elaine, to work for Hagar, the clothing behemoths. Ronnie looked at me obliquely and sort of half-asked, half-suggested, if he could stay with me and my friends. Ooohhh.

"Sorry, pal," I fibbed, "it's a tiny place and I think their Aunt Clara from Wichita is visiting."

"Bummer," sighed Ronnie.

"Yeah, man," I consoled, "you'd be the life of the party." At least *that* wasn't a white lie.

"Say, Steve, I'd be willing to buy the rest of the bottle from you. Full price."

Honor among drunks! The charitable thing, of course, would have been just to give it to him – socialistic code of the Road Warrior, and all.

"I got 10 bucks." He waived a dead Hamilton in my face.

"Sold." *And God Speed, mon frère...*

As he closed the car door and took off, for a moment I pictured Ronnie as a little boy, bawling his eyes out at his grandmother's or maybe his father's funeral. Clearly he'd accepted someone else's propaganda that he was only useful as their collateral. To die for them...or live for them, as another customer at bars, casinos and flophouses. In life's haberdashery, Ronnie's hat was the one on the rack that I knew for sure I'd pass up.

* * * * * *

The highlight of my visit to Dallas was a night at Billy Bob's, the world's largest self-proclaimed honky-tonk in Fort Worth. My back home Blues of Memphis may be dirty and gritty – men are men, and women vixen, by God – but pretentious it ain't. This here Billy Bob $15 cover charge was a bit much; hell, I'd seen the Rolling Stones a few years previous at Atlanta's Fabulous Fox Theater for only $10. These Fort Worth boys even made me tuck in my T-shirt. Life's funny, I thought. Merle Haggard could stumble, stagger, swear and generally make an ass of himself all over the stage (which he proceeded to do in spades), but I'd better look respectable with a tucked-in T-shirt... these are, after all, Urban Cowboys and respectable folk. The Blues may be down-trodden and misanthropic, but at least it was honest. I just didn't know about this honky-tonk, belt-buckle, cow-palace, mechanical bull stuff. Was there some kind of inverse relationship between bulls and balls that I'm just not hip to?

I headed out again on Monday morning. Soon Fort Worth was fading in my rear-view mirror as the stunted mesquites of Central Texas lined up to entertain me. The sky got bigger, the landscape starker.

Everything I had read and heard about West Texas was true; which is to say, I drove faster. Ranches and mesquite trees and barren mesas and alkaline flats just sort of blurred into a mosaic of nothingness. Out there on a curving horizon the edge of the Earth gobbled up this God-forsaken dirt patch and tried to spit it back up somewhere in say, the Australian Outback, or Mongolia's Gobi, or the Argentinean Pampas...where it was promptly rejected and sent back.

Chapter Three

The Prodigal Hipster

As I fought the hypnotic undertow of white-line fever, a willowy shadow caught my eye. It was moving – animate. Too big for an armadillo, too slow for a hawk, too organic for a cop cruiser. Very interesting, this visage. I slowed down; the shadow crystallized into flesh and blood and hustled, almost running with a full load on its back, the last 100 yards to the car.

"Hey man, thanks a million. I'd just about given up hope. Been out here for a fuckin' day and a half, just hangin' in the shade under the overpass."

"Where you heading to?" I queried.

"Prescott, Arizona's home, so I guess anywhere in the neighborhood would be fine. How 'bout you?"

I repeated my Idaho spiel, sans the Canadian red herring.

"You in a hurry?" Shane climbed in and introduced himself. Tall, blonde mane, tumbleweed beard and a lingo pinched right off a Grateful Dead album sleeve, Shane was a cross between the Norse God Thor and one of the Fabulous Furry Freak Brothers.

"Not really. Just seeing the Wild West – ya know, back roads, campgrounds, national parks, some friends and family. I guess it's a nice transitional 'hurrah' before settling in to a new life."

"Listen, dude, if you're not bustin' a gut and are keen on seein' the outta-the-way stuff, it'd be my pleasure to show you the lay of the land. I know New Mexico and Arizona like the back of my hand. Especially Mother Arizona – her deserts, her mountains, old mining towns, you name it. She's somethin' else."

I was piqued, and readily consented. Nothing like a tour guide, and Shane, bohemian/barbarian/bard all fused into one, seemed like a worthy companion. He was originally from Akron, Ohio – *"Home of Joe Walsh, by God!"* – and like Joe, high-tailed it out of there as soon as possible. He landed in Prescott, tending bar for four years and happily engaged to Kathy. But something happened; life got in the way and Shane retraced his way across the country to that great kingpin of rubber tires. Now convalesced, he was returning to Arizona, determined to win her back.

That's the condensed version. The story wove its tapestry slowly and methodically as we passed into southern New Mexico from Pecos. We slept under the stars in the middle of God-knows-where, and proceeded on toward the White Mountains of East-Central Arizona. The road west undulated in sweeping roller-coasters, with roadrunners and crows scavenging road kill as the desert scrub disappeared into the hazy eastern escarpment of the rising hills.

The land was every bit as rugged as West Texas, but wilier, more three-dimensional, more *suggestive*. I felt myself starting to loosen a little. The humidity, carpeted cities and clustered foliage of the East were long behind us now, and the concrete cowboys of Dallas a good 700 miles in the rear view mirror, rapidly fading.

I was still 600 miles from M.C. Escher's freeway systems and the noxious fumes of Southern California. Between those nodes of megalomania, the desert probably looked just as it had when Francisco Vasquez de Coronado passed through, chasing the mirages of El Dorado in the 1540s. My mind's eye saw Wile E. Coyote lurking fiendishly behind a saguaro cactus as the Roadrunner (the real one, not these poor imitators) blasted by – *Beep-Beep!* – at rocket speed; Pancho Villa rode circles around General Black Jack Pershing, while John Wayne punched out a snake oil salesman and gunned down a few Hollywood Comanches. Like me, they were all just passing through. No one stays here for long, except maybe a few sidewinders and scorpions.

A purple, scarlet and orange sky, so different from the east, hugged the mountains like the aura of a people long-departed but not yet willing to yield their ephemeral selves to eternity. It was a kaleidoscope, welcoming me into a new land like a concessionaire at a carnival.

Shane and I passed through the Apache National Forest and cooled ourselves under whispering Quaking Aspens at 8,000 feet in elevation. They teased us with the first yellow of autumn, but mostly still held onto late summer's lime green. We stood on a corner in Winslow, Arizona where Jackson Brown sold immortality to The Eagles, then drove in silence through both the Painted Desert and Petrified Forest, mausoleums from antiquity where even the least human utterance would have seemed like sacrilege.

At Daddy Warbuck's in Flagstaff, Shane chased away old demons and flirted with a few new ones while we shot pool and drank beer. We even accidentally pulled the glass door off the hotel shower stall – but what would you expect for $12 a night? And then, he took me to The Canyon.

Nothing can prepare the psyche for its first exposure to such wonderment. It blows the sockets, grabs the air in our lungs and before we realize it, forces some semi-audible babble through our slobbering lips. Somewhere in the engrams of our cells or in some distant electrical charges lurking in our unconscious memories, we're served notice that this phenomena merits special response. Because it *is* Grand – a vestige of creation so vast, we're shaken by the paradox of our seemingly-pathetic insignificance. We realize we are a living "Koan" – a cosmic riddle – perched in the precarious saddle that girths the Infinite to the Infinitesimal.

Thus was I shaken by that great gorged chasm on the edge of Arizona's Mogollon Rim. I, half of Germany and all of Japan just stared into space and felt the buzz. We were allies that day. No, we were brothers and sisters. No, more like ants. Actually, we didn't think about one another at all; we were too swept up in the timelessness of Mother Nature to even care about petty sentimentalities like the Brotherhood of Humanity. Besides, we were all on vacation and those were taxing thoughts.

"Pretty special, huh, dude?" Shane broke the reverie.

"Yeah," I grunted, too mesmerized for dialogue.

Three thousand feet down and about 40 miles west, by Rim, was an Indian reservation, Havasupai, home of the Supai. In the 1950s they had wisely rebuffed a taxpayer-funded road down to their village, and to this day still receive their mail service via horse and burro. That little green strip of the Colorado River, famous for its white water rafting, seemed so benign from up here when it was in fact, a raging torrent of white, punctuated by the little yellow rafts of the intrepid and insane as they scooted through on their way to Lake Mead and a well-deserved margarita.

Buttressed by the huge rising canyon walls, the river witnessed Major Wesley Powell's prediction in the 1860s that his entourage would probably be the only white faces to explore the canyon from this perspective. With just one arm (the other donated to Confederate artillery), Major Powell can be excused for his temerity. It seemed like a reasonable claim at the time; and several of his crew wrote in their journals that they really didn't expect to come out alive, but were recording the trip for posterity anyway…I wonder what the Major would think today, with dozens of whirly-bird choppers buzzing about in the Canyon's yap.

I watched lightning crack beneath me, as a black cloud passed by. I wondered how many times ("Like the flapping of a giant black wing," writes H.G. Wells in *The Time Machine*) these skits have been played out over the eons. I wondered, too, if Earth First!'s "Monkey-Wrenchers" – eco-terrorists inspired by the fertile mind of Edward Abbey – would eventually be successful blowing up Glen Canyon Dam upstream, and if anyone would then even notice the water rising from up here on the Rim as Lake Powell emptied its houseboat-bilged sewer waters in one cataclysmic rush. I have to believe the good Major would be pleased.

I also wondered if I would have made this side-trip if not for Shane's invitation to be my tour guide…or if the Grand Canyon would have been so awesome had I done it alone. I never cease to be amazed how variables such as a person or event often impact our experiences, possibly even setting us up for the next ones. It's that quantum thing: we choose our reality and also program the players.

* * * * * *

Suddenly one night "out of the blue" Shane confessed, "Not to freak you out, amigo, but I killed a man a while back."

Needless to say, he quickly gained my full and undivided attention. My Marty Feldman-esque bulging eyes must have betrayed my alarm.

"No, no, not like that!" Shane countered. "Sorry to scare you, dude. He was an old drunk that hung out by a parking lot and I backed up and hit him with my truck one night. It was dark and I guess he was just stumbling around. I didn't see him. Went into the hospital and croaked the next day. Holy moly, that weirds you out. Like, I know it's not my rap, but it still drills into your head like a boll weevil and just won't let go. So goddamn helpless of a feeling. Everyone liked him, too. He was kinda like an institution around town. I guess I wouldn't mind so much if he was some sort of bad-ass criminal dude, or just a drifter passing through."

I couldn't help thinking, what if it had been I and not Shane who had accidentally killed this innocent man? Despite our differences in style, I felt a kindred spirit to Shane. He may have been a little rough around the edges, but he had a big heart, keen mind and resolute purpose – qualities underdeveloped in G.I. Ronnie. He was my age – high school Class of '76 – Bicentennial Brethren. We shared a common interest in music and the Great Outdoors. That last night at the Grand Canyon, over a bottle of Peach Schnapps and a roaring campfire, we slobbered about lost loves and waxed poetic about loves we would have loved to have loved. We debated the future of Notre Dame football since the underwhelming Gerry Faust took over. We agreed that Jethro Tull was the most under-appreciated of progressive rock bands on the planet; we naturally agreed that most disco sucked. We reminisced about how cheap a good nickel bag used to cost (5 cents, hence the moniker). Furthermore, we both cast a wary eye toward the Great Communicator who had taken over the White House from that other well-meaning evangelist. Shane was a transplanted-but-committed westerner, back for the long haul, and I was the wide-eyed rookie taking it all in.

"Mother Arizona," toasted he.

"Live long and prosper," I added.

I was also grateful to Shane for introducing me to the serpentine Oak Creek Canyon, the red cathedral bluffs of Sedona and haunted old mining town of Jerome, tilting from the top of an impossible hill. We swigged a few last beers as we watched the sun illuminating the valley below. Somewhere down there was a monastery built by the Spaniards in the 1600s…just a blink ago in the desert's eye, the blink between darkness and light. Finally the last trace of sunset disappeared into the purple-gray of the night.

I dropped off Shane in Prescott the next morning, after staying with some of his friends. He showed me the square where Tom Laughlin kicked the crap out of the bad guys in the movie *Billy Jack*.

"Are you gonna call her right away?" I queried.

"No way, man. Not quite yet. I hope she doesn't catch wind that I'm back. I'm gonna get a job, clean up and get a place, ya know. I want to be worthy. I want her to come back of her own accord. I've paid my dues and sung the blues, but I'm a new man now."

I was hopeful for Shane, though I wasn't sure about the newness part. Sometimes we don't change as fast as our circumstances, and he had more than one weight bearing down on his shoulders. But love, like spring, is eternal and I sincerely believed he had a fighting chance at winning back his fair Rapunzel. Besides, having observed his *savoir-faire* at Daddy Warbuck's back in Flagstaff, there would be no shortage of ladies in waiting. I questioned, rather, if he would want *them*.

"Look me up if you get to Boise, pal."

Chapter Four

Mare Pacifica

The San Bernardino National Forest was as close as I'd let myself get to Los Angeles. I didn't want to get sucked into the morass; something about this hegira compelled me to steer safely away. To the southwest I could see the dragon's breath: carbon monoxide and sulfur dioxide engulfed a sizeable chunk of the horizon. It had been necessary to go through Dallas, but L.A., like Phoenix and Vegas, could be skirted.

Jim, a former college roommate, met me at Lake Arrowhead. We threw down a tent into the teeth of a growling Santa Ana, those capricious winds that often turn an errant spark into a conflagration and terrorize neighborhoods, rich or poor; nature is democratic even though she often acts the dictator.

"Jimbo," one of the smartest persons I know, was getting a doctorate at UCLA. It helped having a photographic memory. I remember several years back in our Atlanta apartment, cramming for tests. Jim had me quiz him from a list of Latin as long as my arm:

Q: "Tetra-flouro-chloro-benzene-methyl-bromide-methanol-penta-sulfate – blah, blah, blah…"

A: "Yeah, that one's purple, smells like a skunk and would eat a hole clear through to China."

Jim was thorough, good natured, and just a tad of an academician. He'd make a great professor, which was his goal. Blessed be those aware of their *dharma*, for they shall inherit the Earth. It takes some of us Gullivers a bit longer to hone down priorities and chart that map…sometimes even several lifetimes, the mystics would assert. Which is why it seems futile to judge anyone; we have no idea where they are on their journey. In this lifetime, Jim and I called out to each other for – what? For me to quiz Jimbo for his finals and my friend to demonstrate the value – and satisfaction – of tuning in to one's natural gifts? It was much deeper than that, and we both knew it…just as we did not question what had not yet appeared in this lifetime for us to know. Maybe this was another insight: to recognize that we not only call certain people into our lives, but also have enough wisdom *not to ask why* and just let things unfold…as they will.

After several days of hiking and exploring, Jim and I parted once again: he, in the direction of the brown mustard gas to the southwest, and I to the northwest toward San Louis Obispo.

The name *Mare Pacifica* was supposedly coined by explorer Francisco Balboa, reputedly the first European to see it from the Western Hemisphere. Francisco saw it on a good day, of course, as I was seeing it now: calm, vast, soothing, patient and a shade of blue that has perplexed the Crayola crayon makers to this day.

She can also be unpredictable, like a mercurial woman, prone to morphing into tempestuous lashes that terrorize everyone in her way. There's a reason insurance rates are highest in paradise. It's the *I Ching* of real estate: "Water under Sky; Sky on Land; and All-Hell-Breaking-Loose…" especially when you least expect it. Had he arrived on another day, Balboa might have christened her *Mare Terriblis*. But then, as now, the lady just yawned. Like a Venus Fly Trap.

After the ceremonial touching of the waves and relieving myself therein – my contribution – the Silver Bullet hugged the coast of the Pacific Highway for the next several hours, playing cat-and-mouse with fog and sun. In and out, in and out…"like the flapping of a giant black wing"…

* * * * * *

It was on that stretch where I'd met Charlie, the Merchant Marine. Charlie just wanted to hang out on the beaches south of Monterey for a while before returning to San Diego and his latest ship. He didn't care for the party beaches – Malibu, Venice, etc. – he wanted the serenity and beauty of Big Sur.

"Besides, I like the people better. They may be misfits and fuckups and a bit lost, but they ain't makin' no fashion statement, ain't there to be seen, don't give a rat's ass about what anybody thinks of 'em. And they treat the area well – they know they got a good thing goin', so they don't go trashin' it or botherin' the folks in the towns."

He was talking about the drifters, not realizing he was describing himself...just as, at that time in my life he was also mirroring "me to me." Maybe we both had ports we were steering toward, but so did the others; they just didn't necessarily know it yet.

The sheer number of available protected campsites on the Big Sur coast, with their generous 14-day limits, made it possible to literally live up and down this fifty-mile stretch basically for free or at most, a few bucks a day. At the end of two weeks, you'd grab your gear, slip on your Birkenstocks and either thumb or load up your VW Van and putter a few miles in either direction. No change of P.O., no back taxes, no worries.

"What do people do?" I asked him. *What do people do?* asked the voice inside. *What do you want to do, Steve? Do you want to do what these people do?*

"Do? Hell, they just live," Charlie retorted. "Hang around, hike, read their London or Kerouac or Kesey or whatever trips people's triggers these days. Maybe a few are planning a palace *coup* somewhere, like those Symbionese Liberation Army dudes a few years back, but most just grow a little weed up in the hills, which they sell to the 'Trust-afarians' and beach punks down in Venice. Sure beats workin' for a livin', I reckon. Ha!"

Dave and Pam from Edmonton, Alberta, were two examples. They'd been camping in Big Sur since March or April. We'd just dumped down our gear next to them.

"Still building igloos up there at home, eh?"

Dave had that irritating Canadian habit of turning a statement into a question. I took the bait the first few times before I realized I was interrupting a soliloquy. He was ragged and nonchalant, with eyes bloodshot beyond casual Visine repair. But he was a gentle guy, the type that gives stoners a good name.

"What do you during winter, when this region gets cold, rainy, and windy?"

"Ah, I dunno know, man, maybe go down to the Baja. Live for today, eh?" He exchanged knowing glances with Pam, snickering between chomps of a brownie.

Charlie's query was hardly casual. I sensed a hidden depth in him that matched the ocean's, and with just as many exhaustible resources. I also sensed it was a depth where monsters lurked. He was a complex Gulliver, with stories untold, cards not played and webs still tangled from some distant time. He was footloose, but not free. Shane's demons may have been on his sleeve and the tip of his tongue, but Charlie's were buried in Davy Jones' locker.

We watched the last flickering light turn the sea to wine, followed by the soft gray of dusk. I could hear Charlie's heart sighing as if being called back to the womb, to Poseidon's lair, where the shrilling of the gulls fades away on a salty breeze.

"Yeah, after a few brain-numbing land jobs, I joined the Merchant Marine and have never looked back," Charlie picked up the thread from where he'd left off. "Those old sailor stories? I can relate, brother. It's a restlessness that won't go away, like the ocean's…this giant tit I can just hang from. Long as I do my job. And I can do scores of jobs, man: I know dozens of knots, I can work rigging, drive forklifts, fix diesels, operate Ham radios, cook, do billing and procurement. I even got a captain's license that I don't use. But I don't know which I like more, the solitude of the open water or the port o'calls. Out on the water, when I'm not working, I've taught myself chess and how to play guitar; I read and write and just watch the fuzz growing in my belly button." He was winding up, releasing some of his loneliness, having sensed I was a both a safe "port" and good listener.

"But on land, oh boy, now that's a different matter. We're like a bunch of pent-up bulls let out of the pen. Not like those youngsters in the Navy, mind you, we're not out looking to pick fights or see how much grog we can swill. Well, not completely. But I tell you what, the ladies know they're in for a treat when we drop anchor. Oh, we're capable of creating a lot of mischief, but generally we don't destroy too much. There's a sense of permanence to us, ya know? Besides, we tip well and always pay our bills, so I guess you could say we do more good than harm, heh-heh."

Charlie stretched out on his back and gazed up at the darkening sky. "The establishments know we're not like the 18-year-old boys that pass through in a whoosh and don't care if they leave Armageddon in their wake. And those bar Sheilas know we'll be back with some outrageous stories to tell – which are *mostly* true, heh-heh. I guess there's something more substantial to us, and this job really is a soul-calling or maybe a soul escape, I dunno."

A soul escape. Yes, that was it…Charlie was bent on poking a hole in his soul-coat so he could let it sneak out and race back to the Cosmic Closet where someone else may wish to try it on for awhile. What Charlie didn't understand was, he was stuck with that soul. It was his, uniquely stamped and addressed to him. To date, I didn't know of anyone who had been able to "change souls," except perhaps in the case of "walk-ins," but that's a subject for another time, and Charlie surely wasn't referring to any of those athletic Gold Medal Olympian events.

"But it sure ain't forced impressment into His Majesty's service, out to police the world or push our country," Charlie rambled on. "I guess you could say we're businessmen, not soldiers. But not that we aren't vulnerable. Hell, did you know the Merchant Marine got the crap sank out of us back in World War One and Two? Like the Kaiser, or Adolph or ol' Tojo's subs cared a whit whether the goods being delivered to their enemies were under a ship of war or a ship of commerce. Merchant Marine ships got sunk left and right. Pay's pretty damn good though. Hell, I almost wouldn't mind a little more extracurricular excitement these days, heh-heh."

Charlie had been everywhere – Dakar, Singapore, Hong Kong, Bombay, the Arabian Peninsula, Brisbane, Wellington, Bergen, Rotterdam, Cape Town, Buenos Aires, Valparaiso, Osaka…I'm sure his passport looked like a dart board in a Liverpool pub, and I, still a greenie, was envious. Here before my eyes was the curtain going up on my future life. Charlie was introducing me to what at that moment I realized I wanted to do more than anything else: travel, see – and *be* the world! I wanted it all, outside and inside.

Unlike me, Charlie didn't seem to know or care about the various cultures of the places he'd visited. He measured everything in latitude, longitude, distance, and time. And in waves and weather, as the sea was his compass and the entire ship his rudder.

Most people, including myself, consider water a transitional medium between land masses. Charlie saw water as his home, and land as little terminus dots representing R&R. People – what they ate or how they dressed, what rituals they practiced – all of this seemed to pass him by, with the exception of a few difficult landmarks such as alimony, from one of those moments when he had accidentally landed in that foreign country of Commitment.

"I know I can't keep doing this job when I'm 60 or 70, man, but it feels right for now. I come back occasionally and do stuff like this just so's I won't grow gills and fins, heh-heh." I could easily picture him hanging out of the Crow's Nest while rounding Cape Horn in the 1500s, or stepping into some Shanghai pleasure palace on shore leave from an 18th Century HMS frigate.

Was it good or was it bad? It just *was*, and I was enjoying the ride of listening to him. Charlie was not my first encounter with Merchant Marines. I'd met some back in 1975 in Bergen, Norway. I was a high school student, in Scandinavia that summer for the World Scout Jamboree in Lillehammer, Norway. Fortunately we weren't always under the watchful eye of our adult leaders, and since Scandinavians have an enlightened philosophy about alcohol consumption that was absent in the Bible Belt of my youth, some buddies and I naturally found our way to the sailor bars by the wharves. Our trip etiquette usually required some article of scout clothing; mine was a red beret. The beret soon became a keep-away Frisbee among the sailors in one bar. I didn't mind; I was pretty schnokered myself. From one sailor to another my headpiece sailed: Yanks, Aussies, Canucks, Greeks, Nigerians, Brazilians, Swedes, Dutch, Argentineans, and South Africans. I wasn't sure what to make of them – no real uniforms like the military. Almost a Hells Angels voguishness, not quite rebels but possessing a rakish self-confidence derived from a lot of interesting encounters; some successful, some not, I imagined.

At my ripe age of 17, I hadn't been able to grasp their profile at the fringes of society, but now Charlie had filled me in adequately. They were thinkers *and* tough guys, self-assured but often reserved (except in taverns). They were also loners, yet totally comfortable in the presence of others. I knew I could never be one of them – and besides, I prefer the revolving hologram of landscape, populated, to the monotony of an open ocean, vacant of all but the seafood part of the menu.

Probably it is just this analogy that I needed at that time in my life…and now again in retrospect, when setting out to write my own *Gulliver's Travels*. It's fine, like my friend Jimbo or like the Charlies, to have the straight path laid out for you, to know what you love to do with a passion; apparently it is inner-directed, almost as if destined. But my own mind, body and spirit seemed to navigate differently.

I wanted nothing cut-and-dried in my life that would take away the need to explore, and the passion for adventure. I realized at that young age that I wanted to indulge in All of It – whatever that was – by placing myself in the center and working through it and outward… through the people, places and cultures. Also I wanted to navigate inward at the same time, melding the two universes and coming out with…what? What?

Ahh, that was the mystery!

I had already discovered my similarities with Charlie, but now I pondered our differences. Both of us were integral to the function of society. The Charlie breed of character has been the vanguard of empires for many a century – not the diplomats or soldiers, architects or musicians; not even the poets – but the Merchant Marines, by God, carrying the world's goods from one port to another. If the old adage is true that "armies go where trade does not," then these guys could rightfully be hailed as our most experienced and expert diplomats… peacemakers…for totally self-serving reasons, of course. But then, why not? And are they any different from most? Why do we make love? Why do we learn how to cut open a person's liver and heart and stitch it together again so it will work better and stronger? *Gulliver*, *there is a certain inner joy, or satisfaction, in the process of following your bliss…and what, pray tell, IS that bliss, except to be in the middle of the journey itself?* It was like a set of Chinese boxes, one fitting into another, into another, ad infinitum.

* * * * * *

I now passed into California's long Central Valley, through the gauntlets of Jerry Brown's fruit inspectors. I guess that's what folks did for fun in Stockton and Modesto (haven't they ever heard of a hootenanny?). But Yosemite was next, and like a mendicant approaching Mecca, I slowed down, reverently fixed on my goal. There it was, the Holy Grail of the early conservation movement, John Muir's dream and Teddy Roosevelt's legacy: Teddy, that ol' firebrand, the last Republican of national stature to look at any landscape without drooling over the "ka-*ching*" of cash registers. OK, maybe that's not quite fair, but certainly he was one of the last members of any political party to possess cojones *and* wisdom.

Yosemite had a reputation of swelling to California's sixth largest city during busy weekends. Thankfully, I was arriving on a weekday in late September. Besides, I'd been seasoned as a youth by the teeming hordes in the Great Smoky Mountains National Park, where on any given summer day half the state of Ohio could be seen leaning out of their Winnebago's tossing peanut butter sandwiches to Yogi and Boo-Boo (who were usually upside down in garbage cans, oblivious to Yankees bearing gifts).

All things considered, Yosemite was relaxed and relatively unpopulated except in Sunset Campground where 50 cents got me a postage-stamp tent site encircled by Japanese, Israelis, Germans, Kiwis, and the regular Olympic-sized delegation of climbers from around the world. English was the common language because it had to be, but at any time a dozen different dialects were buzzing in their own little quarters. I never did feel claustrophobic, but I did feel estranged. After all of my heartfelt one-on-ones in the middle of nowhere, it was ironic to now feel totally alone in the middle of scores of people. Again, it was that kaleidoscopic or "holographic" thing. Touching bodies or camping next to them did not satisfy my curiosity to get to know them, to find out what they liked to do most, what their favorite music was, or what caused them to laugh, or cry...to learn what "moved their cheese," as a later writer would put it.

One night, however, it was the earth itself that moved – physically – and lasting for 15, 20, maybe 30 seconds: shifts, shudders and mini-shudders. The campsite erupted into babble; flashlights scoured the woods and sky looking for some invisible sorcerer. It turned out to be only a low 4 Richter-rumbler, but the next day we were told that several climbers on Half Dome had been badly hurt. Like an idyllic beach garnished as bait to battering typhoons, so did this bucolic backwoods have its tormentors. Can we ever *really* be prepared for surprises?

* * * * * *

The road to Lassen National Park up north looked innocent enough. Judging from the Rand McNally map, it shouldn't have been more than five or six hours of casual driving...but those maps lie! First of all, they can only show so many swiggles per inch, and of course swiggles slow you down when they pertain to roads. Second, the maps don't indicate how many lumber trucks are playing chicken on the swiggles, slowing one down even further. What I thought would be a relaxing drive turned out to be a nail-biting, gear-grinding, bare-knuckled tour-de-force requiring all day and into the evening.

What does one do when the going gets tough? Sing TV commercials? Recite mantras? Listen to personal empowerment tapes? Crawling traffic is surely a test of one's mettle as well as one's patience, especially for a Sagittarian like me. Sag's are notorious for being impatient, for getting a job done fast, and *arriving*. Two-lane no-or-occasional passing highways and getting stuck behind a queue of trucks braking gear to climb upward, was...well, an opportunity to enjoy the scenery, was it not? Which I did...by degrees. It was magnificent. *The real reward is the journey and not the destination*, I reminded myself once again (sigh).

Three hundred miles to the north of Yosemite, Lassen Park sat marooned like a desert isle, a silent specter against a sea of black. The park's main concessions were shut down for the season, as were the showers. I was alone; not even one other camper around. Clear sky sprinkled with thousands of stars, and a steady but respectful wind; otherwise, quiet. Was it worth the trip? It always is…right? What was there not to appreciate about this serenity? I felt as though it was all mine, forever. And it is exactly that quiet "Zen" place that I still come back to, as a Place of Being where no matter what is happening anywhere else, outside or in, *it is always perfect*. Still fertile with possibility, still reassuring me that *all is well*.

The next morning I drove the entire 34 miles of giant firs and geysers without passing a single car or person. About 20 miles outside the park to the northwest I received confirmation that human life still existed when a few cars and trucks appeared on the road; by that time approximately 55 miles and 14 hours had passed since the last sign of human life.

It was a golden, early autumn day as I passed by the volcanic sentinel of Mt. Shasta and crossed into Oregon, south of Medford. Mixed colors of the snow-frosted peaks and turning leaves once more presented one of nature's clever contradictions. Could it be so that the ocean was also nearby, maybe only a hundred miles away, where one could walk the shores in tee shirt and cutoffs? *Are we there yet? Where?* I felt like I had entered into a physical illusion in which I was seeing not only landscape outside myself, but deep within as well: cold spots of uncertainty, oceans of time, and the changing season of leaving home and going out on my own.

Chapter Five

Roots

I'd picked up Chris at a truck stop café about 30 miles south of Shasta. He could have been Shane's brother, only a little stockier, slightly shorter and about ten years older. He was returning home to Medford, on the other side of the gentle Siskiyou Mountains.

"Say, Chris, ever been to the little town of Jacksonville, outside Medford?"

"Sure. I know it well." He cast a questioning glance in my direction.

"Ever heard of Cantrall-Buckley Park?"

"Yeah, I used to play Frisbee there. It's kind of a cute place. Jacksonville and Medford are like two-prong towns – half retirees or farmers, half hipsters like me. Lotsa 'Recovering Californians,'" he chuckled, "but we generally get along pretty good."

"Well, that name Cantrall still belongs to one of the old guards – he's my grandpa's brother."

"No shit?" Now Chris eyed me full-on. "You coming back to search for roots?"

"Not my primary purpose, but I've never met those distant kin and it's a free bed, so I'm gonna check it out. Part curiosity, part convenience, part obligation, you might say."

My mother's father's ancestors had settled in and around this area in the 1850s. The Cantralls and Newlins sailed from England; the Murphys and the Devlins defected from that other tortured island west of Her Majesty's throne. Casualties of the potato famine, I'm sure, but I've never really known. Some came out on the Oregon Trail;

others played leap frog across the Isthmus of Panama, long before the building of the canal – Teddy's long arm, once again. Prior to 1904, that meant leaving your ship on the northern (Caribbean) side – the Isthmus actually runs west to east, contrary to accepted folk wisdom – hacking your way through the jungle and mosquito clouds to the Pacific, careful not to step on the malaria-riddled corpses of less fortunate wayfarers, then boarding another vessel on the southern (Pacific) side, that would ferry you to the Promised Land of Oregon.

My grandfather's forbearers once owned hundreds of acres around the Applegate Valley and Rogue Rivers of Southwestern Oregon. I'd like to imagine the assets were squandered away through whoring, gambling, and drinking; but alas, there were no Wild Bill Hickocks in my progenitors, so I guess they just let it slip through their hands the old-fashioned way.

In my mind, I'd been coming to Oregon all of my life. As a youngster I'd vaguely heard some of the stories about Grandpa's ranch, the cattle drives through the Siskiyous, and floods on the Applegate. Tales of the Oregon Trail and Lewis & Clark had captivated me in the fifth and sixth grades. Prior to graduation from college, I'd even applied to a number of companies in the Portland area, but among my many job offers, nothing had come through for me from this area.

Oregon had an almost mythic call to me – besides, you've gotta admire a state whose two principal universities are nicknamed the "Beavers" and the "Ducks" as opposed to, say, the more common "Tigers," "Bulldogs," "Wildcats," etc. Oregon struck me as an honest state, if a bit whacky.

Grandpa's upbringing could have inspired a Jane Austen novel. Jimmy Stewart, or perhaps Bing Crosby, would have done perfect portrayals. In fact, Grandpa, whose name was Otto, was a lot like Stewart – polite but firm, stubborn but principled; possessing an ineffable humor hidden behind brows of worry. Born the oldest son in 1897, all he wanted to do was stay on the ranch. His younger brother Harlan, whom I would soon meet, wanted to go out and see the world. Instead, their parents, citing tradition or some other supercilious horseshit, declared that as the oldest, my future Grandpa must attend university and stake his claim in the world of commerce. As the dutiful son – and heartbroken – Otto got his Electrical Engineering degree from Oregon State in 1918, thus becoming a "beaver" 41 years before I was christened with that nickname, and eventually the General Electric company sent him to the red clay roads of Georgia. From the early 1920s until his death in 1986, he saw his beloved homeland only once (the other side of the family, known as Grandma, saw to that).

To complete the twisted Greek mini-tragedy, number two son Harlan – the itchy, footloose one – was assigned the ranch, where he grumbled his life away, as I was about to discover, a "victim" of every injustice concocted by scheming bureaucrats, swindling corporations, cheating neighbors, and petty wives. Harlan may have been one of the meek, but he wasn't blessed, he wasn't a peacemaker, and he sure as hell wasn't going to inherit the Earth. He was just a crusty old fart, mad at the world and waiting to die. Although polite to me in a familial-obligatory sort of way and even social to the point of having a wry sense of humor, clearly that twinkle in his eye wasn't playful mischief. It was usually the sadistic malice of the underdog who tries to pull himself up by ridiculing the ineptness of the "luckier" ones – in short, everyone else.

Harlan was contemptible. Was it heredity or environment? Both? And what had caused him not to run away? If he had been born fifty years later, would he have been so obedient and yielded to his father's demands – possibly ending up a happy, self-fulfilled individual? And then, what about my grandfather Otto, who had wanted nothing more than to stay in Oregon on the family ranch? Would he have rebelled also, and refused to go to college, or head east?

What causes people to ignore their destinies and settle for less-than-best? Was it now my duty as the progeny of this most unfortunate mix-up of twisted consequences, to tell the world to RUN before it's too late? RUN…just as I was doing? And not to run *away* from anything, but rather, to run *toward* that inner voice, that Highest Self that already *knows with a passion* how it wants to carve out its Destiny? *"Listen carefully,"* it whispers.

I was not disappointed, however, that I'd decided to visit. Harlan drove me around the valley, tour-guiding me through the cute little town of Jacksonville, preserved on the National Historical Register.

We cruised along the Applegate and Rogue rivers, so benign at the moment but often churning; thus a Mecca for rafters, and the lifeblood of farmers and ranchers alike. He showed me the award-winning winery in Ruch Valley, established on the hallowed grounds of my ancestors. It resembled the Rhine vineyards in many ways, as luscious Gewürztraminers came from this area.

Harlan then drove me out to the family graveyards – family I would never know. Their work here was done. Under those headstones from the 1850s forward, my coagulated DNA was resting in eternity. They had dreamed large dreams, rolled large dice, and endured incredible hardships. But they had received bountiful blessings after settling in their adopted paradise, and from that root stock, one-half of my family tree blossomed. I was awe-struck, and grateful. I even appreciated Harlan, mainly for being my chauffer and narrator, and also for calling me "Boy," the ultimate term of endearment to one's grand-nephew. I imagine he had probably forgotten my name and was too proud or embarrassed to admit it. "Boy, let's go the pancake breakfast," or, "Boy, let's take a ride up the Applegate." Yessuh, Unca' Harlan, suh!

Gulliver had been given another opportunity to ponder what he did not want to include in his own life journey. Better get rid of all the anger, frustration, resentment and pent-up regrets at an early age so they don't spill out into the years like a bushel of bad apples, contaminating the entire harvest of one's days thereafter. Provincialism of family roots that choked off the life force was exactly what needed to be dispensed with – and how better than by travel, exploring the world, to witness the same dangerous sinkholes in every part of the planet?

Uncle Harlan, let me tell you something. There is always a way out; we are not victims of anyone, not even our parents. It is you who chose not to follow your heart, and I'm glad I had a chance before your own dirt bed was dug in that miserable graveyard, to witness the consequences of your choice.

Ergo, my credo. *I say, refuse to submit to anyone or anything except your own heart's desires and investigate every crater and canyon before stepping in.*

* * * * * *

Speaking of craters, it was a beautiful weekend for visiting Crater Lake; the weather was perfect. The Silver Bullet flew over the sweeping curves of highway that sliced an asphalt ribbon through the thick forest of ponderosa pines. After devouring three desserts at Becky's world famous pie shop, I proceeded to the rim of the ancient volcano where I gazed down 2,600 feet upon a surreal world of indigo and cobalt, legacy of the crystal clear water and 600-foot depths. It was flanked by the mini-coned Wizzard Island popping up inside (thus a volcano within a volcano), and crisscrossed by tourist boats carving up its otherwise placid surface. Six miles across and at least 3.14 times that much in rough circumference, Crater Lake was another of those wonderments that either leaves one breathless or causes the involuntary release of trite expressions such as "Wow!" or "Man oh man!" What else could be said? And that was the point. Nothing *could* be said, no words *were* sufficient. It was a sacred place and, as at the big Canyon in Arizona, I vowed to come back.

I rode gravity down through the Umpqua National Forest, reveling in the early fall foliage. At this elevation, considering the latitude, it was more like mid-autumn; Gaia's garments swept the mountains in a collage of red, yellow and orange to complement the thick groves of evergreens. The landscape became lusher now as I moved farther west down the slopes of the Cascades. After a brief stop for parking tickets at the University in Eugene ($2 a pop – Go, Ducks!) I was off to the coast near Florence. Beautiful rolling green hills and simple rustic barns conjured images of an East Tennessee now long behind me. But with saltwater nearby, the seagulls betrayed the fantasy. I spent the night near the Dunes – the Sahara's gift to North America. It rained of course: Oregon Sunshine. One doesn't just sleep under the stars on the Oregon Coast. The next morning, however, rewarded me with real sunlight projecting a kaleidoscope of diffused crystals off a zillion wet leaves and grass shoots.

Oregon, like California, boasts miles of protected seashore. In this finest of Oregon's many fine state parks, I met Greg and Kathy and their two tots. They were moving to Burns, Oregon, from the colossus to the south.

"Like *The Grapes of Wrath*, Steve, only in reverse," Kathy grimaced. She was a school teacher and Greg, a carpenter. They were early 30-ish and the kids maybe two and four.

"We just can't afford to live in California any more – the taxes, the crime, the traffic. Everything's so goddamn expensive and there are so many people now. We're both third-generation Californians, but we've had it."

Greg chimed in, "Yeah, so we started to look around Oregon last year and decided on Burns. Not the prettiest place, but it's dry inland, lotsa elbow room, and we're gonna give these little guys a quality of life they couldn't get in L.A. or the Bay Area – at least, not on our income. So we bought five acres of land and a simple three-bedroom house. Gonna go up there and give it a go."

I assumed they would be successful and wished them happy lives. At the same time I couldn't help wondering what they were really running from, and whether relocation was going to deliver what seemed to be missing in their lives. I was reminded of frontier stories of families of ten or more, living in 2- or 3-bedroom houses without indoor plumbing, refrigeration, heat except for wood stoves, or any of our other modern conveniences…families that not only survived but felt blessed, grateful, for everything they *did* have. Maybe it was the hardship that kept them together, the survival struggle that bonded them. Or maybe it was something else more related to feelings that was in the driver's seat of this young family's decision to flee.

Everywhere, wheels were in motion. Feet burned and hearts yearned to start new lives, forget old ones, or seek fortunes. Some went for the rush of excitement and adventure; others were one step ahead of some (real or imaginary) gremlin in their past. Some walked toward their destination; others ran from their nemesis. The world came alive in the autumn of '81 – pilgrims and vagabonds popped out of the woods and parking lots like the dragon-seeded skeletons of *Jason and the Argonauts*.

But this was an illusion, of course – skewed statistics from a not-too-random sample. We see what we want to see, a fact known to quantum physicists, sages, and used car salesmen. I was on the run, so I kept bumping into runners. Let's face it, when one picks up hitchhikers, hangs around campsites and circumscribes an arc around the greater part of a continent, some interesting characters are going to appear. The reality is, however, that at any given time, 99+% of society are hunkered down in a home, job, school or some other entrenched lifestyle. Most have no desire to upset the status quo or step out of their conventional boxes...not that there's anything "right" or "wrong" about that. Again, it's just the way things are, and who am I to judge? Some dream but don't act, either from lack of resources or lack of temerity. Many do act, in sporadic bursts – like me, now – but with the assumption that the change is either temporary or a step up to something better or more fun.

Shane, for example, would love nothing better than to crawl back into the American Dream with his rekindled flame back in Mother Arizona; Greg and Kathy, to a new community in a new state, with gainful employment. Ditto for Jimbo, once exited from the halls of academia. Ronnie's drunken forays of liberty probably assumed (unconsciously, of course) that the home base of Uncle Sam was always waiting with open arms, as long as he was willing to put himself in harm's way in some Godforsaken wasteland for a few years at a stretch.

The Charlie's of the world, though, were a different breed. But even with him, somehow I couldn't help but think there was one special port – commercial or human – that was his secret Shangri-La...some place where the waters were warm and the drinks cool; where so-and-so's hair and perfume and patience and compassion compensated for all the scars seen and unseen on his persona. The Womb, the eye of his hurricane...that someone/something/someplace representing safety, stability, or even some type of *meaning* in this ever-changing world.

Yet we know this "something" or "someone," too, shall pass in the inexorable march of time, robbing us of identity; so we trump it up by waxing nostalgically or by magnifying the imagery of the good times associated with it. In the end, we must let go completely – ashes-to-ashes and dust-to-dust. There are many gradations of self-awareness for the vast majority of us. But the Charlie's of the world only know two outcomes. Those who can keep their bearings in the maelstrom (their inner sailor) are called *enlightened*, "Bodhisattvas"; the rest end up heavily medicated and laced into straitjackets – or as chum floating in a lonely, gray sea.

* * * * * *

The Oregon Coast soon forgot its manners. Rain fell in sheets. I never knew there were so many shades of gray: charcoal gray, silver gray, black gray, gun-barrel gray, tinted grays, neutral grays, light grays... and I'm sure the denizens of the paint world have a few more dozen among their wall samples. The coast here had 'em all, including the Granddaddy of Grays – "Horizontal Driving Wet Gray." Fortunately, I had long ago mastered my Eureka Timberline tent and could now throw it down, stake it and climb inside in a few moments. Its tarp held up nobly, its zipper struggled but still moved, and the duct-taped interior sported wounds of battles past. Occasionally the floor got wet but an air mattress and musty blanket kept the slush at bay.

The Lighthouse at Lincoln City appeared and disappeared like a ghost in my peripheral vision. The wind whipped curtains of water across the Silver Bullet's windshield and the pavement flirted with the hydraulic friction tolerance of still-adolescent tires. I'd been in plenty of old fashioned "gully washers" in my native Southeast, but rarely had I encountered such an ongoing, fierce, windblown downpour. Driving up the coast, I then cut inland, skirted Portland, crossed the Willamette and Columbia rivers and entered Washington – named after the guy who cut down the cherry tree, a guy who lived about as far away from this present state as is possible in the contiguous United States. There must be a story there somewhere...

I had to see Mount St. Helen's, or what was left of it since it blew its top the year before. I had to see where that crazy octogenarian Harry Truman (not *that* one, the other one) made his last stand before asphyxiating and vaporizing. If there's one thing we like better than our neighbors' dirty laundry, it's disasters. "Oooh – check out that tsunami wave. Twisters, cool!"

I couldn't get closer than 20 miles, as the area was cordoned off in a successive radius of colored zones. Some visitors were allowed scientific or governmental access, but curious citizens like myself were just *persona non grata*.

When Mt. Hood down in Portland decides to upchuck again
– or Rainier near Seattle (or other peaks such as Adams or Baker or
Shasta) – prevailing winds could easily turn those cities to modern-
day Pompeii's. The cascading mud wall alone from Rainier's melting
glaciers, moving like a freight train, would take out Olympia (talk
about urban renewal!). Forget about the ash, fire, and noxious fumes.
Geologists say that in geological time, they're all "due." But we hear,
"not tomorrow, not next week…later." So there's still time for a few
more malls and subdivisions, another lane or three on the freeway.
"Later"…like St. Helen's?

Chapter Six

"Check out my Office!"

I picked up Mike, a young lumberjack, a few miles up the road heading back to his work camp. He had the square-jaw, model look of Lee Majors or Stephen Boyd or one of the other hunk-heroes of '60s and '70s B-grade movies, and was extremely friendly with an ingratiating smile. Mike just wanted to get to a crossroads about 30 clicks, said he, where he'd meet some buddies and pass away the rest of the Sunday afternoon. The sun was shining once more – it seems the Northwest likes to vacillate between steely gray and emerald green, now glistening off the October gold of the encroaching Cascade autumn.

Mike and I stopped at his rendezvous point, the typical roadhouse/cabin-looking place with neon beer signs, fishing worms and questionable food. I was in no hurry, so I joined him for a few Olympia beers on tap.

Mike was third generation lumberjack, but believed he may be the last. "Hard to make a go of it these days, now that the Chinese and Southeast Asians are in the act with cheaper lumber. Also the damn environmental regulations. Hell, I'm sympathetic to the spotted owls or those snail darters down your way in Tennessee; but we've got entire towns and thousands of people here in Oregon, Washington and Idaho who've built America's houses and factories for a hundred years. I mean, does some little fish or bird get more priority than us?"

I was intrigued to hear the other side of the story from someone trying to make a living off Mother Nature's raw bounty; someone who would be hard put to consider the mathematics of extinction, including even his own species.

"I'm sure pretty soon, say 5-10 years, I'll hafta pack up and move to Portland or Seattle and have a go at another profession." He wiped his mouth with the back of his hand and set down his mug for another round. "I'm a pretty good carpenter. I guess that's how I alleviate my guilt – if I can chop the damn trees down, at least I get to make something out of them later!"

We both guffawed.

To go with his good looks, Mike had the Paul Bunyan motif down pat – flannel shirt, jeans, fuzzy hat with the upturned 360-degree rim suppressing a head of unmanageable hair. I asked him where he kept Babe, the Blue Ox. Another round of laughter, and beer.

"I'm a union man, guess I hafta be, but walking a fine line – crap, I tell the guys we're part of the problem. Sensible demands are one thing, but don't bite the hand that feeds you. On the other hand, I sure wouldn't have wanted to be one of those CCC guys back in the 1930s; breaking their backs, living full time in camps that were just shantytowns, away from their families for months or years."

Here was a typical specimen of America's labor force, trying to figure out the best way to survive in a country whose government seemed to be in control of his destiny; a government whose operations he didn't understand; and even if he did...even if he offered solutions, how could he get to the right people? The big amorphous "They" was so far away, what was one to do...except maybe wile away time drinking beer and complaining...

"Anyway," he rambled on, "I'm sure glad I don't have a pack of kids to take care of, like some of these guys. And I'm only 26, so I can move on. But I feel for these guys in their forties and fifties – when the walls come crashing down, they're pretty much hosed up here with no other skills, and dying towns. And Weyerhaeuser, Georgia Pacific, Boise Cascade, they're not sugar-tits, either. They're bottom-line businesses, and only a fool doesn't know that. They'll pack up and move to Alabama or the South Pacific or Latin America or wherever they need to go to keep the ol' shareholder dividend checks going. But I guess I shouldn't bitch too much. Check out my office!" He made a sweeping gesture toward Rainier's summit, about an hour's drive to the north. "Not bad, huh?"

"Cheers, Mike," I lifted my mug. "Two more Oly's, bar-keep!"

As I now write Mike into this story, I wonder what happened to him, if he found a way to survive when some of the big companies did pick up their tent stakes and move on, or how the environmentalists (the "enviro-meddlers," as a future congressman would call them) changed his life. How many times was he married and divorced? Did he become a U.S. Congressman or did he choose alcoholism, religion, law? Anything was possible in America...

* * * * * *

It was dusk now as I pulled into Rainier National Park. I could no longer make out the mountain's buttressed flanks, light notwithstanding, as I was too close. There were too many trees, too much forest, and I couldn't see one for the other. I had sequestered the evening's meal in the little trading post outside of the park entrance – a six-pack of Rainier (best to appease the local gods), a can of Pringles, an apple or two, and candy bars – basic food for basic travels. As with Lassen the previous week, Rainier Park was closed for the season except for a few scaled down campgrounds with flush toilets. Since it was a Sunday night as well, things were all but dead. There was a pup tent here, a Westphalia camper there, and over there, a VW van with Jerry Garcia's sage-like mug radiating from every window.

It was quiet, too. Even Lassen, completely deserted, had treated me to the steady rushing of approaching high-pressure winds. There, the trees had bowed, swayed and cracked in that ancient, indecipherable tongue. Here, sound was muffled; subdued and peaceful, yet serene. Respectful, perhaps – a High Mass for high trees. It *was* Sunday night, after all. Even the occasional visage of a person seemed to emanate no sound, like there was an almost conscious effort not to break the tranquility with idle talk or humming generators.

But I wanted company, dammit, so I wandered about 100 yards over toward a white rental car. It belonged to Lindsay.

"How'z it goin', mate?" he greeted me in the signature Australian hailing frequency.

An Australian sentence without "mate" is like a kangaroo without a pouch. I had always liked that mongrel breed immensely (Aussies, not kangaroos). They seemed to possess the same indomitable spirit of optimism as we Yanks, but without the self-puffing hubris and righteous fervor that has stamped our position in world history with a giant "Reserved – No Trespassing" sign. The Aussies are quick with a drink – or six – and possess a backslapping self-deprecation that comes from living in an upside-down land usurped by convicts. If one can't find humor in that…

I could forgive them and their Kiwi sidekicks for an indigenous genocide program that trumped even our North American disenfranchisement of natives. A Victorian prudishness still lurks in their collective, beer-slogged consciousness and chooses to reveal itself sparingly, like at silly tea parties or the occasional coronation of some monarch overseas. But never at rugby games, nor in the two World Wars. The ANZACs (Australian & New Zealand Auxiliary Corps), for example, had endured the highest Killed-In-Action ratio and captured the greatest amount of yardage per capita of any Allied or Axis army. What I didn't know, as Lindsay informed me, was that "Their Limey commanders just told 'em there was a pub at the end of the field, mate." *For Queen, for Country, for Fosters…Oy!* No Hun or Turk machine gun nest could stand between an ANZAC and his appointed round of "shouts."

Lindsay was a chiropractor from Sydney, on self-exiled "walkabout" to North America. "Six months oughta be about right, mate." Aussies do nothing small or inconsequential.

In his mid-thirties, he was a gregarious guy and splendid caricature of all his country's stereotypes: polite but raunchy, inquisitive, a sports fanatic, and of course he liked beer. Lindsay, too, had a stash of Rainier frosties, and thankfully had purchased a cache of dry firewood for this cool, moist evening on the mountain's hemline.

The custom of walkabout, an Aussie adaptation of an unpronounceable Aboriginal word, was hardwired into every youngster's brain during his or her teenage years. It basically involved traipsing about in a gypsy, nomadic fashion for up to several years, and taking in the larger world. Schools could wait, and employers could go hang themselves. But of course, those institutions understood – they were once young Australians (and New Zealanders) too. For an Aborigine, the journey may have consisted of hundreds of miles out into the barren, orange Outback. For modern-day white kids, it meant Europe, Asia, North and South America, Africa, Antarctica, lots of islands, and the stars and planets, if they could get there.

One might compare a walkabout to the Native American "vision quest," with one exception. The purpose of a vision quest was to meet one's Maker in some fashion or other, a Maker who delivered a soul-to-soul message about one's purpose here on earth, this time around. It was the Leap-into-Adulthood Thing. When you returned to your teepee, you had a direction or inner sense of who you were.

Aussies might spend several years walking about, and return with nothing more than a hangover or empty wallet. But it would be unfair and incorrect to think this isn't also a leap into adulthood: they just don't place any metaphysical significance in the wandering. Truth, however, doesn't give a damn what medium is used or what social construct frames the fable: like water, it seeks its own level.

"No worries" and "Been there, done that" – Australian contributions to Webster's Dictionary – are long-established mantras in that strange land of cheerful, adventurous people. No group travels cheaper and lighter, consumes more beer per rationed dollar, butchers the English language so shamelessly (is there a lesson here?) and is more at ease with themselves and the world body-politic than the Aussies.

The next morning Lindsay was gone, having left a business card on my windshield. Six years later, on my own walkabout throughout New Zealand and Australia, I tried to look him up, but alas, the address and phone belonged to someone else. I'm sure wherever Lindsay had gone and whatever locale he would choose on the planet to call his office, he would be having a great time. Good on ya, mate. She'll be right.

Chapter Seven

Lost

The flanks of Rainier were not suffering fools and Gullivers gladly that morning. Spitting rain and drifting fog stirred up the worst of the Pacific Northwest's weather gremlins – dreary gray and muted green. Although at Cayuse Pass, just under 5,000 feet, a little white was spiced in for the sake of variety. I never did see the top of Rainier that day as I swept around to the northwest toward Puget Sound.

The slow drizzle changed its mind and graduated to a driving sheet of rain. About 20 miles east of Puyallup – (which tickled me as something a southerner might say – "Pull y'all up?") – I saw the shadowy outlines of two dwarves. No, perhaps one was an elf...on closer look, maybe stage extras for Peter Pan's Lost Boys...They were two young boys on their way to somewhere, thumbs out, wetter than Poseidon's graveyard and greatly relieved when I offered my services. The older one was maybe 13, stolid and matter-of-fact; the younger perhaps 10, quiet in a deer-in-the-headlight manner. I assumed they were brothers but had no way of knowing this. The ride took only 15-20 minutes, but it seemed like hours. They offered nothing, just a random litany of "yeah" and "sure." If brevity was a virtue, then I had captured two canonized saints. No questions, no divulgement: not even a name, rank or serial number.

I pulled over at the off-ramp. They mumbled something as lethargically they opened the car door and slid out. Was this slow motion a hesitation, or possibly an appeal? Or just juvenile acknowledgement, "Thanks for the warm seat"? I'll never know. Their secret and/or burden went with them in the general direction of Portland, presumably away from trouble but possibly willing to court it (further?). These are the little mysteries that flit by the radar regularly, if we pay attention. My direction after Puyallup was I-5 North, so I bid adieu, slipped them a $20 bill and silently petitioned their guardian spirits to put in a little overtime.

Yet I couldn't get them out of my mind. What tempestuous forces drove two young boys out onto the open road in the middle of a downpour? Abusive parents? Escape from a "reform" school? They had no possessions except some tattered ponchos, the Sears backroom clear-out type. Shivering, sullen...what fate may await them? I imagined a sadistic twinkle in some trucker's eye; tire treads at 70 miles per hour...or, what was their possible crime? I envisioned two Herbert-and-Gladys-types back on 123 Elm St. in some bumfuck town with their throats slit and jewelry box pilfered. Things are not always what they seem, and I have no idea what wind blew the sails of my diminutive pilgrims.

Should I have questioned more – maybe driven them, surreptitiously, to a police station and forced the issue? Would I read about them in the paper next week while idling around some trucker's cafe? My mind somersaulted – could *I* even be, technically speaking, a kidnapper? Maybe I was a sucker. Or a savior. Or an accomplice in some getaway.

Of all the vagabonds I've ever met on the concrete arteries of America and Canada, I've worried most about these two.

What an easy life I had lived at that age, and all the ensuing years up to my ripe old 22: nuclear family, spin the bottle, requisite pets, Little League, parochial schools. Never mind all the rites-of-passage stuff like teenage broken hearts, zits, peer pressure, sibling slugfests, etc. – those were just a few thorns in the rose garden. I came from the quintessential middle-class town with an above-average educational system, low crime, and ice cream on Saturday nights. I had lived a Utopian life in that little Pleasantville, and even the rough edge of the big city of Atlanta had hardly tarnished society's protective halo around me. This, followed by the ivory halls of academia and collegial playmates; a modest apartment and beer money for weekends...there'd even been a bicycle and a car – for a while, at least (alas poor Horace, gone to the "chop-shop").

I honestly didn't know how to relate to the problems of ghetto kids, or kids with parents incubated right out of Dr. Jekkyl's petri dish. I had no barometer, even though instinctively I supposed that every day in these youngsters' lives looked as gray, sullen and washed out as this Monday morning under the Cascade Curtain. I also felt helpless, and guilty. Maybe I should have done more, tried assertive actions; how could I have just let them get out of the car?

I tried to put myself in their place. My mind raced as I considered all the scenarios that would have caused two kids to be hitchhiking in foul weather, in a relatively rural area…If ever there was a time to count my blessings, it was at that moment. But that did not assuage my uneasiness.

Even though I'd moved way past the spot where I'd left them off on the highway, in my mind's eye I could still see the two Lost Boys hunching under their insufficient ponchos, fading in my rear view mirror. St. Christopher better be well-rested; they were going to need him.

* * * * * *

I skirted Olympia and the southern perimeter of Puget Sound, barely able to make out the gray dome of the State Capitol that appeared suddenly and blurrily. Somewhere in that shadowy building at this very moment, legislators were hacking out compromises, carving up pork barrels and spinning their silver tongues. Taxes were raised or lowered, alliances fused or splintered, conspiracies spun and disputed. I'm sure it was a buzzing hive of frenetic democratic chaos, replete with lobbyists and media; but to me, it was just another navigational buoy, a passing landmark in a foreign land. The houses and schools and donut shops whose livelihood depended so much on the decrees from that hallowed dome were just so many Lincoln logs; the bridges and railroad trestles mere Lego's. It was real, but not to me. Not yet.

I steered around the west side of the Sound and headed north up the Olympic Peninsula. The gray and green were still at war, and it looked to be a stalemate. I was pensive and introspective. I turned on the radio to shake out of it, dialing in to a Seattle rock'n'roll station.

43

Same crap I've had for weeks now – Journey, Foreigner, Blue Oyster Cult, Bob Seger, Moody Blues, the Stones, and that croaky song about Stevie Nicks and Tom Petty draggin' each other's heart around.

In my naiveté, I had assumed that shifting latitudes would mean different tunes from the regional squawk-boxes. Silly me. The big Corporate Cookie-Cutter never sleeps, and you could pretty much tune in the same songs, same regurgitating DJs, the same verbal diarrhea, same schmaltzy ads for discounted waterbeds, and same screaming car dealers exercising their First Amendment rights everywhere you went. It didn't matter if you were in Texarkana or Tacoma, Pecos or Portland. Even the enthralling regional dialects that defined our forefathers' continental babble were now whitewashed over by a streamlined, predictable media vernacular – everywhere and nowhere at once, like the attention spans of my fellow citizens.

The big Quaalude of Consumption says, "I gotta deal for you – wanna demonstrate your individuality, your most excellent uniqueness? Just buy our product, you and 280 million other salivating zombies. Hey, this one's even improved. Now you'll be *an ever better you!* It walks, it talks; it slices and dices, whirls and twirls. Be the first one on your block – everyone's talking about it...they won't last; this offer's not good after midnight unless renewed tomorrow...only $2.99... Wait, there's a new shipment coming of the new-and-improved Yakkety-Yak, and you will want to be the first one to have your own... sooooOO..."

Click. Bring me a bucket to hurl in.

But still, we'll drag him along at 11% year-over-year net profit on the stairway to economic nirvana...

At that moment, I preferred the pattering of rain, the Doppler-whooshing of passing tires and whimsical rambling of my own thoughts. I had what Buddha called "Monkey Mind" – the endless tape deck of inwardly inane babble: warnings, threats, reveries, projections, feuds, rehearsals, conjurings, calculations; *anything* to keep the big reservoir of the cranium chock-full of *everything* but my True Self...because, well, that's scary, and against the rules. Even if it is free, non-syndicated, and authentic.

On the other hand, True Self is a bitch to ignore, always prompting from somewhere right beneath the surface. Damn hard to click off, too, like the button on my Clarion. Pick your poison – WROK, Inc., or your own perpetual teleprompter. Either way's like Chinese water torture. We may have spandex and moonwalks, but unfortunately, peace and quiet won't be regarded by The Next Era as this age's prized commodities. *Silence, where is thy sting?*

Chapter Eight

The Road Worrier

North of Bremerton, another hooded phantom with a protruding thumb split the mist. This one was bigger, although the plastic yellow raincoat lent a comical appearance, like an overgrown kindergartener or an extra from a Ronald McDonald talent tryout.

His name was Laura, because he was a she. Jeeesh – first juveniles, now a chick – what *is* it about Puget Sound hitchhiking that casts conventions sideways?

Me: "Where to?"

Laura: "North, maybe East."

Either way required a ferry crossing, but I assumed she knew that. Laura was in her late twenties, tall, with wavy, dishwater-blond hair.

She explained herself: "I'm from Northern Cal, around Humboldt. Just decided to take a little sightseeing stroll up here. Never been before."

"You're not worried about hitching…? I mean, you know…"

"No problems, ever. I don't buy into all that scare-shit about do's and don'ts. If something bad were to happen, I guess it was meant to be, but I just don't give it a lot of thought."

"So you're just going where the road takes you?"

"Well, kind of, yeah, I'm taking two or three weeks to see the Great Northwest. Kinda hard to see it with all this rain right now, though. But I still appreciate its beauty."

I never did quite figure out what Laura did, but it sounded like she was in some kind of commune: grow your own food, burn a little rope, pass around clothing and furniture, etc. "Sandals and candles," a friend once described it, or perhaps more appropriately, "incense and innocence." And a loathing contempt for whatever represented The System – like anything or anyone who was organized, had a budget, and an agenda had to be a bogeyman right out of Richard Nixon's anxiety closet.

"Governments?" I queried. "Evil despots," the reply.

"Industry?" "Rapacious robber barons."

"Churches?" "Dogmatic lottery tickets to a presumed salvation."

Uh…"Boy Scouts and Little Leagues?" "Homophobic breeding grounds for Nazi-youth."

Christ. "Spelling Bees?" – "Indoctrination for Anglo-American supremacy"…and so it went.

Laura could not have been accused of being bigoted or preferential, because she despised all authority and structure equally. Nor could she be accused of being faint of heart or meek in any way. Her convictions flowed out of her tree-hugging body, and she wasn't scared of anything or anyone – except maybe a distant father, coke-wired ex-husband, or haunting memories of a penguin nun with a mean backhand. She charged ahead with gusto and bluster at all times.

"I dunno, Laura, I'm with ya on some of this Big Picture stuff, but it seems a bit wishful thinking that we can just throw a switch and everything would be OK."

"What do you mean?" Eying me dubiously.

"Well, here's an example. I certainly believe we live in a puritanical society, and I'm all for public nudity. Hey, what's more beautiful than the human body, if indeed God did create Man in His/Her/Its image? But if we threw out all the indecency laws overnight, you truly would have a society gone gonzo, at least for a good long time. For some indeterminate period, there'd be a rash of rapes, car crashes and outright attacks on people. People can't handle it. I mean, think about it: right now you can swing through any video shop in the country and check out enough splatter-flicks to wallpaper the stockyards of Upton Sinclair's *Jungle*, but let a woman's breast blink from a billboard, and you'd think Sodom and Gomorrah was upon us. The same zealots that blow up abortion clinics would turn their wrath on the streetwalker. Those raised under guilt-ridden, fundamentalist Big-tents might figure the new eye-candy just too tempting for their under-appreciated and misunderstood libido. Only through a slow transition over decades, accompanied by unprecedented education and openness, can we shirk our cultural prudishness and still avoid the wrath of the morality police and buffoonery of the perverts. Maybe never…"

"Bullshit," she parried. "I say let 'em get over it. Like it or lump it."

"OK, maybe a better example would be our drug laws." I tried another tack. "I'm a total Libertarian on the issue – hell; legalize all of it, hard and soft, except the truly crazy shit like Angel Dust that turns Mort Meek into Superman. Regulate the drug trade, tax the hell out of it, and use the proceeds to fund educational programs to heal the addicts and trim the recidivism rate. Ultimately you have a healthier society, instead of filling up prisons; and you'd have a greater work force filling the treasury coffers. Not to mention putting most of the bad guys out of business. Right now, the only ones getting well are the DEA and a bunch of Latinos with silk suits and private armies. We've got the highest percentage of our population behind bars of any nation on earth, and most of them for what? Drugs – even pot and hash. Meanwhile, the CEO of a Philip Morris or RJ Reynolds or Seagram takes home seven or eight-figure bonuses for what – killing a combined million people a year through TB, emphysema, cirrhosis of the liver, etc.? That sucks real bad."

I continued my sermon. "It seems to me that addictions will always claim a percentage of any society. Like the French historian Alexis de Tocqueville said, I think we can learn a lot about a culture by how they treat their criminals and addicts. Hell, we don't have to hand out syringes like the Dutch, but if we were truly consistent about punishing substance abusers – and their pushers and pimps – we'd throw every 3-martini lunch imbiber in the slammer, and hang all those CEOs upside down by their scrotums. Which sounds ridiculous, of course."

Was she listening, I wondered, as I continued. "The problem is – what happens if you just change the drug laws overnight? You don't think teen addiction would go sky high, crack and smack and blow and herb would flow in the streets? It'd be like a gaggle of unsupervised three-year-olds laying siege to the Easter Bunny's bottomless basket.

Only those toddlers would just pass out and puke a little; this dilemma would be a bit more serious. So I believe we have to wade in slowly, for our own good. There's an old saying that 'too much socialism leads to totalitarianism, and too much capitalism leads to anarchy.' Anarchy in my book can only work in an enlightened society, whatever the hell *that* is. Everywhere else it's failed – Robespierre's blood purge after the French Revolution; Lenin and Trotsky and their worker paradise, my sixth-grade homeroom when Sister Mary Veronica went home sick, et cetera."

Laura was ready. "Fuck that, it's all Fascism."

King's X. I must admit, I liked her spunk. And her debating *modus operandi* ...

"And that company you're gonna work for, Steve, Hewlett Packard. I know all about them, being from Northern California. I know they make computer systems and cute little gadgets that improve the quality of our lives. Maybe their instruments can even save lives in a hospital. But they also sell a fixed chunk of their toys to the Pentagon. Which means the next time the boys in the Oval Office disagree with the revolution of some brown people in a far away land, there'll be Bill (Hewlett) and Dave's (Packard) signature guiding the delivery package."

I now added "absolutism" and "steadfastness" to Laura's growing portfolio. She'd be one hell of an activist, I reckoned, if a scorched-earth policy were called for instead of, say a benign compromise, a goal of mutual accommodation, or other consensus with "the Enemy." She was hard – not "resiliently malleable" hard or "firm-but-flexible" hard, but the hard that shatters like rock or glass when hit by irresistible forces or gnawed away by the incessant chirping of a billion little waves or puffs of wind – life, in other words. She was anger without activism, principle without passion (at least as defined by *demonstrable* action), force without focus.

In her heart, I believe, she was terribly alone.

Since I've come to accept that all people, institutions and nations do what they believe is the "right" thing; that everyone's behavior makes sense from their unique cultural perspective, debating with Laura wasn't even an issue. Acknowledging the creeds of others does *not* necessarily mean condoning them; it just refers to accepting *them*, as persons, where they are at this time in space. Are we supposed to just shrug and accept Jihad – or the Divine Right of Kings – or Slavery – or Witch-burning – because it's in someone's convenient mythology? As Gandhi said, "I can see the Christ in all men; but sometimes it is necessary to observe from a distance."

In Laura's case, crash landing seemed the most likely outcome. But she was a survivor, and picking up the pieces and moving on seemed well within her capabilities. Would she learn from such crashes? Time would tell.

Laura was also good company and, despite her rhetorically combative nature, she didn't seem to personalize anything or reproach me personally. It was just the thrust and parry of programmed debate, and I think she appreciated my company as well. She'd been riding with short-haul truckers whose mental parameters were confined to stock car racing and Conway Twitty. So I guess even I was acceptable to a melancholy anarchist.

With the likely continuation of the steady rain, we decided to get a hotel that night. Cheap, of course, like $16 a night in post-tourist season Port Townsend. Laura picked up the pizza tab and we wandered the docks, taking in the renovation of old shipping buildings into sandblasted brick with *faux* antiquity, all aimed at sucking tourists into some nostalgic time-warp to the days of whale blubber, harpoons and indentured Chinese coolies. Port Townsend is a strategic ferry point, with regular routes across the sound to Victoria (north), Seattle (southeast) and Oakley/Anacortes (east). The movie *An Officer and a Gentleman* had just been filmed there, and as fate would have it, we stayed in the same hotel where Richard Gere's downtrodden sidekick (David Keith's "Sid") had hanged himself. I sincerely hoped we weren't staying in that same room. I preferred not to know.

In late afternoon, the sky cover lifted and a timely rainbow spanned out across the sound. I guessed the pot of gold ended somewhere near Bellingham, but before I could triangulate, the gray shroud returned and it was back to business. Rain, fog, wind, and gloom – the Four Horsemen of Puget Sound, at least from October through April. And we were definitely in season. With no distinguishing characteristics from the climate and scenery 3,000 miles across the continent in Maine, or Newfoundland...or Vladivostok, for that matter, suddenly I felt displaced. Like a wooden player-peg on a giant board game, the dice could have rolled me onto any coastal spot on the 48th parallel and I would land on a square of look-alike maritime and lumber towns inhabited by the same grizzled old sailors.

After the pizza and stroll, we had a nightcap in a lonely bar where a lonely bard sang lonely Irish ditties and told lonely stories. It befitted the black drizzling evening of a lonely October Monday in one of America's loneliest outposts.

We retired to our clapboard quarters, tired and melancholy, flipped TV channels for a while, performed the ritualistic toiletries, and then slipped onto the respective sides of our bed in silhouetted skivvies. Laura wasn't particularly pretty, but the hardware and software carved a regal presence that had been invisible under the comical yellow raincoat. Must've been all that clean living and healthy eating, not to mention her vendetta against fossil-fuel-guzzling Detroit dinosaurs.

I have no idea what she thought of me; such discourse wasn't forthcoming on either the verbal, emotional or physical planes. She was Xena the warrior - – or perhaps "worrier," but with a little too much bluster and not nearly enough charm. Barely suppressed anger was her master, and whoever got in her way was most likely a target. Besides, I was just another pseudo-fascist giving her a lift down the Road That Goes On Forever. We sipped a last beer and dozed off to Howard Cosell's monologue on TV. Outside, with a steady, driving, torrent of rain, Puget Sound cried its heart out to all who would listen.

* * * * * *

Like many mornings on the windward side of the Cascade Curtain (and leeward side of the Olympic Edifice), we woke to a warming sun foraging its way up through parting clouds. Entire swaths of the sky were even totally clear. Somewhere the tempests were brewing again, but they might not arrive until, say, late morning or early afternoon. Zeus and Hera were in an unsteady truce. The clamoring of seagulls and a few early delivery trucks were the only rankles on the otherwise slumbering burg of Port Townsend. We parked – the drive took about 45 seconds from hotel to cafe – and sipped some of the god-awful swill coffee that cheap diners like to pretend is imported from Vienna and hand-pressed by a pedigreed butler.

Back at the hotel, as I mindlessly clicked the channels one more time – addictions die hard and I didn't know when I'd see one of these again – I came across a breaking news story. Anwar Sadat, the Egyptian guerrilla fighter turned prince-of-peace, had just been assassinated.

The world moaned. I felt a deep hole open up inside, and plunged into numbness. I'm not sure how long I sat there – five minutes, maybe thirty.

I could remember the assassination of JFK…At age five; I was in my brown overcoat, home from half-day kindergarten and playing football keep-away out in the backyard with other neighborhood hooligans. I really didn't know what the killing meant, other than throwing my cartoon schedule off kilter. I remember more vividly the shootings of Martin Luther King and Bobby Kennedy a few years later, yet even then my pre-adolescent mind couldn't equate isolated events with the larger national conscience, and I had no idea what a Promised Land was. My juvenile experiences with grief were largely confined to pets' funerals (tissue box or toilet) or the time my Halloween paper sack burst open and disgorged its rain-soaked contents into a storm grate. *That* was traumatic.

Now, as a young adult, I could no longer dodge the emotional bullet of the latest assassination. Like millions of people around the world, I was numb with the shock and pain of an event that was bound to have serious repercussions. Sadat and his Israeli nemesis, Menachem Begin, had put three decades of animosity behind them to boldly go where no man has gone before, or since: a Mid-East Peace Treaty. They had shared the Nobel Peace prize, emceed by Jimmy Carter, that grinning peanut farmer who still managed to exemplify Lincoln's "Better angels of our nature" when the chips were down.

It's been said that some men see peace merely as the absence of war, others see it as just one of many choices, and still others see it as the *only* way. I suspect Sadat started out in the middle group but had become hardened enough by loss and futility to drift toward the latter one. Grievances aside, the world had been made safer, by degrees, because of him…at least for a while.

Suddenly I realized this global event in Egypt was *my* event. I was part of it.

What had just happened in the Middle East was a long way away from Port Townsend, Washington, USA, yet physical distance didn't seem to matter. I was right there at the time and place of the assassination. And that was the thing about travel that I was beginning to discover: that it was not only physical, but mental and emotional as well.

As I sat there in front of the TV, I was suddenly transported to a time 12 years before during the days of my boyhood paper route when I had first begun to experience "mental wanderlust," in the form of inner conversations that would take me nowhere and everywhere simultaneously.

From age 10 to 15 I had walked my beat, since my neighborhood was too hilly to ride a bicycle with a bulging newspaper bag. It was too early in the morning for a motorbike, so lest I lose all my customers, I walked. Except for raccoons, owls and a few howling neighborhood dogs, I was my sole company. Obtuse, perplexing thoughts ricocheted around in my head (such as "Why did twisters usually hit trailer parks instead of rich people's mansions?" "Why do car salesmen on TV always yell?" "Why do cats and dogs – honorable beasts – live only 12-18 years, while people, ignoble beasts, get 80 or 90?" "Why was the 'Moral Majority' neither?").

And now, seated before the television and watching re-runs of this latest tragic global event, those inner conversations returned. Some were among multiple facets of Me; others were with various political, religious, or athlete-hero figures. Where did all of the world's people come from, and where in the hell are we going? Was there really any hope of progress – what *is* progress, anyway? Do we simply replace one corrupt or inept system with another; obliterating any person or philosophy that comes along to say "there's a better way?" Thoughts, concepts and theses collided in my brain like hyperactive children at a playground.

Think Deeply. Brash, silly and profound thoughts all vied for order or divine logic – something that my teachers, priests, coaches and parents were unable to explain. Here was another example of chaos or uncertainty playing itself out on television, as real as the road before me and unfathomable as the sight of those two little boys yesterday, huddled by the roadside. *Why?* asked my mind, and my heart. Clearly the heart journey was a profound part of what was now taking charge of my response to this world-shaking event.

By Heart Travels I mean not just the romance-thing of seeking an ever-finer complement, friend/lover/partner/companion, or a sharper mirror: the desire to give and receive through one special person. It was also the stumbling through minefields of fear, hate and anger, and their underlings of arrogance and self-absorption. Heart Travel meant learning compassion the hard way – through the school of hard knocks – usually delivered by my own biased 2 x 4s, or through the seeming serendipity (coincidence – *not*) of the Great All That Is; spurring me onto something better or more appropriate, or necessary. Atoning for "Sin" perhaps (Separation In the Now)? Clearing the way for a "more perfect union?" It seemed that my most precious learning experiences – those provoking humbled "ah-hahs" – usually only took root when my defenses had been destroyed and my ego turned inside out. A tough travel companion, the heart – but, oh, so patient. And here was one of those instances of vulnerability. Why?

Why did every peace plan seem to go wrong? Why did people keep beating each other up, when the heart thing was so profound, *so easy to understand?*

At times like these, I have come to realize that full-blown travel necessarily includes the soul and spirit. As Pierre Tielhard de Chardin said, "*We are not human beings having a spiritual experience – we are spiritual beings having a human experience.*" It only makes sense that our cosmic suitcase collects some interesting decals. I don't know it for a fact and I certainly can't prove it, but every fiber in my body, and every cell/nerve/pulse/breath tells me I am a shadow of a Greater Self – that not only can I not exist without the Universe, but *it* cannot exist without *me*. This isn't meant to be hubris: I'm not referring to the petty, Steve-ego-me – but the greater I/Me, the eternal, infinite overseer, occupying many rooms in a sizable mansion.

This Greater Self whispers *Listen Carefully* – because every event-discovery-joy-trauma-breakthrough-implosion-change in my life is a shard of a hologram; and, vice versa. This global event in Egypt was *my* event. I was a part of it. Depending on how I hold it, everything is happening "Now." Not just everything in the Steve-Ego's life, but everything in the I/Me's existence.

Every once in awhile, unusual visitors, "extra-sensory" experiences, statistics-defying phenomena, grace, "miracles," and stories too wild to be allegorical come along and shake things up just enough to send a clear impression that the travel itinerary is more expansive than I may have thought…and enough to keep me reaching. *S-t-r-e-t-c-h-i-n-g.*

This was what was happening now. I was shook up, and the world was shaking.

I sat at the edge of the bed and struggled to hold back tears of helplessness, frustration, despair. Laura came over and put her hand on my shoulder – underneath Xena's breastplate of armor surely a heart lurked, after all. Numbly we watched while the Talking Television Heads blabbered away about the killers' motives, the effect on world markets, Sadat's legacy, Egypt's security, blah-blah-blah. Laura and I may have sparred on the Jeopardy quiz stuff, but we were big kids, reasonably educated, and we both knew the significance of this event. As Bob Dylan said, "*We never did disagree; we just saw it from a different point of view. Tangled up in blueueueueu…*" Amen.

✳ ✳ ✳ ✳ ✳ ✳

A ferry took us across the Sound to the eastern shore, while the Four Horsemen gathered once more for the late morning war council. Their verdict was partly cloudy to partly drizzly, and they stayed true to this theme throughout the day. We drove north toward the Canadian border, the gentle green of Washington blurring by. Off my left shoulder were the shrouded San Juan Islands, named for Juan de Fuca, formerly Apostolos Valerianos of Greece, sailing in 1592 under the banner of Spain. His sponsors dissed his story, although a certain Captain Vancouver – a fine Gulliver in his own right – vindicated Valerianos/de Fuca 200 years later – a bit posthumously but good enough for a plaque somewhere.

Back to the 20th Century, I remembered some controversial cargo I was carrying, namely, bootleg Speed, those white pills with the glittering green specks. Just hyper-compacted caffeine, really, those little babies were the Patron Saint of every architecture student and a long-haul driver's best friend. Be sure you've got a place to crash, though, because when the post-buzz reaper comes calling, your depleted body feels like you've been steamrolled by a Mastodon. In any case, said cargo was also illegal. Or so I suspected. Out the window went my pick-me-ups, along with a few last stems and seeds from Mother Nature's goody bag. I was redeemed. "O Canada!"

The border crossing into British Columbia was supposed to be a simple matter – "On holiday, eh?" or perhaps, "How long you up for, eh?" But I must've hit the ol' random number generator, or fit some profile of a renegade Yank.

"Any firearms?"

"No sir."

"Drugs?"

"No sir." (whew)

"Please get out of the car, sir."

"Wha …?"

"You can wait inside – just routine procedure, eh?" (Was that a question or a statement?)

I asked him why the "routine procedure" exempted the ten cars before me, the ten cars after me, and all three in the other lanes. He just grunted the derisory snort known by petty officialdom around the world when they've got a secret and you don't. In other words: Sit down, shut up, don't touch anything, and if you "pass" you can proceed no wiser but at least not under incarceration. I passed, although I wasn't too fond of having my car trunk, backpack and seats ruffled through, and a scattering of my accoutrement on the surrounding pavement. Perhaps it was the sunroof – there aren't many of them in the Great Ice Box of the North. Or maybe it was my week-old five o'clock shadow, not quite beard and just beyond bristle.

Laura was more than satisfied with this little drama, since it proved her point about the terrors of the Almighty They and Them. "Looks like they've got fascists here, too, Laura," I grinned mischievously, goading her on.

"Yeah. Bastards. I guess they still got a chip on their shoulder from all the Vietnam draft dodgers that poured through their borders 10 years ago. So polite with all that 'sir' and 'ma'am' and 'eh' bullshit, then they pull all these antics without even an explanation. What kind of neighbor is that – the Welcome Wagon Lads from Hell?"

As if imitating Laura's belligerence, the War Council in the Sky had reconvened yet again, and now the saturated charcoal wailed away. Once more camping seemed like a fool's errand, so we pulled into Vancouver hoping there was room at the Inn. We found one of those places where a vertical neon sign was missing the requisite letters. Panhandlers practiced their backhand and bad girls wearing an excessive amount of red hung around the lobby. The front desk guy never looked up from his sports page as he slid me a five-pound key (which I guessed was to prevent me from running too fast if I wanted to get away with it). He pointed down a corridor – *There be dragons* once more came to mind – but hey, it was mostly dry, had a 40-watt light bulb, and had to be heated to at least 55 Fahrenheit – not bad for $16 Canadian. Not good, either, but it beat a stable with baying animals and political refugees.

This place had its own refugees. From anything, everything, and everywhere. A young Amerasian with faraway eyes just grinned and mumbled when I asked him to pass the sugar bowl in the community kitchen. If the needle marks on his arm had been any more obvious, he could've knitted himself a sweater. A drunk wallowed in his own vomit over in the corner. Shadows slinked by on the stairs, shuffling between life and death like reluctant poltergeists, or disappearing into vacant rooms for a quick show'n'tell of the world's oldest profession. If there was ever going be a Salt of the Earth convention, this was the fairground. Surely a warm bowl of soup and bothersome preacher were right around the corner – recruitment potential was just too good here.

We slept in a Spartan cracker box on the second floor. Iron bars only slightly skewed the view, but the dark of night and relentless rain took care of the rest, swallowing the entire hotel and city. Laura took the top mattress, pulled it down on the floor, and sobbed. Xena's armor cracked, but she wasn't ready to surrender completely. Seems like there was trouble in the commune, trouble with parents, trouble with finances, and trouble with an ex-boyfriend, or was it an ex-girlfriend? Life wasn't fair, and that just wasn't, well, fair. I managed a quick hug and word of encouragement before the reinforcements arrived:

"I'll show them all, I don't need anybody, I don't rely on anyone for anything. I'll be damned if I'm gonna live my life for them, or give them one more precious moment of my time."

Xena steeled herself and tossed the night away in a fitful sleep, while I stared at the ceiling and listened to the drip-drip-drip from the gutter outside. Sad, and melancholy.

Whether it's Illusion or Memorex, one can't help but notice the pain and suffering in the world. When I met Laura, I was just starting out on my far-flung journeys, and her plight seemed tragic enough. But since then, I've had a chance to make comparisons. Since that day in 1981 in Vancouver, I've seen people sleeping in cardboard boxes in Kathmandu; eating /swimming / living in the sewage canals of Bangkok; seen limbless babies with bloated bellies in Malawi; peasants yoked like oxen on 60-degree slope hardscrabble Bolivian hillsides; and Maoris, Aborigines and Native Americans just staring into the sunset and dreaming of their next bottle.

Equally gripping and even more perplexing is witnessing children of First World affluence, variations on the theme of Laura, fritter away a life of opportunity and promise to a panoply of false gods – money, power, position, ageless beauty, fawning lovers – all this with a closed heart toward themselves, others, and the world at large.

The bounty? Cancer, heart disease, ulcers and sighing regrets. Lunging like Tantalus after evasive fruit, laboring like Sisyphus up the impossible hill of misguided fantasies, with more money and leisure than most, yet living in fear – living in ignorance.

How could the Laura's of the world be helped? What was it that had triggered her decision to be miserable in a land of plenty, with opportunities galore? Anger and frustration can arise from lack of a plan or not "knowing one's place." Engendering fear that is worn as a storm coat, the end result is pain. In Laura's case, if only that fear could have been tipped in the other direction, toward self-esteem and self-love…After all, her issues had nothing to do with survival, unless she chose to make it into a life and death matter…which happened too often, to too many Laura's, God knows.

Where was I going with this, I wondered then; not realizing yet that my travels had enrolled me in a self-help course in expanded consciousness. Perhaps that was the first time it occurred to me that everything I need is already inside, with or around me. Which is simply the same thing humanity has been told for eons, by those far more empathic and eloquent than I. I knew what was causing Laura's anger and loneliness and fear. I also knew how she could heal it…if she chose to.

I was grateful for the experience of Laura; she was a good teacher who elicited the questions I needed to ask myself at that time in my life when I was first encountering the vast spectrum of human diversity.

Somewhere in our heart of hearts, everyone knows:

We are all 'Everyman' — but Everyman is so f***ing powerful!

* * * * * *

Morning came, and the road east: Highway 1A, Canada's lifeline, spanning a continent. I wondered what percent of Canada's 20-something million people lived within one hour of it – 75, maybe 90 %? Laura was going north to Prince George, maybe even Prince Rupert, then who-knows-where.

"There's nothing in the city I really need," she scoffed as we stared at the display in a department store window after wolfing down sugar, carbs and caffeine at the Dunkin Donuts.

She got off at the edge of town where a labyrinth of concrete tentacles reached out to the vast interior and coastlines of O Canada. Managing a smile and another parting hug, she thanked me for my company. I replayed the "Look me up if you're ever in Boise" blurb, knowing she never would.

As she turned her back and wandered over to position herself on the road for her next ride, I knew I would continue to worry about her as much as I worried about those two rain-soaked little boys; but for different reasons. Laura could take care of herself, even though it was evident that she was spiraling into a dark, bottomless pit: a devastated little girl in the chain mail of a Valkyrie. The boys at least had a chance for redemption. Laura would survive – but at what cost?

Chapter Nine

O Canada!

My spirits brightened and so did the sky as I drove east through the thinning Vancouver suburbs into the encroaching farmlands, green, wet and fresh. Puffy white clouds punctuated the mid-morning's blue and pulled me across the interior of B.C. I couldn't put my finger on it, but it certainly didn't seem like America anymore. It felt different, or maybe I was just feeling unburdened after the last 48 hours of Psych 505. Years later, I would agree: doors were opening inside.

All day I drove, the rolling green giving gave way to the unusual dryer sage and wheat that pushes up from North Central Washington. I wasn't expecting this pleasant surprise.

In Kamloops I stopped to pick up the evening's meal – Labatt's Blue, paying homage to the locals once more. Outside in the parking lot, I opened the Silver Bullet's hatchback, took out my cooler and started to load in the bottles. Instantaneously, two more of Canada's finest came strolling by the car. At first they just smiled. Then, as they walked by the front of the car and saw the infamous Georgia tags, their disposition changed, as did their direction.

"Where are you planning to drink that, eh?"

"Uh…at Revelstoke, in a campsite, my destination tonight."

"Are you sure you're not planning to open it up before?"

"Absolutely not, officer – as they say down in my neck of the woods, 'Don't drink and drive – you might hit a bump and spill your drink!'" I should have known better than to wax sophomoric with two Dudley Do-Rights with a disdain for South-of-the-Border tourists.

"If us or any of our colleagues catch you or anyone with you imbibing while on the road, you're in big trouble, eh?"

"Yes, sir." *Prick.* The Mounties were now 0 for 2 in my book. It might not be fair to judge by such a minimal sample, but well…what about the Good Neighbor policy? All for sight of a license tag! Or maybe they just figured I was Snidely Whiplash reincarnated in a Japanese tin can.

Having grown up in the southeastern U.S., I was used to the crew-cut, hard-assed, no-quarter drill sergeant regimen of southern state troopers. There were the Barney Fife types, comical and bumbling; the angry, pedantic Sgt. Carter types of Gomer Pyle fame; and the strong silent types that just peered out through those silly reflective glasses and forced out syllables like molasses in January. But here in O Canada? Don't they have First Amendment rights up here? It just didn't seem *fair*, as Laura might think.

That's the thanks we get – we protect Canada's southern border from an influx of Mexicans, while simultaneously guarding their Great North with the latest in fighter jets and missile technology; we buy up their surplus beef, timber, and wheat; we loan them the name of our currency; we even provide them with our bastardized Mother Tongue (except for the more refined Quebecois who cling to a version of French that would make a Parisian's ears scratch); we offer them warm places to visit when the Ice Age hits them between November and April each year. We've allowed them two franchises of baseball, our national sport, and we shrug it off whenever their hockey teams run roughshod over our boys. All this, despite the fact that they aided the Confederacy during the War of Secession. One would think they'd be more grateful. Who do these guys think we Yanks are, *foreigners?*

Okay, so they'd struck a raw spot: I disliked making assumptions based on location-location…so what was I doing in return? The same. Ya gatta laugh.

It is precisely my knowledge that the Steve-shell will dissolve into worm food and cosmic dust that compels me to *Laugh Heartily* – to push the boundaries, revel in paradox, confront fear and seek understanding; or, at least, make peace with the temporal nature of it all. Someone once said, "There is no meaning of life – only meaning *in* life."

* * * * * *

I picked up Gerrell, a Quebecois, another hundred miles east. A year or two younger than I, he was a wiry good-looking guy with fashionably long brown hair, an easy smile and measured words. If Gerrell possessed any of the stereotypical fussiness of his disgruntled countrymen – Quebec was the troublesome black sheep of Canada, claimed by neither the eastern seaboard, the western provinces, nor worse, the mother ship of France – he didn't show it. He said he played in a punk rock band back home and had just been out to Vancouver to see some friends. *C'est bon, mon ami.*

We were now into beautiful country of low-lying mountains and shimmering lakes. Not the moist temperate green of the coastal areas, but the clearer air and alpine vistas of the rising Canadian Rockies. That night we camped in a provincial park, coaxing a campfire out of piles of copious, moist wood aided by a half can of Coleman lighter fluid – Boy Scout joy-juice. Gerrell turned in early; I contemplated my future by the warming tongues of flame.

On the entire trip I hadn't honestly thought about my pending work for more than five minutes in any stretch – living in Boise, yes; actually working, no. I assumed I'd punch the corporate time clock for a few years, get a Masters Degree, spin out, and do the wanderlust thing. I really had no other game plan and no other expectations. Fortunately, the rest of the Labatts crawled into my cranium and turned it to mush, relieving me of further speculation. Sagittarians like to think big; just don't bother us with details. At that moment, even life itself could wait if it wasn't all laid out, ready to climb into.

Into Alberta, with a wild rose adorning the welcoming sign that marked the provincial crossing from B.C. The jagged peaks of the Rockies now towered in the background, well fortified by high-country snow and supported by dark green firs and golden hems of aspen and birch on their flanks. In the valley below, the glacially-tinted Bow River wiggled through groves of garnet maples, on its way to crashing the Columbia River. Above, a cerulean sky turned the whole vista into a giant postcard. I imagined yodels and lederhosen, chocolate and cute little cuckoo clocks – no, wait, wrong continent. Wrong hemisphere. But they *did* have good beer here, and spoke their own version of English, except for the recalcitrant Québécois passing through.

I pulled into Banff about mid-afternoon after wishing Gerrell a hearty *au revoir*. He only had about 1,500 miles to go and wanted to catch the tailwind. Banff reminded me of a hipper and thankfully smaller version of Gatlinburg, Tennessee, the hillbilly heaven of the Great Smokies. Not yet run over with trailer parks, Elvis wax museums, UFO mystery places and enough fried food to clog an elephant's arteries. Banff still had a whiff of actual Bavaria to it (even if this actually wasn't Bavaria). The streets were wider than my nostalgic boyhood play town, pedestrians more dispersed, and country twangin' radio stations joyously absent.

For three days I hung out in the vicinity, hiking up to the cute little alpine tea house for a gawking view of nearby Lake Louise's sky blue water. I Christmas shopped, shot pool and of course, drank beer at the King Edward hotel. Banff was the first place I'd ever seen moose and elk walking down the street like epileptic runaways from Dr. Doolittle's funny farm. Coyotes howled at night in the valley beneath my campground at the edge of town. Life was good; I was feeling rested, and whole. I would soon turn right – south, downhill – and the buzz would gradually have to fade.

I passed an evening at the King Eddie bar with Jocelyn, who worked at the Banff Hot Springs Spa, the majestic old sanitarium at the outskirts of town. Not professionally, just clerically – but great bennies and decent pay. Cute, bouncy, brunette and inquisitive, Jocelyn was short in a compact cheerleader fashion, with a hint of a turned up nose and a few angel-kiss freckles. She was the girl-next-door type, a good-looking one, with a wholesomeness that blossoms into impressive womanhood and has guys turning their eyes when she's 30 and all over her when she's 40. Ann Margaret comes to mind. Jocelyn had that signature Canadian way of turning vowel combinations into one long "ooo" – like "hoooose" for house, or "oot" for out.

"What do people do in Winnipeg?" I queried, knowing it to be the capitol of Manitoba and possessing an obscure football team called the Jets.

"Nothing" she giggled, "except maybe get out and travel to Banff."

"Long ride," I commented, reckoning Winnipeg to be maybe 800-900 miles east.

"Yeah, well, you can sleep most of the way through Manitoba and you really don't want to open your eyes in Saskatchewan. Makes your Kansas look like a sine wave. Wheat, corn, choose your poison. What can I say about a capitol city (spelled R-e-g-i-n-a) that rhymes with "vagina"? Just pull out of your driveway with some friends, turn west, and only stop to pee." Giggle, giggle.

"But I have to admit," her coyness vanishing, replaced by a wistful little-girl smile, "Winnipeg will always be home in my heart. I mean it's not flashy and dashy like Toronto, or hip and swank like Vancouver, or snooty like Montreal, or full of bureaucratic stiffs like Ottawa. Winnipeg has just good hard-working people who like to watch the paint peel for fun. But there's like zilch crime, or pollution. My family members will always live there probably, and I'll visit often; *I* just don't want to live there. If I'm going to freeze my buns off in winter, it might as well be somewhere like here. Besides, truthfully it's a lot less cold here than there, and the mosquito clouds are a little less dense here in summer."

We spent an evening sampling whatever was on tap (my treat) and telling life stories, which were surprisingly long, considering just how little life experience either one of us had actually had.

I liked Jocelyn. In different circumstances...well, maybe...no...I already knew the code of the road. You can fantasize and indulge in reverie, but only for a fleeting moment. Stories blow away on the wind and the thrill of that moment lasts only as long as it takes the beer to run through your kidneys. But a quarter century later you might find yourself daydreaming about where they ended up, what suburb of Vancouver or Toronto they settled down in, how many kids they had and how trim their waistlines are. Are they still as free and happy and buoyant and optimistic, or have they succumbed to the monotonous drones of mid-life funk with its endless list of "woulda – coulda – shoulda's"? Had I caught them in their last passage of youth before stepping into the self-imposed hell of assumed responsibility, yielding to some generational prime directive with sonnets to God and country and party?...Or, had I witnessed their launching pad, a tectonic psyche shift into a vaster, exciting world of many gray shades and intriguing possibilities?

Who were they, really, at that moment? The truth of themselves, or someone else's wannabe? *Who was I, at that moment?* Will we defy probability by crossing paths with them years later in some airport, catching a fleeting glimpse of a familiar dimple, hearing a certain chuckle or peculiar lilting accent? We know these things happen, but we also know we shouldn't wait for them. Or even think about them. Yet still, we wonder...It's only human, and after all, we *are* on a human journey.

Choices needed to be made in order to make sure I was getting my money's worth out of this life journey. If I was going to board the scary roller coaster of life, why would I possibly want to miss all the other carnivals by getting stuck at the top of the Ferris' wheel? Yet...if I *did* follow the road code, wouldn't I be denying myself the pleasures of my adventurous spirit, if I passed up all the popcorn and cotton candy along the way?

Although I *do* seek to enjoy myself – pain and suffering suck – - although I do like to go down the rabbit hole of paradox and irony and allow myself to be surprised, knowing full well that life is simultaneously an illusion yet very real – I also want to see if I can make the ride a little wilder. "Wilder" as in not just having lots of fun, even though that's a major part of the reason, but also as a commitment to *put meaning into my life*, rather than try to "find" that meaning. And therein lies the dilemma: Do I choose the one- or two-night stands with the Jocelyns of the world, balancing the titillation of indulgence against the possibility of getting shipwrecked into a major distraction or detour – *or* do I choose to move freely on to the next adventure, where I could still be in the driver's seat...and where that wildness would not have to be put on hold? It's no wonder, to paraphrase Yogi Berra, that "when we get to the fork in the road – we should take it."

Chapter Ten

No Small Potatoes

It was all downhill now, in latitude and altitude. Banff sits at the 51st parallel at 4,500 feet, Boise at 43 degrees north and a hair under 3,000 feet. The Silver Bullet would take me south and down through Southern Alberta and a sliver of British Columbia before crossing back into the U.S. at the Idaho panhandle. I felt welcomed back like a prodigal son, with no Mounties lurking in the bushes or behind trucks.

Idaho, a funny name for a funny state. With a shape described variously as "a hatchet, snub-nosed pistol or pork chop," its entire nearly 500-mile north-to-south expanse was girded by only a 40-mile east-to-west stretch on the Canadian border, rivaling tiny New Hampshire for the least auspicious turnstile with our northern neighbors. Idaho could easily have been carved up and donated to three different states. Washington could take the north, with its shared legacy of lumberjacks, tall forests, blue-collar New Deal democrats and independent sensibilities. (Montana might put up a fight, but the awkward swath of the Bitterroot mountain range would render their stewardship impractical.) Boise and the southwestern part of the state would go to either Oregon or Nevada, with its high sagebrush desert and California emigrants. Eastern Idaho would be bequeathed to Utah, since the southeastern chunk of the Gem State claimed a higher percentage of Mormons than many Utah counties; and not surprisingly, a voting populace just to the right of J. Edgar Hoover. Altogether, Idaho was just quirky enough for me to want to give it a try.

I passed through the bucolic town of Bonners Ferry, and soon the picturesque art burg of Sandpoint promenading out on Lake

Pend d'Oreille. Northern Idaho is a beautiful land – gentle, green, and rolling; punctuated by horse farms, pristine lakes, and rounded mountains. Once more East Tennessee came to mind, but there was more elbow room here. The mountains, lakes and rivers have a benign, non-rugged feel: designer tourism, but way off the beaten track.

Down around Hayden Lake, north of Coeur d'Alene, Richard Butler's Aryan Nation had taken over in the late Seventies. It seems that Butler, an ardent admirer of *Der Füerher*, was impressed by the territory's absence of dark-skinned people and folks with Semitic surnames. And since every Armageddon nut in the country believed Northern Idaho would be Christendom's (and thus America's) last stand against the heathen hordes, here they were. Much to the chagrin of the true locals, I must add, who were as peaceful a bunch of live'n'let live citizens you'd ever want to meet – miners, lumbermen, shopkeepers, farmers, ranchers, artists and retirees. They even had a resident billionaire, Dwayne Hagadone, owner of the resort and golf course with the funky floating green on Lake Coeur d'Alene.

Every year the Aryans would march down the elbow-shaped main street along Coeur d'Alene's waterfront while the salt-earth locals hooted, hollered and pelted them with eggs and tomatoes. The news clips only showed the Neo-Fascists, not the 99% who just wished they pack up and head off to Timbuktu or Neptune. I drove by the compound's front gate and flipped them off. Luckily they didn't see me: this particular breed of Christian didn't have a sense of humor and certainly didn't turn the other cheek.

* * * * * *

I spent my last night at Heyburn State Park, a forested enclave about 100 miles south of Coeur d'Alene. Time for one last campfire, coaxed once more from wet reluctant wood through the persuasion of liquid Coleman. One last six-pack of Rainier (14 oz. bottles!).

Perhaps it was appropriate that this last night was reserved for me. Thoughts, memories, projections and hunches were my guests that night. No Merchant Marines, no runaways, no forlorn returning-prodigals, no carefree service-industry roustabouts, no drunken soldiers, no professionals on walkabout or scholars in waiting, no drifting punk-rockers or denim-clad lumberjacks, no ice queens with a one-way ticket to meltdown, no bouncing pixies. Perhaps appropriately, this last night was reserved for me. A slow drizzle started about 11:00 p.m. and pattered away throughout the night...

BLAM – BLAM!
"Wha...Holy Shi ..." The Aryans had found me! They must have caught my gesture on videotape, scooped the tags, and followed me on down here from Hayden! Or else...I jumped out of my tent, half-asleep and three-quarters hysterical. No one was there...it was dawn, barely...a gray sky hovered over an even grayer lake. All was wet and quiet except for the occasional *quack-quack-quack* of water fowl. Then it came again ...

BLAM – BLAM! Not so many quacks this time ...
As the echoes were swallowed by the sultry gray morning, it dawned on me that I was a privileged party to the first day of duck-hunting season. The adjacent national forest and a few private lands bordering the park were the fields of combat. Shot blasts rolled over the lake like a megaphone. Whoever else planned on sleeping in this Saturday was already rudely awakened. But the joke was probably on me, as I was most likely the only non-hunter hanging out there.

It was mid-October now; time to get a home, an address and a life. I drove south again, past the confluence of the Snake and Salmon rivers, past the gingerbread mountain lake town of McCall (a mini-Tahoe), the pastoral Long and Round Valleys, through old lumber towns searching for a resurrected identity as tourist spots. The Payette River now glided along with me, equally intent on purpose, but far less mindful of destination. The Payette hosted the National Whitewater Rodeo every year, where World-class kayakers (the aquatic cousins of hang-gliders and other action-sport kamikaze disciplines) would converge from far and near to hotdog in the raging rapids, and party along miles of shoreline.

And then one last rise and fall of rounded sagebrush hills dropped me into Boise – "Les Bois" to the startled French trappers, who after traipsing across the rolling prairies for weeks, came upon the surprising and refreshing City of Trees in the early 1840s.

Boise had been the butt of many a joke over the years – some warranted, others egregiously incorrect. But it was shoring itself up nicely as an impressive mid-size town with a bright future. What big coastal cities, like Boston or San Francisco were to ethnic groups, so was Boise to vocational cross-slices of America: perhaps nowhere in the country could you find such an amalgam of cowboys, industrialists, artists, students and ne'er do wells mixed in with ordinary tax-paying Norman Rockwell citizens. It was Boulder without a hundred gurus; Santa Fe sans the Beverly Hill art chic; Burlington without N'yawk; Austin without the summer steam bath; Madison without the Arctic; Berkeley without the anarchists (actually it *did* have a few).

Boise was a town that simultaneously enticed and flummoxed the product test-market purveyors of the consumer industry with its maze of skewed and overlapping demographics. Not to mention hybrid geography, where the escarpment of the high sagebrush desert ran smack dab into a wall of mountainous forest. Last but not least, it had music in the cafes, powder on the slopes and a helluva river running through it.

Right or wrong, good or bad, I said hello to my new home. Things were about to get interesting for both of us.

PART II
MYSTICS AND MANIACS

If you're into astrology at all, you already know about the fiery power-packed straight-shooting Sagittarian energy and determination to do all and see all…and not tomorrow, but NOW. Even my "Virgo-rising" side – the stern, analytical taskmaster – couldn't hold me back.

Always footloose, always itchy, even when pressed for a work deadline or pounding out a Show'n'Tell for my Masters program, the Gulliver in me was always ready for yet another adventure. Escapist? At times. Irresponsible? Perhaps…but by who's rules? Let's just say I wasn't satisfied with the status quo, possibly because the seasons of the soul had other intentions.

Although the landscapes of all these journeys are tattooed on my brain like photographs, it was a long, slow awakening that it took *people* to bring things into 3-D, to put heart into the body and spirit into the memory. And I soon discovered that people – sages and fools alike – can come in many unusual packages …

Moe: *What kind of fool do you take me for?*
Curly: *Why – is there more than one kind?*

Chapter Eleven

Larry in the Sky with Diamonds

The Dog Sled rides were over and the yapping teams hauled off to their pens for a feed and a nap. I guess you could call it a "ride," even if the sled runners were glorified roller skates and the racecourse a dirt parking lot near the intersection – the only intersection – of Tok, Alaska.

Tok was the unofficial Dog Sled training capital of the world. I imagine some colleagues in Murmansk, Siberia, might protest, but their PR guys were still mired in pre-Glasnost days. The letters "yo" were purposefully avoided, since the town was created as a military supply route in the aftermath of December 7, 1941. Tok was where the Alaskan Highway, sweeping up from the Yukon Territory and eventually headed to Fairbanks, intersected a semi-civilized road heading down toward Anchorage and all points southwest. Just east of Tok was the Taylor Highway, a dirt patch heading 60 miles northeast toward the metropolis of Chicken (summer population of 13, winter population 2), an overflow gold rush outpost from the days of the Klondike. Supposedly the founders wanted to name it "Ptarmigan" after the funky bird, but no one could spell it, so they settled on "Chicken."

"Whad're y'all doin, just sittin' there?" asked the stranger of my brother Mike and me.

"Huh?" we answered in unison.

"Big show's over – come on in and have lunch. You can trust me – hell, I'm the cook. Name's Larry." A shaky hand extended from a tattooed arm, which led, indirectly, to a brillo-pad beard, menagerie of twisted teeth and two vacuous eyes.

Larry was referring to a rickety café-looking place about four Winnebagos and three piles of dog turds to our left. It was apparently highly regarded: *Booze – Grub – Rooms* read the weathered wooden sign. Maybe that wasn't good enough for Zagat's Guide, but by golly, it was a virtual trifecta of Far North hospitality.

"You just coming on shift?" I reciprocated.

"Nah, takin' a smoke break and communin' with you Gullivers in your fancy travels."

"Well," I shrugged, bemused. "Don't know if I'd call it *fancy*, Larry – I mean, getting seasick on that pitching ferry for four days from Seattle to Haines. Then getting screwed out of our rental car by the Wicked Witch of the North; then getting covered by mosquitoes every time we surface into sunlight 'cause we're too stupid to take pre-emptive garlic pills and too proper to roll ourselves in bear fat. Oh yeah, and damn near getting run down by that mama moose down in Denali just 'cause we wanted a close-up photo of her baby Bullwinkle."

"Yeah," Larry chuckled, "Guess I should give ya the benefit of the doubt. Most folks come rumblin' through here in their fortified Brinks truck-campers, snap a few Polaroids, then head on down to Anchorage to hobnob at the Captain Cook. That ain't the real Alaska, though."

He hesitated, taking a long draw on his last Marlboro. I wasn't sure if I should be addressing him or the avatar-mug of Jimi Hendrix staring me down from his t-shirt. Guess it was our turn …

"Uh…You a native?" Mike put forth, knowing better.

"Do I look like a goddamn Tlinglit?" he laughed, feigning incredulity, eye sockets temporarily flashing "occupied" signs. "Shit, I owned a gas station down in Lubbock in the Sixties. That went titties-up. Came up here for the Pipeline party in the Seventies and never looked back. Done cashed those chips in, I guess, but reckon I'm a self-made man anyway. Not much to show 'cept my dignity, but crap, look, I got 40 acres and my own place."

He was referring to a provision of the never-ending Homestead laws granting land rights to anyone building a "home" – which in many cases was the equivalent of a 10 x10 outhouse – and hanging around for a few years. This isn't unique – nearly 10% of U.S. land, or 270 million acres was parceled out to "homesteaders" since the mid 1800s. Not all of the Alaskan recipients thereof were a *Who's Who* of society's finest, but they'd probably come in handy in a fight – if you could find them.

"Yeah," Larry continued, "that's about 39.9 acres and one possession more than most of the people on this planet have. 'Seward's Folly,' my ass (the much-ridiculed purchase of Alaska for $7 million by Secretary of State William Seward in 1867). This here's paradise. Sumbitches even pay me to hang around – guess they're worried the Russkies might want their ice-box back. Christ, never could figger the government out, but I guess they're on my side!" He slapped his thigh at the epiphany.

"Tell ya what, pardner, not to be rude, but you ain't seein' shit now. Yeah, the fireweed's pretty and the lakes are glistenin', and all that. But come back up in the winter. Ain't nuthin' like the Borealis when it's minus-50 outside. We'll get my dogsled out, drop a little MDA (referring to the speed-laced LS-Dopey making the rounds for a few years) and watch them northern lights do the Translucent Tango till we can't see straight no more. Big 'ol sheets of green and red and white, like gossamer cobwebs spinnin' 'cross the darkest blue you ever seen. Guess that's how I muddle through – my mind can float away to eternity, then drop me right back down here on this frozen terra firma."

Larry ground out the cigarette butt and spat through a cavernous gap where teeth once resided. A few more errant thoughts sparked where brain cells used to be, but like the wisps of hallucogenia, were soon gone with the wind. I knew he was yanking our chains – building himself up while taunting us comfort-loving sybarites from the Lower 48; knowing of course, that we wouldn't take him up on his offer. He didn't realize, or care, that we all have "our cross to bear" (Had Larry, I wondered, ever been in a parochial school, or had to 'fess up to a squinty-eyed neighbor whose mail box was just detonated by a fuse-delayed M-80?)

"Remember now, when yer down there in the Lower 48 with all them prima donnas, this here's your real friend," he lectured, swiping his hand across the endless horizon. "A man can be what he wants to be, and everyone's a success. And if yer not, why, shit, no one else'll even know! I like them odds. We're all family up here, even if we get all pissy and agitated with each other. I knew I'd find my niche someday. One day I'm gonna write my memoirs – Ah, shit, probably won't sell no how, 'cause no one would believe'm."

He mumbled off, passing into the walls of civilization and a day of grease fires, sweating brows and grumbling pilgrims from more hospitable climes.

I'd read about such characters, either in Snuffy Smith comic strips or John Steinbeck and Jack London novels. There's the salt of the earth, spicy but tempered; then there's the crust of the earth – hard and crumbling. Larry taught me that even a loser was a winner if his story was big enough, and if one is just deluded enough to believe it. Besides, who was I to doubt the integrity of a man who thrived in psychedelic wonderland at the top of the world? We all follow a drummer, but some follow a piper – even if it's a long slow procession into mumbling madness and heart-shackling loneliness.

Chapter Twelve

The Diva of Kailash

I lost Janie in the Himalayas. I'd like to recount that the culprit was something stupendous, like an avalanche or a hungry Yeti (Abominable Snowman); maybe a revolution demanding blood. Alas, the instigator was her free will, and I, her meal ticket.

She wasn't a stranger; far from it. I'd known her for two years. She was a girlfriend, fellow seeker extraordinaire and beholden to no one – and, as I was to find out – committed to no one. Such is the path; at least, her path.

We had spent several weeks looping around some of the lower trekking routes in the Annapurna region of Nepal, several hundred miles west of Kathmandu. This had been a good time to go – tourism was alive and well, but the Maoist revolutionaries bent on spoiling the monarchy's power grip hadn't yet trundled out of the country's far reaches. Peeking through rich rhododendron hillsides or gazing out from open villages at 10,000 feet, we took in panoramic vistas of towering peaks, many exceeding 20,000 feet. The sentinels of Machhapuchhre – sounding, and spelled remarkably like that site of ruins in Peru, but no relation – and Annapurna glowed purplish-pink, the optical illusion courtesy of their 26,000 foot stature. The hiking should have been easy, sans backpacks – we had "sherpas," or porters – and we were not particularly high in elevation; but, intestinal usurpers, known to backpackers the world 'round as the "walking flu," drained our fortitude (and bowels), leaving us stumbling into the lakeside resort of Pokhara to recuperate.

From Pokhara, we continued on to the border of Nepal and India, to Chitwan National Park, one of the world's last refuges of Bengal tigers. This was very much out of the mountains; we were in low-lying jungle now, reminding us that, despite the lofty Himalayas, Nepal was at the same latitude as Florida's Disney World (only with hipper critters). Getting to Chitwan had been interesting enough – first a bus with comical tires, then rowboat, then trucks, then oxen-carts...and once in the tiny camp – miles from God-knows-where and halfway around the world – we walked smack-dab into some folks from Park City, Utah – where Janie and I just happened to reside.

The next several days were spent chasing rhinos through high grass on elephant back at dusk and dawn, while kids resembling Haji from the *Johnny Quest* show thumped on the pachyderms with metal pipes. The beasts were remarkably responsive to dozens of verbal and miscellaneous thumping commands. We passed the daylight hours when temperatures and humidity were in the triple digits, sleeping and just hanging out.

We then returned to Kathmandu, our ending point, to soak in the clamor of this mountain capitol. There we wandered through markets; chanted in temples with the saffron-robed legions of buzz-cut boy-monks; played circle games with prayer flags; teased the hyperactive primates at the Monkey Temple (Swayanabath); and lingered on the steps of 12th Century stupas, those funny-roofed temples where wasted Euro-hippies ended up in the Seventies after taking the Magic Bus from all points west. We watched in humility and awe as cremated bodies – human – alchemized to ash before being sprinkled in the river; then, garlanded by milk and flowers, began the long float "Home."

Janie and I stayed at a quaint family-run hotel, just a few blocks from the teeming market of Thamel. Every morning the trees outside our window would erupt at about 4:00 a.m. with the chirping drone of hundreds of birds; strangely, their noise only nurtured our dreams rather than dashing them, and we woke refreshed while sipping Sherpa's tea – that aromatic blend of Oolong and Darjeeling graced with honey and yak milk. Mmmmm …

One morning in the courtyard, Janie wandered over to where I was scribbling postcards to a faraway world. "Darlin,' (her pet name for me, usually presaging the request for a boon), "I've been thinking a lot about Tibet."

"OK, let's see…North of here…Home of that Dalai Lama guy, though he doesn't get to visit much anymore, 'cause his Chinese guests kind of ate'm outta house and home before destroying, what – 6,000 temples…What else? Oh, the capital, Lhasa, has that awesome ancient monastery…The wind blows all the time…Their McDonald's only serve yak meat, yak butter, yak milk…Uh, if you want to wash the grime off, at 12,000 feet, the best your hotel's gonna offer is an ice cold shower…And, if Mrs. Marshall's Fourth Grade Geography class still serves memory, there's not a tree in the whole bloody kingdom, er, former kingdom…Yeah, so, what about Tibet?"

"Well …" Hesitation turned to sheepishness, which then slipped into a near whisper: "I think I wanna go there."

"OK, I can dig it. I'm always ready for the strange and twisted. How 'bout next year?"

"Uh…well, I kind of want to go *soon*."

"You mean in a few months, after you get back, pay off some bills, and restock?"

"Er…well, no, um, like 'Now'-soon."

"*NOW*? Like tomorrow, Tuesday, next week-now?"

"Yeaahhhh …"

"*WHAT?*"

"Well…remember when I first met you and said I wanted to spend two years traveling around China and India, learning herbal medicines and oriental healing? Well, I may never get any closer than this…my heart just tugs at me, like it's some kind of karmic imperative that I've got to do, darlin.'"

"Cool, I understand your dilemma. But what about our *commitment?*"

"What commitment?"

"Janie, I don't wanna dwell in pettiness, but you agreed to come with me to Bangkok. After all, I've paid for the airfare, the trip packages and a helluva lot more…I mean, if I thought you were gonna torpedo that, I would've just passed or done something different…Can't you do Tibet another time?"

"Sorry, I know this is hard and it seems selfish of me, but my heart says I've got to go."

I had to admit, after the mountain serenity of the Himalayas, dropping into Bangkok and its 110 decibel madhouse would be like getting wakened from a sweet dream by a Who concert outside your bedroom window.

"Really? What about Sage?" Janie's Belgian Sheepdog, a big, handsome fellow, was being kept by some friends on a farm. Upon returning, I would have to get him – and keep him at my covenants-restricted, yard-less, two-story condo...where he'd be miserable, no doubt; and I'd have to do double duty to compensate for his physical needs.

"Sage really loves you...and it would mean so much to me if you could look after him. I know it's a lot to ask..."

Fine. OK. All right already. She was a Virgo, with Leo-rising; a veritable collision course for Sagittarians if ever there was one. Argument was futile; logic, worthless. Guilt-trips, though not beneath me, didn't work either.

I sighed, sipped the Sherpa tea and relit one of my little canned traveling cigars. "So, my dear...what exactly are you going to do, and how are you going to do it?"

"There's a bus from Kathmandu to Lhasa every Tuesday. It sounds like a giant land rover thing with huge ol' tires. At certain mountain passes, or where the roads have too many crater-sized ruts, you've got to disembark while your gear is carried on animals or human backpack to the next waiting rover...providing the vehicle is waiting, and not several days away. This gets repeated a bunch of times, but it's a nice way to pass the 600 miles."

"Uh...why don't you just fly?"

"Nahh...would ruin the effect. Besides, it costs too much." (Uh-huh, I thought.)

"Anyway, my main destination is Mt. Kailash, the revered pilgrimage site. It's holy to Buddhists, Hindus and this group called the Jainists."

I had indeed heard of Kailash – the world's most sacredly regarded mountain. Buddhists called it *Kang Rimpoche*, "The Precious

One of Glacial Snow." Hindus believed it to be the playground of the cantankerous Shiva, who made hanky-panky with his missus and puffed ganja from his pipe. Supposedly, a mere glimpse of his lair would lead to release from earthly suffering and attachment. Kailash was the scene, apparently, of some outrageous cosmic duels between good and bad forces, not unlike Mt. Sinai, or Devils' Tower in Wyoming; or, come to think about it, thousands of other jutting edifices on our battle-scarred planet.

"Yeah, it's 22,000 feet high, but you're not supposed to climb it. The task is to walk around it in mindful meditation." *Yeah*, I thought, with my inner-Guru growling, *What other kind of meditation is there?*

"So I guess it takes about 2-3 weeks to circumambulate, so they say. And that doesn't include heading partway up the mountain to meditate in the caves. Did you know that the truly committed, if they make 108 trips around it and prostrate themselves out at key points each loop, supposedly achieve enlightenment?"

"Why, don't they have *The 700 Club* in Tibet? Ol' Pat Robertson can fix 'em up in a few hours, and they can save all that time for Disneyland and the stock market."

"Come on, Darlin' – please don't be sacrilegious – this is a big deal to me."

"Do you really believe that 108-loop thing?" I probed.

"Well, I'm sure it's just a metaphor for something, but I'd sure like to do it just once…there's something powerful about completing a journey." Just not with me, it seemed.

"Sorry, my little Aphrodite," I sighed. "Uh…what are you gonna do for supplies, food, etc.?" I pushed away a strand of brown hair from a furrowed brow and watched a smile break out a few inches lower.

"I dunno…get by, I guess." Pause. "Say," breaking into her own reverie, "do you have any more of those granola bars from the trek? And can I have some toilet paper…oh yeah, how 'bout some of that dried fruit…also, I don't need all these light clothes; could you take this other duffle home for me? And I have some unpaid bills on the counter, would you mind taking a look at…"

God bless her, my deluded diva. I learned from Janie that the price of commitment is steep, especially if one is running *away* from something more than walking *toward* something else. Seekers of all ages have used their *wanderlust* as a shield and their holy aspirations as red herrings to duck responsibilities to friends, family and tribe. It's a lot nobler to say "I'm looking for God" than to admit, "I'm fucked up and lost and on the hunt for something to make sense out of everything; and once I do, I'll be back to contribute to society in a meaningful way..." Of course, in fairness, the mind truly *does* believe the former – after all, we're all "good,"...right? A little high drama just eases the pain, and what could be more highly dramatic than evasiveness masquerading as spirituality?

Janie was also a mirror for me – cracks and all. There I shone, in a different time and place, also running from the crossroads of karma; not wanting to hear, not wanting to see. Screw guilt, and avoid pain, I can understand – but why do we detour around *what really feels right?*

Furthermore, Janie's gift to me was the introspection of having to evaluate "worthiness" versus its evil twin. I drew it in and blew it out – I wanted to be loved, dammit, for whoever I was. If I was going to give and make sacrifices – indeed allow myself to be taken advantage of – then I had a right to expect, demand more; to respect myself enough to be loved by a committed, equally engaged partner. I don't know what spirit summoned us together, but I felt blessed by that relationship. Teachers wear all kinds of costumes.

There are no victims, I'm convinced, when one looks closely through the veil of the "real" world and delves into the secrets of mysterious being. And I knew that no finer epiphany would ever come from Mt. Kailash...

105, 106, 107...

Chapter Thirteen

The Silly Shaman and the Blessing Bishop

"*¡Mire en el cielo!*" ("Look in the Sky!") "*¡Venus y Jupiter! ¡y la Luna! ¡Que bonita! ¡Que Lindo!*" (How pretty, how beautiful!)

Narciso was in a trance. Just to the left of the snowcapped peak of Mount Veronica at about a 30-degree incline up from the horizon, was a beautiful, heavenly conjunction of the Moon and our two brightest planets. The residual fog from last night's pouring rain was dropping away now, down into the mountain valleys thousands of feet beneath us, leaving nothing but the shining Andes in its wake. Even at this ungodly hour, 5:30 A.M., the encroaching dawn lit them up in regal elegance. It was cold – maybe hi-30s Fahrenheit, and wetter than a sponge in a swimming pool. It was all we could do to stir out of our poly-filled sleeping bags, pull down the tent zippers and rub the sandman away. And gawk.

Narciso hadn't slept. He'd been having too much fun with Pisco, the Peruvian firewater that passes for Happy Hour (morning or night) in the high *Altiplano* of Peru, Bolivia and Chile. He was our guide, and this last night of the Incan Trail, at the precipitous saddle of Phuyupatamarca, was his traditional party time. A bottle of 70-proof hooch at 12,000 feet would render most folks the Mt. Everest of hangovers. Not Narciso. Must be that Quechan or Aymaran blood… or, is it just that practice makes perfect? That was also possible, considering that his normal behavior was hardly different from his celebratory one.

For four days he and his porters had led our band of trekkers over hill and dale – specifically, Huayllbamba, Paucarcancha,

Llullchapampa, Warmiwañusca, Phuyupatamarca, and soon, finally, Machu Picchu – as we snaked through this ancient messenger route, tasked by elevation and amazed at the ever-changing choreography of high-desert and rain forest.

The first time I surmised Narciso was loco was the week before, when he had dared me to jump – then shamed me by doing so himself – into Lake Titicaca. Water at 12,500 feet is friggin' cold at *any* latitude, even our minimal 16° S. bearings. It doesn't help things if one samples the goods on June 21, so benign in the Northern Hemisphere, but, naturally, the shortest day of the year – ergo, winter – in the Southern Hemisphere. I felt a nudge in my ribs, then saw the Mother of All shit-eating-grins wrap around Narciso's long, drooping mustache.

"You jump; I jump, gringo." The gauntlet was down.

"Narciso, you been strollin' in the coca patch again?"

"Hee-hee-hee. Don't touch – evil plant. But I serious here – lake plunge on short day makes man strong – in bed, how you say…?"

"Virile? Bullshit…you're pullin' my leg, you loco Wildman. Or, should I say, yankin' my chain – a chain that would be shriveled down to nothing if I plunge into *that* ice box."

"Hee-hee-hee…"

In Tom Robbins' *Even Cowgirls Get the Blues* there was a wise-ass character named "The Chink" who lived up in a cave. When not leching over young girls (or old ones, for that matter) or expelling vulgar body functions, he'd utter forth just enough timely golden nuggets of wisdom to attract seekers from far and near. (Who said the Profound and the Profane can't be first cousins?) The Chink had a signature laugh – "HA HA HO HO and HEE HEE!!" Narciso struck me as a mere polysyllabic mutant of that guy.

He was short and squat, with a powerful torso and legs resembling bulging pistons. Those weren't uncommon features here, as the Altiplano was a harsh climate where the biological and vocational demands of high-altitude breathing and trekking over passes with bulging packs could easily shape a man into a diminutive spark plug. He could've been anywhere from 35 to 50. His behavior certainly didn't yield any clues; he seemed ageless. Long black hair tumbled down his back, and true to Indian stereotype, not being able to muster much of a beard, he sported the aforementioned cat-tail moustache and little tufts of hair randomly scattered around his cheeks and throat.

But all that was background. Narsiso's eyes were the magnet – sometimes translucent, sometimes a formidable brown wall, sometimes hypnotically spinning around like those mysterious monoliths in *2001: A Space Odyssey*. Modesty certainly wasn't an issue: day to day, his wardrobe would morph from army pants to alpacan sweater, U.S. bomber jacket to a worn-out Sears poncho, or a sombrero to one of those rainbow-colored woolen ski hats that took the North American slopes by storm in the Eighties…(and cost about 49¢ at the source).

Narciso was the Patch Adams of the Andes: a menagerie of outrageous colors, cloths, and cuts. Most likely he didn't care. He kept a grin at the ready; in fact, he seemed totally content – and focused – no matter what he was doing. Like at this moment…

"No worry, no problem. Look…"

Shit. He jumped, his dignity shielded by convenient boxer shorts. Titicaca engulfed him like piranhas on picnic. The game was now afoot – and what Sagittarian can deny a challenge to adventure? In I went, butt-naked of course. Yeah, there were female types on board, but I lacked Narciso's convenient undergarments. Besides, these ladies were the type that could handle it; probably even get a good chuckle at my expense (er, "shortcomings?").

"FUUCCCKKKK…!" It wasn't a coherent exclamation – if I'd had the wits to conjure up a more intelligible response, it would've been a lot spicier than that.

Narciso paddled around, for a good minute or two, amused as usual. I did my best reverse-rocket thrust move, and defying several of Newton's and Einstein's laws, made it back on the boat before I had actually jumped (didn't need no stinking ladder!). No, it must have been an illusion…I was still wet, and sure as Pachakuti *felt* frozen…

That night I got sick. Not head-cold, feverish sick; but the kind of sick that pours Drano through your intestines and cons your stomach into thinking it's Vesuvius laying waste to Pompeii. I don't know if it was the lake trout (from our "Five Star" hotel restaurant), altitude sickness, or Pachakuti's last stand against imperialists; but both ends went turbo, and I couldn't even get out of bed the next day. Which was a major drag, because up the tracks in Cusco was the big Inti Rimi festival. The group had to go on without me. The Inti Rimi Festival is the colorful celebration of the Sun God's rebirth, featuring a cast of thousands dancing, eating, drinking…damn it all, I had to miss it. But Narciso took care of me.

On the morning of the third day, I was again strong enough to walk and he arranged a taxi from the hotel. From there we grabbed the train to Cusco. For twelve hours we chugged through small pueblos while papoose-lugging, bowler-brimmed native women – hitching rides between points A & B by standing on little platforms jutting out from the train's body – thrust trinkets through open windows into my lap. ("*No, gracias, señora – estoy enfermo – por favor, no me moleste – OK?*")

"My people," Narciso reflected. "Train passes them. World passes them. I do what I can."

Peru is one of the world's ten poorest countries, according to the United Nations. A surreal wall of culture – and a real wall of mountains – separates the one percent of ultra-elite and scant middle-class of educated, cultured denizens of Lima or Arequipa from the struggling hill-dwellers and low-land jungle masses – the ones responsible for the predictable cycle of presidential overthrows and revolutions; the ones destined to (clandestinely or openly) grow coca for the insatiable demands of North American yuppie nostrils; the ones caught in an endless tug-of-war (or is it mere collusion?) between Escobar-style crime families, the CIA, the DEA, and perhaps a few pharmaceutical companies.

I stared out the window, too weak to talk, lost in a stark landscape of brown towering mountains pocked by occasional green cultivated hillsides – at 60° slopes – supporting rubble-homes with mud-thatch roofs. How far away; how in-my-face. We crept over a pass where a train station waited forlornly. No, it wasn't waiting…it had no reason to. On the steps I could see a little girl, brown-skinned and dirt-smudged, with a tattered dress and a dolly that had seen better years. Like her doll, the girl was half staring into space. The other half fixated on me. The train chugged the last few feet up the incline to the apogee of the rise – the literal peak of the pass, straddled by the station – where a sign in fading black and white, read "14,025 feet." I reached with some effort for my Pentax camera, feeling like I was in one of those molasses-pouring dreams, where every motion requires attention, and things just keep getting slower, and *slower*...She stared, non-blinking...gradually turning her head to the hypnotic pull of the train. I fidgeted with the camera. There was that incredible moment of sublime "No-Time": we had, like the finest pendulum, temporarily stopped moving. Everything froze...but, alas, I couldn't get the lens focused. (*Was I in fact dreaming?*) She sat stoically; and then – she was gone, as time once more resumed and gravity reluctantly pulled the train down toward Cusco. Narciso sighed.

Reunited with our group in Cusco, Narciso showed us around the impressive Incan capital, the one that Francisco Pizarro co-opted in the 1530s. He couldn't help but smile while he recounted the stories of Cusco's famous earthquakes, whose periodic tantrums always seemed to bring down the Spanish architecture, Jericho-style, while leaving the original Incan motifs in place. "Maybe Christians not respect God right?" mused Narciso.

He even took me up to the high ruins of Sachsayhuaman (we Gringos couldn't resist saying "sexy woman") overlooking the town. It was night, and we weren't supposed to be there, but he had friends. The "Seven Wonders of the Ancient World" guys would've been hard pressed by Sachsayhuaman – a snaking fortress of walls a quarter-mile long, with rocks interlocked like rigid dominos. *One hundred ton dominos – and not room for a knife edge in between them.* Furthermore, the nearest quarry resembling said geology was 50 miles away.

"Spin that one to 20th Century science," challenged Narciso, though in not quite those words. He then sat down in an alcove and offered a half-prayer, half-song to somebody or something. Even the jester had his serious moments.

It's not my place to guess the whole "what/how/why" of Sachsayhuaman. The usual suspects, like ETs and ancient technologies, fill the works of folks like Graham Hancock (*Fingerprints of the Gods*). Naturally, both the Catholic Church and champions of post-Renaissance science claim there has to be a more satisfying explanation. Even Narciso is dubious – "Why reality have to be magic? Incans have better tool, that's all." His feet were always on the ground, even if his head floated around the high mists of the Andes. He was also amused at tourists' infatuation with the Incans, since many visitors just assume the big bad Europeans walked in and raped a peaceful, harmonious group of bucolic hunter-gatherers.

"Incans was like Romans...rule most South America...4,000 miles of empire, from Colombia to Chile...*14,000 miles* of total roads, trails...beat up many tribes, kill them, made great buildings with slaves." Who could blame Pizarro's scout team, when they saw the disks of gold hanging off these dude's chests? But Narciso wasn't nostalgic for the Incans – he considered them late-comers who enslaved his forefathers. According to Narciso, his ancestors possessed some of the original gold tablets left over from the sinking of Lemuria – in the Pacific, 30,000 years ago – and these were buried somewhere in Cusco. Nor was he impressed with the Spaniards. "But were smart – they know to get Inca enemies together, pick Incans apart – do dirty work for them. Final battles was easy. Spanish was – how you say...'thugs'? But very smart thugs."

Yet, "Still, I thank Spanish for bring Jesus. Just have hard time with most that follow Him."

Sipping pisco from my boda bag, I gazed up at the southern stars from the ruins of Sachsayhuaman and drifted back a few weeks to another insightful fellow I'd met...a priest in Copacabana, Bolivia, and a certified "car-blesser." I never caught his name, but we talked in "Spang-lish" for a good half hour or so.

Copacabana is a funky little lakeside town on the southern shores of Titicaca, right inside the Bolivian border from Peru, and home of the weekly vehicle-blessing ritual. It's a big deal – that road has one of the highest fatality rates in the region, which isn't a stretch to imagine, considering the moon-cratered roads and a driving scenario cast right out of *The Road Warrior*. Vehicles of every type plied that road – jeeps missing hoods; 20-year-old rusted Corollas packing in families of eight; pink trucks with bald tires; commercial truckers with actual tread tires; mopeds and choppers...you name it...and held together by every permutation of bondo, bailing wire, rope, bungee cord, coat hanger and plywood that one could imagine. It was Mardi Gras on wheels, but the stakes were high and the contestants serious.

Copacabana, with a noteworthy shrine to the Virgin looking on, puts on the Ritz every Sunday by encouraging drivers of all types to pass through a gauntlet of holy water and rosaries in front of the church located on the tiny town square. Horns honk, people dance, vendors thrive, and above it all, church bells ring. The good padre's job was to sprinkle holy water on the vehicles, but in truth, any liquid would suffice. If the patron requested and handed him the goods, he'd even spew the engine with *Cuszcena* or one of the other local beers.

At the end of the priest's ceremony on this particular Sunday – he was wearing tennis shoes, a brown robe and a fuzzy hiking hat – I asked him about the beer.

"Ah, *si*, one of God's favorite creations." I liked this guy already.

"It's an offering of local products, when you think about it – our own maize and barley from the Altiplano. And to be honest, the more that goes onto the cars and the less into the driver, the easier my job gets."

"The Virgin looks down with beneficence on everyone here. I know, I know, it's crazy folklore to most of the world, and I'm not sure what exactly to believe myself. But it doesn't matter whether it's true or not, *si*? The people *believe*, señor. So I get to – what, rub shoulders? – with my people while doing a great service. And it keeps me young," he laughed, "and sometimes, I even get to keep a six-bag for a *propina* – you call, a tip!"

Lying there near the massive rocks of Sachsayhuaman, lost in space to the Southern Cross, I wouldn't doubt for a moment that Narciso and the good padre could've been kin – the same DNA wired into two different belief systems. But were they really different after all? Both had their integrity; both were flexible and accepting; and both sure as the Holy Assumption worked in mysterious ways. Neither would ever be part of the one percent upper class and maybe not even of the narrowing middle class (though the priest had no doubt been raised such), and probably didn't care to be. Each had a seasoned worldliness about him that reinforced a sense of purpose. Each knew who he was – the God stuff was just the wrapper.

Wasn't that the way life could best be perceived? As a joyous illusion so colorful and exciting, it was enough to believe in and promote, as long as "The Gift" kept giving the same undeniable pleasures, and we hop-skipped over all the perceived perils that threatened to do us in? Well, yes…for some. But for myself, I need a dose of consciousness and mucho self-reflection in order to satisfy my hunger and curiosity to find all the missing pieces of this puzzle called Life – wherever those pieces may have been strewn by that evasive Creator of us all.

* * * * * *

That last night on Phuyupatamarca Pass, while the rain hammered away, a handful of us played poker in the mess tent. There was Stevie A, my Kiwi sidekick from Boise (I was Stevie B); Gina, a doctor from Santa Fe; Linda from Chicago; and an Israeli girl on her own with the smallest pack outside of Stuart Little's toiletry kit (damn, those people are tough – why would *anyone* try to attack them?).

Narciso cleaned us out, which basically meant our Chiclets, a few cigars and a pint of Pisco.

"Life like poker, amigos. Especial, the 5-Card Stud game. Get a hand, you can't help. But you work hard – you watch eyes, you be patient, you make big play when others talk, you risk…and never let mind get in front of heart. You always win" – he scraped his booty into a pillow case – "some just win more than others. *Hee-hee-hee!*"

The next day we descended the last 5,000 feet into Machu Picchu, hiking through the jungle, passing from the cedars and laurel down through miles of orchids and begonias, hobbling over countless stairs (I suppose *somebody's* counted them) laid out by the Incans. We got to see Narciso in action one more time when one of our crew, a quiet guy named Tony from St. Louis, developed horrendous stomach cramps and curled over on the trail. Narciso worked his hands like a surgeon in a clockwise action around Tony's stomach; sharply thrusting at the equivalent of each hour-digit of a clock while our buddy moaned, groaned and rolled in agony. Narciso then went into a mumbling frenzy of Quechan, Spanish, English, Martian and Arcturian (or was it Lemurian?), gesticulating crazily with his hands and weaving some kind of ethereal tapestry twelve inches above his patient's stomach. Slowly, calmly, Tony sat up, recuperated.

Several hours later, we climbed through the great Sun Gate of Intipunki and stared down into the gravity-defying saddle of Machu Picchu, deserted mysteriously by the remaining Incans before Pizarro's boys swept into Cusco for the *coup de grâce.* The Spaniards never did find Machu Picchu. It was so grand from up high: above the throngs of Japanese tourists, removed from the frenetic waving of touts and concessionaires, frozen in time. But not really – it had all just happened yesterday.

One last night was spent at the modest but precious Sanctuary Lodge – the only hotel at the park grounds...the rest were thousands of feet and 13 death-defying hairpin curves beneath us in the town of Agua Calientes. With Narciso's influence once more, we paid "special admission" to (we bribed) the park security guys to let us into the grounds at night. It was different than in the day, sans tourists – and bathed in a full moon. Narciso and a few friends even entertained us with a native dance, a moving trance almost Tai-Chi like, that resulted in several women freaking out with claims of ghost-sightings and strange bodily sensations (hadn't they heard of Pisco?)...

The next morning we pulled out. Narciso hugged, shook hands and addressed us. He had a special surprise for me: feigning a hug, he suddenly reached down to my crotch, grabbed whatever he could find, and gave it a tug...

"See...everything still there! Titicaca make you strong man, amigo! *Hee – hee – hee – hee...*"

Dignity and purpose wear many cloths and guises. They can operate within the bounds of formality or on the fuzzy edge of a seeming delirium. Narciso and the Copacabana car-blessing priest were snapshots for my growing s-t-r-e-t-c-h gallery, rapidly demonstrating to me how limited our views may become when we don't get the benefit of first-hand experiences.

Chapter Fourteen

The Spider Woman of Corcovado

G.I. Joe never had it so good. With our infrared night goggles, we were ready for anything – lions, tigers, and bears, oh my! There weren't any such varmints, but there *were* jaguars, pumas, nasty pig-like peccaries; and, if one prefers long and slimy to big and furry, there's always the 10-foot long boa and deadly poisonous viper snake. None of these were our quarry that night, however; we were after the small and strange. "Small" is a relative term, anyway, considering spiders the size of one's hand, moths like transparent kites, and beetles rivaling Apache attack choppers.

Our escort that sultry night was Terry, a modern day Jane-of-the-Jungle who had built herself an impressive domicile back in the deepest, darkest foliage.

"Hey, y'all," – Terry hailed from the flatlands of Alabama – "Isn't he cool?" Spiders were her favorite, it seemed, and she was introducing us to a grotesque-looking specimen hanging out on his web, staring back at us as if waiting for us to admire him.

Attached to a body several inches in diameter were fuzzy/scaly/ugly legs that seemed to change color with our shifting flashlights. His web was modest, maybe only three or four feet across. I shuddered to think back to the days of my boyhood newspaper route, when, taking convenient shortcuts through my customers' woods on pre-dawn southern summer mornings, I'd walk smack-dab into the wet, fibrous mesh of a spider web and spend the next ten minutes removing it from my face and hair (and neck and torso).

"Wow," exclaimed Heidi, my traveling partner. "Will he bite?"

"Naw, not unless you touch him, or he touches you (*how reassuring!*). 'Course, anything smaller than him is pretty much toast in an encounter."

Jutting out from southwestern Costa Rica's Osa Peninsula, the Corcovado National Park is, by day, a benign postcard of paradise. By night, the place is a Japanese horror flick and an entomologist's wet dream. The stage productions of Alice Cooper's *Welcome to My Nightmare* or Edgar Winter's *They Only Come Out at Night* could easily have been set here. That's what happens when one throws 10,000 insect species (including over 200 butterfly types), 300 bird species (and 50+ of bats), 5,000+ known plants, 120 reptile families (crocs? you betcha), 60 fresh-water fish and 70+ marine crabs, and 700 types of trees into 30 different eco-systems comprising an area only one-tenth the size of Rhode Island. Suffice it to say that, day and night, there's a whole lotta shakin' goin' on.

Heidi and I had veered away from the traditional Costa Rican highlights to check out the Osa peninsula. While the true body count in the Corcovado National Park will probably never be known because new species keep popping up like in-laws at a probate court, those in-the-know claim this little patch of jungle contains the greatest collection of bio-diversity *on the planet*. I wasn't surprised; I was seeing half of 'em all in one setting. Corcovado oozed...throbbed... hummed...chirped...bristled...shrieked...scratched...buzzed... flapped...whirred...It may have been night, but the jungle sure wasn't sleeping.

"Watch out for the cutter ants," Terry reminded us, referring to the incredible, moving "line" that extended miles back to a Wal-Mart-sized staging area where the proceeds – the "cuttings" of millions of ants – would be deposited for safe housekeeping. Industrious but benign, these were the "good guys." Their cousins, the "bad guys" (army ants) will consume reptiles and even small livestock that don't honor the train-crossing signs. Legend has it that the army ants' jaws are so powerful, Indians once used them for suturing up wounds: they'd hold the ant over a wound and squeeze its body until the jaws instinctively shut, clamping the flesh together. The body was then pinched off.

"Watch this, y'all." Terry showed us how to hold our flashlight next to our ear (when not viewing through the infrared lenses), creating a beam on a parallel path to our line of sight. The vision's not bad – a bit blurred and eerie, like a Vincent Price hangover – but what scintillated were the thousands (millions?) of colorful specks; glittering fairy dust in a sea of ersatz black. Orange, red, green, yellow specks.

"Why, this is just like a terrarium, only we're the ones being observed," I realized out loud.

"And just think, you had to *pay* to go on display," Terry laughed. "That's what I like about bugs and reptiles and snakes and all these creepy-crawlies – most were here before us and will probably still be hangin' around long after we finish blowing ourselves up."

We had been at it for about an hour, and another hour or so still awaited us. Our routes were a series of crisscrossing paths that carved lop-sided "Figure Eights" through the surrounding property of the Lodge/resort. It was maybe a mile or two in total, but seemed a lot longer. I thought about Richard Burton, David Livingstone and that voracious conquistador down in the Amazon – Aguirre, the self-proclaimed "Wrath of God." Were they crazy, or was it simply, to quote Samuel Johnson (though he was referring to marriage) "the triumph of passion over reason?" It didn't take much imagination to see how folks just disappear out here. One can literally be five feet from a good-sized trail and never even see it – in broad daylight. "Things" can slither right out of tree branches and into your skivvies. Other things can slither right up your britches and into your skivvies, if they don't stop for *hors d'oeuvres* first.

Terry, the Bug Lady, had died and gone to heaven. Never mind that her heaven looked like someone else's version of hell. Damn, it's beautiful.

Mainstream Costa Rica was awesome enough, even if it was becoming Gringo Retirement-Land. It's hard to argue with cool cloud forests, Class V whitewater rapids, billowing volcanoes observed from *Fantasy Island*-esque hot springs resorts, rolling range land, tropical beaches and Everglades-style jungle estuaries. Not bad for a country of less than four million people in an area smaller than West Virginia. They also had potable drinking water. Average life expectancy is 75 and the literacy level hovering at 96% – several impressive notches higher than their Central American neighbors, and rivaling North America (77 years, and 98% respectively).

Blame it all on Oscar Arias, Costa Rica's extraordinary president and Nobel Prize winner, in the early 1960s. Observing that his larger, pesky neighbors, Panama and Nicaragua, could lay a whooping on his homeland if things ever got confrontational, the legendary Presidente thought, "Well, uh, why waste money on an army?" At great personal risk, he disbanded the military and with tremendous foresight, sallied forth on turning Costa Rica into a stable Central American exception by investing the proceeds into education and a national park system, now comprising almost one-third of the entire country. Did I mention he was far more than a "do-good socialist," but pioneered a model for Enviro-capitalism funded by some of the world's largest companies; and with said revenue proceeds from productive citizens and outside investment, has turned Costa Rica into one of the world's most desirable tourist and retirement draws? So much for Third World altruism. *Things can change.* Not that everything is perfect – witness the slums outside the capitol city of San Jose – but the country has never looked back. Years later, when the Sandinistas and Contras were duking it out in Nicaragua and Bush the Elder was spanking Panama's Noriega (who had ill-advisedly bitten the hand of his CIA and DEA sponsors), the Costa Ricans cruised right on through. *¡Pure Vida!*

Terry, who had loved creepy, crawly things for as long as she could remember, had graduated from Auburn University a few years back. With her dish-water blond hair pulled back, she was sporting a "Bama" tee shirt when we first met. Thus, when I tried to win her fealty through my greeting of "Roll Tide," I was met with a good-natured, derisory snort – how was I to know she'd gone to Auburn and not 'Bama? Even if I was a Georgia Tech Yellow Jacket first and a Tennessee Volunteer second, collegial team greetings in the Southeast were considered diplomatic courtesies…*except* for Auburn and 'Bama, whose mutual contempt bordered on that of the Sandinistas and Contras.

She had never camped a day in her life, went her story, but upon graduation headed to Costa Rica with what few possessions and gear she could round up. As Costa Rica is to the entomologist (attracting as "moth to a flame," pardon the metaphor) like the Holy Land to an archaeologist, it should have surprised no one when she pulled up on the beach one day and commenced buggin'. Before long, she was a resident staff member of a respectable rustic resort. Her duties, which one could assume included wider research into the flora and fauna, also included the nightly Bug Tour...although, I suspect, that was *her* clever invention...

"Howdjall get here?" she queried, knowing there were only two real ways.

"Well, you know, the turbo prop flight, the land rover, the boat thingy," Heidi replied.

We had in fact flown turbo prop from San Jose into a remote strip of jungle, after skirting the rugged-yet-tranquil Pacific coastline for the last 40 miles; cutting over the tops of palm trees so close I could feel my feet tickle. A modest runway and airport shack greeted us and then a van of sorts hauled us through 10 miles of palm plantations to a remote river site, where we boarded a boat for the final leg. This consisted of an idyllic float down river past huts and palms. Then, upon opening into the estuary of the Pacific, we had to cut strategic zigzag swaths through openings in the slanting breakers to gain full entrance into the ocean.

"*Tenemos buen suerte*," said señor captain, referring to our good luck in making it through.

"*Por que?*" – Why? – we had replied in unison, with creased brows and rising voices.

"Because last week, boat hit wave, tip over, two passengers drown."

We had relayed that little story to Terry, who simply remarked it should have been no big deal; the skipper was probably drunk, the boat not serviced properly, tourists not able to swim, etc.

"Do they have Darwin Awards down here yet?" I asked, referring to the whimsical annual prizes given to those who improve the lot of the human race through questionable antics which, while predictable to everyone but them, result in the removal of their genes from the collective pool.

"Yeah, I heard 'bout that," snickered Terry. Well into her twenties now, she had been gone a few years from the Mother Ship but hadn't quite checked out of the media scene. "I'spose a chunk of those awards go to my fellow Alabamans."

"And a king-sized dollop to my fellow Utahans," I followed, having spent the better part of a decade in the former Kingdom of Deseret (or, as social libertarians might say, "behind the Zion Curtain").

That night, Heidi and I were the only takers on her two-hour tour. Jungles are foreboding enough in the day and downright dastardly at night, so the other guests surely can't be blamed for sitting out the festivities. So after dinner, we left the other sensible guests back at the modest-but-culinarily-sumptuous lodge restaurant (which was open air, of course, but with one helluva waterproof roof) picking at their tiramisu and sipping on excellent Costa Rican coffees. Before heading out, we returned to our cabana to grab cameras – and got our first real taste of jungle night life. We had left the bathroom light on – specifically, the fluorescent one above the sink – and upon returning, we were treated to an air show of dozens of moths and a floor show of hundreds of little creepy-crawlies in full raging glory. Many were dead already, fried by light or eaten by the higher rungs of the food chain, but there was plenty enough to go around. We had Mardi Gras in bug-land, and our bathroom was the winning float. It was a freak show, and irritating – no wonder people stick pins in these things: I reckon it's for revenge.

So out we had gone into the night (bathroom light now *off*), flashlights waving, camera bulbs snapping, and goofy-looking mud boots sloshing through the perennially-wet trails.

It was one thing seeing the critter show in our bathroom and quite another seeing a spider the size of your hand. Even tarantulas, hairy monsters that they are, are non-poisonous and make good pets (if one doesn't expect much in the way of loyalty or comfortable lap-purring). But this wasn't PetSmart, and like Franz Kafka's *Metamorphosis*, we sure weren't in Utah anymore.

"Here's a good one, y'all!" Terry was on stage and leading the symphony at the same time. But this refrain would echo for the next several hours as we shuddered, gasped, cringed and instinctively recoiled like shell-shocked veterans returning from Omaha Beach. What makes the jungle so insidious isn't necessarily the obvious; it can often be the small, slimy, and strange: beetles, spiders, frogs, moths, worms, ants, and caterpillars; many whose penchant for weirdness is exceeded only by the length of their assigned Latin surnames. My favorite Corcovado critter was the "Jesus Christ" lizard (*Basiliscus basiliscu*) named after its fondness for "walking" across water. And, truth be known, the percentage of poisonous species in the park isn't really that high; most are harmless, even if looking at them makes you wretch. As is often the case, it's the unexpected that one must expect, and even entomologists aren't immune.

In her zeal to show us a particular beetle about the size of a quarter, Terry had held on a little too nonchalantly before remembering its tendency to exert a toxic brown fluid. "Ouch. Damn, that hurts!" Her casualness, bearing undertones of bravado, indicated to the jungle neophytes in her charge that it *really did* hurt, and whatever had just happened was more serious than our champion was willing to let on, maybe even to herself.

For the next 15 minutes or so we continued our walk, gawking at webs, bending over diminutive carcasses, peering up tree branches, poking around on leaves, etc., while Terry rubbed and waved her hand around, like shrugging off a bee-sting. All the while, the swelling continued, from brown to a dirty orange to a most funky rust color.

"Know what, y'all?" – her voice now measuring *concern* on the Fear Richter – "I better go clean this out."

Off she went, swift of purpose, to a creek we had passed about five minutes ago. Heidi and I stayed behind, in the middle of the path. We waited. Five minutes passed. Howler monkeys were having choir practice in the distance (how does something that small and cute create such a prolonged, rising, primal grunt?). Everything just seemed to settle in around us. Five more minutes passed, then ten and fifteen. Even the infrared lenses seemed to contract their viewing field. The world was shrinking. Another ten minutes. Heidi was shaking. I was concerned..."*Lions and Ti....uh, Jaguars and Pumas and...*"

Then Terry returned. "Well, that helped a little, but it sure stings like the dickens...that hasn't happened very often, but to tell ya the truth, I was scared (*she* was?). If y'all don't mind, I'd like to swing by my place and pour some antiseptic on it."

"Sure, Tarzan and Cheetah follow Jane to hut," I quipped, glad to be heading toward something that represented civilization, as macabre as that might be.

Lo and behold, her place was a beautifully built (technically, still under construction) house, with real toilets (hopefully leading to real septic tanks), real beds, real electricity coming from a generator, and real screens to keep out the invaders. It turned out her Costa Rican boyfriend was well-versed in construction – and obviously not afraid of the jungle. Still, a house like this in the middle of Corcovado's Terrarium would be like building a stucco rambler on top of a Saharan sand dune. Beats me how it would hold back the voracious appetite of the jungle, but I had to believe they had done their homework. Still, I was amazed.

After drenching her throbbing thumb nail in some foul-smelling solution – even worse than the beetle's discharge to my nose and eyes – she wrapped her thumb in gauze.

"I'm sure it'll be all right now. Darn, that was close." *Close to what?* I wondered.

Before we left, she had to show us her "nursery." "Hey y'all, look at these." Coffee cans were laid out like dishes on the kitchen table, each sporting a resident spider, resident beetle, an impaled moth ("they don't cooperate too well when they're alive"), legions of millipedes and centipedes, and red and black ants "Like the Georgia Bulldogs, our mutual enemies!" She high-fived me.

We were done, finally and thankfully. It had been a grand evening – mostly – and one worth remembering, albeit from a distance. We returned to our hillside cabana (light still *Off*), where in the daytime we could lounge in hammocks from an open porch and gaze out over the tranquil Pacific, serenaded by psychedelic-colored parrots and macaws. "So it looks like you're settled down here – even gone native, as they say," I had remarked to Terry before Heidi and I departed that night.

"Yeah, funny thing is, natives aren't even allowed to live in here. I had to pull strings. Executive privilege, I reckon!" (Or was the concessionaire value of a freak show too good for the authorities to pass up, I wondered?)

"Guess you could say I'm into the whole Jane-of-the-Jungle thing. Deserts are too lonely, mountains too cold, flatland too boring. Cities scare the crap out of me. So, here I am…"

"There, but for the grace of God, go you," I added. "Well, you certainly seem at home!"

Terry was commitment and focus. She reminded me of an acquaintance named John, who had known from the time he was four that he wanted to be a pilot and then proceeded to become the youngest commercial pilot in the history of his employer. Terry was committed to be Big with Bugs. Maybe not big in money, fame or notoriety – but big in her heart and giant in her willpower.

Blessed be those aware of their dharma, I thought. They are roadmaps for all of us. They may not all be peacemakers, but they sure as hell make life interesting. I'm honored to know them.

People like Terry also remind us that beauty, rapture, and wonderment can be experienced in the strangest, most unlikely places – though sometimes perhaps best observed from a distance…

Chapter Fifteen

The Barefoot Bohemian

Henri hailed from Normandy, but those windswept, oft-invaded shores were miles and years behind him. He was an American now, by virtue of citizenship – a source of never-ending grief to his proper and fiercely nationalistic Frankish parents. In fact, he had lived for some years in Sun Valley, Idaho; Salt Lake City, Utah; and Sedona, Arizona (dude, you gotta stop following me around!). But in truth, he was one chap who could have just slid into any culture and called it home.

I met Henri through a mutual friend, Avis, who had also lived in all three states and currently called Scottsdale, AZ a home port, where I was living at the time. Henri was in town for some personal business and Avis had thought I might enjoy meeting him to swap adventure stories.

The first time I met Henri and his wife, Carrie, was at a pizza place in town where he had painted the mural on the wall.

I knew I liked him immediately when I observed him playing with his food. "Oh, were you also in Boy Scouts and parochial schools?" I commented.

At the ripe age of 22, Henri had bolted out of his Norman countryside, hit the sunny hippy beaches of Spain's Costa del Sol and finagled his way across Gibraltar into Morocco. Then he kept going. Henri was another "drifter," but unlike those troubled youths of yester year (chronicled in James Michener's *The Drifters*), he wasn't running from anything; he was walking. Toward something. By age 29 or seven years after starting out, Henri had covered much of Africa by foot… barefoot. Then later he took on the Middle East into Afghanistan.

"No shoes? Really?" I gaped incredulously, peering out of the corner of my eye at Avis, then across the table at Carrie to check for the quivering grins that might betray a prank at play. Nope, they were both nodding politely, having heard this story before and apparently long bought into its validity.

"Really," Henri answered with a playful shrug. Surely he had run into this wall of shock before, and I was just one more audience.

"Are you insane?" I segued.

"Oh, *oui* – yeah – but that has no bearing on the truth, *mon ami*," he laughed. Now in his mid-fifties, Henri had the classic aquiline nose of a French patrician and the high cheekbones, slick-backed hair and signature mustache associated with a Parisian *maître'd*. He was also a tall fellow, not imposing but commanding of presence. What he *didn't* have were the less-flattering stereotypes of *haute-culture/cuisine*, the refined snobbery or subtle-sneering condescension of all those who were inferior, e.g., non-French, non-Parisian, and of "common" stock. He was, from my limited encounter, one of the most unpretentious, genuinely friendly, openly expressive, insatiably curious, and thigh-slapping hilarious people I've ever run into. He was even toning it down, Carrie remarked at one point, since we were at a public place.

"Why did you choose Africa and the world's tinder box, the Mideast?" I probed.

Again Henri shrugged his shoulders. "Who knows? Europe was always going to be around, and America would be too, I guessed. Russia and China were off limits back then. So all those magic stories like David Livingstone exploring the dark of Africa sounded good. And despite politics, it was a lot easier then to travel around the Mideast than now. Pick-pocketing is a way of life, and violence always makes the TV, but back then at least you knew the people were friendly, if not always trustworthy. As usual, the biggest worries were sickness, and I was very careful. Or maybe very lucky."

He played for a minute with his pizza, again in a way that tugged at my heart strings. Anyone who has spent time in the presence of boys knows that food has a special allure. You can eat it, of course, although in a number of creative manners. But you can also throw it, reconfigure it, catapult it from a fork, hide it and slip it auspiciously into someone's sleeping bag or shirt pocket, or trade it like the commodity that it is. Food, next to religion and boredom, has got to be high up on the list of "best reasons to go to war," initiated by either those who have a lot but want more, or by those who don't have much and need more. Either way, like gold and oil, it's a precious commodity. Even Napoleon said, "An army marches on its stomach," presumably meaning with food as a fuel source, and not referring to the aftermath of a gnarly case of salmonella or trichinosis. In any case, food has many utilitarian purposes, and sensing Henri's genius, I had a hunch he knew all of them and then some. Besides, he had been a cook as well, as I was soon to find out.

Remembering his story, he segued, "I thought about India, too, but the Magic Bus across Europe, Turkey, Iran and Pakistan was being shut down by then, and besides, I didn't feel like sitting around on one of those Nepali stupas stoned out of my mind for weeks at a time. Mainly, I guess, I had to get out of Normandy, even France. So south I went. South by southwest, then eventually east."

"Whereabouts did you go – I mean, I gotta believe there weren't any Michelin travel guides back then for Africa…"

"Oh, no. But there were maps that showed where roads were, along with mountains and jungles and rivers and deserts and cities. I could read and I could walk, so I figure – shoulders shrugging again – 'Why not?' So I walked down through Mauritania, which used to be called French West Africa – Ha, I thought – what a pompous name – the peoples of Mali were sending regards to their cousins in the Sirius star system (Orion's faithful hunting dog, "Canis Major") back when the ancestral French tribes were hanging out in caves painting animals on the walls. Anyway, I wandered down through Mali, Niger, Nigeria, Cameroon, Ghana and all those tiny little countries whose names escape me."

"How did you, like, *live?*"

"Mmm…very easily, actually. I met people, I stayed with them. They fed me. I would do little jobs – carry some water, plant some seeds. I would meet other Europeans, occasionally, and get little rides. But no big rides – I didn't want to!"

"Wow, I know most West Africans speak French, but surely you had communication problems?" It all seemed too bizarre...

"A funny thing happened. I don't understand. I became very, very sick in the Congo, which had formerly been the Belgian Congo – before it became Zaire, then the Central African Republic, then the Democratic Republic of Congo, or whatever the hell they call it these days..." He sipped his Perrier; he was on a "cleansing" right now, he said, so ix-nay on the wine or beer. " ...and I had a hellacious fever. I also had this incredible ringing in my ears, like nothing I had heard before. It was very frightening. I thought I was going insane, and I thought about all those old stories about people going crazy and trying to kill themselves just to get out of their anguish.

"I thought I was about to die, and there were no U.N. doctors around, or western medicine. I remember the local shaman, a "witch-doctor" Hollywood would call him, chanting around me and burning some incense stuff. I thought that was ridiculous, but I wasn't exactly religious, so I figured – *porquois non?* – it couldn't hurt.

"Anyway, I passed out, I guess. But I felt much better the next day after sleeping heavy. Then, a strange thing happened: I found out I could understand what they were saying. I didn't know how, or why, and I've never been able to explain it. I didn't know the words per se – but I knew their *meaning*. In just a matter of weeks, I could speak it also, although I never saw it written. As soon as I learned words, they were instantly remembered without trying, and somehow, I instinctively knew how to construct logical sentences. It just happened – and that's all that I'm able to tell people to this day."

Henri took another sip of his Perrier, then continued: "Except for one more thing – it kept happening, everywhere I went. Not only the major languages like Swahili, or later Farsi and Arabic, but dozens of regional tribal dialects. Within a day or two, I always knew what they were saying. Learning the words, then speaking the language, would follow effortlessly within a few weeks. I suppose I learned easily over 25-30 languages, and never studied one of them, or even had a teacher or book."

* * * * * *

It was well into evening now, and just a few outside tables still had patrons. "Hey, Henri, you ever hear of Richard Burton?"

"Why, sure…he was one of Liz Taylor's male harem, *oui*? Serious Shakespeare-style actor…always looked like he's passing a kidney stone with that intent grimace…"

"No, no," I cut him off, laughing, realizing his choice was the usual answer to that question.

"No, man, I'm talkin' about the British military commander in the 19th Century. But that's an honest mistake, 'cuz the Welsh actor you're thinking of adopted the *original* Sir Richard's name because he was a huge admirer. Anyway, RB#1 went all over the place – India, Arabia; Iceland; even traversed South America across Brazil and the Andes. In the 1860s, the British Secret Service even had him go undercover to Salt Lake City to check out first-hand the goings-on of a reputed cult called Mormonism. He led expeditions inland from the Kenyan coast trying to find the headwaters of the Nile, which he didn't – but one of his protégés and later nemeses, named John Hanning Speke, did. He spent nasty monsoon summers campaigning in India, where he converted to Hinduism; then blistering hot summers in Arabia where he converted to Islam… snuck into Medina and Mecca dressed up like an Arab. Not for long, though; he was the first to translate and bring the Arabian *1001 Nights* and India's *Kama Sutra* to the West. Ya know, the how-to-in-bed manual for keeping your partner(s) from wandering off to greener pastures?"

"I love that book!" Henri exclaimed. "Great pictures!" (Another thing about genius is its ability to recognize greatness in comics – I wonder if he had ever seen The Three Stooges *A Plumbin' We Will Go*). "Tell me more."

"Well, needless to say, he ran afoul of the proper authorities, as England's 'National Vigilance Society' and the 'Society for the Suppression of Vice' got their knickers up in a knot. Like he cared. Burton lived more in one day than those sanctimonious Victorian hypocrites did in their entire lives. The military of course, being more interested in maintaining empires than pinning starched corsets on proper society ladies, recognized his worth as a spy, diplomat, linguist, cartographer, and when duty called, a warrior.

"It seems to me, however, that the whole 'Officer and a Gentleman' thing was a ruse – oh, he was a fierce fighter and all, and a helluva commander, said his men – but he wasn't really into the pomp and circumstance of Merry Ol' England as much as using Her Majesty as a meal ticket to sponsor his real interests…

"But I digress…The point of this diatribe," I continued, after a particularly pleasing belt of Grand Marnier, "is that the dude learned over 30 languages in his time, many clandestinely, and he never seemed to view the obstacles as hardship. He just kept going, like that Energizer battery bunny on the commercials. And you remind me of him. Only funnier."

"*Merci beaucoup*, Stephen," Henri beamed. "Perhaps the travel bit – but not the soldier routine. I'm afraid I'm more of an artist and player with toys. It sounds like your Mr. Burton didn't mind killing people who got in his way, even if he wasn't caring about his Queen and Country – but I just want to cook and paint for them!" he laughed uproariously.

Henri had done just that, eventually. After the Congo, he zigzagged first across to Nairobi, Kenya, then back and down into Angola before getting detoured by their civil war. Fidel Castro's boys were arming one side, and Jonas Savimbi's UNITA rebels attacking from the other while Uncle Sam and the Russian Bear pulled straws, so that was no place for a barefoot, gun-less hippy, anyway. Somehow, someway in a manner that escapes me, he ended up in Afghanistan. Whether by foot, plane, train, bus, or car, I can't remember, but most definitely without going home to Europe. As he didn't have any money, the middle three options are dubious. I suppose he either walked up through Ethiopia and got across the Red Sea, or hitched a series of rides, crossing Saudi Arabia and then pre-revolution Iran; but I never found out. He then wandered for several more years among the Bedouins of the Khyber and the funky markets of Kabul, before hooking up with Carrie and hijacking a pass to North America and husband-hood. Many years had passed, and they had bloomed in deeper love. She was 14 years his senior, a gorgeous woman, and special indeed to have hooked this live wire. The two were a good match.

"What's all this about being barefoot?" I queried.

"Well, my shoes were stolen, and I had no money," answered Henri matter-of-factly.

"Couldn't you just steal some back from someone else? Everyone else does, I hear…"

"I was too young and stupid then. Besides, I didn't want my hands and feet chopped off in a public ceremony if I got caught. Would be very hard to get home, then," he chuckled.

"The story goes, I 'lost' my shoes in Morocco and found that walking on the sand and rock made them as hard as leather anyway – so why buy more?"

Coming from anyone else, I would have taken that as a joke. Henri continued, "I did rig up cloths or use cheap sandals when the sand got too hot, but I was going toward the jungles of the equator, and once my feet were tough, I knew even the jungle couldn't hurt them." (Shaka, the 19th Century Zulu king of South Africa's Natal region and thorn-in-the side of the British, would have been impressed. Warriors who couldn't keep up with his fast-moving barefoot legions were, well, killed ignominiously.)

"In all those years, didn't you worry about having possessions stolen, getting robbed or beaten?"

"Sure," Henri chuckled, "but God takes care of youth just like he does fools and drunks. And since many of those two *are* youth, I thought I would receive twice the blessings…No, I'm just kidding – I was never a drunk, only a fool! Ha! I tell you the truth…I never felt, or observed that I was in any danger from violence. But I did once have my small pack and all my possessions stolen, including my passport, and I was truly frightened. But I knew who did it, I was pretty sure, so I had to think and act like a Bedouin to get it back…I had been sleeping in a shopkeeper's back room, and he had several teenage sons and their friends who hung around. I knew they were watching me and my bag, when not smiling and offering me tea. I had slept with the bag right next to my pillow, but I'll be damned, it was gone in the morning…*Sacré bleu*, those guys were good!" he laughed.

"Welllllll…so you were kinda like acrost' the desert without a camel, *n'est-ce pas?*" Avis chimed in.

"Yes, exactly like that. So I became rather desperate. As I said, I must think like a desert rat. I had developed a good friendship with the store owner, who was maybe in his forties. I went to him and just kind of smiled, and I nudged him with a wink, and said, 'My friend, I tell you what. My bag? Not here anymore? Here's my deal…get it back for me, please…and half for you, half for me, OK?'

"Within 15 minutes, I had it back. The storekeeper had a 'reward,' I had my bag and what really mattered, the passport. There was even my money in it, which was about 1,000 Afghanis, or like around $20 equivalent. Of course, he got half. What really happened – who knows? Maybe he knew the kids had it all the time, and beat the hell out of them for getting caught. In that case, they didn't deserve the money. Or, because he was a hero to me, he got to keep it. It's a complicated philosophy over there, *mon ami*, but if you play the game right, you get to live and even make friends. Still, it might help if you actually sleep *on top* of your possessions!"

In the several decades since his travels, Henri had become a fine cook and respected small business owner, owning a mini-chain of successful bakeries along the Wasatch Front in Utah. Somewhere along the way, jumping between the alpine snows of Sun Valley and surreal panoramas of Sedona, he had also mastered oil and brush and plied a successful trade painting awesome murals on café and restaurant walls – like the place we were now in.

"How long did it take you?" I asked him, observing the 30-foot long mural.

"Oh, about one week…when I wasn't drinking coffee and cutting up with the owner." (It would have taken me a full day just to figure out what end of the brush to use.) People, landscapes, colors, activity – all there, in one big collage. A little bit of the desert southwest, a little bit of the African jungle, a little bit of the ancient Mideast. Just like him.

It was time to go. Henri and Carrie were moving back up to Idaho; Sedona was getting just a little too overrun by New Age crystal-junkies and retirement Winnebago's. No longer micro-focused on the demanding minutia of running a retail business, Henri found that Utah's stunning scenery was no substitute for a palpable lack of independent thinking on the part of the greater masses. "It's actually very comfortable in Salt Lake," shaking his head wistfully, "besides the beauty…and I also have many wonderful friends…but it no longer quite fits. So I must say *adieu* to that well-organized, very gracious culture."

He needed more than foot space; he needed heart and head space in order to keep creating and evolving. He always needed to poke his oversized Norman proboscis into new and challenging things.

Henri was certainly one of the most unique individuals I'd ever met. He was proof-in-point that Spirit always provides for those who follow their passion. He was also a role model for flexibility. Guys and gals like Henri teach us that knowing how the game is played is often more important than the "good or bad"; and those, in fact, are often arbitrary cultural paradoxes. Like Burton, one needs many disguises to flesh out the real truth – or at least what passes for it.

More than anything else, however, Henri drove home the fact that one doesn't have to stay on the fringes to explore the Strange & Mysterious, but can incorporate those into everyday contemporary culture: in the board room, in a suit and tie, in the market place, and in a suburban cul-de-sac. Henri was a reminder, as author Dan Millman remarked in *The Way of the Peaceful Warrior*, that there is no "Ordinary."

Chapter Sixteen

Beethoven's Last Stand

"**A**nd where are *we* from, my quixotic pilgrim?"
The voice was slightly effeminate, demeanor animated, and ethnicity tinted with Asian genes (part Chinese, part Filipino, perhaps?). The eyes were sparkling but direct.

"Uh, Rotorua, most recently," I responded, referring to the sulfur-reeking town of hot springs and semi-dormant volcanoes a few hundred clicks up the road in North Central New Zealand. I had slowly climbed the handful of stairs to the front porch to inquire if there was room at the inn.

"No, no, no, sir knight, I mean before *that*." My host put his hands on his hips in that Betty Davis, well-tell-me-more posture.

"Oh, in that case, then Auckland, the Bay of Islands, and all the normal highlights."

"My, you are a *difficult* one," feigning indignation while reaching for my pack. "I'm referring, dear boy, to your country of origin; your home port; the place where you pay taxes if you're so unfortunate as to be sullied by the reins of employment."

"Oh, I get it!" I winked at an amused German couple, fellow backpackers maybe in their mid-twenties, as I grabbed a wobbly chair on the rickety porch and accepted my host's offer of a cold Steinlager.

"U.S., mate – the land of the free and home of depraved."

"Ummm...let's see...hmmmm...Yes! I know the one," his finger wiggled like a theology professor with a sudden epiphany..."Say, don't you guys usually stitch that cute little red Canadian leaf on your packs? I mean, to throw off the scent of the hounds; to well, how shall we say, avoid being labeled as one of the *bad* guys?"

"Yeah," I laughed, "but those guys are a bunch of pussies. I'm referring to my turncoat countrymen, pal, not my fair-handed Canuck cousins, whom I love and tease in good sport. Nobody criticizes my country more than me, ya know, but damned if I'm not gonna own up to her. I'm proud of all those fiery speeches and enlightened manuscripts from way back when. The fact that we wander off the path from time to time – well, often – and occasionally turn those creeds upside down, is no reason to duck and cover."

"Bloody noble of you, I'll grant, if a bit misguided. In any case, welcome to *Beethoven's Hostel*. My name's Walter."

Walter presumably was the owner and all-purpose caretaker, cook, accountant, philosopher and greeting committee for this creaky once-Victorian house on a Wellington hillside. I can't remember how I heard about it – probably word-of-mouth from fellow backpackers and gypsies – but it was convenient and the price was right. It had a semi-impressive view of the harbor, which encircled New Zealand's House of Parliament and other diplomatic consulates from the wide world. It was also within walking distance of strategic docks, terminals and eateries, as well as much of commercial Wellington. That may not be saying much, but like hoofing the hills of San Francisco or Nice, a saunter about town could pack quite a wallop on inexperienced calf muscles.

It didn't take long to surmise how this backpacking hostel got its name. This guy was a Beethoven freak, and like a run-down tribute to Graceland's Elvis, Walter's hillside former-manor was ground-point-zero for all that was odd, quirky, trivial, enchanting and eccentric about his main man, Ludwig Von. The entire establishment was a museum of busts and posters, tee-shirts, newspaper clippings, paper weights, books by the score, and replica musical scores, of course…every form of kitsch and *tchotchke* gathered from who-knows-what tour, mail order catalog, trinket shop, et al.

Beethoven symphonies, sonatas, concerti, operas and masses bounced off the walls during the day, waking up boarders in the morning and sinking in smoothly like a fine cognac in the evening. Beethoven's Hostel was a mandala of the mad; a medicine wheel for maniacal musicians and footloose foreigners.

At first glance, one might believe if the ghost of Herr Beethoven were lurking about, it would be severely disappointed. The Maestro was, after all, a brooding perfectionist who always reached for the highest pinnacle of creation he could render. He *had* to compose and had to orchestrate, not because he was a loving person or considered it "fun," but because it was the only medium that bridged the fine ether between his genius and his insanity, which often ran in tandem. Fierce-tempered and unforgiving, nothing would or could stand in his way – not even going deaf. Furthermore, to say he didn't suffer fools gladly would be like claiming Hitler had an anger management problem. Witness the time Beethoven and Goethe, walking together, crossed paths with a party of nobility. The proper Goethe, two decades his senior, stepped aside and bowed, while Ludwig V. blustered right on through, hands behind back, forehead lowered. When Goethe asked him why he was so disrespectful, the headstrong youngster retorted, "There are many nobles. There are only *two* of us."

Walter, on the other hand, not only suffered fools gladly; he seemed to relish playing the part of one. He threw food (another soul mate!) – "*Yoo hoo, incoming, me landlubbers,*" often in the form of pancakes or taco shells, across the kitchen to the waiting tables of breakfast patrons. He philosophized with the neighborhood dogs that stopped by daily to check out the happenings – "Why are you here for only 10 or 12 years, my slobbering friend, while those selfish, mean pussycats get to live for 18 or 20?" He also gave mild-mannered sermons about everything from A to Z, treating his guests as itinerant disciples or like wayfaring pilgrims of old who sought sanctuary in the House of the Esteemed.

He lived and breathed chaos; and like a living agent of entropy, had no time or respect for petty cultural refinements, such as curtains on windows, vacuumed rugs, washed dishes, clean sheets and functioning shower doors. Apparently he was also in a continual tussle with health authorities, who had the audacity to hassle him over little things like vermin sightings (rats in particular). Those matters, in his estimation, may have been the stuff of Empire but "don't add one scintilla of wisdom to a man's nature." Besides, house care would have required work. Instead, he was a type of global diplomat, accepting each visitor not just as a fee-paying boarder, but also as his personal "guest" or ambassador. He possessed the showmanship of Liberace, the persistence of Socrates, and the flitting movement of a firefly.

Certainly, this was a far cry from the malcontent Beethoven, who in the words of author Jeffrey Dane (*The Beethoven Mystique*) was "misanthropic, impatient, ruthless and rude with servants, suspicious and distrustful of friends, sometimes vulgar, and could be unethical in business dealings."

But on closer inspection…*were* the two men really so different? Beethoven, like Walter, was prone to mercurial, spontaneous outbursts in public, and many escapades, apparently, were humorous, although he didn't necessarily *intend* them to be. He either didn't care or didn't know that he was considered "odd." Also like Walter, Herr B. wasn't impressed by title or nobility, instead treating each person he encountered according to his own perception, ignoring other protocols or what might be called "political correctness." For example, he had remarked about his friend Goethe, "The Court suits him too much. It is not becoming of a poet." He also shredded the front page of a symphony devoted to Napoleon, after surmising that the "champion of the common people" was really a tyrant masquerading as a PR agent (he then substituted a third person, generic name – *d'un gran uomo* – "a great man"). Beethoven's firm and principled stands, like Walter's whimsical and often non-flattering observations, were products of a fierce personal commitment to right and wrong that often defied convention or cultural standards.

Ludwig's admonitions were delivered by a thundering fist on the table; Walter's with a flippant, exaggerated *je ne c'est quois* that left Scarlet O'Hara's "Fiddle-dee-dee" gasping for air.

Although Herr B had plied his trade in the great symphony halls of Europe and Walter in an avant-garde backpacking hostel 10,000 miles removed, both were absent-minded professors of sorts. Ludwig's idiosyncrasies manifested in forgetting to button his fly, spitting "out of" closed windows or trying to pay a restaurant bill for a meal he hadn't ordered (after furiously scribbling notes in the corner all day). Walter's sins of omissions revolved around leaky roofs ("When it's sunny, they don't leak; and when it's raining, it's too icky."); dog fur in the kitchen

("Dogs are people, too"); and the occasional toilet jammed with last week's turds ("Oops – we have another one upstairs, I think"). Beethoven needed people to hear his *music*, even if it "was for a later age," as he once told an awestruck protégé about the underlying significance of his quartets. Walter needed people to hear *him*, at this very moment; and creditors, health agencies and tourist boards could go hang themselves.

I had arrived in Wellington from the north, traversing down through the rolling emerald green of the North Island, and was traveling by myself, although that's a bit of an oxymoron in New Zealand. Traveling in that part of the world is like a free electron bouncing around in orbit – you're gonna get scooped up pretty quick by the ever-morphing gypsy crowd if you have half a pulse and no discernible disease. Hitch-hiking was a convenient mode on the North Island, and rides usually appeared quickly, either from the bulletin board walls of hostels or out at the edge of town. I had long ago quit Hewlett Packard, and upon finishing my MBA at Boise State University in Idaho (with a "Student of the Year" award, no less, on the wall) decided it was time for a break. A long one. New Zealand seemed appropriate, since it was summer in that inverted part of the world; and because Australia was in the neighborhood, I figured I'd stop next door to sample their beer as well.

Although Beethoven's Hostel was bizarre by anyone's standards, the guests were fairly typical for the Down Under backpacking scene: lotsa Europeans (especially Germans, Swedes, Dutch, and of course Brits); Canadians with maple leaf flags on their packs; cowardly Americans with maple leaf flags and proud Americans with Stars'n'Stripes; Israelis on tour after risking life and limb in the world's sternest military for two years; and a handful of local roustabouts from Oz and New Zealand. There were occasional South Africans, although the travel restrictions of Apartheid from both their own country as well as from disapproving other countries, made the logistics dicey. There were even Japanese around too, as their economy ruled the world in those days. But they tended to stay in legitimate hotels, either too refined or too befuddled by the culture clash to fit into the hostel community. Besides, they could afford it. Most of us were living on about $8 U.S. per day, which after subtracting beer money, meant we were basically indigent.

We crashed on the floor with our sleeping bag and pads, although Walter was resourceful enough to come up with the occasional foam mattress. We would sleep side by side, both genders and all ages, possibly 20 or 30 people on a given night, scattered throughout the house in a number of different discombobulated rooms. One room even had a TV, which didn't work, of course, but did suffice nicely as a placeholder for a clay bust of the Master – wild hair (powdered wig be damned!), stern nostrils, blazing eyes and rumpled tie.

But much of the activity was out on the front porch, where Walter met guests and boarders hung out with tuneless guitars, slugging on whatever beer was cheap, and scribbling in travel journals. Wellington is blessed with temperate climate, so with daily summertime highs hovering around only 70° F. and usually a cool harbor breeze, it was a most pleasant way to pass a stay. Many of the lodgers were overnighters; this was just one more page in a long list of bookmarks. Others, like me, would carve up our trips by staying three or four days in one place, which made it a lot easier to sightsee, meet friends and get a general delousing from the road.

My interests in Wellington were 1) pragmatic – I had to jump the ferry to the South Island; 2) cultural – I wanted to see the Chinese Xi'an Terra Cotta warriors at the historical museum; and 3) strategic – the U.S. football Super Bowl was that weekend. Since it was the last weekend of January, as a capitol city, I figured there was a good chance some pub or diplomatic ex-pat place in Wellington would serve up the game on satellite TV.

"Say, Walter – ever heard of the Super Bowl?" I queried my host.

"Hmmmm…He shifted weight suddenly and resumed a pensive posture, with finger to chin and brow curled, staring a bit long, I thought, at a cockroach in the corner…"Isn't that something the Maori's drink out of?"

"No, mate…it's like, well, you know American football? It's kind of our World Cup, only it's played every year, and they call it a bowl 'cuz it's played in a, well, round-ish coliseum, and it's just one match, for all the marbles."

"Oohhhh…like that Babe Ruth guy, or the Wilt Chamberlain fellow…aren't they famous football players…?"

"Well, right country and right ego…but different sport and different era. Anyway, you know, our guys wear all kinds of pads and protective stuff, unlike your rugby and soccer guys, or the Australian-rules football chaps."

"You know"…he shifted again, and gave up on the cockroach… "Yes, I do recognize the game. My word, those are really big guys, all dressed up like stegosauruses! You live in such a violent culture, Stephen…when you're not blowing up other countries, you're beating up on each other. I *guess* that's a fair trade!" I glanced obliquely, looking for a punch-line.

"Oh, my, I'm just teasing you, silly." He nuzzled up and put a playful, bony elbow in my ribs. "At least most of your fellows have their teeth left, which is more than I can say about our Rugby and Oz-rule jocks. So…what about this Super Bowl match – are you going?"

"Hah, I wish. It's like in Miami or L.A. – don't even know, to tell you the truth. It's today, being a Sunday – no wait, it's tomorrow, which is Monday here but Sunday at home, because they're like 6 days behind you…or is it 8 days behind…?"

"Oh, so *that's* how it works! I always wondered…" feigning shock and enlightenment at the same time. "You're such a trickster. You're even weirder than me, my son."

"Thanks, perfessor!" I circled back around, not sure if I was being chastised or complimented. "Anyway, I was wondering if you knew any establishment where I might watch it; ya know, some place where U.S. diplomats or foreign workers hang out, some huge sports pub?"

With that, he had directed me to the Prince of Wales Pub, a mere handful of blocks from Beethoven's Hostel, and at 8:00 the next morning, I and curious Klaus, a German from Düsseldorf, got to the Prince of Wales just in time to get two of the few remaining bar seats for the 11:00 a.m. kickoff. By the time that rolled around, we had sampled every "yardarm," "middie" and "schooner" of ale in the place, usually in pitcher form. The game was a blowout (as were our brain cells) even after Denver's improbable first quarter. Soon, experience and depth of payroll had emerged, and by the game's second half, Phil

Simm's New York Giants were pasting John Elway's Broncos. But all of that was the sideshow, anyway. The real sociology experiment was observing 100 or so New Zealand sports fanatics, mostly unfamiliar with American-rules football, staring starry-eyed at the television screen.

Their first objects of attention were the cheerleaders: "What's she in her swimmin' suit fer, mate?" yucked Frankie to Clive. "That there's a pasture, not a beach, Sheila."

"Yeaahhh…but I'd rather graze with *that* livestock any day, Frankie."

"And whadda ya call them things, mate," lurching over into my face…"pom-poms? Don't know why she needs to shake'em, when her other assets are so obvious and a lot more shake-able!"

Then, there were the umpires, and a plethora of mind-boggling penalties. "How come them referee zebras look like prisoners, mate? Ya'd figure they'd be dressed more like *wardens*." Or, "Wazzat flag for – he didn't hit 'em *that* hard…dint even break nuthin' fars as I can spot…if that bloke can't handle his face guard bein' twisted around, he shouldn't be in the bloody match."

And so it went, through pitcher, pint, shot glass, and of course, the commercials.

The commercials were even more mesmerizing. Sleek cars, beers guaranteed to find Mr. Couch Potato the perfect doll, Mr. Clean and his White Tornado (or was it the Man from Glad?), the new and improved Apple McIntosh…all wrapped in Madison Avenue's finest trappings and delivered, thousands of miles away on a Monday morning, to a jam-packed bar full of homesick Americans and spellbound, drunken Kiwis.

Richard, a grizzled-but-erudite local, meaning he wasn't slobbering or yelling, leaned over and remarked, "You know, I've always admired Hollywood and America's grasp of the aesthetic. No one, not even the Brits, can pull that stuff off so audaciously. But I hafta tell you – nothing personal – there's times when your whole country seems like one bloody advertisement. I used to travel widely in America, as I'm with our diplomatic corps, and I do love your country, but once I got over my initial shock-fascination with your telly commercials,

I had to click the bloody box off. I mean really, do we *hafta* have the second-half kickoff sponsored by the Poulan Weed-Eater company? Or the time-out sponsored by the guys that make the potty bowl the bluest? I say, at least put the tits and ass back up there so an old man can enjoy a commodity with *real* value!"

Klaus nodded, although he did think the new Cadillacs were pretty cool.

"The commercials have strategic value, pal," I responded to Richard. "They put 'em up there to give viewers a break so's we can refill our popcorn bowls, thus aiding the cause of sobriety, or at least we won't burst from bulging bladders. Why, legend has it that more than one U.S. city has experienced plummeting water pressure levels from too many toilets being flushed simultaneously during Super Bowl commercials."

"Hah! – well, lad, better pissed off than pissed on, I reckon. That's rich." Even Klaus was amused.

The game was over by 3-ish Monday afternoon, and after stumbling around Wellington's pristine Botanic Gardens in fuzzy reverie, six-sheets to the wind, I managed my way back to the hostel in time for an impromptu lecture by Walter (weren't they all?). His sermon was about the evils of the French Secret Service blowing up the Greenpeace *Rainbow Warrior* ship the previous year in Auckland harbor. All, ostensibly, because the noble watchdogs of Greenpeace were scouting out alleged French violations of nuclear non-proliferation treaties in the South Pacific. The sons of Charlemagne were, after all, the guys who vaporized Bikini Atoll, revered shrine of a great swim suit…(whereas Uncle Sam just blew up Nevada back in the 50s – and who complained? Creative American advertising to the rescue once more; we called it "urban renewal").

"How uncouth; how savage," he pontificated to me and Klaus, as well as a hairy-legged Danish femme named Lise, and a young bandana-sporting Dutch couple. "And those incompetent Froggies didn't even have the wits to not get caught. What amateurs…Where *do* they get their training – from your CIA, Stephen?" Wink – nudge. "I'll bet that James Bond fellow never would have gotten caught. I mean, *really* (voice rising) if you're going to do a job, you might as well do it *superbly*."

"That's because he just wants to save the world, not destroy it," suggested clever Klaus, my cantankerous Kraut and fellow inebriate. I was too polite to say anything, but I was tickled by a German asserting that the French were predatory.

"Well, that's the world, for you," declared Walter, making a point either too sublime for our neophyte grasp of philosophy, or too empty to deserve comment. "I just want to stay home and play with you crazy travelers."

And thus he did, and has, apparently, for many years running.

* * * * * *

But all good things must end; or least, continue on in a different place and time. I was off to the ferry the next morning, the one that hopped over to Picton on the South Island. It was a three-hour 60-mile jagged line of splendid scenery, the zigzagging necessary to navigate the treacherous depths and wild currents. But it was only the first leg; the one that would propel me on to the regions of World Class whitewater, fjords, glaciers, trekking paths, and millions of sheep dotting hillsides like manna on rumpled green table cloths.

Hitchhiking would be more problematic there, I reckoned, but no worries, they had modern amenities like buses; and of course, there were always my salubrious brethren in beat-up jalopies, looking for company and a shared fare.

From the South Island, it would be on across the Tasman Sea to that larger island, the Land of Oz, or "Australia" in English…a place completely different from New Zealand in geology, geography, flora and fauna.

Walter offered me a ride to the ferry, sparing the 25-minute stroll down to the Quay. As we headed down the walkway toward a beat-up van, with me stuffing half-washed laundry into my oversized pack, I was treated to the *Ninth Symphony's* "Ode to Joy" blasting out of an upstairs window. I shivered. The *Ninth* was – *is* – Man's magnum opus; a transcendental leap into unknown (or, perhaps *forgotten*) zones; and the "Ode" never fails to send goose-bumps through me from stem to stern: consummate perfection, it was, is, and always shall be.

"For me?" I asked, with feigned eccentricity, "a grandiose farewell, perfessor?"

"Of course, my merry traveler – for you, and everyone else, all the time, everywhere. Crazy Ludwig *knows*, even if he did huff and puff and behave like a big bully sometimes."

"Uh…he knows *what?*"

"Why, that perfection is here *now*, silly. We don't have to look for it. We *are* it. If that wasn't true, dear boy, how could Mr. B ever have written such perfection in the first place?"

We pulled into the quay, and I shook hands with a beaming Walter. "Well, be good, my sunny Yank. Or at least, be good *at* it."

I admired that little firefly. He may have skitted around a lot, but he blazed brightly. He also knew his place – not because anyone told him what to do or where to be, but because he chose it; compelling himself to serve the world from the den of his own ramshackle kitchen and front porch of an imploding house. His opinions, which were simply candor wrapped in semantic ribbons and compounded by endless gyrations, were nonetheless non-judgmental and never to be taken as a personal affront. His suggestions and elucidations, likewise, were meant to raise the bar; to excel and nudge everyone to a higher cause of action, a wider path of selection – even if such selections resulted in ignoring inconsequential things like cockroaches and pesky health board bureaucrats; or cluttering one's house with banal, even childish, memorabilia. Those weren't the measure of worth, in his mind, and they thus deserved no attention.

Chapter Seventeen

The Wistful Walkabout

"Bub" (Bob, I think) wasn't a bad roommate; he was just sort of *laissez-faire* about the etiquette of putting things away or hanging clothes up. Besides, his attention was fixed on a map of Australia, that of his homeland – and his world, solar system, galaxy, and Universe. That didn't make him, in my estimation, either parochial or unkind. He was just indifferent to everything else, and figured since he'd been born in such a quirky continent, it therefore deserved his undivided attention.

"Sorry, mate," pushing some papers away from my side of the shared table and kicking his dingo boots over into the corner, "Kinda lost in me own world here."

Taking a swig off an oil-drum sized can of Victoria Bitter, his eyes returned to the map. It was huge; probably six feet wide and four feet high.

"Ever hear of an American named Steven Wright, Bub?" I queried.

"Nah…whad he do?"

"Said he once had a summer job as a cartographer – a map drawer. His task was to make a map of America. The scale for his project had to be 1:1."

"Yeaahhh…so…?" Fortunately, he was grinning.

"Uh, well…(not sure if to continue)…"His job the next year was to fold it."

"Bloke sounds fuckin' loony, mate. He should try comedy; at least maybe could make a livin' at it!"

Bub stretched out; he'd been bent like Quasimodo over the map for two or three hours, he reckoned. His six-foot, five-inch frame with outspread wings took up a considerable chunk of our quasi-Quonset hut. He sported the latest mullet, the shorn-on-top, scraggly-on-the-sides motif popularized in America by football jock Brian Bosworth. His body, likewise, was a proving ground for Tattoo styles; a giant advertising sign for punk bands, motorcycle groups, and naturally, his dear ol' mum. His body was also rock-hard, from an adult life of breaking rock, digging ditches and any other occupation favoring brawn over brain.

He stretched out again – "Oops, sorry, mate," – nearly knocking me over, as I quickly ducked over into the unoccupied two feet of the room. Decorated in the "Early Bomb Shelter" look, our quarters were really just a fan-blown square of concrete, maybe 12 x 12-foot, with a creaking World-War II style bunk bed against one wall, the aforementioned table on an adjacent wall, some hanging hooks on the opposite wall, and two metal chairs. It had a window – that is, a place where light came in, if the blinds could be worked just right. The toilet and shower stalls were outside in a central facility, down on the corner of this Spartan complex, the services consisting of a central locker and restroom. This row of domiciles and a few others like it formed a cluster comprising the backpackers' hostel here at Uluru Kata Tjuta National Park (the former Ayers Rock, before it was reclaimed by the original tenants), in brightest, hottest Australia. There were better accommodations to be sure – a few – but the $7 ASD (about $5 U.S.) allowed budget-conscious, beer-swilling travelers the opportunity to, in the words of W.C. Fields, "not have to dine on an empty stomach."

The highlight of Australia so far, besides dodging the pesky "cyclone" (a storm with an attitude) was celebrating Jack Daniel's birthday party at a pub in Sydney's Kings Cross. Funny, I thought; I grew up just a few clicks up the turnpike from that hallowed distillery and had never even been there; but here I am halfway around the world, getting two shots of Tennessee Tranquilizer for a handful of quid while black balloons sporting the birthday boy's mustached-mug swirled around me. Sometimes, I reckoned, one must travel far from one's home to appreciate its native genius.

Leaving stylish, sensual Sydney, I had then proceeded up the coast, jumping back and forth between reefs and island groups and landing in the tropics of the Northeast. Deciding that a bit of dry air would do me good, I knew that I had to get out to the quasi-desolation of the mid-continent.

Opting for the air instead of 36 hours of bus delirium across red, flat wastelands, I had flown into Alice Springs first, and then, after a few days of acclimatizing to flies and buffalo steaks, had bussed the final 300 miles down to Uluru and "The Rock."

Some perspective is in order here, especially for my fellow Americans, many of whom consider Kentucky and Connecticut next door neighbors because they, well, sound the same. If one considers that Alice Springs occupies the continent's geographic center, say the "Kansas" location, then the next town of any consequence to the north (save tiny outposts like Tenant Creek or Katherine) would be Darwin on the coast, at about 1,000 miles / 1,600 kilometers; equating to somewhere in Saskatchewan. From the east, the plot thickens. One would have to go about 400 miles up to Tenant Creek (equating to say South Dakota's relative location); then encountering only occasional petrol stops (about every 200 miles), one could head east and eventually end up in Townsville – about where Cleveland is.

South? The first stop of any size is at Woomera, about 700 miles, then finally Adelaide, (at about the "Houston" location) at approximately 1,000 miles / 1600 Km. West? *Major* forget-about-it. There are *no* western roads across the Great Victorian and Gibson deserts, unless one is coming counter-clockwise, south by west along the coast, from Darwin; or clockwise along the southern coast from Adelaide. Imagine an area the size of Colorado, Utah and Nevada with absolutely no roads; hence no rest stops, no Waffle Houses or Sinclair dinosaurs, no Lotto, no forests to topple, and naturally, no people. A true wasteland, although I imagine the occasional lost Aborigine found some sort of solace in it. Way over on the coast sits Perth, down about San Diego's relative bearing. But *only* if one could get there from say, a "Houston" or a "Seattle" – not across the middle.

No wonder these blokes were ready to jump into the fray with Johnny Turk in the Great War – they were bored out of their freaking skulls…The King Father's clarion call from faraway London was, methinks, simply a passport to another world: it was sumthin' to do, mate…

* * * * * *

My rendezvous with Bub was chance, as the landlords stuck people two-per-room into the little quarters. It was pot luck, if one didn't have their own travelin' Bruce or Sheila. We had been out to The Rock that morning, but he didn't want to climb it, like I did. "'Cuz I don't wanna crawl up through all them bloody Jappos, babblin' away and flickin' their Nikons like there's no tomorrow," he sagaciously commented.

This was in the days when the Yen was king and Japan was buying up Oz and Hawaii lock, stock, and barrel – until their crony-riddled financial system imploded like a house-of-cards, and the tour buses suddenly developed a lot more leg room. So Bub waited at the bottom, X-raying through halter tops (a distinctively *non-*Japanese fashion) and scribbling postcards.

I had bolted ahead, first up the assistance-chains, then across the smooth, sloping sandstone, so I could have a 15-20 minute personal audience with the caretakers (wind and rock, mainly) before the jabbering shutter-flappers arrived. It was also sunrise, and a wonder to behold from atop the highest thing for hundreds of miles in any direction. Later on, after Little Asia reconvened once more at our air-conditioned buses, we drove around The Rock – which, by itself, measures about two miles in length and one-and-a-half miles in width (thus about a six-mile circumference), and 1,300 feet high; though, like an iceberg, much remains "underground." Not bad for 600 million years and an occasional rainstorm. These rainstorms, sometimes occurring only every decade or so, were capable of carving impressive swaths in the fragile sandstone and had created awesome caves at the bottom, many of which possessed amazing drawings from deepest, distant Aboriginal antiquity. After all, the Abbos (the locals at Uluru Kata Tjuta are the Anangu tribe) had been on the continent a bloody long time, with estimates ranging from 30,000-65,000 years to perhaps several *hundred* thousand years. But who knows? They weren't builders, after all, and "The Dreamtime" – *Tjukurpa*, or the Aborigines' mythical bible – isn't talking…at least not to us visitors and the other 98% of non-Aboriginal Australians…

The Dreamtime is oral of course – what tree or papyrus could they use for paper? It is sewn into the fabric of every youngster's psyche before she chases her first dingo or blows into his first didgeridoo. It is the ethereal playground of huge animals that once roamed the earth – snakes and moles and lizards – that are now immortalized, impressively, on a myriad of red rock clusters. I was particularly drawn to the cave of *Itjaritjari*, a mole on steroids; and then, the skillfully sketched fight scene between *Kuniya* (a nasty looking python) and *Liru* (a poisonous usurper). "*Wandjina*" – otherwise known as God, Allah, Krishna, Zeus, Watan Tanka and Yahweh in other tongues – had created it all, scattering "seeds" from faraway places, dropped by "sky gods" making "celestial descents." These seeds were like a cosmic record of other places, other memories, other "personalities" and are called *guruwari*. Their blueprints shaped every landscape and delivered unseen energies into the manifest world. Thus, physical, metaphysical and intellectual powers have left an imprint everywhere on the planet, say the Abbos. Some of these powers are seen, others are not; consequently, everything is magical. But that's no big deal; that's just how it works.

The dreams were clearly nightmares, however, for most of the 19th and early 20th Centuries, because a genocide agenda by the Anglo visitors decimated the natives. In fact, it was legal to shoot Aborigines as "vermin" up until the early 1900s. The government is now making earnest reparations for health care and education, and the Aborigine population has gradually increased to about 400,000 people. Like the Native Americans or New Zealand's Maoris, the natives are now celebrated for the incredibly rich cosmology that lurks right under their deceivingly primitive personas. They're also a good tourist draw, and the Welcome Wagon folks over in Canberra aren't about to let that one slide.

Everything seemed bigger than life out here. The Rock, and nearby Olgas (a few dozen handsome, rounded, orange-red mini-mountains) were the only perturbations on an endless horizon. The sky and world went on forever, the Martian soil only occasionally interrupted by a Grass Tree (yes, a combination of both), a couple of Gum Trees, and other sparse vegetation. It was easy to relegate time to a "circular" thought, no beginning or end. The idea of linear time was as abstract to the Abbos as was a round world to Dark Age Europeans. Thus the Dream Time wasn't so much "in the past"; it was, well…in the time of dreams…No Time, All-the-Time, and the "All That Is" just beyond our reach.

Bub and I later strolled in the Olgas, about 20 miles to the west of The Rock. They reminded me of another landscape, thousands of miles away.

"Tell ya what, pal, this is amazing country, but if you want to see the most bizarre concoction of desert anywhere, come to Southern Utah."

" Wharzat?"

"A few hundred clicks north of The Grand Canyon – I'm sure you've heard of that one."

"Yeah, sure – so what's this Utah gig?"

"Same kinda colors as here, but it's a fantasy world, man. There's these "slot canyons" which make you pitch, roll and yaw just to get through 'em. There's giant cathedrals of pointed rocks, like Gothic churches in Europe; there's mountains several times the heights of the Olgas, orange on top but full of vegetation between them; there's fresh water streams and giant swim holes, fed by snow-melt from high green plateaus bordered by yellow aspen trees. Or even better in the winter, cross-country skiing along the rim of these canyon beauties, with a white mantle of snow accenting the brilliant orange like a fine hem line. Tell ya what, it's damn near surreal, walking through these creeks with your backpack, bordered by waist-high wildflowers, being towered over by these Old Testament-style red bluffs. One could get lost in there and never found. Hell, many *have*. It reminds me of those old bible stories about the wandering tribes coming into Canaan, full of milk and honey. Just jumpin' back and forth between the rusted, fiery reds of the desert, and soothing green trees, both the leafy type and those big ol' cedar bastards. I guess what makes it all happen are the extreme altitude differences."

"Wow, sounds bitchin'," Bub sighed, "but I reckon I got all I can handle here. See, I been at it for four years now."

"Been at what?" I asked, as we took a path between two of the more accessible Olgas – The "Valley of the Winds" to the Anangus.

"Walkabout. Ya know, just movin' around the country."

"Looking for work?"

"Nah, never for long," he winked. "I mean, I get it when I need it, right? Don't want it to be a goal or anything, just a little pick-me-up 'tills I can be movin' again."

"What's your goal?"

"Well, mate, the only real goal's to see the whole bloody country. 'Course, I'm not sure that's so much a goal as a purpose…I came from down in Victoria, a few jumps west of Melbourne. Got married, got divorced, ya know, been there / dun that. Got tired of hangin' round. So I took off, ya know? Worked a fishin' boat down in Tassie, but too fuckin' cold and rainy there. Besides, I get seasick too easy, and I can't understand them blokes – I mean, they speak like wankin' Ubangi's, ya know?"

"So then up to Sydney. I wanted Fair Dinkum civilization, I told meself. Tended bar, drove delivery trucks and dug a lotta ditches that year, all that rot, but Syd was just too crazy big for me. So's up the coast, and inland a tad, onto Lightnin' Ridge, ya know where all them black opals come from? Tourist trap, but I could tend bar then disappear out into the wild to muck about. Gradually, came at peace with meself. Started to like just doin' the day-to-day thing, ya know? Stopped worryin' about tomorrow and just got to know my temporary home a little better."

"Went out to the Whitsunday's next, them islands near the reef. Much more my kinda climate than Tasmania, tell ya what. Gorgeous water, gorgeous bodies, if ya know whadda mean. Well, some are." I nodded approvingly, having cut a wide swath through there myself just weeks before.

"Did the boat thing again, only not fishin' this time, just droppin' blokes n' their Sheila's out on islands for the day and then pickin' 'em up in the evenin'. From there I went up to Cairns and worked two jobs: slammed nails by day, buildin' houses, and poured beer again

in the evenins'. Liked it a lot too. Same thing for Darwin, but bloody
hot and humid there, worse than Cairns in the summer, especially
for workin' construction again. But the place I liked best was down at
Kakadu Park – a lot like your Utah stories, mate, only it's real jungle-
like mixed in w'the desert. But strange animals, and waterfalls, and
forests and huge fuckin' rock faces w'lotsa Abbo art carved on 'em;
'roos everywhere like fleas, and them funky Baobab trees, all upside-
downsy. I couldn't get no work in the park, but I got some grunt gigs
in the little villages near it. Hell, I didn't care; I ran around in that big
ol' playground every chance I got."

"And then Alice, me dear ol' Alice Springs. Pushed a broom
there, for Christ's sake, but it was a good go for a party. No pressure,
no brains, right? But there's sumthin' not right about a cushy city
in the middle of the wilds, so I came down here to Uluru. I'm part
of the buildin' crew, and sometimes shillin' beer on weekends. The
construction company pays for me rent, which ain't sayin' much, but
I also get little stipends for me meals and laundry and such. And the
pay's good, real good, mate. Union scale at that, and out here in the
middle a nowhere's an' all, a fellow can stash some loot. Of course, I
spend most of mine on shouts a' tinnies (Australian for "rounds of
drinks"), but I'm never at a loss for mates! Even had a bloke want me
to work at one a' them camel ranches where the Jappos stop and take
rides. But I can't take the smell – I mean, the camels, mate – and who
in their bloody right mind needs three jobs if the whole idea's to be
not tied down, yeah? Fair dinkum right, that is…tomorrow can wait,
and yesterday's history."

"Speakin' of 'tomorrow' where will that be?" I risked a snatch into
his future.

"Dunno…but probably out around Perth or Freemantle area
– see the Indian Ocean, ya know. All them boat races got me fired
up, yeah?" He was referring to the America's Cup, as big in Oz and
New Zealand as the Super Bowl or World Series was in the U.S., and
this year (conducted every fourth year, like the soccer/football World
Cup), it was Down Under. "Reckon I'm destined to give Perth a go,
sooneralater."

"I must say, pardner, you've covered some ground."

"Bloody right. About 6,000 miles of loop so fars, and when I make it out to Perth and back, reckon that'll bring it to about 10,000."

"Back? Where to?"

"Ha, Good question, mate!" He stopped to swat several flies away. Outback flies aren't quick and aggressive like their jungle cousins. Instead, they land and then stumble like drunken sailors into lips, eyes, nostrils, noses and any other orifice offering the possible purchase of moisture. Killing them is easy; the problem is that reinforcements, in triplicate, are always just a buzzing lurch behind. Some clever merchants figured out how to sell hats with little corks hanging off them to tourists, I reckon to confuse the invaders. I've heard they work, if one doesn't mind looking like a dork for days on end.

Bub seemed momentarily befuddled. After a rare pause of pensiveness, he continued. "Guess it's just habit to think of Melbourne and Vic Territory as home, but come to think about, I don't have any particular reason to go there any mores. Guess we'll just hafta see, eh?"

After an afternoon of sloth and indolence at the community pool – strategic defense for 108° Fahrenheit – we walked down the path to the makeshift community village of Yulara. There was no real "city" here, just a collection of eateries, tourist amenities and questionable entertainment. It was a typical scene, I came to understand, so low-key it made Alice Springs seem like the glitter strip of Las Vegas's "Miracle Mile." Bub's friend, Chrissie, tagged along with us. She'd been hanging out at the camp, and with Bub, apparently, for some time. I wondered more than once if my bunk bed had been graced by her presence over the last few weeks.

"Howzit goin', Steve," she had introduced herself at a local pub, where she'd been waiting. Chrissie had the Annie Lenox / Eurhythmic look down pat, a band I had coincidentally caught a while back in Sydney after I first arrived from New Zealand. Her spiked blond hair was cropped like Bub's, only longer, but without the rooster tail mullet-thing down the back. Her tattoos could've given him a run for the money, however, and her tongue was a turbine for churning English into raw sewage. A nose ring occupied one nostril; a diamond (surely zirconium) graced the other; and some kind of mascara stuff slept under her bloodshot eyes. Chrissie was a "piece of work," confided the affable and honest Bub. She had wanted to get "pissed," since it was Friday night, even if she had to work the following day. Bub, likewise, was living testimony to comedian Bill Maher's observation that the male body "is simply a machine for converting beer into piss." The sons and daughters of the UK were one up, though, simply referring to beer *as* piss. "No need for small talk; it's just being recycled anyways, luv." (Uh, please pass the piss...)

I could see how Bub and Chrissie might hit it off. They both answered to no one, easily being able to tell a quarreling superior to "go stuff it" if he got too meddlesome. They were also the types to pick up and move around, just because "It was there," and "It" consisted of Mother Oz (perhaps, someday, a voyage back to Chrissie's distant New Zealand). They weren't going to win any Nobel Prizes or lead any movements; they were probably never going to live in suburban cul-de-sacs and breed 2.3 children. But they were also not the type to end up on the welfare dole or in anyone's prison – halfway houses, maybe, but that's another story. They'd throw in their sweat equity pretty much anywhere there was a ditch to be dug or a truck to drive or cash register to clang, as long as there was a shaded pub, punk-rock club or sporting match at the end of the day. They sought little in return and were reasonably content to just tread a wistful "walkabout" across the dusty pages of their lives. At least for now. Yeah, there was a future out there somewhere; but like the Mexican "mañana," it didn't *really* mean "tomorrow," it meant "not today." It could wait, in other words.

We stepped into an open air pub, anchored down with huge white canvass "reflectors" to keep the Sun gods at bay during the day. The America's Cup was on the satellite TV and Bub, Chrissie and every other red-blooded outcast-convict from Down Under was tuned in and turned on.

"Jibe, you bastard," shouted Chrissie, the displaced New Zealander, urging her homeland contestant to make up the distance to Dennis Conner's boat, the *Stars and Stripes*. "He's gonna fookin' lap ya if ya don't' git yer pecker oudda yer hands and put 'em back on the rudder. Jeezus, c'mon, mate, either plow ahead or bag the pissin' race, you wanker."

Yada, yada, yada. The woman was gifted. Bub just smiled. He was too interested in the scenery on the beach (whenever the cameras broke away) and the alluring pull of the cerulean-teal waters off the coast of Perth.

In 1983, the Australian *Kookaburra II* had wrestled the trophy from Conner after a century-plus of Yankee domination. Now, four years later, the gamesmanship Down Under was verging on "Waltzing Matilda" prepping for the Great War. When I had been in New Zealand, Conner's boat had popped the Aussie's bubble by wiping out the defending *Kookaburra III*, much to the satisfaction of the Kiwis, the latter gathering in neighborhood pubs like flies at a barbeque: not that they gave a tinker's damn *who* beat the Aussies, mind you, just that they got their comeuppance. It was reversed here, in the Great Outback and 1,000+ miles from the closest ocean, as most of the bar (sans the fuming Chrissie), accepting of Conner's victory, cheered on the Yank who was easily dissing the upstart-but-outgunned Kiwis (who would lay claim to glory four years later in San Diego). Besides, Conner, as a no-frills son of a fisherman, had an aura acceptable to the psyche of Down Under: They were the underdogs, the gamblers, the outcasts. Even though Conner would later brazenly wear on that psyche (during years of fractious lawsuit), he never engendered the scorn heaped on future gazillionaires like Oracle's Larry Ellison and Microsoft's Paul Allen, who heralded the Gilded Age of Sailing by buying up sailboats and captains at stratospheric prices to quench their even-larger egos.

Later that afternoon, we had grabbed a ride out to view the Rock at sunset. Neither Bub nor Chrissie had to work that day and I was glad for the company.

At the time of sunset and for about 20 minutes afterward, I clicked off shot after shot on my Pentax, each a slightly different color, shattering any illusion of this primeval landscape as "timeless." It *could* change, and did in the wink of an eye, and my Pentax caught it. Uluru glowed, morphed and faded through the most incredible array of orange, red-pink, scarlet, rust, purple, brown, and then finally, black – darker than the soul of *Mokoi* (a not too pleasant spirit of the Outback). Like it has for 600 million years.

"She's better on cloudy days," Bub remarked, once more referring to the rock. He wasn't trying to rain on my parade but just put things in perspective. "Moody skies make for moody mountain, I 'spose. Check out them pix back in the tourist shops, mate. They ain't superimposed, believe me. But I never mind seein' the sunset, 'cuz she's always different, every night. I'm just glad to be along for the ride."

"Yeah, freakin' awesome, eh?" contributed Chrissie, who had kept one eye on the morphing mountain and one on her makeup mirror.

Back in the Yulara settlement that evening, it was still too hot to hang out in our Neanderthal barracks. Even with a fan, the metal-framed construction and harsh exposure rendered the place a virtual oven. So back out into the night we went. Our first stop was a cowboy-sort-of-bar, Outback style, where a tall bearded crooner right out of *Lonesome Dove* served up the worst folk songs I've ever heard. There was nothing wrong with *them*, just him. I had never heard my beloved *Shenandoah* butchered so shamelessly, and even the tear-jerking part about civil war veterans departing their homelands, crossing the wide Missouri – " ♪ Away, you rolling river . . ♪ " couldn't keep my Appalachian butt glued to the seat any longer.

"Shiiiittt...I'm bored outta me buggy mind," the gold-spiked princess offered. "But reckon I'm gonna call it a night. Gotta be on the clock at 7 in the bloody a.m. G'Night mates, see ya on the boomerang" (presumably, "later?"). Up above, the Southern Cross, considerably older than 600 million years, looked down in detached amusement. Talk about being bored. I wondered, did the Dream Time explain him, too?

Bub and I made it safely back into our bungalow without burning our hands on the door or asphyxiating. With the overhand fan prattling away on its last few breaths, the place was a bearable 85-90° or so – not too bad, considering a non-existent relative humidity. I felt dreamtime coming on – or possibly the other Dream Time, *Tjukurpa* (or *Mura-Mura*) summoning me to probe even deeper, into something. My little walkabout Down Under had a purpose and an ending, supposedly; at least there was one probable scenario etched on my mind, with airline tickets and so forth. The rest was all details and subject to change. As usual.

Bub, however, had no ending in sight; nor was he sleepy. His mind was still on Walkabout, despite his modest intake of 12-15 beers that day. He was *Googoorgaga* – the "Laughing Jackass," who came and went at his own pleasing like the North American coyote. Not a trickster though; he was just passing through…restless at first, like *Tjinimin*, the ancient ancestral father; but now satisfied, and just on Walkabout "to see what he could see."

There on the table, the gargantuan map of Australia was once more unfolded. It was old and worn, obviously handled hundreds if not thousands of times. Like a giant handkerchief, it was nearly threadbare and served as a dartboard for red X's, scribbled notes, lead-smeared circles, coffee stains, cigarette burns, coagulated snot, and the dozen other assorted accoutrements that blessed it. To Bub, it was a relic; his own Shroud of Turin, as special as the blanket of *Peanuts'* Linus. The map was as much a part of him as his tattooed Mum or his spiking, bleach-blond hair. And considering the subject matter was pushing a billion years old, there was no need for a new one. "She ain't goin' nowheres, mate."

With a pencil, he was pecking away at one place with the steady monotonous tapping of a sculptor. His attention was focused. "Perth…Perth…she'll be right. Might just need to give'er a go."

"So think you're gonna go, after all?" my fading voice drifted across the room.

"Yeah, sure. I dunno know when. Maybe next week. Maybe next month. Maybe next year. She'll be there when I'm ready, I reckon. No worries."

Chapter Eighteen

At the Cross-Rhodes: Greeks, Turks and Other Intruders

The little old lady could hardly be blamed for sleeping on the job. It was hot outside, and there she sat, like a disheveled Babushka, spread out on her chair with neither modesty nor care. Her head bobbed momentarily, then went *plunk* to one side, while a few flies did warm-up laps around a mountainous swirl of white cotton-candy hair. Her stall was surrounded by religious icons, cheap historical trinkets and beach towels; the latter flapping around in the mid-day breeze. I sneaked surreptitiously to just the right vantage point and clicked away with my camera, for the sake of posterity. A German tourist took cue from me; then, a few Brits followed him as well. We whispered to each other, "Would she mind if she knew?" We surmised not; this place has seen more visitors than Santa Claus at the mall. All loiter awhile on the beaches and in the markets. Then they're gone too, and the history books add another footnote. Or not.

If anyone could be excused for having an identity crisis, it was the Mediterranean island of Rhodes. Consider it the birdie in an endless game of tag-team badminton; the quarry, tool and bargaining chip of every king, duke, emir, sultan, caliph, pharaoh, chief, viceroy, prince, general, emperor and potentate who ever had reason to pass through the cobalt waters of the Aegean Sea on their way to glory and headaches elsewhere. Rhodes was a coin that said "curse" on one side and "blessing" on the other, and could never stay in anyone's pocket for long. Like the first retail store, it was the epitome of

"Location, location, location," but, like a K-Mart Blue Light special when the pickin's are good, she's always had a tendency to attract some interesting characters.

Hanging like a teardrop off the southwest coast of Turkey, Rhodes is currently in Greek hands. Again. At least for now. Not as large and well-known as its other Mediterranean siblings, such as Sicily, Crete, Cyprus, Sardinia, and Corsica, she's nevertheless managed to nab her fair share of history. Long before Paul preached Christianity to the Rhodesians there had already been a lengthy list of caretakers: Mycenaean Greeks from Peloponnesia; Minoan Greeks from Crete; Achaean Greeks from the Mother-mainland (see a trend here?); the Persians, under Darius, the greatest empire the world had ever seen back then; Macedonian Greeks under Alexander; Ptolemy's Egyptians; and everyone's favorite landlords, the Romans. "*Veni, vidi, vici*" – they all came, saw and conquered. Then they, in turn, got humbled, either through intermarriage or a bad day at the war.

But it didn't stop there. The Romans had to wrestle Germanic visitors, the Goths, before throwing in the towel and handing Rhodes over to Constantine's Byzantines. Eight centuries of intermittent intrusions by Turks (Seljuks and Saracens) and more Persians led to the Byzantines passing the lease to Crusaders (Richard the Lionhearted's boys), more Crusaders, those quarrelsome Knights (the Templars and Hospitallers), Italian city-states (Venetians and Genoans), Ottoman Turks (under Süleyman the Magnificent and his quibbling descendants), Italians again (Mussolini's minions), Nazi Germany (who *would* have made the trains run on time, but there were none), England as a caretaker following WWII, and waddayaknow – back to the Greeks again. Not to belabor the point, but there are even more names in the footnotes: Phoenicians, Lydians, Hittites, Carians, Carthaginians and Napoleon's Franks, for starters…

As mentioned earlier, the little old lady had seen it all. And my tenure was sure to be shorter than those other guys.

* * * * * *

Archie was in his late forties by my reckoning; a short, mustached man in conservative dress: Dockers, top-siders, dark sweater, beige-brown windbreaker and non-descript beret that split the difference between the Greek and New Worlds…neither a fedora nor an item from Anthony Quinn's fisherman collection. He could have been president of a fraternity (Greek, at that!), or the local ward leader of Pipe Fitters Union 101. Actually, he owned several hamburger franchises in Florida and having spent 15 years there, now considered that state, and by default America, his home. "My allegiance is to the U.S., my head and feet are in Florida, but my heart is here on Rhodos. I come and go, just like all my ancestors. You will see why, I'm sure, if you stay long. It's like a baptism that I must renew every 5 or 10 years to come back here to Greece again. Maybe it's like those swallows down in Capistrano that always know when it's time to fly to or from their winter home in Mexico."

He stopped to light a cigarette and watch the combat antics of the gulls following our ferry as we approached the harbor. It was almost sunrise now, and after ten hours of putting across the murky deep from the island of Mykenos, we could finally see the outlines of Rhodes City taking shape on land.

"I grew up here, but it's more than that. They say some places leave imprints in your genes and brain cells; like silent messengers with their own tune. It is a blessed man who knows how to hear these certain pitches and tunes and get the message." He shifted his weight on the railing, where I'd met him moments before. The two of us, and my sister Sarah were awake and antsy. We'd taken up lookout on the exposed ferry deck, while most of the other 100 or so passengers were still inside and asleep.

"Maybe I'm homesick or just crazy, but Rhodes has a magnetic pull like no other. It's one of the few places I've been where the land itself is more important to me than the people who occupy it. Or maybe, it's because the people have the land in their bones, and the sea in their blood, that I can see transparently through them to the source of it all. I love my family and friends, so that's a convenient excuse to come back and visit. But really, it's the pull of Rhodos. It used to be watched over by Helios, the Sun God, legend has it, and I'm sure that wears into your mind over many years. Even if one doesn't believe all that ancient mythology nonsense," he winked.

Sarah and I had spent the last three weeks jumping around the Aegean Sea, playing hopscotch between polluted, chaotic and dour Athens and polluted, chaotic and charming Istanbul. In between the clamor of those cosmopolitan magnets, thankfully we were able to soak up the shoulder season of the Cyclades Islands and the western Turkish coast; sinking into sun-bleached sloth on the islands, exploring without hassle the tourist-bereft mainland ruins and bartering without pressure in the post-horde markets. The days were warm and sunny, the water just starting to sport a hint of cool, the nights breezy and refreshing – away from the cities, that is. Ferries were our steeds across the islands, and we had seen and rested on so many: Andros, Tinos, Mykenos, Patmos, Samos...We never tired of "The Blue": the deep, cobalt blue of the sea; the endless powder blue of the sky; the streaking grey-blue of the porpoises frolicking alongside our boat; and the handsome royal blue of all those shutters adorning simple white buildings. Never mind that the landscape was boring. The rocky brown hills and occasional patch of olive trees are just the right accent piece for this island landscape.

Everywhere, history oozed – every island or mainland city had its great philosopher, general, statesman, inventor or playwright. And, everywhere, naturally, natives were ready to make a quick buck off that history, with all the souvenirs and trinkets that tourists are eager to bring back as proof they were really "there." These islanders' history was "Now" and all that stuff from the past was just that – the past. They wanted to know about NATO and the E.U., about their chances at the World Cup; about getting into universities; about traveling to *other* places that had history (say, the "New World" with its big skies and its own ancient cultures) and glistening amusement parks. But make no mistake: they were Greeks, or Turks; and all the blunders, deprivations, scorn, accusations, embarrassments, abuses and other exchanges or goings-on, real or imagined, weighed heavily on their cultural psyches – as did their pride, accomplishments, and past glory. That's because they were astonishingly proud of their long and storied histories, even if they didn't quite understand the details. So help them God; so help them Allah.

Like the cab driver in Izmir, up the Turkish Coast, who just had to show us the fortress that Alexander had built, even if that same cabbie had to come flying back down the hill "Streets of San Francisco"- style through winding dangerous curves, dodging kids and wash ladies, because he virtually had no brakes. We still tipped him; how often does one get to have that much fun? *Güle-güle* ("good bye"), counting the thousands of Lira, about two dollars, we had handed over. "*Allaha ismarladik*," we replied, another form of goodbye which means "we're damn lucky to be alive."

Or the cabbie in Istanbul, who kept driving us in circles around the "Old Town" of Sultanahmet, partly because he couldn't find our destination and partly to offer us an unofficial tour – and what a tour it was, passing by Topkapi Palace, the Blue Mosque, and the 1,500 year old Christian-turned-Muslim Aya Sofia. Or the gentle Amarani family, vacationing from the Greek mainland at their villa on Andros Island; buying us drinks and speaking in broken English about their homeland. They lived in two worlds: the frenetic pressure cooker of Athens, the nerve center of Greek commerce and finance; and the idyllic, tranquil world of the islands, steeped in mythology but always just one swat away from a pissed off Poseidon or heckling Harpie (bosses of the waves and winds, respectively). The Amarani's, too, came and went, straddling a proud-but-tempestuous past with a promising-but worrisome future.

Even Suat, a witty, industrious Turk in the coastal town of Kusadasi, considered himself torn between two worlds.

"I live here now, to make some money, then maybe up to Istanbul. Or Ankara, which is clean but boring. I don't know. I have a degree in mathematics from Wittenberg in Germany. I can teach perhaps, or even do research and programming for a computer company. I shall see; for now, I will help Mustafa," referring to his employer, the warm and benevolent inn-keeper of our hostel ($5 per night for a private two-bed room with hot shower). Mustafa, by the way, would send me personalized Christmas cards for the next three years…had I been able to find a "Ramadan Greetings," I would have reciprocated.

Suat spoke seven languages, and if his English was any indicator, he got at least a B+ for all six of the non-Turkish ones. Nothing seemed to bother him; not even when on the road to the ruins of Ephesus I had to slam on the brakes of his ramshackle jalopy, pasting his face in yogurt from his kofte sandwich and sending scalding coffee all over his crotch.

He took care of us like a doting mother: changing money at the bank, for the smallest of tips, overseeing laundry dispatch, playing taxi at our every whim, dispensing practical advice and providing helpful history lessons: "Ah, yes, the Greeks; our good friends." He was a masterful poker-faced straight-man. I believe he was referring to the little tussle on Cyprus, scene of recent U.N. refereeing between the Greeks and Turks. Well, "recent" is a relative term. He also toured us around Ephesus, the impressive ruins of one of the world's most populated cities at the time of Christ. Libraries, saunas, amphitheaters, marble walkways and a race track to make Daytona blush – this place had had it all. It also had St. Paul, who rounded up quite the block of believers before moving on to Rome, Corinth, Athens, Thessalonika, and wherever the Spirit pointed him. More controversial, some legends have Ephesus as the final resting place of Mary, mother of you-know-who.

Suat was at his own crossroads. In his late thirties and single, he was light on his feet and not bad looking. Highly educated and worldly, he could hang around and try to help wet-nurse Turkey into bigger and better things. They have the firepower, with a modern trained army. Turkey is a secular country, which, despite its classic Muslim union card, displays an incredible tolerance for alcohol and Western living. And, despite the fundamentalist tendencies of Eastern Turkey, the country also boasts a proud tradition of religious tolerance as well. Nowhere in the world except in Constantinople/Istanbul has there been such long-standing *relative* peaceful co-existence of Christian, Jew, and Muslim. The Turks sport literacy rates in the high 80 percentiles (better than many U.S. Appalachian coal mining towns and northern factory boroughs), which would certainly be higher without the diluting influence of the semi-nomadic Kurds in the east. The downside is that when one lifts the bonnet, things don't quite work as well as in Europe. The Turks employ a different definition of criminal justice, for example; and they seldom hesitate to use whatever force considered necessary to whack those deemed "terrorists" (like the Kurdish PKK), whether actual or presumed. Perhaps this treatment is understandable in light of their shared borders with Syria, Iran and Iraq.

Furthermore, despite the Turks' lofty education levels, unemployment continually drives the disenfranchised – those who *are* poor or semi-literate – out of the country. Finally, the real thorn in the side of those who are attempting to establish a totally integrated European Union was that little spat with Armenia, whose genocide at the hands of the Turks during WWI cost the Armenian citizens 1.8 million lives. Problem is, until just recently, Turkey wouldn't even acknowledge the incident and still seems to choke on "apologizing" for it. So the Turks remain adrift, stuck between two continents and hamstrung by conflicting ideologies, all the while buttressed by a crazed pack of imams and ayatollahs just off to the southeast. One gets the feeling the Turks are trying to sniff the winds to seek movement in one direction or another.

Likewise, Suat kept waiting, watching and mulling things over. He knew Berlin and Amsterdam were options. Or maybe, Copenhagen or Stockholm; or Toronto or Boston…"But very cold. Brrrr. I am a Mediterranean Man. I like the sun – it's good for my tan (he smiled, already possessing olive skin) and really good for watching bikinis on ferry boats." He would make his choice soon, to stay or leave; another infinitesimal immigrant on the timeless shores of the Mediterranean.

✷ ✷ ✷ ✷ ✷ ✷

It's a widely accepted axiom that the very size and shape of geographical features can influence the thinking and cultural activities occurring nearby. One only has to look at the history of the world's great crossroads to see that principle at play: a Gibraltar, Isthmus of Panama, Khyber Pass, Straits of Malacca, Golan Heights or Cape of Good Hope. Wherever sea, mountains, deserts and forest push folks into a constricted nexus, or conversely, open them up to wider expanses, it's just a matter of time before immigration, trade, warfare, housing associations and meddlesome bureaucrats follow. It's the way of things. Many of those venues burst on the scene for a century or two, sometimes even a millennia, then quietly retrace their way back to being just another dot on the Michelin Guide or thousand-dollar *Double Jeopardy* question.

Then there's the Aegean Sea, Mother of all Crossroads and Bathtub of the Ages. One look at a map practically recites its legacy. Technically part of the Mediterranean, the Aegean pinches up to the north like a mighty wedge, separating Greece, Turkey, and Crete while continuing on through Turkey's Dardanelles and Bosporus straits, into the Black Sea (on whose other side sits Romania, Russia, Georgia, and Armenia). Oh, if the Gods still talked, what they would say...

For argument, they would offer up Troy and Gallipoli, two of the planet's greatest battlefields, separated by a mere 30 miles despite the gyrations of 3,000 years of history. (Never mind that Troy is as much myth as fact. So much so, say some revisionists, that they present "proof" that Troy and Homer's *Iliad* are a recounting, handed down by refugees, of a battle in *England* in 1,500 B.C.) *Something* definitely happened in Troy; a rather nasty confrontation of some sort, say the peeled-back digs, multi-leveled redoubts and the bones and arrows. Perhaps it wasn't the full blown war of the *Iliad*, but there was a sure 'nuff battle for the history books, probably between Achaean Greeks and a powerful city-state of the Hittites. According to Manfred Korfmann, Director of Excavations at the site for nearly two decades, the true footprint of Troy City is now believed to be 75 acres – *15 times* the size previously thought, just a few decades ago. And Korfmann's research from as late as 2003 indicates that Troy indeed may have had the largest arsenal in all of Southeastern Europe. So perhaps the revisionists need revising. And with photos of Yours Truly inside the 60-foot-tall Trojan Horse – who could ever doubt its authenticity?

Gallipoli ("Gelibolu" to the Turks), may have lacked Homer's poetry or pageantry, but what it lacked in fancy it made up for in stark, cold blood. It was all too real, and recent enough that the photos don't lie. Gallipoli was Churchill's World War I brainstorm to backdoor Europe by knocking the Axis-aligned Turks out of the war, then hooking up with the Brits' allied Russians and subsequently trapping the Germans and their Austro-Hungarian mates between two fronts. It was a classic case of "Brilliant Strategy, Lousy Tactics," however, and with the Turks holding the high ground, His Majesty's boys and their ANZAC surrogates spent most of 1915 penned down in hell beneath the bluffs of Gelibolu. By the time Winston's charges realized they couldn't take the high ground, there were nearly 380,000 combined casualties (120,000 killed). The Allies withdrew in the dead of night, soon to be deployed in a different kind of hell in the trenches of France; and the Turkish hero Atatürk (Mustafa Kemal) began his ascendancy to president, a move that sealed the casket of the Ottoman Empire and launched secular democracy in Turkey.

In between the Achaean Greeks and Churchill's visitors, Gelibolu and nearby places played host to a number of other strategic clashes; sometimes with Russians, Bulgars or Egyptians, and sometimes with each other. And then there were the visitors from the island of Lesvos, namesake of female love trysts ("Les-bian") and distinguished incubator of poetry and music. The Dardanelles Strait is just one little strip of land, a mere 40 miles long and five miles wide – so peaceful and bucolic today, but so blood-stained over the ages. It is like a gate swinging in both directions: to heaven and to hell.

Constantinople / Istanbul, too, has been a trophy for the ages, though it seems relatively content in Turkish hands today. There's perhaps no more strategic crossroads on the planet than this convergence point between Asia, Europe, the Black Sea and the Mediterranean. If Rhodes has been a testimony to "Location," then Istanbul is the Mother Lode of all Empire, stealing the glory from Rome long before the latter handed the keys to the Visigoths in 476; and long after the final emperor, Constantine XI, fell on his sword to the Muslim usurpers in 1453 – after turning down numerous offers from the soon-to-be victorious Mehmet to spare not only the lives, but most of the *property and possessions*, of the inhabitants. Pride before pragmatism, we must surmise! Nowhere is the collision of crossing cultures more evident than Istanbul: the architecture, food, clothing, secular intermingling of religions, et al; she's a menagerie of sounds, tastes, aromas, colors and feelings. Not to dump on their Greek rivals, but next to Istanbul's splendor, Athens is, in my opinion, a faded black-and-white photograph; a sound byte (albeit a noisy one).

The whole region reeks of paradox. The cradle of western democracy, Greece has seen very little of it the last 2300 years and Athens still can't get the traffic flow worked out. And for a nation (well, collection of city-states) that pioneered quantum advancements in arts, literature, and philosophy – not to mention sending Alexander out to conquer the known world – they're still muddled around the periphery of Europe, not just geographically, but where it really matters – influence. For a people who created the concept of *Eros* – the desire for all that's good and beautiful, the innate appreciation of quality – they can be one tough bunch of cusses to deal with; often dour and gloomy, often fighting, and prideful to the point of ridiculousness. Further, for a people also known in the good ol' days for turning a blind eye to sexual mores, there's a chest-puffing "macho-ness" there, perhaps a product of the stultifying effects of orthodoxy, almost fundamentalist in its view of human relations. To top it off, for a culture renowned for food and drink, someone really needs to set the Greeks straight about Retsina (pine-pitch masquerading as wine), Ouzo (nitroglycerine scented with licorice), and Metaxa (an obsequious blend of embalming fluid and turpentine). I'd like to meet the Greek PR guys someday and shake their hands – they've overcome unfathomable odds.

The Turks, on the other hand, have historically been Hollywood's idea of the Bad Guys: wild-eyed assassins with curving scimitars, sadistic sultans, the soulless prison system of *The Midnight Express* movie, aforementioned expunging of the Armenians, occasional public hand-chopping of a thief. "Barbarians!" we say. Yet, collectively, the Turks – well, mostly Western Turkey and Istanbul in particular – are some of the most genuinely ingratiating people one could ever meet. A camera I left sitting on an outside café table was still there two hours later – try *that* in New York (or Athens). A farmer and his family drove me back to the ruins of Troy from miles away to retrieve my forgotten glasses. A young man in a Brooklyn Dodgers jacket (did he even know it was a nostalgia timepiece?) grabbed our suitcases and walked us around Izmir looking for the right hotel. A smiling cop gave me directions in the middle of an Istanbul intersection; I, foolishly clinging on to a bottle of *Ahududu* ("ahoo-doodoo"), raspberry liquor. Waiters smiled, hotel clerks smiled, cabbies smiled, even public servants smiled.

Sure, some of the stuff didn't work – this wasn't Germany, after all. But even beyond their personal virtues, the Turks' collective history has its good points: despite the touchy issue with the Armenians, Turkish conquerors through the ages have shown great magnanimity in victory; which, while still seeming philistine or medieval by the later standards of the Geneva Convention, were much more "humane" than most other Christian, Arabic, Incan, African or Asian aggressors of those times.

From my novice sociologist standpoint, it seems to me that the Greeks have entire handfuls of *minor* challenges, while the Turks have just one small handful of *major* challenges. Which way things evolve is as wild a guess as predicting the next "snap" from the colliding seismic lines of the Anatolian Fault, which girths the Bosporus Straits and wreaks havoc indiscriminately on Turks, Greeks, Bulgarians, Georgians, Armenians and tourists. Don't be fooled by the apparent still-scenes of history: everything is in motion there, even if it looks unchanged for thousands of years. Witness Greece's recent resurgence, with white-washed Athens and a truly spectacular Olympic games; while Turkey, so close to the edge of "breakthrough," now wrestles with a resurgent demon: growing pressures from an Islamic party determined to do away with their secular state. What will happen? Stay tuned and then we'll all know.

* * * * * *

Rhodos City was getting clearer. The late-September sun was now up, and the hodgepodge of Byzantine, Ottoman, Roman, and Crusader architecture splashed together to form an inviting scene. A little over 100,000 people inhabited the island, with about half of them here in the main city; but the historic "Old Town" where we would be hanging out was much more quaint and manageable, winding alleys and all.

As we passed through the ancient gateway to the harbor, Archie nudged me. "Do you know what we just did?"

I said something banal like, "Uh, entered the harbor?"

"Yes," he continued, with obvious pride, "But we also just passed under the spot where one of the *Seven Wonders of the Ancient World* stood." I looked up but saw only sky and seagulls.

"Well, it's long gone, but I'm talking of the Colossus of Rhodes. He was giant, made of bronze, iron, and marble, and supposedly he straddled the harbor." I cringed instinctively, thinking it a bad omen to pass under the crotch of a toga-ed giant.

"He was Helios, that same Sun God. You can imagine how dazzling he was from miles away when the sun hit him. Like now. But in truth, he couldn't really have straddled the harbor. We're pretty sure he stood off to one side. And he only lasted 50 or 60 years, until a giant earthquake brought him down. The rubble sat half on the bottom of the harbor and half on the side of the wharves, for about 900 years. Then one day in the 7th Century, some clever Arab entrepreneurs loaded up the rubble, hauled it away on thousands of camels, and sold it to a Jewish merchant in Damascus."

There was time for one last cigarette before the moorings came up, and Archie seized the moment. "The Colossus was surely symbolic of the history of Rhodos. Some things happen in massive scale, very quickly; while others unfold themselves, unnoticed, over millennia. Like those earthquakes you mentioned, coiled tensions just under the earth. But there's always something that can be taken from the experience, I guess. Did you know that your Statue of Liberty – I guess I should say *our* statue, since I'm now an American citizen – owes its very look and message to the Colossus of Rhodes?"

"Get outta town – you serious?"

"Yes, much so. A French artist named Auguste Bartholdi, who traveled widely in Egypt and Greece, was so taken by the story of the Colossus, he borrowed ideas from our native mythology to copy for the statue, which of course was a gift from France. I'm not sure how he superimposed the idea of a proud Egyptian peasant woman seeking liberty on a male Greek Sun God, but it worked in his mind. There's even a poem, "The New Colossus," written by Emma Lazarus, commemorating Lady Liberty. The funny thing is, no one really knew what the old statue looked like! But I guess artists are like we Greeks. If we don't like one story, we make up another – isn't that how Socrates and Aesop did it? And despite our serious scowling faces, we *do* know how to make fun of ourselves – surely you've read Euripides and Sophocles and Aristophanes?"

"Yeah, I really liked that one about the women of Athens and Sparta conspiring to withhold nuptial favors to call bluff on their warring men-folk."

"Very good! *Lysistrata*. I tell you what, my friend, if the Greek and Turkish women could line up like that today, the whole Mediterranean would know at least one generation of peace! Ha! We could even export that idea to the Russians and the Ukrainians, then to the Iraqis and Iranians, then maybe the Israelis and the Syrians; even perhaps the Indians and Pakistanis? …Ha, that's great – what a fantastic idea!" His laugh caught some cigarette smoke going down the hatch; he hacked and sputtered for a moment, then continued: "We always know, that's the funny thing. Sometimes we're just too damn proud. Sheessshh, that's really stupid."

We were mooring now, and Archie fidgeted with a notepad and pencil.

"Today, I climb the hills over Lyndos to peer down on that beautiful harbor, where all those dozens of white boats bob around in that gorgeous aqua water. St. Paul spoke there, too, you know. It grounds my soul to go up there and peer into all that beauty, and into all that history, and know that no matter how many miles I wander or places I live, or how many crossroads I pass through, I'm always Greek and can always come home."

Archie scribbled a phone number on a piece of paper and handed it to me. "You and Sarah call me tonight for dinner. I'll grab my friend Phideas, he's a crazy bastard; you'll like him. Hasn't had a vacation in years, because he works like a mule – he's 38 but looks 50 – amazing, eh? But he knows how to have a party, and I love him like a brother. We'll show you a good Greek time, OK? Eat some Souvlaki and Moussaka, go dancing, pour some Campari?" (Even he knew better than to imbibe Greek spirits.)

The ferry moored and Archie grabbed his bags to skedaddle down the plank. He patted me on the back and winked. "See you tonight, yes?"

We nodded. "Absolutely!"

"Great, my friends. *Opa!*"

He was glad to be home – even if just for a week or two.

PART III
I MUST HAVE BEEN DREAMING

Those inspirational best-sellers about making lemonade out of lemons seem to fall into two camps. They are either 1) works of fiction or 2) distorted artifacts of a true-life episode that, when originally occurring, actually depressed, frustrated and/or pissed off the author. Salvaged by time and soothed by a late night brandy in the comfort of one's den, the saga is recreated with unwarranted humor, danger or luster. Embellished, in other words.

Just as "History is the lie most commonly agreed upon," (sayeth Voltaire) so does the amazing story incubate in the authors' minds, aggrandize itself through their heads like a gauntlet of Chinese Whispers, and emerge as Truth on the other side. And since truth is relative...well, a good story is a good story.

Memories, good and bad, are subjectively crafted into an entertaining but often distorted story, repackaged for sensational book reviews or for garnering adulatory *oohs* and *ahs* from a captive audience of friends and family. The storytellers, like good politicians, simply *forget* they're lying and puff their way into literary hubris with the conviction of a zealot and synapses of an advanced Alzheimer's patient.

The following stories are so wild and bizarre, I'm compelled to vouch for them by the letter: although at times I still ask myself – could I have been dreaming?

History is herstory, too.
– Author unknown

Chapter Nineteen

Sitiveni and the Kick-boxers

Flashlight? Check. *Hiking Boots?* Right here. *Poncho?* Uh-huh. *Imodium & Cipro?* Yeah, yeah, got 'em (you never know when the "foul bowel" is gonna flare up…).

Duffle bag, toothbrush, camera, camp soap, et cetera. It was all there, and I was ready to tackle Fiji's largest island, Viti Levu. The trek would take about four days, over hill and dale, along sharp ridges, thick jungle, pine forests, sweeping palm plantations and a smattering of tiny villages. My swarthy guides, natives all, would provide food, shelter, and company. It would count as good leisurely recreation with plenty of cool photo opps. And it was now, thankfully, dry season.

I had arrived in Fiji in early April of 1995, aiming for that window that separates late summer monsoons (this was upside down, remember) from the Melanesian version of winter. Dry and warm, in other words. I must have rolled loaded dice, because the wet tarmac that met me in Nadi (pronounced "Nondy") that night was the last moisture I would see during the next two weeks. I had missed the season's last rain by several hours, and the sky was already clearing. I put this phenomenon in the Good Omen basket if for no other reason than it confirmed the strange predilections that led me to Fiji. For about a three-month period that previous winter (now right side up), I had been flooded with imagery of Fiji: dreams – many of them; overheard chatter at the café, a news blurb on television, the proverbial travel page opening magically while I was waiting in the dentist's chair, the postcard on a company bulletin board. I had also recently read about an informal survey of independent travel agents at a national conference, who when asked the question, "Of all the places you've been, which is the one you would most like to return to?" ranked Fiji first. Too much temptation requires indulgence, and having both a cat's curiosity and Sagittarian's impetuousness, I did the only sensible thing. I decided to check out that four letter F-word in person.

I had been in the neighborhood eight years earlier, visiting some larger island sets named Australia and New Zealand, but had avoided Fiji due to cultural turbulence. About every decade or so, the natives go berserk, conduct a *coup* and threaten to throw out the minority Indian subculture. Then everything calms down while the travel agents keep Fiji on the blackball list. But like investing in a low trough of the stock market, the intrepid explorer can take full advantage of this lull to slip into a low-profile paradise for next to nothing and not worry about Fodor-spouting tourist herds & hordes.

I soon discovered that the "folkgeist" of that independent travel agent conference was not trumped up. I found Fiji to be a paradise of breathtaking beauty, stewarded by some of the most genuinely friendly people I'd ever met. With most of the population centers swelling around Nadi and Suva, the remaining 800,000 inhabitants were spread out over a rugged archipelago of 330 islands occupying about four times the size of Connecticut – remote, totally undeveloped backwaters of Eden chock-full of waterfalls, emerald forests and a colorful palette of cobalt, turquoise and teal coastal waters harboring some of the world's best coral formations.

＊ ＊ ＊ ＊ ＊ ＊

One day while bumming around Nadi, I came across a tour organizer promoting authentic "Fijian experiences": treks, village stays, Habitat for Humanity-style volunteer projects, teaching gigs and a whole smorgasbord of Cultural Immersion 101. Since most of my previous week's exercise had consisted of jumping in and out of water and hoisting beer bottles to my mouth, I decided a walk would do me good. I selected a ridgeline jaunt, an excursion of about 40 miles that connected little villages; the latter providing room and board with host families at night.

The promoter was an Indian-owned enterprise with a nice air-conditioned building and attractive glossy photos. The term "Indian" refers to ethnicity the way an American may be said to be Irish or Italian. These Indians – actually known as Indo-Fijians – had in fact been in the country for well over 100 years and were a well-established minority comprising almost 45% of the population. Their forefathers had been brought over by the British in the late 1800s, either as indentured servants or passage-paying customers hoping to make their own killing in the sugarcane fields. The British, in turn, had been requested by the Fijian king to "annex" the land to stop tribal bloodshed. The plan of the Indian visitors was, in addition to staying out of debtor's prison, to return to the Subcontinent with enough rupees to launch one's own dream: land, wives, cattle. In other words, class, prestige, and distinction – another notch up the barber-striped pole of the Hindu caste system. Unfortunately, upon arriving, they were informed by the ships' captains of an unfortunate clerical error – seems like their stints would need to be a bit longer, say five years instead of two, etc. (*"Sorry about that, lads. Pip, pip, cheerio."*)

The condensed story is that the Indians stuck around, not unlike the former indentured British/American colonists of Georgia and the Carolinas. Eventually they cajoled some females to make the voyage from India – a mere 6,000 miles away by ship – and settled down. Enterprising and industrious, they established an impressive infrastructure of goods and services, essentially creating what then became the merchant class. This was easy, considering the average Fijian native's idea of work is to catch just enough fish to have dinner, and then watch the sunset. Nothing wrong there, but one can see how cultural ideologies might clash at fractious angles. Unlike the polyglot cultures of Brazil, Hawaii and other Polynesian and Melanesian islands, Fiji's peoples have remained somewhat stratified. To this day, the Indian descendents run the show and the natives tolerate them, except for the occasional aforementioned revolution.

A well-dressed gentleman named Ravi drove me in a SUV to my disembarkation point. In his late thirties, about my age, he was dressed in linen pants and silk shirt; on his wrist was a Rolex. Business must've been good. Ravi was a pleasant person; it must be said that despite their demonizing by the natives, the Indo-Fijians were relaxed and congenial compared to their estranged kin in Mumbai, Calcutta, or Delhi. These were still the tropics, but food was plentiful, malaria under control, and life crept along in a monotonous slumber of deep-knelled satisfaction. The Australians call it *Troppo* – "He's gone troppo, mate" – referring to that slow-shuffling, shit-eating-grin demeanor of a bloke who's tossed too many barbiturates into his Mai Tai cocktail. He's not bored as much as "blissed."

But the Indians did have a penchant for a buck, and generally ran tight organizations. Certainly not the type Tom Peters might write up in a sequel to *In Search of Excellence*, since customer service tended to be mechanical and was likely to produce diminishing returns after the customer had paid his fee. Nonetheless, they generally showed up on time, which means in South Pacific chronology on the appropriate day; dressed professionally (for the tropics) and had acquired enough education to talk about the world beyond Fiji. Or at least, talk *to* a world beyond Fiji.

Ravi drove me through miles of sugar cane. Gradually the land rose, leveled off, then became elevated once more as we passed small farms flanked by steep cliffs and encroaching jungle. Like General Patton or the IRS in April, the jungle never retreats, it just encroaches, answering the primal urge to "advance at all costs." Even the indigenous banana and pineapple trees, many of them surrounding patchwork plantations, would be consumed by the jungle's voracious appetite if not for the wonders of John Deere; or, lacking such technical accoutrement, hundreds of sharpened, swinging machetes. Over yonder was an orchid plantation that actor Raymond Burr, or at least his philanthropic spirit, once lorded over. Palm trees, then pines escorted the dirt road as it climbed higher. Despite the mud from recent rains, it was in decent condition and we made good time. After about an hour we had arrived at the Nausori Highlands, a good 4,000 feet higher and 15° Fahrenheit or so cooler than seaside Nadi. Nausori had a stunning view of the Pacific and the reef of coral breakers about a mile off the shore, accentuated by parallel scallops that frothed white against the indigo background. But we were well inland now, 15 miles or so as the Pink-billed Parrotfinch flies.

The village looked like a pleasant enough place for a drop-off point. Here, I supposed, they would hook me up with my guides and off I'd go, to be picked up four days hence about 40 miles to the southeast, where the spine of the ridgeline drops off to the ocean.

Ravi's SUV caused quite a stir. I could only imagine that it usually portended something interesting from the outside world – a visitor from faraway lands, sweets – some diversion from sweating with hoe or shovel over meager hardscrabble crop rows. As soon as he parked, throngs of curious children surrounded the two of us. The aggressive ones yelled, of course; the benign ones smiled, and shy youngsters lurked in the background with curious eyes. There must have been at least 30 of them, a clamoring cacophony of shouts and greetings growing by the minute. Fijians, like Australia's Aborigines, possess a much more pronounced African look than their Pacific neighbors from nearby islands – a neighborhood is measured in thousands of miles – such as the Maoris of New Zealand, Tahitians, Samoans or Tongans. I was surrounded by a brown blur of Melanesian pygmies, obviously on a sugar high.

"Now, now, my friends," laughed Ravi with the easygoing countenance of a benevolent favorite older cousin. He'd obviously done this before. "This is Steve. He is your guest. Be kind to him and don't beat him up," chiding them good-naturedly and winking at me as if to infer "what did you expect?"

"He is from America – a long way away. Perhaps you can even practice English with him. Maybe he can introduce you to Michael Jackson or Madonna or Rambo…"

"Yay! Good-good-good," responded the swarming beehive. Fijian children start learning English at about seven years old and were fairly conversant by 10 or 11. It looked like I was their mark.

After I grabbed my gear out of the jeep, Ravi introduced me to a teenage girl named Mary. The Fijians weren't just bilingual, they were also bi-religious, adopting a Christian name as an alternative to their tribal heritage. Which was a good thing, unless the visitor enjoys polysyllabic pretzels and anagrams. Mary was about fifteen with a round face, high cheekbones, signature kinky hair and an even, pleasant smile. She reminded me of a young Tracy Chapman. Her

English was good, although she spoke slowly, probably more because of shyness than lack of verbal acumen.

"Hello," she greeted me with extended hand. "I will take you into our family house. We have a lunch for you."

Ravi drove off before it struck me that it seemed unusual to leave me, a foreign visitor, in the company of a teenage girl who wasn't exactly a tour guide. Or a male. Or very athletic. Oh well, she must be an appointed representative, maybe a younger sister of one of the guides. "Go with the flow," I told myself. "You have no choice," said the self on the other shoulder.

Mary led me into the village. Nausori was one of the larger of a handful of settlements that peppered southwestern Viti Levu. The prevailing architectural style was Early Junkyard, a housing equivalent of the bondo, bailing wire and rusted out clunkers that dot many a U.S. southern-backwoods hamlet. The dwellings were hybrids of houses and huts; discombobulated boxes of stone, plywood, corrugated concrete, visquine and other sundry plastics, thatch, and God-knows-what. *Bures* was the popular term, but I soon learned this could mean anything bigger than a shoebox that had four walls and a make-shift roof. It was like the whole village had gone on a scavenger hunt, with points given for creativity.

We entered a house, stooping low for a short door while simultaneously stepping over a six-inch high curb at the foot of the door. I guessed it was to keep water and mud out. We were in what must have been the family room – a large open area with oval-shaped, threadbare carpets covering clanking floorboards. There was also a small wooden table used only for placing objects, since it wasn't large enough for family dining. In one corner was a bed and in a side room, another bed. At the back was a kitchen with a pot over some coals. The wooden cupboards bulged with ceramic cups, wooden bowls, plastic dishes, dried spices and other mysterious organic matter in bunches and bags. If the Old Lady in the Shoe were going house hunting, this would be her digs, be it ever so humble.

Mary introduced me to her father – Emori. I never caught his Western name. He was a large burly man with about a 48-inch waist and legs like tree trunks; a gentle, kindly person. "Hello, Steve." A calloused catcher's mitt grasped my outreached hand.

With the exception of the coastal dwellers, especially in the larger cities like Nadi, Suva, or Lautoka, Fijians over 30 didn't speak much English. The occasional visitor like myself often had to communicate either via a young teenager (the older ones were off at trade schools), a 20-something prodigal returned from city vice to raise a family, or the occasional graybeard who'd actually dabbled in commerce with the outside world.

As Emori and I sat on thatch mats on the center carpet, Mary brought out lunch, which consisted of canned tuna, pineapples, mangos and breadfruit, that bland blasé hybrid of banana, potato and plaster-Paris that passes for starch in much of the world. It didn't taste bad; it just didn't taste at all. My kindergarten Play Dough had yielded more flavors, especially in the salt category. But breadfruit was their mainstay, like rice to an Asian peasant, or maize to a Sub-Saharan African.

Through Mary, I inquired about my pending travels.

"When will the guides arrive?"

Mary/Papa: "What guides?"

"The ones who will take me on the trek."

"I will take you on trek," Mary responded, interpreting for her Papa.

"All the way?" I asked incredulously.

"As far as you want to go."

"I don't understand. We must go south and quite a bit east, toward Suva. It's quite a distance."

Mary and Emori looked at each other with bewilderment, then mutually shrugged. Must be a translation thing, I decided, like when those crazy Spanish conquistadors in the Americas started asking the indigenous ones about Cities of Gold.

"Yes, trails go that way," Emori chimed in, "Mary walk you on one." Whereas Mary's English was halting but grammatically correct, Emori's was direct and riddled with bullet holes. He didn't care; he was Papa, master of the *bure* and sure-of-self.

"On *one?*" I probed, more perplexed than annoyed. There were alternate routes?

"Yes, all children know woods here. It safe."

"But…but…will she be carrying a pack?"

"No need pack...would be heavy." (*Well no shit, Papa-san, but nonetheless...*)

"So...will we meet up with others?"

"Yes, if you want" (*if I want?*) – many peoples walk on trails in woods."

"Will they be going with us?"

"Perhaps for little if you need friends." (*Need friends?*)

I was flummoxed; way off the deep end of linguistic limbo-land. I felt like a Monty Python record being played backward. Now I knew why there were wars. With all due respect to Mary's command of English – we understood each other's words – neither of us knew what the hell the other one really meant. It just didn't make sense. Oh well, I was still sure it would all work out okay.

Mary continued, "When you want hike?"

Me: "Well, uh...when should we start, in order to finish by dark?"

"Oh, we can go any time...maybe you finish lunch and we go?"

So it was. I excused myself to the family privy, an outhouse behind the main family dwelling, after which I drank from the two-inch diameter pipe that brought treated water down from a protected spring high on the nearby mountain. It wasn't that old, I was told, a gift from some benevolent UNESCO or other well-meaning philanthropist.

Then I grabbed my backpack and laced up my boots.

"Why you carry much, Steven – you train for big contest?" Mary had made a funny.

"Big contest?" I laughed – "No, just extra clothes, flashlight, small things. Necessary for four days, ya know. "Will I see you again, Emori?"

Again a perplexed exchange between father and daughter, Fijian telepathy, more pronounced than previous.

"Yes, Steven. I see you when supper."

"Whoa...how...is that *possible?*"

Their eyes got bigger. They stared at each other. Mary's head dropped just a little. She almost spoke in a monotone..."When we come back..."

"But...not...tonight? We'll be in the next village...How...?"

Eyes on full alert. Uncomfortable breathing. The Tower of Babel translators took a holiday as body languages provided all the meaning necessary...

"What you say...next village?"

Concern yielded to panic. Confusion bowed to shock. An unbelievable thought started to hatch somewhere in the back of my head, and proceeded to grow longer with fangs, talons and really bad breath...*I wasn't going anywhere.*

"Wait a minute...isn't this just the beginning point – aren't I going to end up about 40 miles from here?"

Emori coughed. Mary giggled, the awkward giggle of astonishment wedded to embarrassment; whether for her or for me, wasn't clear.

"Uh...no...Steven...you are guest here. Ravi will drive truck here in four days to pick you up. You stay, please, be our guest, OK please?"

* * * * * *

When I was eight years old, I had slipped on some black ice in my neighbor's driveway while shooting basketball. I fell straight back, arse over teakettle, landing square on my head like some cartoon character, complete with stereophonic sounds and circling tweety-birds. The impact was so unreal I literally didn't feel it. Since I was alone, I stood up, probably having endured a concussion and been "out" for a few moments. Stunned and wobbling, I navigated my way home. I was there, but not really *there*; watching myself, ambulatory through another's will, thinking but not opining; an automaton with a conscious homing device but no sense of "oh, shit, I crashed and am in trouble." I guess I was in shock.

Flash forward 29 years to 1995, here in Fiji. Stunned and disbelieving, I felt a similar shock reverberate through me. I was in the bloody Third World with no communication mode, no plans, and apparently was someone's "guest." I wasn't expecting them, but by God, they had been expecting me. I don't know which thud was louder – my derrière collapsing back onto the floor or my heart swan diving into my stomach. I was to stay in Nausori Highlands. *Troppo,* hell – I was marooned...and these people were only a few generations removed from cannibalism...

I guess I shouldn't complain. Poor Robinson Crusoe had only a dog for company the first dozen years or so before subjugating his slave Friday. Tom Hanks' Fed-Ex character in *Cast Away* spent four years talking to a goofy volleyball named Wilson. Those guys in the Donner Party and in the '70s, the ones who crashed up in the Andes, were forced to dine on human *hors d'oeuvres*. I was only going to spend four days, in human company, and if things got dicey, I could step back on the winding road and walk or hitchhike the twenty miles or so back to Nadi, a swimming pool, and a San Miguel draft.

And yet: I must have been dreaming. It was a joke – yeah that's it, and the entire village was in on it. Emori and Mary had been trained as impromptu comics in Sydney, and this gag was called "Yank the Yank."

"Steven, you no want stay here?" probed Emori. *Oooh, no fair.* The look of incredulity was not practiced on any world stage. It was distressingly authentic.

"Why it's a lovely house and so gracious of you to ask and I appreciate…"

"Good," Emori segued, "You sleep there." He motioned with a frankfurter-sized finger to the bed in our same family room and flashed a cavernous, toothy grin. He was glad to share his castle with the rich American. All praise on his *bure*.

Slowly I regained my wits. Clearly this was Ground Point Zero and I'd better make the best of it. About that time two boys came through the front door – Samuel, age 12, and seven-year-old John. Samuel, tall and slender for his age, was reserved but congenial, and seemed to possess an unusual confidence in his instincts. He had fond memories of other guests, Mary said. His English was halting but grammatically correct. John was shy and seemed star-struck (what, at me?), lurking in the corner as if to allow the shadows to conceal his brown skin and render him invisible. But he hung on every word and erupted in a spontaneous combustion of smiles whenever looked at. He didn't speak any English yet, but seemed to empath everything around him and reflect it back in a cascading eruption of brilliant teeth and brimming eyes. He was like a puppy – an ounce of love yields a pound of adoration and lifetime of commitment.

Mary explained that these were only two of the boys. Another, in his early twenties, was in the military; still another, in his teens, was off at a boarding school in Suva. Mary also said her mother would be arriving home soon with another child in tow.

Despite the initial impression of random chaos, the village was laid out with great practicality. Small ramshackle houses, glorified huts (the *bures*) and their requisite outhouses lined the perimeter of a cleared field. Most of the houses, like Emori's, had a gravity-fed shower hooked up adjacent to the house – cold water only, needless to say, but refreshing jungle cold, as opposed to, say, water from a melting glacier…although I could imagine in the winter, with nights dropping into the 40° Fahrenheit range here at 4,000+ feet altitude, it could be a tad nippy in the morning.

Troweled causeways allowed monsoon rains to siphon off harmlessly, down sloping escape ditches. A church was located at the back of the village, on the highest ground, protecting family graveyards (in the newly adopted Christian tradition) to the rear. A clinic occupied the other end. In-between were tiny family plots for gardens, and an empty turf for makeshift soccer.

Nausori had about 200 people, sprouted out from three family branches, or clans. Everyone was related through blood or marriage, sometimes both. I was never too good at that "fourth cousin from my mother's side" stuff, but this was a true genealogical jigsaw puzzle. Everyone was someone else's auntie, third nephew, second uncle, brother or sister, and in-law thrice removed. And of course, each could tell you his or her exact relationship to everyone else, like weaving Ariadne's thread through a *Who's Who* of the tribal yearbook. I have no idea how many generations lived and died here, building, destroying, mingling blood and bone into the Earth and spawning forth the flame of their clan. Or, like so many tribal peoples, this might end up being just a transitory spot on their endless migration. I guessed it was likely the latter, despite the stolid, almost regal imminence of the white church. This village just happened to sport the fetishes of Anglo predators. Maybe it'll last another century or two before the jungle reclaims its birthright and the tribe morphs into a more appropriate environment.

Mary, John and Samuel escorted me across the village, with young Johnny now brave enough to take my hand. Suddenly we were surrounded.

"*Eee-Yah!*" shrieked the first Ninja, administering a swift but playful karate kick to my upper thigh.

"*Ayyyy!!!*" answered a second, placing a foot across my backside. Gads – there was a mob of them, martial-midgets using me as a punching bag. Their grins betrayed their mannerisms, but their feet and hands were no less bothersome.

"*Yi-eee!!!!!*" came a nine-year old's karate chop to my chest. Samuel and Johnny jumped to my defense with primordial grunts of their own, sprinkled with Fijian tough-guy jive to ward off the predators.

"Ay-yee!" *Whoosh.*

"Ee-hah!!!" *Chop, slice.*

"Uuuuu-eh!!!!" *Whack.* These Ninjas had entered the dragon, and come out the other side – just a little stunted, that's all.

I soon found out from one of the village elders that brainless martial art kick'em-ups were the rage of the village – courtesy of a 16mm projector, run by generator, used for movies on Friday nights. The movies were a steady diet of the Steven Seigal, Jean-Claude van Damme, and Chuck Norris variety. And if comedy didn't work, there was always Jackie Chan…The whole village would gather in a large Quonset hut next to the church, and soak in the culture.

Naturally, this image of America as a land of kickboxing heroes thwarting sinister forces was assumed to be real. And in light of the World Trade Center bombing of '93 and the just-recent Oklahoma City debacle, who had the greater grasp of reality? America's blockbusters were no secret even in the backwashes of Eden.

Steven Seigal was their favorite. As "Steven" roughly corresponded to the Fijian name of "Sitiveni" – I soon became known to the village of Nausori as Sitiveni…and since I was from America, this automatically meant I knew that other swashbuckling Steven; and of course that meant I knew Kung Fu…which naturally invited a testing of my skills. Thus it was for the remainder of my stay, I was continually forced into thrusting, parrying, deflecting, or downright running, if I could escape the gangly-limbed, shrieking, giggling marauders. I was a marked man.

I was also the village mascot. Maybe it was because I was from America, that Shangri-La of unlimited verticality; the promoter of great truths; addict of sound bytes; peacemaker and warmonger;

moralist and hedonist; land of 48-ounce steaks, game show millionaires, cross-dressing movie stars and pet rocks; the Alpha and Omega of attraction and repulsion, where any Texas oil brat or Massachusetts Trust-afarian could grow up to be president, and any jive-talkin' pimp could sign a rap contract.

Or maybe it was my age – at 36, I was old enough to be the father of these kids, not to mention the peer of the village elders. But here I was – sans wife, sans offspring – hanging out like a dilettante playboy. What was up with *that?*

My little disciples followed me everywhere, whenever I stepped out of the *bure*: to the showers, though waiting patiently (but not silently) outside; to the swimming hole, about half a mile into the woods; on nature hikes (is there any other kind?) as Mary or Samuel showed me different fruits and talked about their studies. I could have been a troubadour or messiah spouting the usual nonsense. At any time five to ten kids trailed behind me, flanked me, scouted out our path, and occasionally landed a well-placed "Yee-ahh!" on my bruised body. After about the tenth time of arresting the abuser and tickling him profusely to a clapping jury of giggling playmates, I gave up and just absorbed the blows. The chances of a stalemate or truce were increasingly against me.

Inside the house, however, the rules were different. The *bure* was apparently considered off limits for my fan club, sacred ground where I wasn't to be messed with. Thus for refuge I would nap, or write voluminous verse in my tattered travel log. Occasionally a beaming face would appear in the window above my bed – there were no screens, of course. The face, sometimes in triplicate, would lean closer and a curious voice would venture forth…"What you write, Sitiveni?"

"Well, let's see…words, sentences, paragraphs, the normal stuff." *Snicker, giggle.*

"What about?"

"You, mostly." *Double giggle; triple chortle.*

Then they poised for attack…"*Eee-iii…!*" I braced for onslaught, knowing the sanctuary of the house would deter violation of my space. Sure enough, *zooommm*…they were gone.

Once I did make it out, miraculously, without an entourage. Having been shown the path to the "mountain" – a peak about three or four hundred feet over the village, I managed to escape to do my own exploring amidst the high sugar cane, emerald green from the recently departed rains; and on through pine and evergreen woods that also sported groves of banana and mango trees, even at this advanced altitude. I climbed to the top of the rocky mountainous slope and surveyed the village below, then beyond, to where the deep indigo of the Pacific crashed into the coral barrier before transforming itself to the soothing turquoise of the inner coast.

Off in the distance were the Mamanuca islands, which I'd visited the week before. I had tagged along on a three-day, two-night tour, courtesy of a revamped 19th century schooner complete with cooks, singing musicians and a bevy of Australian divers. At night we camped on empty islands that were little more than glorified coral outcroppings with protected overhangs in case it rained. In traditional style our hosts prepared pit feasts (*Lovos*) that consisted of an amazing assortment of meats, fish, cassava, and of course breadfruit, all wrapped in banana leaves and simmering on coals for hours. The singers were good, too – they knew the ballad of Gilligan's Island (whose fate we hoped to avoid), the Beverly Hillbillies' theme song, and even a few Beatles ditties.

We sailed out to some islands where the natives, just as on Hawaii's Niihau, still lived traditionally. We bought up their trinkets and "ooh-ed and ahh-ed" while they danced around – *meke* – and smiled a lot. Most wonderful, however, were the diving and snorkeling. Several times daily we anchored for glorious jumps into some of the world's most beautiful coral formations, complete with perfunctory schools of rainbow-colored fish. It was paradise, found.

* * * * * *

In truth, a great deal of my reverie was spent on Alexis, my latest flame. We'd met on a blind date just weeks before. She'd just returned from Nepal, and since I had visited there the previous year, a mutual buddy introduced us. Our first date had produced a number of shared interests, including the fact that we were both schooled in the discipline of Industrial Engineering (not that two wrongs make a right). We obviously had a mutual love of traveling, and she seemed to share my inquisitive nature about the world and its people. And yes, she was a babe, had brains to spare, and found me, uh, "intriguing." That was about three plusses-up from my usual blind dates, so several more dates ensued, and by the time we camped in the red rock plateaus of Southern Utah a few weeks hence, I was in the full-throttled rapture of *l'amour*. I knew then that she would be – correction – I would *want* her to be, my *Femme d'Vie*.

Thus my Fijian sojourn came at a most awkward time – too late to cancel, no chance for Alexis to join me – while our budding emotions balanced on the edge of a very sharp knife. She had other suitors, and I had taken off halfway around the world to chase the wisps of a mystery (my premonitions). Was I a fool, was I in love? (What's the difference, anyway?) But I *was* infatuated, and I passed long hours scribbling my intentions, fantasizing and pondering the circumstances of life with all its flux, that it would have produced our meeting. But there it was, and I reveled in it. Dammit, I *was* in love, and I prayed to Cupid, Hermes and Venus that Alexis would be there smiling when I returned.

* * * * * *

Meals were served by Mary, and I ate all breakfasts and lunches alone. There was always breadfruit, to my chagrin, but also plenty of Nabisco cookies, pineapples, bananas and mangos. Ovaltine, Nescafe and Nestlé's chocolate mixes were served in abundance in bright ceramic mugs. There were chicken stews, beef with yams, and canned tuna (never fresh, not up here). And of course more breadfruit, in case one was starving and bereft of taste buds.

At dinner, Emori would join me – Papa's prerogative – and I was glad for it. Sometimes Mary would sit off to the side and translate. Other times, Papa would just grunt and we'd find a way to gesticulate our way around the inadequacies of language. He was a warm person, all heart, if you didn't count the 350-plus pounds of mass, with effusing eyes and characteristic stand-at-the-ready Fijian grin. Not to say he didn't have brains; they just didn't seem to be employed in any productive enterprise.

Mama still hadn't shown up and it wasn't my place to inquire. A number of friends – village elders, mostly – dropped by to inquire about the Yank and exchange pleasantries. A few spoke decent English, but most were as mono-linguistic as Emori and myself; my pigeon Spanish would get me by in the Philippines maybe, but not here. In those cases I was the grinner, while my two village hosts would ramble on in the verbal torrents of mysterious Melanesia: lotsa vowels, just like their Oceanic cousins, the Hawaiians – and equally meaningless to me.

One key food-stock missing from the village's humble larder was alcohol. They didn't imbibe, partly because the missionaries had cursed its evils over the last century, partly because (like many tribal cultures) they didn't handle it too well, and partly because it was difficult to obtain. But most certainly, and for the best reason of all, the Fijians had something superior: Kava-Kava.

Kava – *Yaqona* – is an indigenous root, which when ground into fine powder and mixed into a soup-like slurry, yields a fine numbing buzz, sweet dreams and a long snooze. Never mind that kava concoctions taste like pepper-tinged mud. It is a religious ritual, a sacrament actually, shared most nights in "Ceremony."

At the Ceremony, attended primarily by men, incantations would be uttered to deities near and far, in the old days at least (Jesus now was the Main Man). The men wore their trademark skirts, really towel-like wraps, and sat around in a semi-circle while the host of the house, perhaps stealth shamans, I never found out for sure, conducted Ceremony. Coconut shells were used as the vessel. The drinker – uh, initiate – would say "*Vinaka*" – thank you – clasp his hand, proclaim "*Bula*," and glug down the contents. This would be followed by "*Matta*" (loosely meaning "get this foul thing out of my face").

After about three half-shells, coherent thoughts would lose their edge. After say, six half-shells, a sublime grogginess would envelope the devotee in a gentle shroud of numbing stupidity. After about nine slurps, one was damn lucky to get home to bed for a 10-12 hour hibernation. At least that was my experience. With their cultural conditioning, and in some cases prodigious girth, many of the men guzzled 15 or 20 coconut shells. "High tide," no beginner's rations for them.

But there was no hangover, no headache, and no sugar whiplash depleting one's blood system. The active narcotic of kava, known as kavalactone, is as benign and pleasant a sedative – uh, sacrament – as ever yielded by forest, field, or jungle and ground by pestle in man's medicine bowl. Sociologists and anthropologists credit it for taking the edge off the Fijians' predilection toward cannibalism – the "happy natives make calm natives and good citizens" theory. Personally, I think the menu change can be accredited more to the firearms of the British Empire accompanied by the stern admonitions of the newly adopted Jesus. In any case, it became a lot easier to attract tourists to Fiji's smorgasbord of earthly delights when visitors knew they weren't going to be the specialty *du jour*.

The role of kava in Fijian folklore is debatable, but it does seem that at one time it was a play-toy of the elite and used in the strictest of rituals. Like the Native American peace pipe or a Norseman's runic bones, kava was imbued with special powers. Supposedly a shaman could predict weather patterns or crop yields by observing the miniscule ripples of the liquid in its coconut shells. Chiefs would be exalted or overthrown. A smooth surface was surely a propitious sign from the gods for a boy child. A splash could mean the bad guys' war party was on their way. Such was the stuff of legends. But like the amulets of Allah's Evil Eye or the Christian crucifix, whatever special force occupied said object probably fled when it was co-opted by an ecclesiastical council and pedaled in the market.

Unfortunately, the commercial trivialization of kava, now a New Age wonder drug in Europe and the States, and the acerbic lamentations of missionaries have now commoditized it as a household item. To be sure, the robes, invocations of ancestors and the clapping and chanting all yield a regal veneer to Ceremony. But substitute an aluminum can for the coconut shell, pasteurized Pabst Blue Ribbon for the kava slurry, a double wide trailer for a *bure*, denim Levi's for a skirt and a rebel yell for a clap, and any good ol' boy from Mayberry would be right at home for Monday Night Football.

Furthermore, kava has a downside. Two, in fact. The first problem was that the imbibers – men, naturally – slept until about 11:00 the next morning. If there's anything that sloth and indolence love, it's to have religious rituals as a scapegoat for one's own innate lack of inertia. "Kava is sacrament – men drink kava," ergo, tradition requires that half the village elders stay zonked until the sun is overhead.

It's a known fact that in all of the world's industrialized societies and many of the developing ones, women perform the lion's share of the work. There's nothing wrong with this; personally, I approve. But I suspect even tradition has its limits, and more than one Fijian husband has been awakened by a frying pan across the noggin. Without a doubt, the modernization of the village and reservation-like entrapment of a people who no longer hunt has done its damage to the collective Fijian male ego, now bereft of purpose and diminished of stature. Ceremony – *sevu-sevu* – helps them maintain the illusion of a past when they had more purpose than mere procreation.

Besides, Ceremony was heavy shit and women couldn't possibly understand the grave responsibilities required therein. Papa *needed* his 10 hours – it was his burden to bear, for the good of the family and all. Meanwhile, women dressed and fed the kids, dug trenches for seeds and yanked crops out of the ground, ran to the market, repaired the *bures* and thumped invading vermin, all the while being knocked up for nine months of the year for about 30 years running. Or so it seemed to the novice sociologist.

Ceremony took place almost every night at a different *bure*. In a town lacking telephones, MTV, computers or any electronics (not including the previously mentioned generator, which required fuel) it was as good as any of these. I vowed if I ever returned, I'd bring a few decks of cards and some plastic chips, and show them some new ceremonies. I was honored to be their guest – "Sitiveni from America."

I was a good acolyte; I said my *Bula* and *Vinaka* and *Matta* lines flawlessly and kept up with the prolific circulation of coconut shells throughout the evening. They didn't know I had practiced in college for this very thing. I did stick to "low tide" portions, however. True to word, I slept the deepest of hibernations and dreamed outrageous things, only to wake up mid-morning totally refreshed.

The second ill effect of Kava is more insidious. Over many years, it dries out the skin. Men in their thirties would start to develop the scaly, calloused skin of a reptile, and by the time they were in their forties or fifties, would resemble the bumbling brute in *The Creature from the Black Lagoon*. Dehydration was the culprit. Kava, like the slow drip-drip-drip that wears down a rock, gradually sucks up the body's moisture and withers the skin into a shroud of sandpaper with the sheen of a chafed leather purse. I'm not sure what the real health downside to this is – kidney stones? Ulcers? Perforated livers? – But Fijian GQ has a long way to go before threatening the salons of Tokyo, Sydney or Sunset Boulevard. I suspect daily Ceremony leads, at least indirectly, to an earlier death. But it sure beats the point of a spear, or a heart attack in a stressed-out Manhattan high-rise. And I suppose if one could spend a majority of his life partying – uh, ritualizing – and sleeping blissfully, then could not that be successfully argued to be the more enjoyable life?

Who needs corporate stress, deadlines, bottom lines, lines to the theater, coffee machine, Brooklyn Bridge and supermarket cashiers? Who needs life in the fast track with all its trappings?

I do, like most of the people on the planet…and why? I suppose it comes back to that stickler word *meaning*, and my passion to "make," not "find" it. I could make myself peaceful with kava ceremony every day for the rest of my life and wile away the years in a state of semi-oblivion; close to nature for sure, and somewhat like an animal. Yet was I not more endowed, since I had brainpower that was lacking in the 4-leggeds? It was that Western mentality thing.

All my life I'd been taught to save, not just spend – but also to invest at least a portion of what I'd earned. Here, such standards were simply non-existent. What was earned? Saved? So, why *not* spend all the nothing, night, after night, in the same boring monotonous ritual that praised the gods and saints and whomever else had signed their guest list, for giving them this opportunity to sleep until noon and let someone else do all the work?

Was this not a grand scheme to cheat one's way through life? Cheating whom? The Universe – or myself?

* * * * * *

There's another side to the story, however, that needs to be presented. Although, like many of the village men, Emori didn't work, gainful employment wasn't really an option. Some men chopped sugar cane or helped out with the occasional odd jobs around the village that were subsidized by UNESCO or the Fijian government. But most of the males simply had nothing to do.

Emori spent his day puttering around the village and having council with other sages. His clipped speech and subdued animation in conversing with me were no more than the awkward reservations of his limitations in English. He was genuinely polite, courteous and inquisitive: definitive Fijian trademarks. They effuse warmth, greet every stranger as friend, and seem totally captivated by the day's activities. A fisherman I had met on the coast the previous week practically adopted me, taking me home to his wife and family. Among a pile of sweet cakes and tea in his humble hut, he looked at me squarely with eyes that could only be described as "smiling" and said, "Fiji people always speak from heart." He gave me a gentle thump on my left breastbone. "Always from heart, my friend. Fiji people love life, love God, love friends." Grin-City, from the heart.

That was the refreshing thing about them. They could be so shy and demure, but when curiosity got the best of them – which was often – they'd look at you with a laser-like gaze and ply you with questions like a garrulous four-year-old fidgeting in the back seat:

"What are snow like?"
"How far away are America?"
"Is you rich?"
"How old am you?"
"What you eat in you home?"
"Why people explode city in O-kla-ho-ma?"
Why, why; what, what; where, where; how, how…often for hours.

But of all the tall tales I've encountered from travel literature and the wagging tongues of gypsies, none have been truer to the mark than the legacy of Fijian friendliness. Exaggerating their amiability is not possible. From the smallest children (Kung Fu antics aside) to leathered graybeards, they are the most authentically warm, spontaneous people I've ever met. Having spent time with the gentle hill peoples of the Himalayas, shy Quechan villagers high in the Andes, mellow Aborigines (well, some of them) in the Great Outback, effervescent seaside Turks, and a gaggle of African tribes scattered around the Sub-Sahara, I thought I had seen the extent of human kindness. But the Fijians push the chart off the scale. The ubiquitous "Bula," akin to the Nepali "Namaste" or Hawaiian "Aloha," is a verbal gateway with doors swinging in many directions: "Hello," "Goodbye," "I greet the God within you"…take your pick.

I try to never judge a culture's intellectual (or social) acumen by the extent of its vocabulary. A single word can conjure a multitude of meaning depending on when and where it's used, as well as its pitch or intonation. Words are simply placeholders to many Oceanic languages – the real meaning is embedded in their heart and flutters in vibrations the ear can't detect. But few words are necessary, as the honored recipient can almost effortlessly intuit the deeper meaning. *"By their acts ye shall know them."*

Emori had one overriding question for me, administered through Mary. He wanted a "Track Suit." I surmised this meant sweat pants, sweat shirt, etc. Cold season would be here soon. Lacking an Eddie Bauer's – K-Mart hadn't even made it across the pond yet – warm clothes from the industrial world were appreciated, especially if it had a logo on it, like that garish Nike swoosh. Fijians may be humble, but they did have their pride – especially the papas. Every day for four days running, after he learned how to pronounce it, Emori would hit me up with "Please…to remember…track suit?" I could have been Santa Claus at a suburban mall.

Emori's petitions were small and awkward, but what they lacked in firepower they made up for in frequency.

"Yes, Emori, I will send you a track suit." He beamed – he'd be the big man of the village. He was already the biggest, physically, but this would be *real* stature.

* * * * * *

I'm sure somewhere a social hierarchy existed beyond the men's kava ceremonies. A council, a board of elders, chieftain, someone. It probably had to do with male representatives of the three family lines, but I couldn't figure it out and it wasn't disclosed to me. Perhaps it was communism in its truest form: "From each according to his abilities, to each according to his needs."

This already flew in the face of social welfare, however, judging by the extent of the government's artificial support of the village. Maybe it was an Oligarchy of the Many. On the other hand, taking into account the work that got done, or not done, probably it should have been a *matriarchal* society. But impressions are often misleading. A joy of life should not be interpreted as docility; gentility, never measured as subservience. Just ask the Indo-Fijians who have to thwart off an uprising every decade or so – all because they've had the audacity to create enterprises and proceed to staff them with – *voila* – family members and friends (such nepotism!).

Whatever form of local government existed, it wasn't without challenges. The clan was losing its young – the soul of its future – as the trade-school educated young increasingly sought greener employment pastures (that is, *any* employment) and the club scenes of Suva and Nadi. Then there was Mother Nature, the tempestuous alter ego of idyllic island paradises everywhere. Fiji is no stranger to typhoons, and the last one to lay siege to Viti Levu in 1991 killed four villagers, as the high winds collapsed buildings on friends and family alike. Since they are all related, grieving is profound.

In a land of poverty, weather isn't the only threat to health and well-being. Despite the minimal presence of malaria, Fijians still died at the modest age of 69. AIDS, the love bug, had found its way into paradise, and if that wasn't enough there was always hepatitis, cholera, typhoid, and a *Who's Who* of killers both quick and slow. But the lifespan is most assuredly lower in the remote inland villages.

With death such a constant companion and the employment scenario so muted, it's no surprise that the villagers are a religious people. And like so many other facets of island living, their spirituality reflects a crossroads of the old and new. The old was the traditional native animism with its polyglot of deities representing fertility, crops, war, anger and love. But this was fading away under the burgeoning influence of Christianity, and the latter has garnished the lion's share of the village's icons, artifacts, prayer books and other vestiges of faith. The Methodists got the franchise rights in Fiji, beating the Mormons to the punch by a few years (the latter sticking with their pluckier pickings in Samoa and Tonga to the northeast). All the villagers of Nausori were ostensibly Methodist, and the modest church at the edge of the village, along with its concomitant cemetery, was the center of activity on Sundays…and very much the center on Easter Sunday, when I happened to be there.

Three times we trundled across the village green (which was brown, and actually, a mud patch). At 7:00 a.m. the "warm up" service brought out about a third of the village. This was followed by a huge breakfast, and then the main show from 11:00 a.m. to 1:00 p.m., which everyone attended. Then a huge lunch, maybe a nap, and more ecclesiastical fireworks at about 4:00 p.m., attended by probably two-thirds of the village, getting out before dark and just in time for supper. For my part, three times I donned a cotton skirt (*sulu vaka taga*), wrapping it around my waist and tucking it in (safety pins were a luxury), and my finest (unsoiled) white linen shirt. I even shaved (cold water, of course). On all three occasions I stood – everyone stood, at all times – in their humble church and vibrated with the joy of their songs. Other than the occasional "Jesus" or "Amen," their God must only speak Fijian, because not a note of English was either spoken or sung. I prayed for their health and vitality, for their peace and tranquility. I petitioned their deities (the traditional ones along with the new one) to bless their households, and, for crissakes, to lay off the typhoons and epidemics for awhile. May their children win the Nobel Prize someday, may their crops bloom large; may they find amiable fellowship with those industrious Indians down on the coast who prayed to Vishnu, Krishna, Shiva, Brahman, and even Allah (about one-fifth of the Indo-Fijians, or approximately 9% of all Fijians, are Muslim).

Most of all, I prayed for my own deliverance back to the mainland of Uncle Sam, for I had lost my return airline tickets and sure hoped Qantas Airlines' good-humor lady would be working the day I showed up at the airport. But then, remembering there were a lot worse places to be marooned than Fiji, I prayed for forgiveness and said ten Hail Mary's in English.

On Monday morning, the fifth day, a truck rumbled into the village. Some supplies were being delivered. Considering the magnitude of the communication *faux-pas* with my "hospitality brokers" in Nadi,

I contemplated what the chances were of Ravi or his next-of-kin showing up at the right place at the right time. Deciding those odds were not high, I cast my lot with the returning truck.

I said goodbye to Emori and thanked him for his hospitality. He embraced me like a gorilla hugging a teddy bear.

"Track suit, please?" One more for the road. I consented, for the last and probably twentieth time.

Johnny hugged my leg and cried the purest crocodile tears this side of Pago Pago. He was the poster child for the *Blessed be the Children* psalm. Samuel, quiet but smiling, wanted to see me again – in America. I gave him my parents' address, since my Rolodex of domiciles looked like Johnny Carson's suit rack. Mary feigned the proper subdued female role her culture has assigned, but reached out anyway and gave me a big hug.

"Goodbye, Sitiveni. Thank you for blessing our village." (Wow, I did *that*?)

I threw my (unused) gear into the truck, and as I looked up from the side panel, one last *"Ay-yeee!"* pierced the air. I intuitively ducked, missing the final kick. A small army of five-to-nine-year olds vamoosed like roaches in a Raid factory, giggling, flailing and chopping like there was no tomorrow.

♫ *Everybody was Kung Fu fighting, those cats were fast as lightning...* ♫

* * * * * *

Nearly a year later, long after the perfunctory package of tracksuit and miscellaneous photos had floated slowly across the Pacific, I received a letter with Fijian postage. With my live-in fiancée Alexis at my side, I opened it and read aloud:

Dear Sitiveni [The handwriting was surprisingly legible],

"*Thank you very much for coming our house to stay as guest. I wish I could have meeted you, but I was in hospital having baby. We arrive home day after Emori say you leave. God has bless my house with you visit. We hope you always live strong life, and please to remember you family in Nausori Highlands, Fiji.*

Emori look so handsome in his tracksuit. He is very proud man and wears tracksuit everyplace. I must make him take off when he goes to bed!

Sitiveni, school season is come soon. Is it please OK to send children lunch boxes with Disneyland animals on side? Thank you so much for be such jenerus!

You greatful friend in Jesus,
Sarah, Emori wife

Chapter Twenty

Dharma in a Delusional Age

*T*he following was written "real time," a journal of sorts in 2001-2, and reflects a turning of the tides in my exploration of Who I Am and What is Life. As is often the case, these breakthrough/turning points derive from stimuli beyond our control and often contrary to our wishes. Rather, they seem cast upon us, and it's up to us to decide what they mean and more precisely, what we want to do about it. What does it mean to live a life of Purpose: to live an "ordinary" life in an "extraordinary" manner…and is this what is really meant by "dharma"?

* * * * * *

The "Dot.com" Crash

For nearly a year I watched them drop like flies around me: my own employees, testimonials to the laws of physics ("What goes up, must come down"); first savaged by the collective insanity of an industry gone berserk, then subsequently slain by the budget reaper. It was hard to imagine at the time that a year later, having joined the exodus, I'm sighing relief and dusting off my traveling shoes.

In retrospect, it's amazing that only some gadflies on CNBC or a few "old school" curmudgeons relegated to the back pages of a boring business rag, saw it coming. But greed wears its own blinders, surely as every gold mine eventually goes bust. Most industry captains were all too happy to hail "I.T." – Information Technology – as the new Klondike, and most institutional pundits were all too eager to jump on the Little-Train-That-Could without wondering where it was headed or even if it had any brakes. Real trains do need to be on track with real tracks to follow in order to go anywhere, but suddenly in our new space age of virtual reality, this factor seemed to be irrelevant. Countless venture capitalists threw caution and dollars to the wind for the New Economy's promise of market supremacy and unbridled profits.

Not to be outdone by these 3ʳᵈ Millennium Ponzis, employees got in on the act, too, demanding 20 percent annualized pay raises and stock options with a buy-in ("strike") price just a few pennies north of zero. And woe be unto the boss who wouldn't or couldn't honor the insatiable demand of these high-priest technocrats. Swaggering with the hubris of inflated self-worth, they would indeed cross the street into the welcoming arms of another employer – in regular three-to-six-month cycles.

I knew the party was getting out of hand when a 24 year-old lip-pierced, unshaven, tattooed "senior consultant" leaned across my desk and asked me: "What can you do for me, dude?" (I showed him the door, the incorrigible swine.)

Soon these rivulets of greed, naiveté and miscalculation would merge into a mighty torrent. Capital budgets would be slashed, unused software would sit on shelves, inventory pipelines would jam full of unwanted components. "Dot.coms," the latest incarnation in a long list of get-rich-quick-without-a-business-plan-or-funding schemes, would evaporate back into the ethers from which they had come, and Human Resource turnstiles would soon stop fluttering.

Every decade or so we get reminded of the dark underbelly of capitalism, its rhythmic bulimia rattling our economic gridiron and societal psyches like a great tide that rises, ebbs, and sucks back capital, people, and dreams across the world's shorelines. If it's not a technology implosion, then it's a financial collapse; if not an energy crisis, then a commodity panic. The excesses and shortages left in the wake produce such extreme inequities between countries and industries, it is safe to conclude that capitalism truly may be the worst possible form of economics – except, to paraphrase Winston Churchill, "for all of the others."

It was inevitable the I.T. swoon would exact its own body count. Faces became fading names and now they're statistics. Numbers and percentages in the *Wall Street Journal's* business section, embellished resumes and pleading cover letters jumped off the underscored links of every headhunter's web portal. Many are angry, frustrated, or guilty; others are terrified, depressed, or just plain relieved. However, for every self-aggrandizing *wunderkind* (e.g., the aforementioned 24-year old "senior consultant"), there are also hardworking, serious folk in that bevy. Behind the numbers are flesh and blood, friends and enemies, loners and socialites, veterans and rookies. Many are damned good at what they do, are (were) loyal and cared deeply about their employer's success in an old-fashioned altruistic sense. They're the ones I have cared about.

I remember feeling lucky during the early months, even as rosters were trimmed, cubicles vacated and parking lots emptied. Although the market's fortifications were stiffening against my company's services, I was still getting paid (albeit on a leaner diet), and projects seemed to be in the docket (read: cash flow) for the foreseeable future. But it was a pyrrhic fortune. As the company's infrastructure stretched like a rubber band, a burned out CEO soon lost his vision, fortitude, and resources, in that order. Good money (what little there was) followed bad, good employees bailed, and disillusionment became the order of the day. Even then, it seemed like it wouldn't get any worse, and the long-trumpeted economic recovery would arrive like the cavalry in the nick of time.

But the Fates would have none of that. First, it seems too many Wall Street magicians had been pulling too many rabbits out of their hats for too many years. Enron, Global Crossing, WorldCom, Andersen, Perot, Tyco, Adelphia, Dynegy, Kmart, even Merrill Lynch for chrissakes. Like that old Burger King commercial asking "Where's the Beef?", Main Street has now taken Wall Street to the woodshed. Public trust has pummeled (yesterday's rock-star CEOs, like Tyco's Kozlowski and Enron's Lay, are now considered bums, or worse, possibly crooks), the financial "bears" are roaring louder and capital budgets seem frozen in limbo – or slashed into shreds.

Meanwhile, India and Pakistan are revving up the nuke rhetoric, and once more Israel and the Palestinians are amplifying their grudge match of asymmetrical attrition. As if that's not enough, the Bushies, with Democratic complicity in this post 9/11 election year, are priming the home-front security pump and uttering all the requisite scare warnings (whether from true convictions or as fertile fodder for a voting populace of manipulated sheep, we'll never know), while they beat their chests menacingly at our old nemesis, Saddam. It'll be interesting to see how this one plays out...

To borrow a recurring line from a Tom Robbins book, "The world situation, as usual, was desperate."

The I.T. industry is at the unfortunate end of that whip-cracked tail – not "out" but big-time "down." I've little stomach for the new playing field. Maybe it's a blessing in disguise – there's something about ennui and stagnation that flies in the face of this wander-lusting Sagittarian. Once again, I hear the sirens of the open road whispering sweet seductions in my inner ear, and impatience burrowing like a feisty ferret into my heart and guts. I wonder what Sisyphus would really do if he could lay down that damn rock, what Tantalus would do if he could sink his ravenous chops into that smorgasbord of fruit and flesh. Probably make for boorish company, but it sure would feel good...

Around the time when the first hunter-gatherer traded in his club and flint for the clustered chaos of the city-state, our vocational identities started the slow morph from "what I do" to "what I am." Millenniums of bureaucratic hair-splitting, trade specialization, and subordination to a greater gestalt (feudalism, capitalism, socialism, communism, mercantilism – doesn't matter) have placed "self worth" squarely in the crosshairs of society's fickle field glass: we are described, measured, evaluated and rewarded or shunned through the perspectives of our career. Even if our neighbors were clueless or couldn't care less about our vocational calling, the programming is so pervasive, we carry it around with us anyway. It is the narcissist's pacifier and libertine's jailer. Only seldom, it seems, do we peek out from beneath that wet, heavy blanket to catch a glimpse of our true chariot: the one of unbridled passion.

Oh, but that programming demands to be heard and employs many messengers, such as midlife crises, passive daydreaming, and phantasmagoric nightmares. And then there are those loose tongues that unwittingly leak out "woulda / shoulda / couldas" to our family, neighbors and confidantes.

* * * * * *

The concept of *dharma* is an old one. It may be a funny-sounding word, rhyming with that other overplayed New Age tome, "karma," – but it is an extremely simple idea…aye, there's the rub. For is it not sometimes life's simplicities that are most difficult to embrace?

Dharma, which means "statute" in Sanskrit, refers to the principle or law that rules the universe. Buddhism interpreted this to mean knowledge of or duty to undertake conduct set forth by the Buddha as a way to enlightenment. Today, we use it in reference to the practice or state of mind and being that allows us to cultivate inner strength and peace in a calamitous, cacophonous world. By recognizing that our perceptions are amplified by the inner turbulence of our fears, clearly a calmed mind through disciplined practice not only alters our perception but also allows for the possibility of *creating more peaceful physical manifestations*. Individually, this may result in passionate dedication to making the world a better place and harnessing our talents and abilities to a vocation or profession that reflects this goal. Among the rewards are the by-products of greater communication among all people on the planet, reduced tensions and enhanced relations with our cultural and worldwide neighbors.

Embracing *dharma* doesn't require an admonishment of material wealth, but it does stress a supreme responsibility. Without inner peace, *outer peace is impossible – for outer peace is simply the manifestation of our individual and collective minds*. Inner peace is achievable, even without material acquisition – as we have been told for centuries by many "masters" both within and outside of, established institutions. Regardless of wealth or status, outer peace will come naturally *if we train our mind* – accepting that we are at least co-authors of our own Passion Plays, and that we tend to cling to habits and belief systems, including stale or repressive dogmas, because they are familiar and often the unknown is too frightening to confront. Or perhaps because we just don't know of a better replacement.

When we start to remember who we are and why we are here, we begin to connect our inner world with the outer one, and life starts to be experienced from a wholly different perspective.

* * * * * *

A year later, gainfully unemployed and $5,000 poorer from the enrichment of counseling, I think I'm a step closer to solving the work / vocation / career / *dharma* conundrum…or at least, making peace with it. Sort of. Well, maybe.

I've always found Jack Kerouac and his buddy Neil Cassidy to be entertaining characters, and I respect that the social straightjacket of the 1950s required special navigational tools for independent thinkers. But I'm just a little too far removed from the *On the Road* or "Dharma Bum" epistemology. Besides, I've been there & done that. It was fun in a pretentious, sophomoric kind of way that relieves the "doer" from ever having to confront those demons in the bathroom mirror. But hitchhiking, sleeping in fields, pickling my liver and pursuing the perfect jazz note aren't really my idea of self-actualization.

Emerson had a feel for it, pontificating about self-reliance, compensation, intellect, et al. But his transcendental aphorisms never quite wrestled this enigma to the ground – there was just a little too much ivy on that tower (never trust a man whose hands aren't dirty). Ditto Kahlil Gibran and his metaphor-soup about the virtues of labor – great writer, lousy career counselor. Even the Buddha's "Right Livelihood," a great code for living, doesn't grind the occupational grist, either. I can see my résumé: "Carried water, chopped wood, contemplated belly button."

Oscar Wilde gets the most points for honesty, with his poignant observation that "work is the curse of the drinking class." Maybe that was palpable from the perspective of 19th Century smokestack drudgery, but it is insufficient these days to the modern *dharma* seeker with a bundle of options and freedoms that were sorely missing in Oscar's gilded age. In fact, the "analysis paralysis" of indecision (too many choices!) can be its own special kind of hell. Surely not a hell that would be recognized or respected by, say, a starving beggar in Calcutta or a landmine-amputee in Cambodia, but one nonetheless that haunts and torments the restless children of First World affluence.

I believe The Turk in Voltaire's *Candide* came closest to capturing the essence of *dharma*, commenting that we must "cultivate our own garden" to fend off boredom, vice, and poverty. I'm intimately familiar with the first one, danced around a little with the second, and have no desire to sleep with the third. But one man's garden is another man's weed patch – so, what to do?

I surmise that we're left to make the most of things, like an on-going game of five-card stud poker. Here's what yer dealt kid – now read your own bones, sort your own tea leaves, and shuffle your own "Death" (*change*) card. In 43 years I've traveled five continents spanning upward of 30 countries. I've wandered the ivory-towered parapets and Elysian fiefdoms of higher learning, and severed myself away from a handful of employers, including my own entrepreneurial *L'enfant Terrible*. Yet, I've had the satisfaction of creating dozens, actually several hundred, jobs for people, selling innovative business solutions to some fairly progressive companies, and bringing quality food products into a culture predisposed to devouring processed swill. Throughout the long journey, I've managed to entertain friends, outrage enemies and collect a dandy set of photographs. A good measure of success by anyone's standards!

Still, I've had a tendency to see myself as a malcontent, fidgeting at the "three-sigma" deviation point (on the fringes) on the statistician's behavioral curve. Friends and colleagues see the engineering degree propped up with an MBA and corporate pedigree as the Standard & Poor's 500 seal-of-approval, while considering my sabbaticals and wanderings as the exceptional diversion. *Funny, I always looked at it the other way around.* But money and fear are powerful motivators – or should I say, inhibitors?

An extended travel may once more be in order. Maybe Africa – now there's a big hunk of real estate. Far pavilions, cheap beer, different 'tudes. America can suck you into her voluptuous arms, smother you in her cushy largesse and pump your head with mush from her frothing, frenzied media. She can also insulate you from the ugly side effects of "Americanism," the great juggernaut on steroids: *Consume. Entertain. Preach. Ignore.* Like a Dickens epitaph, we're the best of countries and the worst of countries. There's no place I'd rather hang my permanent shingle, no graces I'd rather succor…and no place more comfortable to return to. But confining oneself to her borders is like looking through a kaleidoscope with one eye closed or attending a symphony with an ear full of wax. Many of our "self-evident truths" aren't necessarily seen that way by huge chunks of humankind (not that *they're* right either...!). Many of our practices are held in even less esteem.

The times of Kipling, London, Burton, and Hemingway may indeed have changed. No lands are truly un-traipsed and not many people(s) are deeply mysterious anymore – on the "outside," at least. Certainly the world's neuroses are ever more amplified through the spider web of the Internet, CNN and the World Trade Organization: bringing us together – tearing us apart. Still, the landscapes haven't changed that much, cultures don't turn on a dime, and, as Mark Twain reputedly said, "Travel is the bane of all prejudice." And...I have itchy feet and no anchors weighing me down (caveat: my wonderful wife Alexis says she wants to go, too). I'm not exactly sure what I'll do "out there," or back here. Perhaps I'll teach English, write a little, or offer some S&M advice (uh, that's "Sales and Marketing") to fledgling companies.

Quite honestly, it both exhilarates me and scares the hell out of me. Is this really happening to me? *Am I dreaming?* This is the first time in my adult life that I don't know what vocation to pursue next. There's still that tug backward, into the safe, the known – and the deadly. The manacles of identity don't relinquish their grips that easily, because they'd rather rule in hell than serve in heaven. It's one thing to say "You wanna do *what?*" It's another to consider "Just what in the hell *am* I going to do?"

Maybe *dharma* is just an attitude, and vocation merely an armored vehicle for a roaring engine. Among all the uncertainties, one thing is surely certain: it'll all work out OK; it always does. Now if I could only figure out what I want to do when I grow up...

Chapter Twenty-One

Because It Was There

ZINNNNGGGGG…Here comes – and there goes – another one. Like enraged granite bees, these peripatetic missiles approach with little fanfare: first, a low-humming drone, and then, a rising, almost-metallic "twang" as the airwaves compress in a spasmodic Doppler-jam. No sooner do they flicker an image in the back of the brain than they're gone, heeding the same insatiable siren call to gravity as that famous apple that clocked the noggin of Sir Isaac Newton. But this was no mushy organic goop snapping off some dainty branch in an idyllic orchard – it was another goddamn rock, released from the melting ice a few thousand feet up the culvert. That's a few thousand feet *vertically up*, having covered about five thousand feet in actual landscape.

We were lucky this time, especially Alexis, whose head was spared a physics lesson by a mere three or four feet. The irony is, she never knew it, since she was lurched forward into a precarious toehold, the wind blowing the wrong way. Like a well-placed neutron bomb, these rocks leave no mess. Some are grapefruit-size and could probably perform a nice clean decapitation. Others are like basketballs, indiscriminate enough to take a whole torso with them, and render any cleanup impossible.

So we trudged on a few more feet, our lone ice axe chipping away tenuously in alternating hands; our toes wet, freezing inside of saturated boots; our calf muscles precariously close to cramped rebellion from weight shifted forward against a 55-degree pitch. All the while, the fog above shrouded its game plan cleverly – was it snowing? Sleeting/raining/shining? Somewhere about 3,000 feet above was our destination, the smiling yap of this insolent mountain. We couldn't go back if we wanted. It was too steep, too icy, and we lacked proper gear – a sure pinball ride through a minefield on the way to a gruesome "Tilt."

* * * * * *

It wasn't supposed to be this difficult. Despite the embellished folklore of Hemingway and a pretty cool Swahili moniker, Kilimanjaro is the gentleman of world's summits, a scant 19,320 feet give-or-take a few clicks of satellite error. It probably *would* be easier, too, during dry season, along the well-trodden "Coca Cola" route. But it was rainy season (hadn't we always been lucky?) and we had taken a more "interesting" route.

Truth be known, Kili would be just a mere asterisk in the Olympian lofts of the Himalayas, or just one more anonymous vertebrae of that anorexic millipede named The Andes that stretches from Colombia down into Tierra del Fuego. It is, however, the world's tallest freestanding mountain, edging out Turkey's Ararat and a few other challengers. Kili even rivals Alaska's Denali (McKinley) for sheer gain from the bottom. It also has the tourist draw of the nearby Serengeti Plain, that giant fenceless Disney Park where the animals don't smile. So a Kili-tour fits nicely into a three-week vacation – some mild exertion followed by a photo shot of big game; and if you've planned well, a side jaunt down to Zanzibar on the coast, to rest weary bones in the soothing waters of the warm Indian Ocean.

But our circumstances were different. Fitting Kili into the greater three-month itinerary of our Nairobi-to-Cape Town circuit required some seasonal planning, and this November – the "little" rainy season (the bigger one comes in March) – was the only time that would work. Even then, we were assured, that usually means the rains stop at about 13,000 feet, you break through the cloud layer, and – *voila!* – smooth trudging to the top. "Usually," however, doesn't always mean "always," as we were about to find out.

We also chose the hardest route – the Western Breach – as our taskmaster. Not because we were masochists (fools might be a better word) but for what seemed like some compelling textbook reasons: it was the prettiest route, it afforded the most time to acclimatize with several strategic days bouncing between 12-14,000 feet; and, it was the least-trodden path. The aforementioned Coca-Cola route, named for concessionaires who once staked their goods at the trailhead, or traditional trail, was a hiker's highway – wide and boring, with makeshift shelters housing a herd of beer swilling, twenty-something Germans and Aussies. Hemingway would've scoffed (booze notwithstanding). Surely Gregory Peck and Maureen O'Hara wouldn't have been immortalized in such circumstances. So we eschewed safety and boredom for the route less traveled.

Our first clue that something might be amiss was our U.S. booking agent saying something like, "I can schedule you to start on whatever day you want, and I can almost assure you that you'll see very few others on that route."

The trip started harmlessly enough. The first stop was Nairobi, that ancient crossroads converted into a center of British mercantilism. There's nothing romantic or exotic about Nairobi – it lacks Cairo's steeped history, Marrakech's casbahs, or Cape Town's geographical assets. It looks like some bureaucrat threw together a bunch of streets and buildings and of the resulting maze retorted, "You figure it out." Nairobi was chaotic but benign by day, chaotic and sinister by night. I guess it doesn't help being the lone white faces in crowded plazas that are unlit and swarming with pickpockets, scam-mongering orphans and unemployed malcontents. The three of us stood out like icing in an Oreo factory – Alexis' blonde hair, my collage of boring European browns and the Asian gene pool of our friend Conrad, along for the stroll from San Francisco. His features didn't hide him any better than us. We were a long way from Ellis Island or the Golden Gate.

The atmosphere was also charged by the general Kenyan election which promised to replace the corrupt Moi administration with a bevy of slogan-spouting, populist, soon-to-be-corrupted successor/candidates. The battle lines were drawn and the ideologies parried, but other than a handful of fatalities and mayhem, the whole thing played out okay. Democracy, African style.

Our most interesting encounter was a distinguished gentleman who bought us tea and inquired if we would be so kind as to "sponsor" the border crossing of an exemplary colleague, who had done something – quite innocently, of course – to piss off the authorities. We respectfully demurred. Sad to say, but the most interesting building in Nairobi is one that *isn't* – the hole in the ground, now a converted park, where the U.S. Embassy once stood before some deranged Son-of-Allah blew it to Kingdom Come in 1998.

* * * * * *

A four-hour bus ride took us across the border into Arusha, Tanzania. It was a smooth crossing except for the unfortunate Nigerians who were refused entry without proper papers. It seems like the citizens of West African countries, with the exception perhaps of Ghana, are pariahs of "proper" Africans everywhere.

"They're all addicts, guerillas, or drug dealers," said a sari-wrapped Tanzanian woman of obvious pedigree, in much the same way a 19th century Boston blueblood matriarch would've collectively dissed the entire Irish and Italian cultures because of the turbulent cauldron stewing in their immigrant shantytowns. "Bad people all; mustn't trust…"

The village of Arusha is a deceivingly industrious city of several hundred thousand people located at the outskirts of Kilimanjaro. Kili is not a mere mountain, but a grouping of three peaks, of which Uhuru is the tallest, with a giant massif of girth covering hundreds of square miles. The preternatural, irregular thrusting of its footprint upon the Tanzanian plain combined with the country's poor roads, required the better part of a day to circumnavigate by Jeep. So much rain falls on the mountain, especially the first 6,000 feet of sylvan jungle, that huge swaths of the country have come to depend on it for irrigation, with streams and rivers fanning out for hundreds of miles like spokes from a dark green hub. Until recently, climatologists and U.N. agricultural experts were mortified that Kili's melting glaciers, an Ice Age legacy, would leave the country bereft of water in a few decades and lead to mass starvation, displacement and general unrest. There is now a revisionist twist on this, however, as further research points to the steady rains at lower elevations – not the shimmering cornices above – serving as the fountains of life for man and beast alike. But the jury is still out.

Arusha, nestled in the moist rain curtain of Kili's shadow, gives the impression of being at the foot of the mountain, but in fact is still a good 30-40 miles away. We arrived on market day, Saturday, where every color under the rainbow leaps from clothing, food and sundry. It's lively – a cacophony of haggling, blaring horns and tooth-flashing "Jambo's" to us *Mzungus* (whiteys with money). We stayed at a comfortable lodge away from the bustle, at the edge of town. The lodge, we were told, was the site of an old coffee plantation. Here we enjoyed a last shower, a buffet, bar, European sensibilities and smiling waiters. We rested and dreamed forward to a looming trailhead leading to a hidden summit, just a vulture's flight away.

The ride to the trailhead was interesting in its own right: slowly climbing, asphalt yielding to dirt, then mud; tiny roadside villages hugging this solitary artery, and eucalyptus and giant palms jutting ever higher. Everywhere children waved emphatically as we snaked through the small thatched villages that lined the road like sluice gates. I'm not sure why the kids are so entertained – surely they've witnessed this a gazillion times? Maybe they're hoping for some goodies jettisoned out the window – or maybe it's really their true disposition in full view to a jaded Westerner.

As the climb ascends to 5,900 feet, the road curves even more; precipitous drops hug the roadsides with deep V-shaped ravines separating them from parallel ridges with more thatch huts. If this were West Virginia, the bottom of these saw-shaped hills would be plumb-tucked full of old Chevvies, rusted-out washing machines and an occasional still. These guys had their own refuse, I suppose, but I couldn't quite make out the discarded stashes of Pepsi and Bavarian Ale bottles that presumably littered the bottom.

At the trailhead we met our entourage consisting of our guide Daniel, his loyal assistant Peter and a host of a dozen porters to support the three of us. For nine days of trekking, this ratio isn't unusual, considering food, tents, pressurized stoves and fuel, and gear – ours and theirs. They were mainly veteran climbers from Arusha and Moshi, which basically means they worked when a party showed up, trundling out of their villages in tennis shoes and (somebody else's) discarded army jackets. Daniel, in his late twenties but looking ten years older, had a wiry build and firm jaw. His piercing gaze belied an easy-going countenance not to be confused with nonchalance. Peter, on the other hand, could have been the poster child for *The Lion King's* "Hakuna Matata" – "What, me worry?" – the Chaggan tribe's version of Alfred E. Newman. He could have passed for NBA star Karl Malone's identical twin, possessing a giant grin and a surprisingly soft, lilting voice. Daniel had climbed Kili maybe 20 times; Peter, about a dozen. Hakuna Matata.

The first few days took us to 12,500 feet, as we witnessed the jungle transforming into the high green Veld. Long behind us now were the shrouded purple jacarandas and graceful palms of the valley. The taller dense trees of the jungle took over: camphor, myrtle, eucalyptus and balsam competed with a tangled network of vines, ferns, mushrooms and orchids. These in turn had to fight for survival with the ever-present "Old Man's Beard" – a shaggy moss that hangs like a mosquito net over the forest. Somewhere in the shadows colobus monkeys and baboons raised vocal hell, but we never saw them. The occasional view out through the canopy only revealed layers of undulating green ridges disappearing into the tropical haze. Amazing…you'd never know that a glacier lurked only 15 miles away as the buzzard floats.

At about 9,000 feet, the sylvan canopy yielded to heather grass, some so tall, in comparison it seemed like we'd been shrunk to the size of a rodent in one of those really bad Japanese Sci-fi movies. It's not unusual to see heather exceeding *40 feet* in height. Above 11,000 feet, moving well into the Moorish expanse of mid-mountain, one is then treated to the bizarre senecio trees – weird, spindly spikes resembling cigars with asparagus jutting out the top like porcupine quills.

We'd been forewarned about frequent rain along this stretch, but it wasn't until the jungle yielded first to a pine-laden belt, then to a band of high sturdy grasses at about 10,000 feet, that the clouds appeared. First was the telltale *plink-plink* on a hat, an arm, a nose. Then the accelerated *plink-plink-plink-plink*, followed by a whole chorus of *plinks* ever louder, harder, and wetter; and now, because of elevation

– cooler. But all in all, things were temperate at this elevation, and the ubiquitous senecios lent a surreal, fairytale aura to the landscape. By the end of the second day, at Shira Camp, the rain and mud were pretty much established. Other than a fleeting glimpse of Uhuru Summit mocking us from on high, we ate, slept and roused about in shrouded fog. All the while it rained, occasionally stopping to reload and then dump again. Our Ascente tents with their protruded vestibules did an admirable job of keeping the sludge out of the insides, but only for a while.

The chief entertainment at this camp was watching the gargantuan ring-necked ravens swoop over us like forlorn drone planes (or more accurately, winged garbage scows) landing to forage, and then lifting off with a giant rush of air and monotonous thudding of black wings. These are huge birds twice the size of their North American cousins, a handsome blend of white, black and brown. They didn't really cause any problems, but I reckon if they ended up in the middle of a dispute, woe-would-be unto their antagonist. As we climbed, we would see them for thousands of feet of elevation yet to come until finally, unlike their foolhardy visitors, they refused to tread or flap any higher.

* * * * * *

Days Three and Four roller coasted us between 13,000 – 14,000 feet, solidifying our metabolisms by first exerting our lungs and circulatory systems, then, backing off in subtle massaging infusions of oxygen. We were to stay two nights at the Barranco Camp, a peninsula-like outpost jutting from the side of the mountain. Cascading streams dissected the mountain in a macabre network of varicose veins, converging together at key junctions and leaping in tremendous waterfalls down through chasms, meandering for a while, then disappearing as far as the eye could see out the flank of the mountain, destined for some pineapple plantation and a far-away rendezvous with the Indian Ocean.

Other than the senecio trees poking out like so many toothpicks of saguaro cacti on an Arizona hillside, this was barren volcanic tundra. We were definitely zeroing in though, feeling the inexorable pull "up"; a sense of Kili's energy concentrating its focus just below that next fortress of rock…the one that extended thousands of feet up into the fog. By now, the *plink-plink-plinks* had coalesced into a steady patter, the patter frequently punctuated by torrents, gusts, and the brittle biting sound of sleet. Wasn't this about where we should have pierced through the mountain's foreboding underbelly into exalted blue skies? Well, "usually" – usually, the bane of speculative investors and old pilots, the mantra of optimists. We were, after all, in "Little Rainy Season." And we had just seen a leopard.

＊ ＊ ＊ ＊ ＊ ＊

The spotted leopard, a loner and wanderer, is the most mysterious of Africa's big cats. They're not prone to ham it up for tourists at the big game parks; in fact, rarely do people see them – especially above 9,000 feet. Yet here was this bad boy skulking around 13,500 feet, about a hundred yards from our tents, pre-occupied with something he was stalking. Something non-human, we hoped.

If God protects fools and drunks, she was working overtime that afternoon. Alexis and I wandered closer, debating his pedigree.

"It's a cheetah," said I – hadn't I watched Mutual of Omaha's *Wild Kingdom* enough times to qualify as an amateur zoologist?

"No, I think it's a leopard," said she, and pulled out some obscure African critter guide to distinguish its anatomy.

How cute, and prancing after little field mice or whatever quarry. We even told Peter, who just smiled and diplomatically said, "You make mistake."

An hour later, a wide-eyed Peter pulled me aside. "Stevie, you right, him is leopard ('Leo-pard'). I saw."

His twinge of excitement couldn't quite conceal a quivering uneasiness. Leopards are generally more aggressive than lions and will take on all-comers at once. They're particularly prone to fearless ambushes from tree limbs, or in this case, rock outcroppings.

How high can a leopard jump? Hint: never patronize a zoo whose leopard-retaining wall is less than 18 feet high. I guess that makes sense if you consider a house cat's vertical *fait acompli* and then multiply that by the proportionate size of a leopard. But how stately, lithe and graceful they are! We didn't see him again, although we kept a steadfast watch, trying to reconcile relief with disappointment. Surely he saw us, but opted that night for the finer delicacy of fresh rodent.

Patter-patter; plink-plink-plink; thud, thud. Rain, sleet, and ice serenaded us in three-part harmony. Most of the afternoon was passed in our tents, buffeted by sleeping bags and copious amounts of tea delivered by nonplussed porters. Boredom and monotony teamed up with apprehension to create second thoughts, which spiraled into the first murmurings of mutiny.

"I'm wet, cold and hate this," proffered a tearful Alexis.

I chimed in fatalistic "what ifs" – projections about hypothermia, death slides and freefalls that could await us. To this were added the prospects of becoming the chief entrée for a leopard smorgasbord. Furthermore, having now endured rain for the last three days, I also interjected a few pissing dollops about my cold wet boots. They never did get completely dry for the remainder of the trip.

Conrad, a marathon runner but cursed by the handicap of living at sea level, was suffering in silence. He never complained, but like a Jesuit at confessional, was prone to flagellate himself in the style of a seasoned masochist. His knees bothered him and he was sick, partly from mechanics and partly from altitude. And we still had a long way to go.

It was inevitable that someone would lob out the eventual heresy: "What if we just bagged this? We didn't pay to suffer, we're obviously having uncooperative weather, and our boots are now soaked and caked by ice and mud."

"Yeah," someone else chimed in, "there's no shame in not seeing this through; why, hell, our intuition's yelling at us. Ya know, discretion's the better part of valor, and all…"

I, for one, have never been so metaphysically blessed to be able to discern the murmurings of intuition from the insidious hissings of fear. Given a fair shake, I inevitably side with stupidity over wisdom every time. Somehow, out of the awkward void where mutinies bubble forth and resolve clamps down, came a timid half-ass compromise to proceed "one day at a time" – knowing full well that at some point it would be logistically (food) and physically (terrain) impossible to turn around. But it steeled our honor, with the same brash hubris that conspiratorial con games have won the day since times immemorial. "Group Think," "Pride cometh before the Fall," et al. We were steeled – at least for one more day.

In retrospect, I can now understand that the challenge we were presenting for ourselves and from which we refused to back down was another opportunity for a metaphor: the steep upward climb, seeking the greatest obstacles imaginable…knowing what we were getting into (ah, but did we really?)…and now at the apex of decision when common sense would have instructed us to turn back, we *knew* we could not *not continue, until we had reached our goal.*

Whether for the sport of it or for some other reason linked to business, profession, health or wealth, we were proving to ourselves that we were not quitters…that no matter what, we could do it. Never mind what others thought or said or did: if we made up our minds that this was something we needed to accomplish, by gum, that's just the way it had to be. The future had not yet revealed how valuable this quality of perseverance would prove (and *need*) to be.

✳ ✳ ✳ ✳ ✳ ✳

As if to reward our resolve, that evening we were treated to a brilliant sunset. The clouds parted for about a half hour, revealing the glistening peak above us. A mere 6,000 feet more, shucks, less than half our climb differential. The departing sun's rays danced across the face of Kili's fortress, the sky momentarily blue in just the right places, followed by the majestic purple afterglow. How serene and peaceful it was – just like the eye of a hurricane. We stretched our legs and explored the area, mindful of the potentially lethal kitty.

About 200 yards away from our encampment was a hut, so we wandered over to inspect. Kilimanjaro is a national park, and not unlike the national parks of North America or Europe, outposts have been established in strategic places. This shelter was a glorified lean-to, a Spartan box masquerading as a cabin. As we approached from around the backside, we came upon Joseph, itinerant housekeeper, who was a ranger, sort of. He and colleagues spent two-week shifts at designated huts where they ministered to errant hikers, warded off poachers, recorded scribbles of meteorology and biology, shivered next to an insufficient stove, daydreamed and engaged in banter with the outside world.

Noting we were Americans, Joseph was predisposed to banter about G.W. Bush and Saddam Hussein:

"Why your president want bomb Iraq?" asked Joseph, not an ounce of enmity lurking behind his curious eyes.

I muttered something about Texas oil barons, misplaced testosterone and four-year election cycles before inquiring about his lack of a TV, and whether or not he had seen the leopard. No dice, Joseph wouldn't take the bait.

"Is bad to bomb innocent peoples."

"Well, Joseph…it's complicated. Some people are convinced that after 9/11, any dictator who's done the things Saddam has done, treats weapons programs like high school Chem lab, who plays cat-and-mouse with U.N. inspectors, is bound to be holding a few aces. Remember, this is a guy who attacked two of his neighbors, committed genocide on his own citizens and tortures his own Olympic losers."

I was winding up. "Other people see our president as a simple-minded dolt, wrapped in a flag and pounding a bible. Some see him as a programmed mouthpiece for oil and gas cartels. They believe Junior's itching from embarrassment at Osama's escape, and his handlers have him convinced that he's some kind of Churchill making a defiant last stand in the wilderness. They say Saddam was hemmed in by the U.S. and British no-fly zones, that he's been defanged since the last Gulf War, and is now a convenient foil. Even his former war toys – supplied by Reagan and Bush, Sr. back when Iran was the neighborhood bully – are long gone, and gee, that transnational pipeline running across Uzbekistan would sure make his Daddy's buddies happy…and the cleanup in Iraq could be handled by no-bid contractors from a company once run by his Vice-President…but I'm out on a limb, Joseph, these are mere speculations…and like many of my countrymen, I'm strictly non-political…"

"France, Germany, Russia say no help," Joseph chimed in, implying their reasons were sane and their motives honorable.

I reminded him, or perhaps informed him that those countries had been routinely flaunting the sanctions programs for many years, were swilling at the same trough, and lining the coffers of their national or corporate treasuries in a manner much the same as Bush's buddies. Perhaps their opposition had less to do with being good world citizens and more to do with caressing their piggy banks.

"But, alas, Joseph, I concede – that doesn't mean they're necessarily *wrong* in opposing the war – or that Dubya and his buddies are *correct* in pursuing it…"

My mind was aching to explain to Joseph that because we had been attacked on our own soil, the tumultuous aftermath produced a murky line between programs of prudent protection and those calculated for political advantage by misinforming, manipulating, and unnecessarily scaring the Bejesus out of many of us.

But then the absurdity hit me, along with a twinge of shame and embarrassment, about even trying to discuss with Joseph our geo-political conundrum. In a serendipitous moment, as the last rays of twilight pierced the calm of Arusha below, I remembered what was happening at our very feet.

Arusha was hosting the Central African Council on Truth and Reconciliation, to deal with the pesky aftermath of the 1994 "disagreement" between the Hutus and Tutsis. Seems like some seething differences had gotten out of control when local DJs, with a call-to-arms moxie that would have made Rush Limbaugh blush, urged the dominant Hutus of Rwanda and Burundi to address their grievances by taking up machetes, knives, axes, shovels and whatever other household accessories were lying around, and administer a serious lesson to the Tutsi tribes. When the smoke cleared and the blood dried, about 900,000 people had been massacred – roughly 300 times the body count of 9/11. Absent CNN and FOX, absent the BBC, absent the U.N.: the revolution was not televised.

The border of Rwanda and Burundi, maybe 400 miles distant, was a killing field of tribal *angst*. Like the borders between so many other African countries, it was an artificial boundary calculated and shaped by European voyeurism. These "borders" were nothing more than temporary holding pens at best and porous sieves at worst, for fratricidal grudges that faded into antiquity. Blood is indeed thicker than water and heavier than a flag. When hunger and disease – AIDS, tuberculosis, malaria, cholera and polio – pile onto the already prevalent class discrimination, one can expect the worst. Old Testament wrath, whether named Jehovah or Nyaminyami (the Swahili god of raging waters), is alive and well.

Joseph knew and understood far more about this plight than I ever will – God willing.

This wasn't the first time I've had to walk that razor-edge that defines U.S. culture and by default, our policies. We are the most benign of benefactors and the most demanding of donors. We create a Declaration of Independence, a paradigm-rattling manifesto that truly shifted human consciousness (as well as being a helluva piece of sedition), yet we were one of the last nations on earth to abolish slavery. For every Marshall Plan, subsidizing vanquished enemies into merely quarrelsome allies, there's a Vietnam. I'll call your Vietnam and raise you two Roosevelt's.

Like ancient Janus, we stare in two directions. We may have a Peace Corps, but we also arm the world. *Our defense budget is, in fact, larger than all other nations combined* – that's quite the hat trick for less than five percent of the world's population! Never let it be said that Uncle Sam doesn't operate on a grand scale. We are wonderful, benevolent, creative, optimistic and (individually) peaceful; we are also destructive, arrogant, naïve and rapacious. We're schizophrenics in a hall of mirrors – for every Michael Jordan firing the world's fancy, some clod at an Olympics game insults a host nation. Most of us would truly die for the values our country *purportedly espouses* – but many of us see our flagship institutions displaying less of those values every year. I'm privileged and damn lucky to be an American, the recipient of our many liberties and opportunities – but other times I want to crawl under a rock and yell "time out!"

America may yet usher in the next Era of Brotherhood – if we don't break the straw of our environment's back first. Like no previous civilization, we've empowered our citizens through the vote, referendum, initiative and recall; meanwhile, our Two-Headed Political Dinosaur and its suckling whores at the Federal Election

Commission and Federal Communications Commission have created the most restrictive barriers-to-entry (for third parties) of any democratic, industrialized nation. It is the ultimate irony-of-ironies that President (nee *General*) Eisenhower in his 1961 farewell speech so presciently warned about the pending excesses of the Military/Industrial complex. Wasn't it that poster boy of Italian virtue, Benito Mussolini, who said "Fascism is simply when corporations run the government?" God Bless America, but please, God Help America...

We Americans, it seems to me, vacillate between xenophobic isolation and earth-quaking internationalism, depending on whatever or whoever's goring our ox. Africans, on the other hand, are much more concerned with getting clean water from the well, watching their backsides and adding a few more gray-haired people to their villages. We see through the eyes of a nation, calculating policy on a macro scale, while they see through the eyes of a clan or a tribe (*never* a nation), trying to figure out daily survival and occasionally whomping a neighbor. But if a mercurial angst defines a tribe's good-neighbor policy, no such quicksilver scars them individually. Over ninety-nine percent are humble but open, quick to smile and laugh, and curious but polite. They love freely and suffer bitterly. It's the other fraction of a percent you have to worry about – those with the RPG's and stinger missiles; cunning usurpers like Robert Mugabe down in Zimbabwe or Charles Taylor running amok in Liberia and the Ivory Coast (*Cote d'Ivoire*). When anarchy is always just a step away, a strong minority can cause great damage.

I thanked Joseph for his hospitality and wished him well. Tomorrow would be the end of his two-week stint at this lonely outpost, and he would head on down for a shower and a stipend, then a round of Tusker brews before being redeployed to some other lonely outpost where he could contemplate his good fortune. He was educated, employed and healthy – a rare trifecta for African citizens. At that time, neither one of us could have possibly guessed that one week hence, the Kenyan port town of Mombassa would be decimated by a terrorist's bomb; the mangled corpses and grieving survivors graphically splashed across the front page of Kenya's national newspapers.

* * * * * *

A starlit night buoyed our spirits, but morning once again brought fog and the portents of gloom. Destination camp: the Lava Tower, 3-4 miles that-a-way, an eerie 700 foot outcropping of volcanic vomit that girded the path like Mordor's Bar-a-dur Tower in Tolkien's *The Lord of the Rings*. The so-called trail didn't suffer the pilgrim to tread casually. There may not have been any nasty Orcs lurking about, but one sure wouldn't want to piss off its guardians. It lurked at 15,000 feet, where vegetation receded and ice-tinged trails yielded to total snow. The views *should* have been stupendous as we wove like a lethargic serpent up the spine of the ridge. We moved slower – one, two, breathe; one, two, breathe – the brain sending nasty-grams to the lungs that it was being cheated of precious oxygen and wasn't going to cooperate as seamlessly with muscles and limbs anymore.

It was crucial to slow down in spite of what adrenalin and ambition dictated. In fact, the mental discipline to adjust speed was most challenging for Alexis and me, as we were used to routinely going up to 12-13,000 feet. Our natural inclination was to keep pushing, supposedly immune to the laws of diminishing returns, that sneaky degradation of ATP (adenosine triphosphate) and blood sugar; and naturally, willpower. But at this higher elevation, the routine 2-3 foot step up a rock outcropping, or quick thrust through a sharp crack would be followed by a three-second delay and then an inevitable metabolic backlash. Muscles didn't spring; they *strettcchhheddddd*; lungs didn't draw; they "gulped!" and "gasped!" It's like one of those dreams where the Blue Meanies are chasing you and you respond by desperately trudging through molasses at the breakneck speed of one mile per hour, or half a mile per hour on the vertical stretches. One, two, breathe; one, two, breathe. Hakuna Matata.

Thankfully, we had a secret weapon: Diamox. Along with duct tape, Velcro and the Electric Blues, Diamox has to be considered one of the great inventions of the 20th Century. It inhibits the consumption of oxygen, calms the heart, and generally boosts your performance by a few miles per gallon at high altitudes. Diamox is the mountaineer's Viagra, the drunk's nightcap and Methuselah's secret youth tonic compacted into one tiny little pill. What the ribbed condom is to sexual gratification, Diamox is to the tentative climber. The trademark high altitude migraine becomes just another numbing headache. No more waking in the middle of the night, gasping and wheezing, not sure if it's a residual nightmare or just a heavy blanket wrapped around your head. Diamox is, in fact, a wonder drug. Surely, Sir Edmund Hillary and his Nepali guide Tenzing Norgay had no need for it back in 1953 on top of Everest. And most assuredly, Rheinhold Meissner and those freewheeling, oxygen-starved Italian/Austrian climbers of the 1970s would've dissed Diamox as so much lazy man's lung candy (never mind that some of them are now as brain-addled as a punching bag in a prison cell after having suffered too many rare-air cerebral jabs). But to the rising class of today's REI mountaineers, it's manna from heaven. And there's no side effect, really; just a tingling in the finger tips and increased bladder activity resulting from the extra 25% of water required to push it through the bloodstream. Deep sleep and steady rhythmic breathing are well worth zipping one's fly down a few more times per day. Long live the Big D.

* * * * * *

Now all was gray, white and black; an opaque, visceral scenery for visceral emotions. Step, step, step, with slow interspersed breaths separating the steps.

Out of the mist approached the silhouettes of fellow travelers. The party consisted of several porters and a lone *Mzungu* – a Brit.

Me: "Traveling by yourself?"

He: "Well, I am now. My wife had never camped before, and she didn't like the whole tent thing, ya know, especially with the bloody Zambezi River flowin' through it every time it rained, which of course has been continuous. So she went back, silly girl. I'm sluggin' through, though."

Good on 'em. I just hope the couple – if their marriage outlasts this experience – never takes tandem skydiving lessons together. (He: "Arch your back, count to three, and pull the chord." She: "You can't make me.")

There's a version of Murphy's Law that dictates "The one thing you don't bring you will most certainly end up needing." We had parkas, windbreakers, fleece and capilene long-handle undies. We even had umbrellas. But we really could have used a simple poncho: resistant, but not too warm. Instead we improvised with alternating layers of relative discomfort as we trudged toward a black cornice. One, two, stop, breathe; one, two, stop, breathe. For the first time, the trail was purely on rock now – hard rock, crumbling rock, black rock. The steps were no longer smooth and linear, as abrupt mini-ledges required a sudden large step, a lunge forward, and a reach for a handhold to hoist oneself up (no tree branches here). Conrad forced his way through like a tortoise on a mission, adjusting his ski poles marionette-style and cursing under his breath. But all things considered, our slow, gradual gait delivered us unspoiled to our camp at the base of Lava Tower. A menacing black façade of night, it nonetheless provided shelter from one side of the blasting frigid winds. We were basically in a saddle now, with the two ways "down" exposing us to more tantrums of the Weather Gods, and the way opposite Lava Tower, our path to the unknown – up.

Driving horizontal sleet and bursts of tempestuous wind confined us to our tents once more while our industrious porters set up the makeshift dining and kitchen tents, which were also their sleeping quarters. A sporadic sunbeam would occasionally diffuse the valley below, casting off a surreal tapestry of beiges, browns, golds, tans, rusts and greens. But like Tantalus lurching for forbidden fruit, we could never quite grasp hold of the evasive Sun, and soon it ducked cover again for the long, long night.

* * * * * *

Morning, Day 6. Brilliant skies – *huh?* Destination: the Arrow Glacier, at 16,200 feet. Baby steps, alternating with measured cycles of inhaling and exhaling, defined the hypnotic trance that propelled us through the rocky face of boulders and fresh snow. But the path was reasonably safe, and our boots had been somewhat dried in the cook's tent the night before. All were in decent spirits upon arrival at camp, where once again clouds suddenly materialized and it started to snow, blow and reduce visibility to about 20 feet. Once more, our trusty porters preceded us, and tents with warm sleeping bags lay waiting.

Once more we grumbled, napped, sipped tea, and waited. Once more the Sun broke through in a teasing taunt, enough to illuminate the massive cathedral of Arrow Glacier behind us; a beautiful castle-like edifice of glistening ice/snow with protruding rock columns like the bellows of a Herculean pipe organ.

We were truly tired now, Diamox or not. Alexis didn't feel like dinner; I had to drag her into the mess tent. A sure sign of the altitude trickster: just when one should be consuming maximum carbs, your tummy decides to go on holiday. Hunger abates, interest wanes and nothing even smells appetizing.

In fairness to our entourage, the meals were good and wholesome. Cajun TV chef Paul Prudhoe wouldn't feel his culinary manhood challenged, but I'll bet he never hauled his kitchen on his back up a glacier. Breakfasts consisted of an assortment of eggs, toasts, cereals, pancakes, pineapples and mangos. Lunches, taken along the trail, varied from a range of soups, cheeses, dried meats, pineapples and mangos. And for dinner, once more in the sheltered canvas, hunkered over folding tripod chairs, we devoured soups, stews, pastas ("sopa-getti" was Daniel's favorite), rice and yams; and of course, pineapples and mangos. It was delicious, prodigious and reasonably well accented by local and international spices. There were always hot tea, coffee, and tang-like fruit beverages to go around, with ample mixes of biscuits, crackers, dried fruits and "Gorp" concoctions that could have come from any Albertsons or Kroger's back in the States.

In Nairobi we had eaten at a place called Carnivore's, a gastronomical hit-parade of Big Game: Warthog, Impala, Crocodile, Hartebeest, Zebra, Ostrich, Springbok, Gazelle. No such luck here, but there were few complaints except for some grumblings from Alexis, who can torture the most professional servers with a never-ending litany of creative "requests." We usually ended up leaving much of the food on our plates, which I'm sure got surreptitiously gulped down back in the cook's mess tent. *Bon Apetit, mes amis.*

This evening was a solemn melancholy affair in the mess tent. It was, after all, "a dark and stormy night." Our tripod chairs seemed unwieldy, whether from unstable ground or unstable occupants, I wasn't sure. We stared half into space and half into our bowls of mush, only marginally making a dent in the food. Talk seemed precious and sacred, though it consisted mainly of grunts, and had to compete with coughs and sneezes. Outside the wind howled as the canvas flaps of the mess tent whipped like agitated ghosts. Only Daniel and the cook broke the routine, periodically appearing with another plate or kettle. I imagine it could have been like this in the cabin of some old-time mariner ship hacking through choppy seas, or on Lindbergh's solo flight across the gray night skies of the Atlantic (well, sans waiters). We were deep in our own thoughts, cold and only marginally ambulatory; zombies preparing for a long night and nervous suppositions about tomorrow's adventure.

* * * * * *

Morning, Day 7. Brilliant blue sky – again! We were elated; our spirits soared. The sun climbed over Kili's crater and threw its effusions on our camp, warming us with lovely-but-deadly ultraviolet rays. It had snowed most of the night, and our red tents bulged inwardly like concave strawberries. Today was the big push – from 16,200 up to 18,700 feet; destination "The Crater," inside the horseshoe-shaped caldera where Kili had erupted in its prehistoric past.

The first mile or so consisted of serpentine zigzagging up through the gap that separated the glacier. The fresh snow was just temperate enough to re-wet our newly-dried boots, and once more toes rebelled while lungs whined.

At the ridge of the gap, a funnel-shaped culvert stretched nearly two miles up toward the crater's rim. This culvert was probably a half-mile wide at the bottom, narrowing to maybe 100 yards wide at the top. But it was impossible to tell. Funny thing about too much white: your visual acuity becomes the optical analogy of a blathering idiot; things just don't make sense and disorientation is your constant companion. A pile of rubble 50 meters away can be mistaken for an outcropping on a distant ridge; conversely, a mountain across the valley lurks so viscerally in your peripheral vision, you unconsciously reach out your hand as if to deflect passage in a tunnel.

Buttressed by a phalanx of brown, orange and black towers rising several thousand feet on each side, we felt like we were being sucked into the vulva of an archetypal Ice Age Earth Mother. The converging field of white assumed an ethereal, mirage-like glow as it disappeared into the mystical vortex. I'm reminded of astronaut Alan Shepard, who in the early Mercury space program once described the psychologist's white paper when held to his face and queried about impressions, as "two polar bears fucking in a blizzard." People thought Shepard was being a smart-aleck. I believe his prescience just wasn't appreciated.

Anyone who has ever peered through an electron microscope or seen greatly magnified photographic blow-ups, knows that ordinary objects like skin or paper are pocked, scarred and irregular. So it was with our phantasmal culvert, as the irregular geometric realities of nature once again trumped the artist's imagination. Aristotle's ideal of planets as perfect spheres of the heavens was so much mythological horseshit, as those orbs' crater-pocked surfaces and elliptical orbits attest. Our culvert – the Western Breach – wasn't the nice, symmetrical, smooth tongue depressor the mind would conjure – it was a prehistoric battlefield of undulating rock outcroppings and mini-ridges running parallel up the funnel, stopping and starting, broken and jagged, like a ruffled potato chip. These disruptive geological mutants ranged from one foot to ten feet in height and often ran for hundreds of yards. Some were completely covered in snow; others sported protruding nodules like sinister warts. As any skier knows, barring trees and cliffs, the only thing worse than rocks hidden under snow is rocks *and ice* hidden under snow. It seemed like no two steps were the same, and they were all wet and cold. Now we were going slower, not so much from exhaustion – yet – but from a disappearing trail. Daniel and Peter did their best to conceal concern and bewilderment. No worries, we had ice axes and ropes – *didn't we?*

Daniel: "Not suppose to snow this much this time of year. Not this high."

Peter: "Yes, is strange. But Hakuna Matata." Peter would say "Hakuna Matata" if he was standing at Ground Point Zero in Hiroshima.

The vanishing trail left just a few visible reminders of steps dug into the malleable ice. This was just enough to put half a boot into, while the other boot crouched halfway into the previous toehold. Daniel reached inside his rucksack and pulled out an ice axe. The *only* ice axe. He started flailing. Every 10 chops or so, we could take one step forward. Whatever rest was afforded the lungs was countered by the incredible exertion of maintaining posture for 30 seconds to a minute at a time, praying that those weeknights at our 24 Hour Fitness gym had strengthened the calf muscles enough to withstand a controlled, forward-lunging arch at 17,000 feet. Cramps would presage death, either slowly or rapidly...

We maintained this regimen for the next three hours, moving like snails, a handful of specks inching up to where the sea of white engaged the encroaching fog. Coming our way.

Another thing known by skiers is the illusion of the gradient, the slope. This route was a helluva lot steeper than it looked from below. Our angle of ascent and compromised-crouching was even more exaggerated now.

Me: "Daniel – why don't we rope off?"

Daniel, after a sheepish frown: "We don't have rope. Too much weight to carry, usually don't need." (usually, again)

Alexis: "Oh, shit."

The worse thing one can do (other than actually falling) is to look down.

Conrad: "Don't look down."

Telling a Sagittarian not to do something is like asking a rooster not to crow. So naturally, I looked down – half stupefied; three-quarters mortified. It was steep; F'n steep. And slick. A slip here, whether from exhaustion or miscalculation (often linked) would be fatal – eventually: after a minute or two of adrenalin, terror and well-petitioned Hail Mary's. Unlike the aforementioned pinball, the descent would be no straight shot of singular fury, but rather a lot of sliding, cart-wheeling, flopping and bouncing around like a sack of potatoes. Until the bag broke loose, of course. Two hundred yards – a mile, perhaps? I thought of Robert Frost's epic *Fire and Ice*, the human choice of demise. Either way would suck, I concluded.

ZIIIIINNNNNGGGG...a volcanic golf ball passed by, within ten feet. The sun's rays, like the melodies of the Muses, now carried daggers of deceit. The ice above was melting and releasing its prehistoric captives – hard, calloused inmates, jettisoned to the whims of gravity.

A magical survival instinct lurks in some obscure part of the cranium, which, if one's really lucky, lets you know that some line of demarcation has been passed in a crisis. A watershed moment, a critical mass (not necessarily "good"), a whispered *Eureka*: "There's no going back, you have now passed the point of no return." Furthermore, if you're really lucky, this recognition won't instigate outright panic and abandoned reason.

We knew we had entered that phase. Somehow, someway, we kept going, one toehold at a time, no anchor to the world or to each other. But no muscles cramped and no wills froze. Instead, there were flaring tempers.

"Daniel," I suggested, "why don't we just angle over to the far wall – there's a ridge we can go up and over."

Daniel's answer: "No good, Stevie. Wall is higher than you think." Indeed, optical (dis)illusions abounded, like mirages on a white desert. The landscape was real enough, but how far away? How tall? How deep? How *steep*?

Another half an hour or so passed, which was good for a few hundred yards. We were taunted by "zinging" marbles and baseballs, some ironically resembling Aristotle's perfect sphere. But after awhile, one must just stop looking – if one of these projectiles *did* have your name on it, it would be too late anyway…there'd just be a "Kili" tattooed on one side of your skull, and a "Manjaro" on the other. If your skull was still attached to your neck, that is…

* * * * * *

We were now well above 18,000 feet, and countless little specks of dandruff started swirling everywhere. We were ready to be finished with this culvert before it finished us.

Alexis diplomatically offered, "I don't see why in the hell we can't just scoot up that easy little ravine over there, wedge our way out through that gap, and get our asses out of here." (I had married her for her subtlety.)

I chimed in something like, "Yeah, this is a load of crap. We're lost and these guys don't know what they're doing and they're trying to save face, and we're all gonna end up on the sleigh ride from hell. Or into hell." Conrad just grunted, lost in the stoic hinterlands of a pilgrim's private purgatory.

It must be said with respect, that all successful guides have expanded sensory powers. Daniel, through sonar, intuition or sheer luck of the wind's direction, detected the simmering cauldron in our ranks, wheeled on us from a good fifty feet away – and let fly with a rebuke so firm, so rational and so pleading, we could have easily melted from embarrassment.

"Look guys. We here now, we get out alive, OK? That way you mention is bad. Dead end. People easy die. This way is good, is right, and where we go. I don't want responsible for you to die – I don't want *me* to die. We go this way, almost there. Please come."

OK, Danny, you da man.

"Hakuna Matata," added Peter.

Sure enough, about ten minutes later we had wheezed our way through a crack in the fortress, about 100 yards from where the culvert dead-ended at a vertical wall. Sliding through, with a lot of moaning and groaning, we made it up a ridge. A good vantage point illustrated just how futile was the path-not-taken – and how much we would have suffered, had our guides succumbed to the short-fused felicitations of Alexis and me.

But we weren't safe. The ridge was short-lived, and now we could make out through the fleeting gaps in the mist that there were hundreds of vertical yards still ahead, leading somewhere or to something. Only now we were no longer in boulder-strewn minefields, but among twisting chasms of rock, cornices and precipices; volcanic minarets edging up the sky's dark underbelly by leap-frogging over one another. Instead of death by sliding and tumbling, we now courted mortality via the short quick fall followed by a mercifully snapped neck (although, bouncing and thrashing was still a possibility). But more to the point, the climbing was very difficult. Each step required a calculation of the body's ending position. Each upward thrust burned a handful of Gorp; each pounding in the chest sounded like Grateful Dead drummer Mickey Hart (pun coincidental) in overdrive. Whereas the task of chipping away the ice field below had necessitated waiting between steps, now we stopped from sheer exhaustion. Handholds had to be secured, a foot wedged in properly, goggles wiped off in order to see. Then a lunge forward, upward, careful not to go too far. Or to the left, or to the right. Conrad's water bottle scraped a rock and dislodged. Twenty seconds later we could still hear the high-pitched *whack* of frozen plastic on rock, somewhere in the shroud below.

We stopped for a late lunch and flailed ourselves out on an unusually flat, table-sized rock. The sun flirted with the clouds. Rivulets of sweat stayed their flow, froze and crystallized into another layer of salt cake. Ice sculptures and nostril noodles snuggled into cavernous cracks in my week-old stubble and my voice rumbled like Froggy from *The Little Rascals*. We laid out a makeshift table and pondered the sky above, wondering if we were already dead (funny, I thought this place was supposed to be *hot*).

We were ravenous, despite the aforementioned tendency of appetite to wane with greater altitude. We devoured every morsel of grain, candy, meat and a few inanimate things as well. Voices from below – surely devils. We saw the silhouettes of a dozen Quasimodo's, big gray hunchbacks protruding behind them, shuffling alone. They were babbling in an alien tongue – didn't Dante say this is how it would be? No, wait…it was Swahili, and they appeared to be human. They were…our porters.

Thunderstruck, flabbergasted, all we could do was stare. In our *angst* we had forgotten about the porters. Here they were, somehow following in our footsteps with 60-pound packs (some heavier), sporting tennis shoes, scaling ice and rock like wind-up toy soldiers on an afternoon stroll. They resembled an ebony shade of those silly dwarves – Hi Ho, Hi Ho! We Mzungus paid thousands of dollars and came from halfway across the world to sweat and curse our way up Kili, carrying nothing more than a camera, a water bottle and a rosary, whereas these homeys had strapped on everything including the kitchen sink, and lumbered up and down this ancient volcano for a mere three dollars a day, pre-tax. Can't say I know whose M.O. is the wackiest, but I do get a glimpse of how revolutions arise.

"Whew, I'm glad you guys made it," exclaimed Alexis, her nurturing instincts always looking out for the huddled masses, the downtrodden, the tired, cold and hungry.

"Whew, I'm glad you guys made it, too," I added, realizing what a drag it would have been to spend a night in a crater with no food or shelter. I am as practical as Alex is compassionate. Conrad grunted an unintelligible soliloquy.

"Hakuna Matata," replied the visages, and disappeared into the mist above.

Getting back up after lunch could only be compared to Rip Van Winkle waking to a pure-grain hangover. Force of habit more than willpower got us going again. Well, gilded self-interest, too – our stuff was all ahead of us now. Like Oz's Tin Man after a few squirts from the oilcan, we gradually limbered and now somewhat refueled, exerted ourselves once more. Up again, through narrow shoots. *One, two, heave.* Grab here, insert foot there, wiggle and hoist, moan and groan. Pause, and wait for the metabolic backlash. Then repeat process…

We had yet to experience the most formidable challenge – snow, ice and unpredictable footing highlighted a 10-foot stretch reaching up at a 50-55-degree gradient at least, listing precariously toward a one-way ticket to the belly of the whale: total exposure, nothing to grab. Not what our Tanzanian Michelin guide had described. Not what Daniel and Peter had hoped for…and sure as hell not what we three paying customers expected. How we made it through still mystifies me. That little voice that says "you have no other choice" must have shot liquid amphetamines through every cell, neuron, lung cilia and muscle in our bodies. Conrad in particular has a history of mild agoraphobia and had been known to freeze up and turn around. "Not this time," his inner taskmaster said, and somehow he bridged the deadly impasse.

We collapsed on the other side in a drum roll of heartbeats and swamps of shimmering sweat.

Another assault, less perilous but equally draining, put us up over a cornice. Then we saw it: we had accessed the open rim of the horseshoe – we were above the crater, opposite the peak. It couldn't be real, but here it was. Euphoria and relief nearly overcame us; we reveled in this most beautiful of Ice Age panoramas. A stark barren tundra of volcanic dust, dirt, and rock sloped several hundred yards away to a blue massif of ice, the latter a 9,000 year-old legacy from a more frigid era. Nothing grew up here – not even lichen could tolerate the twin killers of cold and alkalinity. It was so desolate, we could have been in the Sea of Tranquility on the lunar surface. Or Antarctica.

On the other side of the horseshoe, lurking behind a fine curtain of vapory white silk, lay our quarry – the summit, Uhuru, now a mere 620 feet above us. But it could wait until morning. Tea and biscuits beckoned down in the crater, where the red shells of our nylon igloos were already popping up. A campsite never looked so good.

* * * * * *

As if to reward our stamina – or perhaps because they were depleted – the local gods kept the clouds away for the remainder of the evening and night, except for the final shroud on Kili's peak. We stumbled into camp like drunken sailors, tuckered to the bone and grateful to whatever Juju looked over us. Peter sauntered around camp in sweat pants and flip-flops. Why not? It had to be at least 15° Fahrenheit.

Me: "Aren't you cold?"

Peter: "No. My feet like animal hide, I no feel weather."

Me: "Are you insane?"

Peter, with his biggest canary-eating, Cheshire cat grin, just shrugged. "Hakuna Matata."

The night was colder still, of course – somewhere between 0 and minus 10 Fahrenheit. Not bad for just off the Equator. The crater was a perfect sinkhole for frigid thermals to settle in and harass trespassers.

But the greatest harassment came from one's own bladder. It's a cruel joke of nature that the higher in elevation one climbs, the more water is required to ward off dehydration. Thus, the more one needs a polar sleeping bag to stave off ever-increasing cold and exhaustion, the more one finds oneself driven by nature to night-time forays out of the tent into Arctic conditions – blacker than the devil's iris; colder than a mortician's handshake. That night in the crater witnessed no fewer than four such maneuvers on my part, and at least that many by Alexis. But we were getting good at this, and having long ago eschewed any pretense of modesty or dignity, we mastered the "Power Pee" in impressive fashion. Zip – two-three-four, right in front of the vestibule. Never mind the yellow snow; there was plenty of fresh camouflage to cover it up…You got used to seeing little snowdrifts piled up in front of each tent in the mornings, most peculiar when there were no winds in the night.

Putting boots on wasn't an option, anyway – most nights they were drying in the kitchen shelter. So the trick was to jump out of the bag, slip on the back-up tennis shoes (think: plastic ice cubes), unzip the tent and one's own wardrobe, in that order, conduct one's mission and back-tail as rapidly as possible. At least the bags were warm, aided by the trick of a warm water bottle inserted at the feet each night at bedtime. But I swear if I ever do one of these high-altitude death marches again, I'm going to invest in one of those NASA bladder bags or those cute little wee-wee tubes sported by REI and other comfort-minded retailers. "Better pissed off than pissed on," sayeth the prophet.

Better neither one, sayeth I.

Morning light revealed a splendor. On the eastern escarpment rose the equatorial sun, splashing across the bowl of our concave refrigerator. On the western horizon, disappearing over the open end of the horseshoe ridge we had trudged up the day before, was the moon, only one day post-wax. Two wonderful spheres, one for day and good possibilities; one for night and dark secrets. Yin & Yang balanced across our glowing crater like an ethereal celestial pendulum. Across from our tent opening, about 500 feet across the rubble field, was the wall of opaque blue ice, reaching 40-50 feet in height and extending for miles. Massive, and beautifully quiet. It sure didn't give the impression it was shrinking, but in geological time it was in its final death throes.

The air was perfectly still, with our frosty breath just hanging around with no place to go. All was silent – no whooshing wings of ravens, zinging of aeronautical rocks, clanking pots of porters, nylon zippers; no gusts of wind scraping their ghoulish fingernails across our camp. Behind us stood Uhuru in regal stoicism, beckoning: "Bring it on, my friends – what are you waiting for?"

Well, breakfast for one thing. There was a small hitch. Most of the porters, including the cook, were snow-blind.

It seems like a number of them lacked sunglasses on yesterday's frontal assault. Considering the six or seven-hour window of blazing sun, the pitch of the gradient, rare atmosphere loaded with ultraviolet nasties and a surface whiter than Snow White's tush, it wasn't surprising. I've never been snow-blind, which thankfully is usually temporary, but an unfortunate ski buddy of mine in Utah once remarked: "Imagine taking a vial of water from the Great Salt Lake, adding a dollop of Tabasco sauce and a shot of tequila, mixing, then administering a drop per minute into each cornea for some hours, or until you either pass out or die first." Every sliver of light, particularly sunlight, is like someone holding a cigarette lighter to your eyeball.

Our merry dwarves were miserable, and Daniel and Peter were in a pickle. Last night's dishes were still dirty in the mess tent, and the cook's tent – the sleeping quarters of the entourage – was silent. Daniel went into overdrive, excusing himself and disappearing at double speed. Like a parent straddling the fence that separates diplomacy from wrath, or a frustrated football coach at halftime, he cajoled, pleaded, warned, cheered and accursed his charges.

Peter, at a loss for the trademark "Hakuna Matata," flashed a Chaggan "Uh-Oh" deep in his brown eyes.

For the second time in two days, we witnessed real emotions from Daniel. "Guys, I apologize. This is very bad. Please I ask you favor. If company discovers, I lose job. I suppose to check porter's gear (he didn't mention his own ropes and extra ice axes). I thought they had glasses. Please be kind and do not mention in your survey – I have family, baby."

We acquiesced, harboring some guilt about not deterring future would-be patrons with incendiary feedback. But our reasons were more self-serving: we wanted to kiss Uhuru's nipple. Besides, we surmised it was unlikely Daniel would forget the protocol again any time soon…

Slowly the porters rose, some slower than others. Out of the ominous number of 13, only three were unscathed; the other ten were in different stages of torture. They moaned, groaned, stumbled and somehow got up. What they lacked in common sense or couldn't afford – sunglasses – they compensated for with courage. Miraculously, we were fed and summit-bound only slightly behind schedule. Double lucky, our invalids were not summiting *with* us, but swinging around the flank of the mountain – no climbing – and would catch up with us as we came down the other side, after 180 degrees of circumnavigation.

It would be incorrect to say the stroll to the top was anticlimactic after yesterday's flirtation with premature mortality. A subdued but anticipatory excitement carried us almost effortlessly, as we tread the final 620 feet of vertical up to the ridge line: the curving slope of the summit. Hanging a left, we proceeded in silent reverie toward the Grail. We weren't even breathing hard. No muscles tensed, no swearing. Everyone was in their own space of distance, time, feeling and thought. I thanked whatever patron saints delivered us from the throes of yesterday and whatever guardian spirits sped us to our destination on a clear blue morning, to peer out at Earth's sloping curve ("There be dragons…") from Africa's highest summit, the world's tallest free-standing mountain, Uhuru Summit, 5,895 meters (19,320 feet): just like the sign said.

We all had harbored doubts, even before the pesky monsoons and previous day's gauntlet. Alexis had been above the Base Camp of Mt. Everest, at Kalapathar, rivaling Kili in height and requiring several weeks of coughing and headaches. I had likewise sojourned in the Himalayas and the Andes, and had been victimized by nasty intestinal usurpers that would've left me too weak for this altitude, Diamox or not. Conrad, who ran more miles in a week than I did in a month and possessing the calf muscles of a Sumo wrestler, was handicapped by a sea-level residence. We weren't novices. It would have been easy, prudent, rational – *hell, even highly recommendable* – to have high-tailed it out of there before we had crossed No-man's land into the Culvert from Hell. But here we were, for better or worse, in sickness and in health, triumphant at last and whirling in our private thoughts.

We were the only ones there, and would be for the next 30 minutes until a Dutch party arrived from the opposite direction – the easy way, the smart way, our way down.

It's a rare treat to have anything but a fleeting view from the top; it's even rarer to have it all to yourself. We were blessed, fortunate, and grateful. Shutters clicked as we buddied up in two's and three's by the sign while Peter and Daniel did the honors. Then, the first vapors of morning started their circle dance around the summit.

* * * * * *

From this vantage point, it would be easy to imagine that the vistas below were peeks into the polyglot of Africa. Up to the north, past the electoral chaos of Kenya, a resurgent Ethiopia courted tourists while their Sudanese neighbors were cowering under ruthless Arab militia called the Janjaweed. To the northwest, past Lake Victoria and the elusive Nile headwaters that so beguiled Burton and Speek, Uganda was emerging in the post-Idi Amin era as a renaissance of stability – the only country on the African continent besides Nigeria to reduce its AIDS count. Its capitol, Kampala, was now considered the safest large city in Africa. To the west, though, past the killing fields of Rwanda and Burundi, Congo and the Central African Republic continued their sad legacy of war, sliding further into the cultural morass of deepest, darkest Africa. Bereft of trade, scourged by disease and devoid of all but the most delusional missionaries, this region was a great malleable holding pen of seething tropical misery. Their civil war, dating back to the 1960s when the Belgians waffled out, had claimed about *three million* lives so far – many in just the last few years.

Angola, to the left, was extricating itself from Portuguese colonialism and Cuban meddling, as well as the usual business of warring tribal leaders. Then Namibia's (formerly Southwest Africa) orange dunes – the closest thing to Mars on earth – and her orderly towns of German sensibility, welcoming tourists from afar. Swinging around to the south, there was Botswana. They had the good fortune to discover diamonds the year the Brits pulled out, plying the proceeds into infrastructure and now sporting the most respected civil service on the continent – even though they had one of the shortest life spans, courtesy of AIDS and Malaria. Farther south was South Africa, that mighty amalgam of brains, brawn, and turmoil; a stunningly beautiful country unshackling itself from Apartheid and tiptoeing precariously back into a welcoming world market. Johannesburg's provincial region alone, an area the size of a small U.S. state, produces one-quarter of the GDP *of the entire African continent* – another example of The Golden Rule (aided by its corollary, the Diamond Rule). But alas, Johannesburg was one of the murder capitols of Africa as well.

Sweeping around counter-clockwise, my vision extended up the coast of Mozambique with her 1,800 miles of unspoiled Indian Ocean shorelines. To the east, the turquoise coast of Zanzibar, the exotic spice center and cultural crossroads, and shameful slave-trading capitol of an Old Africa. Finally, wedged between Botswana and Mozambique, was the former Rhodesia, now fissured into Zimbabwe, Zambia and Malawi, all going their separate ways. Once the breadbasket of the Sub-Sahara and playground to David Livingstone and Albert Schweitzer, our southern neighbors were as divergent as the mighty Zambezi river carving their borders: Malawi, regarded as the poorest-yet-friendliest country in Africa (are the two related, or is it the copious ganja?); Zambia, carving a nice post-colonial life for itself with the safe, bustling communities of Lusaka and Livingstone; and finally, Zimbabwe, "Mugabe's Folly," stripped of its productive European farms by back-to-homeland "reformers" who then realized they didn't know how to deliver the goods…but were too proud to admit it. Naturally, they blamed their woes on those intransigent Brits.

Of course, this was all in the mind's eye. It seemed an appropriate image from this sentinel straddling the equator, blown by capricious winds and jolted by tectonic thrusts, face ever changing, basking in sun and shivering in blizzards. Even the overachieving Cecil Rhodes, imperialist forefather of the nascent Rhodesia, once envisioning a transcontinental railway – British, of course – from Cape Town to Cairo, had to settle for a few lousy diamond mines and a scholarship fund for smart kids.

Hope and despair: the twin-edge razor of Mother Africa…that paradox of life wherever we happen to be situated. And in this momentary birds'-eye view of the continent, a vantage afforded only through challenging every fiber in my body and mind, I knew I would always choose hope as my elixir to move me even higher, to the next rung up of whatever fancy I chose as destiny. Right now, it was gratitude for having won that battle against the elements, and for being alive; also gratitude for having a wonderful partner to share it with…a buddy in every way.

Could there be more? Well yes…and that was the beauty of viewing *myself* from the top of the highest mountain on the continent. Much more. The only requirement was readiness: an open mind and willing heart.

* * * * * *

From Kili's top, what I really could see was, in fact, a tiny sliver of northern Tanzania and southern Kenya, a mere postage stamp on a wall map. Tea plantations and Masai villages dotted the landscape in front of me. Almost at my feet, across from the shadowy haze of Mt. Kenya, lay the Serengeti Plain and Olduvai Gorge, where *Homo Erectus* (*Australopithecus*) and his progenitor, *Zinjanthropus*, trundled out of their caves to slay their first gazelles and open the first Waffle House. In the other direction I could see banana and pineapple groves sloping down to Dar es Salaam, where another U.S. embassy had crossed paths with one of Osama's minions.

* * * * * *

I could also see a column of ants arcing around our flank. Tall ants, hauling packs. It was our porters – the blind truly leading the blind. Even from this distance, a mile or so away, one could detect their hypnotic somnolent gait. I'm reminded of the story of some ancient Persian king who, after vanquishing his enemies in battle, poked out the eyes of his prisoners, leaving every one hundredth man with one good eye, then dispatched them in a bumbling column back to their homeland (talk about low-budget imperialism). Our guys didn't have it quite that bad, but there they trod, each man's right arm out on the shoulder of the guy in front of him, chugging along with little baby steps and presumably cursing up a storm in Swahili.

It was all downhill from here. Precisely at 8:30 a.m., the wispy clouds coalesced into a curtain; we pitied the poor schmucks just arriving who would purchase nary a glimpse of a shrinking world. But we had seen it, by God, soaked it in and captured it through Nikon and Olympus shutters.

Eight thousand feet below, a good 11 miles for those without wings, was our next campsite. But now we were on scree, sun-soaked volcanic shale or loose rock that gives away gingerly to the well-applied boot. Once you get the feel for "surfing" (twist the hips, bend the knees, thrust the boots…*slide*…rise, shift weight, reverse twist, continue: twist-bend-thrust-slide-rise-reverse) one can easily cover huge swaths of distance. Ski poles help, too, buttressing the occasional over-thrust and compensating for the insatiable appetite of gravity. Down and down we went, almost giddy and stripping off clothing like Lady Godiva on laundry day – and we were still at 15,000 feet. But we were also out of the wind, in the sun and ready for lunch.

A few sandwiches later, the porters stumbled in. Some collapsed right on the trail. Others threw up a makeshift tent where they could get out of the light, as the smallest amounts of sunlight would produce piercing pain. The normally white parts of their eyes were bloodshot red and even a vacuous stare was a precious commodity. They closed their eyes whenever possible and suffered in silence, half embarrassed and totally drained. But they had made it, one more testimonial to indomitable will power overcoming "short-sighted" planning.

After a prolonged break to let the home boys recover, we were off again. The scree now yielded to hard trail and slowly vegetation returned as we dropped back into the gentle green Veld of the mid-mountain. For miles in all directions, sturdy plants and miniature trees swept the landscape like a fine emerald blanket. Between 14,000 and 13,000 feet they were perhaps knee-high; by the time we arrived at our camp at 11,000 feet they had stretched to shoulder and head height. We had returned to the world of the living.

* * * * * *

That night was relaxed and joyous. I smoked a celebratory Habana Montecristo #4, straight from Fidel's own humidor. It had been waiting for just this moment. We laughed in the gentle rain shower that now felt like a benign warm mist after what we had been through. At last we could get rid of the hot water bottle at the bottom of our sleeping bags and strip off fleece and socks. We buzzed, drifted around camp and uttered inane nothings like I imagine would emerge from a convalescing infantryman after a fortnight on the front lines. It was a dull bliss, not euphoria; welcome relief, not ecstasy. Even Conrad, nursing hobbled ankles and burning knees, seemed content.

Thoughts of a mindless amble to the bottom, however, proved naïve and premature. The next morning, after a sauntering descent of a couple thousand feet, we left the high grasses and entered the beginning fringe of the jungle – what can only be called "The Mud Luge."

The trail at this point essentially became a giant orange tongue that sluiced through the woods for the next 4-5 miles. Still descending, we were now in a sea of mud, a semi-tunnel like a crosscut pipe, varying from 4 to about 15 feet in width. The trail was criss-crossed by tricky, gnarled branches that resembled Medusa on a bad hair day. Our ski poles, which had provided such good purchase on yesterday's scree, were now more hindrance than help. They kept getting stuck or caught on a submerged tree root. Some steps forward produced skids; some steps sideways resulted in lopsided tilts. Using the roots was particularly tricky, as they provided no friction, and our boot treads were rendered useless under a gooey cake of earthen plaster.

Then the lactic acid kicked in: right on cue, 24 hours after yesterday's 8,000-foot drop. Quads burned, knees quaked, calves rebelled, and expletives spewed. Other than the knowledge that we were no longer in danger, this final jaunt was every bit as demanding as the culvert episode. And even more painful. All thoughts of the pending trail's end were vanquished to the needs of expediency: full concentration on every step we took, a calculated measure that required shifting of balance and likelihood of a quick Texas two-step. Even the reek of nine days trekking awoken now from our skin and hair by the warming, steaming jungle, evaded our olfactory senses (thankfully). Mindless jingles of show tunes gave way to grunts and sighs. We were in the zone – *Zen and the Art of Mud Tunneling*.

Peter and Daniel, of course, were unfazed and singing the Hakuna Matata song. Incredibly, the only mud on their entire bodies was confined to their boots and socks (tennis shoes, in Peter's case), whereas Alexis, Conrad and I wore a montage of orange, brown, black and beige splattered as high as our chests and equitably applied to the lengths of our arms and legs. We were a mess and we ached; but we plowed ahead. We thought about our half-blind porters taking up the rear a mile or so back, and conjured up horrendous images of them doing headers into a tree, breaking a neck, twisting ankles and writhing under inhuman loads with no traction.

After a short eternity of about three hours, the mud tapered off, an actual trail re-emerged and soon we were on dry ground.

Daniel said, "We make good time."

Whether he meant that statement as praise or rather that we were a source of entertainment for himself, I think he was blowing smoke up our chutes. But we soaked it up anyway and limped along through the pine trees and first groves of palms. We soon came upon a ranger's hut – the trail's end – next to a tiny village. There we signed out, receiving a patch of authenticity and certificate of insanity.

We then shuffled across the dirt road to a fly-ringed tavern and quaffed down several Tusker beers, patiently waiting for our squinting porters to emerge from the jungle. They showed up, miraculously within several hours, returned our gear and sang a boisterous round of the Kilimanjaro anthem for us, pantomiming with their hands our serpentine ordeal. We tipped them, increasing their bounty well beyond the standard suggested daily fee of $3. Enough for tennis shoes and a round of Tuskers – or perhaps some sunglasses?

I gave Peter my boots, possibly the only pair he would ever own. After a quick wash in the creek, they appeared to have a few more Kili ascents in them. He was a happy guy.

"Hakuna Matata," I said with a grin.

"*Kwaheri*" – "thank you" – he replied with a bigger grin.

Freed of our burden and thoroughly exhausted, we waited for our driver who arrived soon and drove us down to Arusha. We enjoyed a shower, a shave, some great Kenyan coffee and a few more Tuskers. Then it was time for bed and *"Lalasalama"* – Sweet Dreams.

* * * * * *

Was it worth it? Of course. Would we do it again? – Asking this question is possibly as irrelevant as our souls asking us before birth if we want to take on a physical body and venture back into the physical plane once again. Would we do things differently? Well, yes, from a practical standpoint – like, how about *dry season* next time? But then, if we do indeed create our own reality, would we not also create other obstacles just as challenging as those we just overcame, in order to prod ourselves forward to yet another level of competence/self-awareness/ JOY? Consider the memories. Consider the photographs…and now, this book and the fun I've had sharing this unforgettable experience with whoever's wild and crazy enough to go along for the ride. Reasons for doing something don't have to be complicated, and we may not even know what they *are* at the time we embark on that perilous journey. But the Voice says to strike out anyway…

'Shore is purty 'round here – but the dagnab mountains block the view!
– Anonymous

Chapter Twenty-Two

Nyaminyami Throws a Tantrum

Travel is fatal to prejudice, bigotry, and narrow-mindedness."
– Mark Twain

The Stairway to Heaven...The Devil's Toilet Bowl...Commercial Suicide...Oblivion...The Terminator...Ghost Rider...The Gnashing Jaws of Death...The Washing Machine...Overland Truck Eater...Deep Throat...

The Best of Mötley Crüe? Video games for the truly demented? Hardly. These were the bad boys of the Zambezi and the world's longest stretch of Class V rapids, churning out of Victoria Falls before sending the mighty Z to well-earned slumber in the Indian Ocean.

The rapids, first gazed upon by Bandu and Losi natives in times lost to antiquity, were exposed to the Western world by the intrepid David Livingstone in the 1850s. It's probable that some Arab slave traders knew about them, too, but failed to commit the account to papyrus. It's also quite possible the visitors never made it back to the pressroom in one piece.

For 18 miles, this crashing torrent of South-Central Africa carves through a basalt canyon. The rapids include a total of 23 subsets, over one per mile, which is doubly impressive when one considers that some of the stretches last for over 500 yards at a time. American, British and South African rafting expeditions laid siege to the place in the 1980s and today play host to a small but growing number of death-wishers: either those over-endowed with testosterone or under-endowed with common sense. And even if one *is* clever and talented, there's no accounting for the third calculation: the mood of Nyaminyami ("Nyami-Nyami"), the itinerant River God.

* * * * * *

The Zambezi was no stranger to us. We had just canoed a run of it several hundred miles downstream as it meandered along the lowlands of the Zimbabwe-Zambia border. It often expanded to a mile wide, with plenty of photo opportunities for the casual canoeist, as elephants, hippos, storks and crocodiles watched us with disinterest; the latter posing no problem as long as your humble guide knows which swimming holes are "safe."

The highlight of that excursion had been running over a hippo quite innocently (same for him) – while ferrying back upstream in a motorboat. We bucked like a bronco, but fortunately the boat kept going and no one got ejected.

"Does it hurt them?" I inquired, knowing that possibly the boat's prop had taken out a chunk of hide.

"Happens all time," responded our driver with a nonchalant shrug.

But that bucolic stretch of river was the tranquil *Yin* to Vic Falls' *Yang*. That is, it had been the safe part: Nyaminyami's smoking lounge, his morning-after hiatus, the eye of his storm and pause cycle between the gear-meshing frenzy of his aquatic agitator revving up for mischief.

* * * * * *

We had pulled into the region of Victoria Falls in Frankie, our diesel-powered Mercedes battering ram. Named after Frank Zappa – the fleet's other steeds included Janis (Joplin), Buddy (Holly), Jimi (Hendrix), Jerry (Garcia), John (Lennon) and Jim (Morrison) – Frankie resembled a miniature school bus welded onto Caterpillar tires and sported the Mother of All "Cow-Catchers" in front. One didn't just hit cows with these; they were more for bouncing off of elephants and hopefully landing right side up – ostensibly to then outrun the enraged pachyderm.

We were tired, bedraggled and thirsty; a Rogues' Gallery of English-sounding mongrels from the remnants of Her Majesty's far flung dominions: Aussie walkabouts seeking the next thrill or the next beer (often one and same); British students on leave between semesters before a life of drizzly monotony; New Zealand schoolteachers on generous four-month sabbatical; Canadian divorcees reconstructing their lives; South African surfers taking an inland break; and, of course, Americans seeking CNN and the neighborhood Starbucks (both notably absent in Vic Falls). We even had a few Belgians thrown in for the sake of cultural refinement.

Our escorts included Christopher, a native Kenyan and all-purpose driver, mechanic and border-crossing palm greaser (visas, African-style); and Rebecca, a cheery, white South African country girl and darn good cook. She was a 21-year old chain smoker committed to killing herself from lung cancer before malaria did her in first (she had been hospitalized twice).

We had been together six weeks so far, starting out in Nairobi, Kenya, heading toward Cape Town, South Africa via a circuitous route that covered nine countries and nearly 7,000 miles. About six out of every seven nights were spent at the equivalent of a KOA campground. These sported a shower, cabana/bar with music, reasonably cold beer and a high fence to keep out both four-legged and two-legged intruders.

Occasionally we splurged for a cheap hotel or A-frame lodge at some family-owned safari resort, like the place where we'd spent Christmas outside the Zambian capitol city of Lusaka. We'd pit-barbequed a pig, washing it down with rancid local wine and capping the snow-less Noël with various smokes, teas and brandies. But these interludes of revelry had been few and far between, so it was with gleeful anticipation that we approached the New Year's holiday break at Vic Falls, a semi-civilized outpost and home of one of the world's "Seven Natural Wonders."

In addition to a kaleidoscope of Sub-Saharan geography, flora, and fauna, the trip put us face-to-face with the natives: their markets, villages, ceremonies, etc. There were ample diversions for us as well, that ranged from snorkeling and diving to hiking, parachuting, canoeing, and now – soon enough – white-water rafting.

Some of the experiences to-date had not been expected. While camping primitively (read: no KOA-type fence) on Tanzania's Serengeti Plain, we had been stalked by a lion. He slowly circled our encampment like a maddened insomniac, kept at bay only by hastily-made campfires and sharpshooter-rangers, the latter urgently summoned by walkie-talkie. The fact that they'd spent most of the night asleep in their jeeps (must've been union men), Kalashnikovs and M-16's balanced on their laps, didn't detract from their deterrence. Kitties big and small alike can smell a trap...

This particular menace was an old male. He was bereft of females, who'd abandoned him for a younger more vigorous male – a trait found in animals and humans alike – and who traditionally did the hunting. Therefore, he was hungry, possibly having gone as long as two weeks without food, figured one of the rangers. He also weighed the standard 450 lbs. Cats this desperate will attack any/all comers with no regard for the odds and hoping to scatter the flock and prey on the easiest. (Old safari axiom: "You don't have to be the fastest – just don't be the slowest").

The fact that in 20+ years our Overland company and Christopher the driver had never encountered this situation, didn't exactly dispel our apprehensions. If you've never heard a lion roar, don't try for the experience unless said creature is well behind thick metal bars at a zoo. A male lion's roar can be heard up to *seven miles* away – without benefit of wind. And the bloodcurdling yelps of hyenas, hoping to clean up the aftermath of his buffet, likewise pierce the air for several miles.

There's something so powerful, mysterious and foreboding in the primal lion roar, every basic-instinct flight/ fright /fight cilia in the body goes on overtime. "Fight," however, is not recommended. Those B-grade Tarzan movies lie; there's not an ambulatory adult *Panthera Leo* alive that couldn't tear Johnny Weissmuller or Fess Parker to shreds. So we spent the night awake in our tents, scared spit-less (and bladders bulging) while our unwelcome guest circled counter-clockwise from only about 50 yards out, booming forth his Do-Re-Mi's at regular fifteen-minute intervals.

* * * * * *

Victoria Falls – *Mosi-oa-Tunju* ("Smoke that Thunders," to the resident Bandu and Losi tribes) – is both a waterfall and a town. Two towns, in fact; the Zimbabwean namesake and its Zambian counterpart, Livingstone.

The falls extend over a mile wide and 350 feet high – not as high as Venezuela's Angel Falls or as wide as the Iguaçu Falls that straddle Brazil, Argentina and Paraguay – but impressive all the same. Next to Victoria Falls, the U.S./Canada Niagara Falls is a mere tempest in a teapot. The plume of Vic Falls' mist can usually be seen 15 or 20 miles away and has been reported as far as 50. The Falls can also be *heard* from a distance of 15 fifteen miles away, as approximately 240 million cubic feet of water per second pour over the precipice, taking precious silt downstream along with animal carcasses and the effluvium of Angola, Congo, Botswana and the highlands of both Zim & Zam. The Big Z winds for over 1,600 miles, earning it Africa's honorable mention after the Nile and the Niger, but Victoria Falls is certainly more than just a hiccough. It's a line of demarcation between landscapes, countries…and between Heaven and Earth.

In the early 1900s, Cecil Rhodes – he of the scholarship fund and namesake of Rhodesia, a country now splintered into the twin Z's and Malawi – commissioned the bridge over the falls for railroad visitors. These days, bungee jumpers (until recently, seizing the world's longest jump) hang their cookies over the side while smiling border guards, a rarity in Africa, greet tourists. The guards know who butters their maize, Robert Mugabe notwithstanding.

We spent several nights on each side of the falls, arriving first in Zambia's Livingstone. Pulling in that first night next to a modest but comfortable tourist lodge along the upstream riverbanks, Christopher backed Frankie into the campsite sector we had reserved.

"Tents there," he motioned with a head bob.

"Showers there," he segued with a finger gesture to the right.

"Bar there," a hand pointed in the opposite direction.

The Holy Trinity: sleep, shower and bar. We knew Christopher's routine by now and could mimic it with proper intonation, meter and Swahili/Kikuyu pitch. The only thing that ever varied was the direction of the pointing or nodding. Christopher would have been a great straight man in an African vaudeville show. He took incessant needling from us while keeping the straightest of faces through the entire interrogation – until, finally overwhelmed, he would burst out laughing. He spoke in short rapid-fire phrases, usually only conveying the basics but obviously holding onto a lot more.

Christopher may have been in our employ, but we were no "Bwanas" – he was every bit our equal and then some, speaking a multitude of languages and boasting of the unofficial African Overland record of having driven Frankie 50,000 miles without a flat tire. That's like playing hopscotch blindfolded in a minefield and not stepping on one of the buried detonators. Although these deterrents, resembling moon craters, weren't hidden, they were ubiquitous. When Christopher's streak finally ended a month later – with us, of course, in the middle of nowhere in a Namibian desert – we found to our chagrin that Frankie lacked a jack. *Hey, no one's perfect* .

✳ ✳ ✳ ✳ ✳ ✳

"Booze Cruise!"

"Hey mates, there's this Booze Cruise thing tonight on the river (we were now above the falls several miles)."

Brian was excited. There's nothing a 22-year-old Australian male enjoys more than getting schnokered, unless it's getting schnokered on holiday between Christmas and New Year's.

"Yeah, they do it every year for several nights before New Year's," added Christopher, referring to the resort lodge's Yule festivities.

"We've simply *got* to go," chimed in Rebecca, who wasn't averse to letting alcohol tag-team with tobacco for the dibs of killing her before the malaria did. "It's tradition. Besides, you've already paid for it, so ya might as well indulge!"

So for the next two hours, before/during/after a fine sunset, our party and about 50 others boarded a ship – okay, a big boat…the wealthy uncle of Bogart's *African Queen* – and floated around the tranquil waters upstream from the falls. The uninitiated in critter-watching – some had just flown into Vic Falls from civilized places and hadn't yet seen any big game – "oohed" and "ahhhed" at the hippos, crocs, occasional elephant and virtual aviary of strange-looking birds. All that was old hat for our group, so we made a beeline to the libation servers.

There was wine – mediocre South African stuff (too peppery, like Argentinean Malbecs) and downright nasty Zimbabwean hooch, likened to the worst of amateur distillers: sweet, full of tannins, yeasty, etc. Rhodesia may have been the former breadbasket of the southern continent, but the semitropical weather and clueless apprentice guild have made a mockery of its vintages. There was also plenty of what we used to call "jungle juice" – the irony seemed pronounced here – in my freshman (broke) college days. This was a concoction of cheap vodkas, rums, gins and whiskeys filtered through a sanitary landfill and dissolved into a montage of sickening fruits. There was beer as well…good beer, thankfully; one of the few lasting contributions of European hegemony from back in the good ol' days. Naturally the Aussies and Kiwis sampled – quaffed – 'em all, while the more refined British and we cautious North Americans paced ourselves. We had to – our circulatory systems actually cycled hemoglobin instead of the barley-and-hops blood mash of our upside-down brethren.

A beautiful sunset capped off the "cruise": not brilliant or flaming, but a calming cantaloupe-orange that morphed into the fine vapors hovering over the treetops. Not everyone saw it, though, as eyes were reddening, vision blurring and speech slurring.

"Coventry'll rip you wankers," challenged Martin, a Midlands Brit, to Ian, a South African from the Stellenbosch region near Cape Town.

"In your pissin' dreams, mate," retorted Ian. "Buncha prima donnas. I wouldn't let 'em lick the salt offa my sack if they was dyin' of thirst."

The Boer War obviously hadn't ended for these guys. Rugby's just another form of organized warfare, anyway, sans the machine guns and bombs.

Then, not to be outclassed, the Aussies and Kiwis got into it. Tony, a strapping farm boy from New South Wales and possessing a cockney delivery, started, well resumed, needling Allison, a gregarious New Zealander, about *her* accent – 'Fush'n'Chups' (presumably "Fish and Chips") he called her – in obvious reference to her colloquialism-flavored syntax. Allison was old enough to be Tony's mother.

"Fair dinkum, Bruce," she winked back. Calling an Australian male "Bruce" is like the German "schwienhund." Far more vulgar things *could* be said, but few are more insulting.

Daphne, a very inebriated Brit, got into it: "Hey, Banick, whadda ya thinka that prick, Bush?"

Like the cultured belles of my native South, when alcohol collides with the British female bloodstream, the façade of gentility drops from their Victorian personas like an anvil in a vacuum. Manners, civilization and "dreadful me" class-consciousness all take a holiday when liquid truth serum runs pell-mell into exhaustion.

"He's a wanker, luv," I testified, translating my American opinions into British verbiage.

"Yea, he's quite the troglodyte, eh?" she continued. "He's like this gushin' oil well that all his cronies can suck off. He plays the whole Bible and Cowboy thing up so well, but it doesn't take a bleedin' rocket scientist to see through the invisible strings. Reckon if he was Pinocchio, he couldn't even turn around in a room without his nose whackin' somethin'"

"Well, Daph," I responded, "that's a bit harsh, but probably a lot of truth to it. There's a saying in my country that the only thing worse than a knee-jerk liberal is a knee-pad conservative – the pads for always groveling before the rich and powerful. But I reckon Dubya's only heeding his hidden masters, just like Clinton did before'm. Only Dubya's dumber and more obvious in his *faux-pas*. Actually, come to think about it, it wasn't too smart for Slick Willy to debate the semantics of the word 'is' on national television. And *his* handlers must've forgotten to tell'em that cigars are for smoking, not playing forensic putt-putt with the intern staff."

"We also have another saying," I added. 'A fool and his money are soon elected.'" I paused for a sip of Lion Lager. "With Clinton we had a buncha sophomoric events called 'File-gate,' 'Travel-gate,' 'White-water-gate,' 'Buddhist Fund Raising-gate,' and of course, the eventual 'Zipper-gate.' With Dubya's boys, it seems the lunatics are in charge of the asylum, and anyone questioning their actions are deemed either heretical, non-patriotic or weaklings. I dunno, the whole Electoral College thing we have in my country is an antiquated joke anyhow; it just leaves states open to be carved up by whichever party has the better-greased machine and can stir up fears the best. I only preferred Clinton's buffoonery because it made for better fodder in the *National Enquirer* and late night comedy shows. Unfortunately, with this current cabal, there's no humor in environmental degradation, 'pre-emptive' war or runaway deficit spending. Seems to me that Dubya could learn a lot from Clinton about the *entertainment factor* of the office. The worst thing a clown can do is not play the part well."

I was about to inquire why, if the U.S. government was so irreparably toxic and that of my mates so enlightened, then how come *their* leaders, Britain's Tony Blair and Australia's Johnny Howard, were groveling up first in line for the Iraqi signup sheet…

But I was interrupted by an inhuman, gurgling choking sound. Agonizing, pathetic unnatural grunts…then it heaved, choked, gasped…and reloaded for more…

It was Brian, hurling his jungle-juice – recycled, that is – off the back of our *African King*; seeing the Old Year out (a day early) with both a bang and a whimper. Paying homage to Nyaminyami. Water boiled, frothed and bubbled where he spewed forth. Funny, those were the first fish I'd seen on the river…We sure hoped Nyaminyami approved of the offering.

* * * * * *

According to an unofficial Zambezi rafting consortium, the mantra for Class V waves reads as follows: "Long and violent rapids. Large waves that are unavoidable. Complex course. Scouting is a must."

Alexis and I had been on Class Vs once before on Costa Rica's Pacuare River, an exhilarating rush that lasted just a few minutes. Never for the better part of a day.

We had also done, collectively, an assortment of North American specialties: the western king-pins such as the Salmon, Snake, Colorado, Green, Selway, and Arkansas; and their southeastern counterparts, such as the Nantahala, Ocoee, and Chattooga. Although all of these include some nasty stretches of water, most of our rides had consisted of long stretches of lazing interspersed with quick thrusts through Class II, III and the occasional Class IV chutes. The Vs of the Big Z were not only numerous – nine out of 23 were Class V, and another six were Class IVs – they were often lonnnngggg…If a life can indeed flash in front of one's eyes in a split second, imagine how many lifetimes may blur together over the course of several minutes, or say, hours.

What makes Zambezi rafting possible – other than Africa being a far less litigious place than Europe or North America – is a freak of geography. The canyon, deep-carved basalt sculpted in a very short geological time (a few hundred thousand years) has very few rocks in it. Not counting, of course, the V-shaped slices that adorn the sides. To be sure, there *are* rocks, but as long as the water is high enough, one is far more likely to die from getting thrashed about than from actually getting pummeled into pulp by a basalt 4-Iron. In other words, your chances of surviving prolonged stretches of the Big Z are far greater than a theoretical counter-part; say Peru's Urubamba, Chile's Bio-Bio or China's Yangtze. Even those North American IIIs and IVs, for that matter. But that shouldn't stop one from trying…

* * * * * *

To have a town named after you is a great honor. Such befits Sir David Livingstone, who along with Bob Marley (a more recent edition, but alas, no town yet), is still highly esteemed throughout Sub-Saharan Africa. In fact, after Livingstone died in 1873, his embalmed corpse was carried for *two years* through the jungle to Dar es Salaam, Tanzania, then sailed home to Westminster Abbey for safe housekeeping. These days, Livingstone's namesake is the unheralded alter ego of its big brother, Vic Falls, across the falls. The town has just a fraction of the tourist baubles and lodging provisions compared to its rival, but, by African standards it's safe, clean, and orderly.

After the breakup of Rhodesia in 1979, Zambia took modest steps forward: agricultural co-ops and research farms, UNESCO sites, etc. Although most of it certainly is still considered poor (no less immune to AIDS or malaria than any of its geographical neighbors), Zambia nonetheless seems to have a chance at a better future. The capitol city of Lusaka had amazed me with its busy but orderly shopping malls, European cars and professional people. The residents took an extreme interest in the outside world. One night at a private campground, the bartender, resembling a well-pedigreed Uncle Remus, told me he was Harvard-educated and the country's former Minister of Labor.

Who knows? His eyes said he was truthful and his voice was matter-of-fact. Although that sort of thing just doesn't happen in the western world, it was no surprise here, where allegiances and patronage shift like coursing rivers and blowing sands. Besides, who wouldn't rather shill beer than listen to political blowhards all day?

Zimbabwe, on the other hand, held most of the cards after the breakup. The former Salisbury, now renamed Harare, had been a bustling commercial center full of professionals and diplomats. Unfortunately, two decades of Robert Mugabe's draconian paranoia and calculated greed had depleted Zim's larder and zapped its vitality. He's no dummy – the man has a handful of degrees from Europe and South Africa alike. But he learned long ago that to get your way with crowds (i.e., take advantage of them), you needed them on your side. To get them on your side, you needed an enemy. Multiple enemies, if you were lucky. That meant the UK and other western governments – white people in general, imperialists, the whole lot of them.

First he manufactured a currency crisis, simply refusing to repay his lessor's loans – why reward imperialism? Then the government confiscated the land of the productive white farmers – great enterprises that had fed millions. Like Lenin and Trotsky at their best, the land was "generously" shared with the poor country folk. Until of course, they found out they couldn't operate the machinery, couldn't get spare parts and didn't know how to rotate crops or use fertilizers and pesticides. Or sell commodities. Meanwhile, Mugabe rigged elections, hoarded fuel and grain for the military, all the while driving the professionals – white and many black alike – out of Harare and Zimbabwe altogether. A ranger I had met – now living on the Zambian side – told me there were less than 10,000 whites left in the entire country, whereas there had formerly been over 200,000 (out of a smaller population). *Viva la revolucion* – let 'em eat cake, said the Boss. He's got his.

The town of Vic Falls had been a great tourist magnet for much of the 20th Century. The poshest British hunting lodges were there, and the best restaurants. It even had an international airport. The commercial area – a small checkerboard of cafes, pubs, and tourist shops, still abounded with frenetic energy. This was one place Mugabe's long arm didn't want to tweak – the town brought in hard currency and put out a smiling face to the world. But even here, dissension and desperation simmered, and sometimes not just under the surface. A palpable tension was in the air as merchants went about flaunting their wares and vendors took orders. Not the heavy-handed, jack-booted tension of visible troops; rather, the visceral *angst* that poverty and delusion engender, and the uneasy feeling that violence lay waiting in a not-too-distant future.

It was – is – such a shame. The wares are an amalgam of the Sub-Saharan's finest: ornate soapstone sculptures, exquisite ironwood carvings, tight-pointed tapestries, glistening jewelry and intricate handicraft such as world-renowned basket work. True, much of this could be found in the western tourist shops of Cape Town's Victoria and Albert Waterfront, but for about five times the price. In London, New York or Sydney, these items would sell for 20 or 30 times higher than here. Elaborate baskets for which we paid several dollars might cost several hundred in swank Seattle or Melbourne tourist areas. The 40-pound carved elephant – gorgeous ironwood going for (well, negotiated for) $20 – would go for $300-400 in a trendy Midtown-Atlanta African import store. The shoulder-high giraffe, for which we paid $7 – a guy came running after us after we walked away; we really didn't want it and only purchased it because he was desperate – would have cost $200-300.

That's the good news, if you're a budget shopper and your house looks like David Livingstone's garage. The bad news is that this was a truly worsening scene. Maize, like the Irishman's potato or the Cambodian's rice is the staple crop, and $10 of hard cash keeps an entire family in maize for a month. So everything was up for dibs. It's a disheartening scene – not the normal, hustle-bustle, friendly chit-chat found in casbahs, kiosks, bazaars and *bures* around the world – but mercantilism in its lowest common denominator. Here was fear, anxiety and "Darwinian competition" as vendors battled, both physically and mentally, their brethren in the next shop, or hundred shops. Having bartered in some pretty strange outposts, this was nonetheless new to me. I've seen plenty of beggars, but never in a commercial market have I seen such huge swarms of very desperate people.

"Please what you give for basket?" asked the woman, sweat and dirt caking out beneath her head wrap, baby on her breast.

The piece was beautiful, intricate reed work with a mosaic of geography; almost an M.C. Escher complexity to the overlapping and interlocking dark brown patterns that adorned the center of the lighter brown 18-inch bowl. Tough-but-pliable, it would hold anything, even liquid for quite a while and last for ages.

"Please you give me five dollars?" she filled in her own blank.

Before I could answer, a chorus started.

"I sell you my basket for only $3," said the upstart from the kiosk next door...unsolicited, of course. Her basket was completely different but equally impressive.

"Please you take mine for $2?" clamored a third contestant. Then $1...then two for a dollar.

The cloud of locusts thickened, the clamor grew, anxiety gripped the air and the whirlwind intensified. Not quite the Warg/wolves of Tolkien's Isengard or the beggars of Calcutta – these were merchants, after all – but cacophonous and unnerving all the same. My stomach flipped as I felt their pain and gazed at the circle of pleading, piercing looks, the outstretched hands sometimes holding two or three baskets – and sought out the expression of warmest countenance. Desperate, yes, but dignified, calm, trusting...I found her, and one more. I gave them each $5 and took one basket apiece.

You could hear the air "pop" a mile away. The *angst* had roared to a crescendo, peaked and plummeted – then all was calm and quiet. Besides, they now had a new mark. Up came two Afrikaner newlyweds with questions and a camera. The pitch started revving up all over again, and I got the hell out of Dodge.

All of this was confined to the Central Market, the officially zoned bartering place. There were many other cute little stores and mini malls on the major streets, with air conditioning, clean glass and Western epicurean delights. These shops tended to be owned and operated by Brits, South Africans and/or the dwindling class of white Zimbabweans who were trying to figure out how to haul their assets out of their imploding country.

The most common bauble, however, was an interesting white carving about the size of a shark's tooth, and worn as a pendant. This was Nyaminyami, or *"Mudzingu,"* the Loch Ness monster of the Zambezi valley, and everyone wore one, especially the river boys who toiled daily under his bemused but mercurial temperament.

* * * * * *

Many have claimed to have seen Nyaminyami – dragon-like, with a snake's body and fish's head – but no one has come up with definitive photos. In any case, like most gods, he can be beneficent when the mood moves him, or he can be a real bastard.

The Tonga and Batonga peoples, cousin of the Bandu and Losi, claim he's been particularly peeved since the 1950s when a dam was built upstream at Kariba. Apparently the only thing that would satisfy His Honor would be the total destruction of the dam and restoration of things "as they were." Although this idea has only received lukewarm consideration in the capitols of Lusaka and Harare, the tribes have history on their side: in the late 1950s, directly after the Kariba dam's completion, record floods nearly destroyed the project. Only a fool or a blind man couldn't see that those events were a warning from Nyaminyami.

The Tonga's reverence, however, is based on much more than fear. There is a real affinity between god and tribe. Rumor has it that Nyaminyami, during times of famine in distant antiquity, made offerings of his own flesh to feed the starving people. Moreover, it's said that the completion of the dam severed him from his better half, his female spirit squeeze, and now he wanders the valley (or Gwembe Trough) forlornly; thus engendering the sympathies of his loyal-but-cautious subjects.

Nyaminyami has one vice, however. He enjoys puffing an afternoon bowl of *dagga*, known elsewhere in the world as atshitshi, bud, bush, bobo, burnie, cannabis, cese, coli, cosa, dimba, doja, dubbe, doradilla, dom jen, dope, earth, funk, ganjah, gage, gong, grata, grass, gungun, hemp, hay, hocus, hooter, juanita, kali, kaya, kiff, kitchie, leaf, lobo, lucas, marijuana, method, mutha, moodos, muggie, oregano, owl, pot, pack, pine, pod, rasta, reefer, root, siddi, sassafras, sativa, shmagma, sinse, snop, stinky, straw, vipe, wooz, wuwon, weed, yeh, ying, yerba, zambi – and even some slang terms. Who said being a god meant all work and no play? And being a god, what could be more natural – *more appropriate* – than partaking of the most prolific, versatile plant on Mother Gaia? Not to mention the most practical, used for clothing, rope, paper products, medicine, etc., and found as far north as Scandinavia, as far south as Chile and in every jungle, farm, forest, prairie, pasture, college dorm and mountainside in between?

Only deserts seem exempt, and even then, a little irrigation can work wonders. Something for the reader to consider: would one rather trust his upcoming river-run to a deity with a slight buzz and a bemused, mellow grin – or an angry Jehovah ripped on Kentucky corn filtered through a rusted radiator and whispering to the brain that "I'm invincible?" Or, perhaps, that Mexican joy-juice known as "To-kill-ya?" (There's much in a word…)

These days, despite the fact that no one can actually locate him, Nyaminyami's image is everywhere, not least of all in the tourist shops of Livingstone and Vic Falls. In addition to the protective pendant, another favorite pose is on top of a walking stick. A beautiful wooden depiction of the people's folklore, these sticks place Nyaminyami on the handle top with carvings of rings, magic amulets, fish, the Mopani tree, the dagga pipe and grateful people occupying successive "rungs" of the stick. Great fanfare, but he'd probably give it all up in an instant, if he could just return things to the good ol' days. It's not easy being a god in this new millennium.

＊ ＊ ＊ ＊ ＊

Our quarters on the Zimbabwean side of the town of Vic Falls were a little more problematic. It was a pleasant enough setting, inasmuch as we were staying in a backpackers' hostel complete with dorm rooms and kitchen/mess hall. It even had a swimming pool, sort of. "Overlanders" passing through from the distant reaches of Africa convened here, so the air was always buzzing about places near and far – Morocco, Egypt, Ethiopia, Nigeria, Ghana, Namibia, South Africa – wagging off the tongues of guests and employees alike. There's a certain camaraderie engendered on the road, especially when the whoppers start flying and members of the group can up the ante with one better (true or not). But that's the fun – tall tales, like elephant grass, grow richer and taller the more they're nourished. It's all part of the Overland mystique.

It was hot – we were in the peak of the Southern Hemisphere summer in the middle of a friggin' jungle – and the rooms had no fans. Unfortunately, opening the windows at night wasn't an option, either, because there were no screens, and mosquitoes are relentless insomniacs when there's flesh around.

I pulled Christopher aside. He was nursing a beer while refereeing an arm-wrestling contest between Tony and Richard. Richard was a chipper Brit enjoying one last fling of freedom before joining the Accenture sweatshop back in London.

"Christopher, sorry to bother you, but, like, how do we keep from being mosquito smorgasbord?"

"Huh?"

"There are no screens to keep the mossies outta the rooms," I explained.

"Close windows."

"It's fuckin' hot, mate. We've got no fans, and it's stickier than a brothel in the Congo. Or so I would imagine."

"Drink lots of beer, Stevie," he chuckled, "You'll sleep good dreams then. Pull sheet up over you to make sure." Wink-nod. The Kenyan vaudeville act was quickly losing its charm.

Alexis and I were tired, buzzed by the six percent lager (recipe courtesy of the departed British and German Empires) and more than just a little irritable. We considered getting out our designated company tent – a canvas cocoon that was tucked away in Frankie's bowels. Our assigned domicile, resembling a giant version of the bulky Baker tents from the 1950s, had been our bedroom most of the way down from Nairobi, barring the few aforementioned hotels and lodges. It was okay most of the time, as the 5,000-plus foot elevations of Kenya, Tanzania, and Malawi had kept the temps cool at night. But we were at lower elevations now, farther south in this upside-down summer, and trying to sleep in a canvas cave would be like wrapping up in a warm, moist straightjacket.

We knew of one possible remedy. Alexis, bless her heart, had purchased (over my objections) a tiny lightweight tent before we left the states. Correction, it wasn't really a tent but a glorified mosquito net with a footprint just adequate for two intimates to lie down in (with no room for gear). It weighed a grand total of 1-½ pounds and was made for just this type of occasion. We had already used it once, on a beach outside of Dar es Salaam, where similar sultriness had set in (try sea level at the equator with no breeze).

The downside of this featherweight bedroom is that it's just a little too revealing to the outside world, as the entire sidings consist of paper-thin transparent mesh. It hadn't mattered on the beach, where we simply moved 100 yards away from our comrades. Here, however, there was precious little grass and we had no desire to be on display in the parking lot, strategically smack dab in the middle of a gravel walkway. It just wouldn't work.

We trudged defeated back to our dorm room. "Hon, I'm exhausted." Alexis didn't give up easily, but this was too much. "What are we gonna do?"

"Well, let's coat the hell out of ourselves with mossie juice, open the windows, pull the sheet up and hope for the best. Maybe a snake will fatally bite us in the night so we won't have to worry about slow death from malaria."

"Shut up, Steve, I can't handle it."

Malaria is right near the top of African killers. AIDS and sleeping sickness (from the tsetse fly) are high in the mix, followed by civil war, cholera, irate husband/fathers, irate wife/mothers, hippos and crocodiles, in that approximate but non-scientific order. Somewhere on the list should also be *schistosomiasis* (or, *bilharzia*), caused by lake-bound microscopic worms burrowing in through one's feet (hence, stay out of stagnant water) and proceeding straight to the tummy, kidneys and liver where they bide their time before throwing an outrageous party about a year later, when it's too late to combat this intrusion. Poison snakes are near the bottom of the list, Tarzan-hype notwithstanding. Same for elephants, who are slow to temper but take a lifetime getting over it (true to myth, they don't forget a usurpation).

I don't know where Nyaminyami fits into the hierarchy of killers, but he doesn't suffer fools gladly. Overlaying this entire tapestry of killers are the specters of (dysentery) dehydration and malnourishment, usually hitchhiking with one of the others. One thing's for sure: the sight of gray hair in a village will soon turn visitors' heads.

Mosquito deterrence is an art unto itself. Natives, sadly, don't have the means, or in some cases even the *knowledge* to deal with the havoc it causes, and unfortunately, one cannot build up immunity to malaria either through genetics or conditioning.

To contract malaria, one has to be bitten by a mosquito that has bitten *another* infected carrier within the last 24 hours. So a mosquito bite, of which one endures many, doesn't mean anything. But needless to say, the concentration of a few zillion winged zealots, like starry-eyed investors in a Ponzi scheme, greatly increases the odds of spreading the bad news.

Ideally, First World visitors deal with it through a four-pronged strategy. First, orally, such as daily (or weekly, depending) doses of Malarone, quinine or Larium (the latter often conjuring depressing nightmares). This doesn't prevent one from contracting malaria; rather, it just stays dormant and subdued within one's immune system. Second, by washing clothes periodically in a god-awful smelling batch of stuff resembling kerosene. Amazingly, when the clothes dry, there's no discernible odor except to mosquitoes, and the treatment lasts through multiple washings. Third, coating one's tent, including zipper, every two weeks with a special repellant made just for that fabric. Fourth, through a topical repellant, such as Off, 6-12, etc., especially at dawn and dusk. *Not* the 95% DEET stuff that'll shrivel your skin like a reptile – one simply can't keep up that regimen day in and day out for three or four months (experiments reveal that prolonged use will strip paint and erode metal) – rather, through a minimal, say 20%, concentration – placed lightly on ankles, wrists, neck and face. It actually works.

Into the room...Dreading every step...Surely an agonizing night awaited us. We sat apprehensively at the edge of our twin beds. My imagination was already producing those sadistic little *Anopheles Quadrimaculatas* revving up their McCullough chainsaws and polishing their proboscises. Imagination, hell. Their scouts had already arrived. I reached for the bug juice.

Suddenly I had a flash...not so fast, my tempestuous tormentors! For every problem there is usually a solution. One either has to be sufficiently inebriated or desperate enough (again, often related) to seize the vision.

Quickly I yanked the mattresses off the twin beds. With the surging adrenalin of a man possessed ("Eureka!") I propped up both bed frames vertically against the wall – out of the way. By that time the light bulb over Alexis' head had tripped on, also. We put the mattresses together, in the middle of the room, and placed our mossie-net-cum-faux-tent on top of them. In two minutes' time, we had secured our home.

The inability to use stakes to secure said domicile didn't really matter, as the skeletal-like poles created enough of a fixture, and our weight upon the tent/net and mattress would be sufficient to prevent the transparent cocoon from moving around. We even left our room's door open, for whatever ventilation wished to visit. We were at the outskirts of the village and thus very secure, barring a drunken Scotsman bumbling into our room by accident. We relaxed and slept a very sound sleep that night. Earplugs kept the chainsaws at bay.

The next morning, bloodshot eyes and stifling yawns filled the camp. It could've just been hangovers from the copious libations of the Castle brewery, but the scarlet welts and incessant itching of our comrades betrayed the culprits: buzz-bait. Our fellow travelers had been mossie-ized. I hoped they were up on the four-step program...

* * * * * *

"Awright, let's see a show of hands. How many have rafted before?" Maybe 10 or 12 hands rose, out of a good 35-40 people present.

"Really?" the interrogator addressed the hand wavers. "What's the matter, didn't you suffer enough the first time?"

Eamon clearly enjoyed his role as master of ceremony for the pre-rafting orientation. He was a Brit, with a personality well suited for his effervescent swim shorts and tumbleweed hair perm; the term "Afro" seems appropriate under the circumstances. He had under his employ a handful of South African and local guides who would assist him, and us throughout the day.

After subjecting us to a propaganda film – surely to minimize our fear of being churned in the washing machine from Hell; and to entice us to buy the thrills-ville photo plunge at the "Commercial Suicide" rapids – Eamon fit us for life preservers.

"This is your best friend," he lectured, "more valuable than your captain, more handsome and certainly less quarrelsome – right?"

"If you get launched into the river – as you most likely will sometime during the day – this wonderful little bag of foam and air will keep you floating. All you need to do then is keep your feet forward and ride out the storm – er, waves, sorry – and our helpers will be available to grab you."

"Likewise, if you're one of the so-called rescuers, never imperil your life or that of others by trying to be a hero. Wait 'til the next calm waters. Then, like so," borrowing a helper and simulating the act, "yank them like this (*pull…ugghhh*). Under no circumstances pull out someone who looks wild-eyed like a raving hyena – they're in shock, and you need to get us pros to assist you. Otherwise, you'll be right in the drink with them, and they will probably consider *you* a raft. If you get my gist. And at all times, please keep these vests tight – like so (*yank – gulp*)."

He spoke in a rapid fire fashion, which was a good thing because there was a lot he wanted to say. He brandished a form of humor if it can be called that, because, after all, he *was* an entertainer.

"For hobbits and other wee folk, we have the small life preservers. For physically fit normal people, we have the medium size. That large pile over there is for you athletic-types and buxomous Sheila's. Finally, just in case anyone needs Exhibit D, the extra large units, we have a fourth stack. We call these the 'American pile.'" Wink-nudge.

I shot my hand up. "Good sir, if I suck in my 32-inch waist, could I please have one of the skinny English ones?"

Eamon blushed. "Oops, sorry Yank, I thought you was a Canadian."

"Naw, I stink at hockey and never could learn the words to *Alouette*. Besides, every time the Canucks let me in they can't wait for me to leave."

Perhaps Eamon didn't know it was an American expedition, the Sobek Outfitters in 1981, that first ran the Zambezi, but I let it slide. My life was soon to be in his hands, so diplomacy was in order. After all, he was mostly correct: you can usually spot a Yank in a multinational crowd, and not because our mouths are moving. Sad to say, it's our collective waistline, chest and wherever else coagulated calories go to lounge – thanks to the Colonel, Ronald McDonald and our other cultural icons.

✳ ✳ ✳ ✳ ✳ ✳

We arrived at the river after an ambling 15-minute ride, followed by a ½ mile hike down from the cliff. We had dropped about 400 feet; the Batoka Gorge cuts an impressive swath deep into the river valley.

Our raft was to be commanded by Choongu, a very dark Bandu with a flashing grin. He spoke the basic necessities of English: "man overboard, paddle, rest, left/right," etc. Our team of six spent the first 10 minutes or so paddling around the eddy near the "Boiling Pot," the churning efflux of the falls, which were about a mile upstream. As this was the maiden voyage for several in our group, the whole shtick of oars, body rotations and commands had to be introduced and practiced.

Off we went! For good measure – and as ritual demanded – we aimed through the first set of rapids to bounce off of "Against the Wall," a large vertical basalt slab that girded the side of this Class IV chute. It's considered good luck if your "bounce" leaves your raft uptight. We successfully bounced, though five of the other seven were somersaulted. First blood. But it was harmless; everyone laughed, the water was a pleasant temperature and the river immediately calmed into another eddy as we all got psyched for the "real ride."

Choongu was a tad smaller than me, possibly 150 lbs. dripping wet. Unlike me, he hadn't an ounce of fat on his entire body. Every muscle was taut, every sinew tuned to perfection. It comes with the territory, and he had run this river hundreds of times over the last decade or so, applying exertion to oar-strokes thousands of times per day. Not to mention the adrenalin required to brace oneself against Nyaminyami's unpredictable tantrums. I was thankful for someone with Choongu's personality and experience. When he wasn't grinning he was dead serious and seemed to realize that not only his vocation but also his guests' lives were largely in his hands and oars. He took proper orders from Eamon regarding group solidarity and such, but otherwise, he and the other guides had to follow their instincts as required. Just as no two rapids are the same, neither are two consecutive runs of the *same* rapid. Flowing, crashing water is the ultimate Zen – no two moments ever exactly the same. The worse thing a guide (and some would argue, a normal functioning human being) can do is fall into hypnotic complacency – or assume that the solutions of the past are the best remedy for the challenges of the present. All is not as it seems.

The next 10-15 minutes were a blissful rush – fun, challenging, not too scary. We glided over the Class III water of "The Bridge," a reference to the plain-sight waving of spectators and bungee jumpers hundreds of feet above us. Our first real rush was Rapid #3, curiously unnamed and surprisingly "quick." *Feel stomach enter heart and throat...* It's not uncommon for drops of 12-15 feet of gradient over an even lesser amount of horizontal distance. Of course, it's never linear, like a well-greased hypotenuse; rather, it's a series of quick thrusts and jerks followed by crashing, foaming white water bursting over the bow. This would be followed by a momentary roller coaster ride, then another whoosh-like drop. *Lather, rinse, repeat.*

"Morning Glory," a batch of IV's and V's, was even more challenging. It required strategically bouncing off walls (again) as rafts had to plot the current's diagonal impact trajectory just right in order to shoot around a crunching "hole" underneath. In my native Southeastern U.S., these holes were also known as "hydraulics," which with minimum surface fanfare can pummel someone to death and not even relinquish the body until minutes or hours later. Best to stay in the "gentle agitation" cycle.

"Left forward!"

"Right forward!"

"Back left!"

"Back right!"

Choongu sounded off. I kept waiting for the bit about thruster engines and dilithium crystals. He may not have been Arthur Fiedler of *Boston Pops* fame, but his vocal precision achieved the same symphonic synchronicity. We obeyed and Nyaminyami acquiesced.

We then coasted for awhile, like a congratulatory cigarette break after a romping round of the Horizontal Bop. We had earned it, and lay back in our rafts. We were deep in the gorge now, bathing in the late morning sunshine, although on either inside of the narrow V-shaped gorge was a dark imposing jungle. Located considerably farther south of the equatorial sun, the Zambezi River drainage isn't quite the jungle of Tarzan's deepest, darkest Africa – but it's a close second. There weren't too many large mammals here because of the steep canyon purchase, but any zoologist could write a thesis on whatever creepy, crawly things invaded his tent or laid larvae in his porridge. Vines and dense grasses, monkeys and baboons, huge canopies of trees – it was all here in spades. Eagles soared overhead and kingfishers dive-bombed the river like ravenous kamikazes. I suppose if truth be known, the guests were really the entertainment. More than one set of curious eyes were watching us, and they sure as Nyaminyami weren't human.

The river at this point fanned wide, perhaps 150 feet. Supposedly it was over 200 feet deep in the middle, which made sense, considering the descent trajectory of the canyon walls. We simply had to stop to revel in this illusion. We jumped off our rafts into the cooling green water. We even jumped off the nearby cliffs a few times. We then reinvented what every 12-year-old boy instinctively does with an oar: applied just right, at 45° degree drop to the water, you can successfully drench someone up to 30 feet away. And since 22-year-old Aussies are basically 12-year-olds with an overdose of testosterone, thus commenced the raft wars.

Five minutes later, the canyon narrowed. Not surprisingly, the water started moving again – cigarette break was over. We shot through the "Stairway to Heaven," which drops nearly 25 feet over a mere 30. Massive, rolling waves tossed us like a Dixie cup in a four-year-old's bathtub as we paddled furiously to Choongu's barking orders. I'm not sure if we actually *accomplished* anything other than the illusion of control. But we made it, after nearly a minute of what seemed like an entire morning. Mechanical bull riders in those *Urban Cowboy* honkytonks would have appreciated the sensation.

"The Devil's Toilet Bowl" was now upon us. Presumably the name reflected the activity level and not the contents. It wasn't long, but the rapids plunged suddenly into a boiling cauldron of geysers, whirlpools and cacophonous waves – the type that don't harmoniously merge into a sculpted larger wave, but rather seem to duke it out in random chaos, like pit-traders at the Chicago commodities exchange. We were very conscious of our breathing at this point. And our biceps, triceps, lats and pec muscles. What was all in a morning's stroll to Choongu represented the most exercise – in some cases the only exercise – any of us had had in along time. It had been over a month since Alexis and I had summitted Kilimanjaro. Other than the several days of canoeing the previous week, the lion's share of our exercise the last month consisted of putting up and taking down our tents. Fine British ale and Rebecca's bread puddings just added insult to the inactivity (and the dreamy beaches of Zanzibar added even more inactivity to the insults).

* * * * * *

Then the day turned interesting. Ahead of us lay "Gulliver's Travels," 2,300 hundred feet of Class V with travails worthy of its namesake. There may have been no Yahoos or Lilliputians lurking about, but Lemeul Gulliver never had to reckon on Nyaminyami.

We entered the dragon, for how long, no one knows. Maybe 30 seconds, maybe a minute. We knew better than to feel invincible, but there's a false confidence that arises – whether from skill or luck is debatable – after the first dozen successful navigations of wave and hole. In fact, those crashing white waves start to resemble the passing landscape one might see out of a train window. But alas; it only takes one errant wave, and we found it. Rather, it found us.

We've all heard stories about someone's life passing in front of their eyes: the "slowing down" of time; the very non-panicked state of, well, not "peace" but matter-of-factness that accompanies one's actions and reactions; the big projector of the brain and light-meter of the eyes just clicking on one more stimulus. Somewhere in the depth of our consciousness (certainly not on the surface) is the realization that all of this hoopla is one giant entity unto itself; that no actions are separate; that it's all the same thing but with a lot of perplexing spokes masquerading as separate realities. But when "reality" hits or loses one of its sprockets, metaphysics goes to hell in a deflating raft. And reality hit us in the form of the Mother of All Waves.

Poseidon and Triton of old, those quirky Mediterranean sea gods had nothing on Nyaminyami. I know how Odysseus must have felt whenever he got close to his home and some capricious deity pulled rank on him. Over our bow the intruder came, white and curling, with frothing lips and snarling teeth. The buckling raft must have resembled a crushed piece of paper. Alexis was on the front left and she went flying past me like a banshee in a wind tunnel. I saw oars, loose helmets and other debris go airborne. I was on the far right and followed her – I guess, because I have no memory – by a few milliseconds.

At some later point – either a quarter second or 10 seconds, I became aware that 1) I was in the "drink," 2) the drink was sloshing violently, and 3) all was dark. The latter was explained by the fact that I was under an upside-down raft, which in turn meant no one else was in it, either.

Instinctively I grabbed the side of the raft and managed to duck under it, liberating myself from captivity but now totally at the mercy of the mighty Zambezi. Trying to position oneself feet-first is a joke when your torso is being tossed around like a rag-doll. The only thing I was certain of was that I was moving downstream. Everything else was "pitch, roll, and yaw." Life vests are amazing things, and I continued to bob helplessly as wave after wave crested me, dropped me into the next hole and then lifted me to the next. But it wasn't nearly that linear. All the while I was being rotated like a top, intermittently swallowing drainage from Angola to Botswana; my peripheral vision catching snippets of oars, clothing, sideline tree branches, and occasionally a colorful helmet adorning another bobbing body.

I'd been in the drink before, but not like this. Rocks, yes, even perilous – but not the world's longest roller coaster commanded by an angry god. It just kept coming, wave after wave; every brief interlude of precious calm (lasting maybe three seconds) followed by another drop, another twirl, another gulp, another hacking choke, a lunge. I'm an excellent swimmer and have never been intimidated by water, but this was getting old. Furthermore, I was getting tired fast.

Ahead – ahoy! – a boat bobbed. Mouths moved, arms gestured. Was I at the movies? *Was I dreaming?* Who were these guys? Slowly it dawned – they were motioning *to me*. Oh yeah, I'm in the water and flopping like Flipper in a tsunami. The little voice that runs the show said "Go right, Flipper," and somehow I made it to an outstretched oar. With the help of four gangly arms and an extreme burst of adrenalin, Flipper flopped into the raft, hyperventilated, and proceeded to return a half-gallon of Zambezi water the same way it had entered (only in reverse).

We were still rockin' and rollin', but now in the relative calm of Class IIs. A good 500-600 yards had passed, and gradually the scene revealed itself. The river was littered with a combination of empty rafts and those possessing only two or three people. Here, a blue helmet bobbed; there an orange vest; over yonder an oar went zipping by. Slowly, body by body, rafts were refilled with grateful, breathing corpses.

Then it dawned on me – where the hell was Alexis?

I knew not to panic, but since when do emotions listen to brains? I scanned the horizon with its ferocious gradient and its nips, tucks and curls, the mirage-like gaps between holes disappearing into some momentary rendezvous with a watery Hades. I yelled at other boats, which were mainly preoccupied with assembling their own cargo. What seemed like another eternity (Zen koan: how many days are in two eternities?) passed before I caught a puff of blond hair streaking out from under a helmet, and a pallid face that must've just kissed a ghost – or more accurately, Nyaminyami. I don't think Alexis even knew her name at that moment. She was half-wild and totally in leave of her senses. I did the unconscionable with an acquiescing guide (another boat, of course, had picked me up, as Choongu was nowhere in sight) – etiquette and common sense be damned – we reached over and grabbed her vest straps, hair, arms and anything animate or inanimate that offered purchase.

Her 115-pound frame didn't present a problem as much as the piercing pain in my side. She came on board easily enough; I writhed in the boat. Ribs, dammit, either broken or deeply bruised. What I hit I'll never know: a helmet perhaps (supposedly with a head still in it?), an oar, a thrusting foot, the rare rock – or maybe it was just from being inverted yogi-style like a kundalini pretzel.

Safe and sound aboard now, Alexis babbled, shivered, cried and did all the other things that revived overboard (wo)men do. I'm sure Jonah was no different. But she was okay. All troops eventually re-gathered at the next calm, and we counted the damage. No fatalities, no contusions, just a bit of posthumous barfing and coughing. In fact, my ribcage was the only real casualty, and I apparently would live. All in all, Nyaminyami had just played with us. But this was a warning only: he had thrown far worse tantrums.

* * * * * *

Another break and then it was time to resume the gauntlet. Next up was "Midnight Diner," spanning three different approaches: Star Trek, the Muncher Run and the Chicken Run. We asked Choongu about our chances:

"Star Trek best."

"Let's do it," we declared. "That's the route. What do you think our chances are?"

"Better than 50 – One-Half" (presumably he meant "50-50").

A word on linguistics: just because one speaks, hears and understands the words of another language doesn't mean they catch the underlying context. If so, the Tower of Babel would never have been built and U.N. translators would be driving taxi-cabs in Queens. Perhaps Choongu was the product of a fatalistic culture, or maybe he assumed that Anglos from faraway continents expect, *even desire*, to crash, like a scary ride at Disneyland. In any case, Choongu really meant greater than a 50-50 chance *of crashing*. Wasn't that what we wanted? Accordingly, we chose the most difficult route, by virtue of its 16-foot hole.

Actually, Choongu was wrong; we crashed with 100% certainty. The approach was gradual; benign, almost loving – up, up, up, curled the wave, slowly even. Like surfers wanting to pass over the breakers on an outward paddle, we held our breaths…then lost the gambit. Ever so gracefully the Zambezi's infantry curled over us – plop – and Alexis and I (in different seats than before) were in the drink again. Luckily, we weren't entering an aquatic minefield of 300 yard rapids. It was all over quickly, and considering everything, gently.

Thankfully, the next set of rapids – "Commercial Suicide" – was impassable, thus requiring portage. Impassable, that is, except for a few suicidal kayakers who disappeared into the midst of Class VI chaos (not commercially sanctioned) only to miraculously emerge alive, 10 seconds later about 50 yards downstream. Mad dogs and Englishmen, take note.

The "Gnashing Jaws of Death" wasn't as bad as the handle implies. Class IV, yes, but predictable and of course, no rocks. We then collapsed for a long lunch and an unexpected snooze.

After lunch, it was more of the same, but we were spared further humiliation by Nyaminyami. "The Three Sisters" (known as "The Three Little Pigs" to kayakers) were great sport, as was "The Mother," a rolling train of standing waves modeled after a NASA flight simulator. The two Terminators (I & II) were benevolent; we were forced to portage "Double Trouble," otherwise known as "The Bitch"; we even made it through "Oblivion" – responsible for more raft flips than any other commercial stretch of water in the world. Choongu conquered it; one of the lucky 25% who do. "The Washing Machine" and "The Overland Truck Eater" likewise were stern tests, but we passed without incident.

Finally, we were done. After a painful 750 foot ascent using tree roots and horizontal 2 x 4s as ladder rungs up the 45° incline, we stumbled back to our pickup trucks. There we paid homage to Nyaminyami, slugging down three coolers of ice cold Lion Lager – a humble but sincere token.

* * * * * *

It was now New Year's Eve. Rested up from our masochistic mayhem, we decided to do the town of Vic Falls in fashion. That would be the Victoria Falls Hotel, the "Classic African Grand Dame in an unbeatable location," according to the propaganda peddlers.

But they were right. The hotel was a regal timepiece of days gone by, when Britain's empire – in truth already shrinking – still spoke of grandeur, elegance, and refined taste (whatever the hell *that* is). A half century after Livingstone's "discovery" and a few short years after Cecil Rhodes' railroad could haul the bourgeois into have a look, Her Majesty's minions naturally did the sensible thing: they built a playhouse adjacent to the falls. A true luxury hotel, it was complete with winding staircases where the stern gaze of the truculent namesake queen stares you down ("I detest plebeians…*harrumph*") and busts of Julius Caesar and African notables (Nelson Mandela? Shaka Zulu? Robert Mugabe, his Most Excellent Thuggery?) adorn banister landings. There were also tea rooms ("But of course, love!"), crystal chandeliers, afghan carpets, mahogany furniture and marble floors.

For the *Better Homes & Gardens* crowd, the manor had lily ponds, swaying palms, swimming pools with cascading fountains (but why, with a wonderful river nearby?) and richly manicured lawns (croquet and crumpets, anyone?) blending into sculpted hedges and luscious gardens. For naturalists, there were animals grazing on the stately lawns, whether for show or for the kitchen I'm not sure; for the athletic-type, there were floodlit tennis courts. The pampered, rich and shameless could choose from any number of amenities: a beauty salon, wedding chapel, impressive wine list, smoking rooms, masseuse staff, and the *coup d'grâce* – satellite TV (Motel 6 had nothing on these guys). Finally, if anyone got bored of roughing it, there was always a pleasant stroll down to the falls. They were a slow 10-minute walk away, while the plume – the gift that keeps on giving – was always in view.

All of this was yours – 181 rooms to choose from – for just $327 U.S. Not a bad stipend if one can get it, here in a land where a $1 basket whips vendors into a frenzy like drunken gamblers at a Carolina cockfight. The visitor shouldn't be shocked if some of that $327, say, about $325, ended up in the capitol at Harare, or even in Mugabe's Swiss bank account.

It would also be correct to assume that the hotel didn't exactly sit on Main Street. It was about a mile away, enough of a buffer for guards, fences and other deterrents to keep out the riff-raff. But the employment base of locals was substantial, possibly in the hundreds. The front line helpers, impressively, were every bit as refined as *Batman's* "Alfred" without any of the cynical baggage of, say, *Arthur's* "Hobson" (John Gielgud).

There were six of us that night. The under-30 crowd preferred the pubs and discos that fired up in town around 10:00 p.m. and went until just before sun-up. The over-30 crowd sought a more sublime experience, sans the jackhammer drone of Hip-Hop music and reek of regurgitated Mai Tai on one's shirt. In addition to Alexis and myself, there was Allison, the New Zealand schoolteacher; Andrew and Daphne, professionals from Brisbane, Australia; and Tracy, a Canadian grad student.

We started out with a wonderful dinner in the hotel restaurant. It was solid Four-Star quality and worth every farthing of the $10 entrée prices. At about 10:30, we went outside to the veranda. The mist from the falls was in plain sight even at night, and a recalcitrant moon muddled about in the humid sky. Coffee, liquors and desserts – for six – came to $22. It seemed quite the dichotomy considering the room rates, but I never could figure out this black market translation stuff.

It wouldn't be fair or accurate to say that the elegance was a charade, but it surely was yesterday's glory. No longer were the guests movers and shakers from Cape Town and London (although any guests obviously *did* have money), the empire shakers of old, puffing cigars and sipping scotch, while deciding how to best pilfer resources and quell uprisings. No longer were intelligent and honest explorers, such as Livingstone, Speek and Burton, seeking knowledge and adventure for their own sake. Besides, whereas statistics may lie, occupancy rates don't. There were only perhaps 25-30 rooms rented out that New Year's Holiday – leaving about 150-plus vacant. Our superb dessert and café trimmings, as cheap as they had been, required four servers: meaning this was either the ultimate patronage system or the welfare state at its ugliest. They were polite and mannered, yes; friendly, sort of; busy, not remotely, for the simple reason that our group and one other were the *only* guests at this beautiful outside veranda overlooking one of the world's Seven Natural Wonders. It was like a giant party had been thrown by a grand mistress who just happened to forget to send out invitations.

I almost wished I could have seen the fine carriages, liveried stable boys, corseted Victorian dresses, smoke-filled rooms and hearty "huzzahs"; the scheming bureaucrats plotting their railroad routes and fingering diamond and gold mines; Sunday croquet matches with century-old Daguerreotype "flashes" capturing nobility before it faded into the sunset, absorbed by the history books: with a whimper, never a bang. Just as in India, North America, Australia and New Zealand, the benefactors had withdrawn from here, too, either via revolt or financial necessity. But unlike those other boisterous offspring, here the experiment was very much in doubt. I wouldn't even give it "50 – One-Half" odds at this point.

Right before midnight we caught rumor that the hotel was sponsoring a raucous New Year's Ceremony, complete with native dancers. We trundled a few hundred yards across the massive lawn to a ballroom courtyard, a pleasant outdoor place with columns, marble, tile and other pleasant furnishings. Surely we would find vitality and *joie d'vie* here. We entered the courtyard amidst a gala flood of balloons, streamers and fine cakes and beverages (alcoholic and the other kind). We heard singing, shouting and clapping. Our festive juices flowed – this would be a great finale to our lonely/lovely evening! – but the place was practically empty. About 20 dance members were giving it their all in front of no more than a dozen guests, the latter spread out over six or seven tables. James Brown's *Soul Train* couldn't have delivered with more passion, more shimmying hips, more effervescent life bellowing from lustful lungs. But like so many others in Mother

Africa, they were practically singing for themselves. Cecil Rhodes' train had pulled out a long time ago (airport notwithstanding) and the jungle was encroaching once more.

Alexis and I tried to jumpstart things. Compared to their fluid hypnotic movements, we danced the white man's "Funky Chicken." We were received with...humor? Sympathy? A few other hesitant Mzungus – our vanilla-colored brethren from northern climes – got out of their wicker chairs and joined us. *Auld Lang Syne* was sung at midnight, followed by a tribal chant for peace and prosperity the coming year. They sure could use it.

Our entertainers were strikingly handsome. They wore a type of skin, possibly real, possibly synthetic, with a leopard or cheetah motif that was cut off raggedy-edged, Fred Flintstone style; exquisite bracelets jangled on their arms, wrists and ankles. They moved gracefully and smiled from the heart. Yeah, this was just a job – but they lived it without a trace of indignation or resentment. They took our hands and danced with us, thanking us profusely for jumping in – that was the whole idea, anyway. Many of the dancers, we learned afterward, were former professionals from Harare, or unemployed grad students. Or, they'd done something quite innocently that landed them on Mugabe's dung list. These were serious citizens of the Motherland, disenfranchised by the old and new guards alike. Country after country, the game's the same. The skin may be darker or lighter, names pronounced differently and the gods of a different ilk; but ultimately power, like cream or scum, rises to the top. It doesn't take much to stir it up.

These are the kinds of vignettes that spark my *joie d'vie*. My observations aren't necessarily "adventures," but rather, a way of allowing my heart, mind and body to participate at a deeper level of human connectivity. If I hadn't recognized it before now, it was time to point out to myself that we are living in a "mental" universe. Perception and mind power: beliefs and belief systems are the two strongest controlling forces. Class systems are merely *embedded beliefs* placed there by controlling forces and accepted, sometimes unconsciously, by acquiescing believers. Once figured out, everything else becomes simple, since there's only one way to tear down the walls and remove the barriers: a smile, a knowing word or expression in one's eyes, the delivery of trust through a handshake or hug, and the accompanying love that conveys acceptance, understanding, forgiveness and perhaps, common tears.

All people really *are* the same. ("We share the same biology, regardless of ideology"). That we find ourselves in controlled and controlling circumstances this time around, has more to do with our choices and with something we want or need to learn. In another lifetime a slave might find himself sitting on a throne and ruling a country, or playing the lead role in a Hollywood blockbuster.

* * * * * *

A month later, after fun and games in Botswana, Namibia and South Africa, we were back in Vic Falls, the nerve-center junction in Sub-Saharan logistics. Which isn't saying much: like, three roads intersect there. Good thing Christopher had loaded Frankie up with petrol in Botswana. The lines of vehicles in Vic Falls waiting for fuel stretched half a mile long, vehicles that were empty, because no one knew when the precious juice would arrive...this afternoon? Tomorrow? Next week? Almost as bad were the queues at the grocery, as rumor had it that bread, even raw millet, was about to come in that afternoon.

I thought of the stories of Russian food lines in the early Nineties, when the conversion to capitalism hadn't worked out the distribution kinks yet. It struck me that in neither place, Russia nor Zimbabwe, was "supply" the actual problem. Russia had one of the world's largest breadbaskets, and the former Rhodesia was likewise blessed with prodigious crops. But incompetence and cronyism are deadly allies: the Russian shortages were generated by disastrous five-year mandated plans; Zim's disaster after ousting the co-op managers (which greatly diminished the output) was amplified by Mugabe's slight of hand: his warehouses bulge with grain and fuel to feed and supply the army and defeat "imperialists" aligned with London, Washington, Johannesburg and Sydney. *Huh?*

Walking back to our hostel that evening, Alexis and I ran across a fellow named Rudo. We recognized him as one of the teenage helpers from the rafting company. He wasn't a guide but more of an assistant or first mate, like Choongu's "Gilligan." He was noticeably limping and had a gash over his eye, sewn together with something resembling thread. It wasn't sewn by any doctor, either – it looked like my one high school stab at Home Ec needlepoint. Rudo was also missing several teeth, and dried blood was caked around his mouth. Bandages were spread liberally around his arms and legs. *Wait 'til Workers Comp hears about this*, I thought.

"Wow, what happened to you?"

"Big crash – even rocks – many boats. Many people hurt."

"What about Choongu?"

Rudo pointed to his knee and exaggerated it sticking out at a 90 degree angle. He then pointed to his ribcage and stabbed each one with a closed fist.

"Choongu go carry out on stretcher from Zambezi."

It was a day to remember – and one to forget. Legs had been broken. Noses smashed catawampus. Teeth blasted out. Big time concussions. The town even buzzed with rumors of possible fatalities.

"Why?" I pressed on. "How did they crash?"

Rudo shrugged. He was obviously exhausted and wanted to go home. "Maybe Nyaminyami have bad day," he sighed. "Who know?"

I pointed at his pendant. The white amulet stared back, blankly. "How come Nyaminyami didn't protect you today?"

Rudo managed a polite smile: "He *did* protect. If I no wear necklace, I be dead now. Instead, I am lucky man."

Without a pendant for protection, without any type of recognition of native deities, Alexis and I just happened to choose a different date and time to test our own destinies. Who really was in charge here?

At that moment I wondered if that meeting with Rudo was, in fact, the real reason why we had embarked on our white water adventure in the first place. I realized once again how little we really know, when relating it to the large scheme of things. Even crossing the street when the light is green could turn out to be fatal if an oncoming car fails to stop. "There, but for the grace of God, go I."

Part IV
Mindscapes and Soulscapes

To the well-organized mind, death is but the next great adventure.
– Albus Dumbledore

It is the Father's good pleasure to give you the Kingdom.
–Luke 12:32

In probably every Western graduate finance program, the parable is told of a drunk's "random walk" – a statistical parody attempting to predict a stock's next move. The theory goes that, after accounting for all the variables (e.g., staggering this way and that), the drunk's next "ending place" – that is, the stock's future value – is just as likely to be exactly where he started out.

At some point in my travels of longitude and latitude, it struck me that most of us live our lives like the drunk's random walk.

Sure, our wallets may get fatter or thinner, just like our waistlines and hairlines, but for the most part tomorrow's "ending place" would continue to look much like today. This is true not only for the nonchalant and brain-dead, but also for the folks with all those day-timers and "goals," rules and regulations: *often, living someone else's life.* Even those of us with a lot of frequent flyer miles and cool decals from far-flung ports o'call often live a two-dimensional, self-limiting life.

Why? Maybe because we don't know any better, or maybe we've numbed the pain and enjoy wallowing in our own self-proscribed victimization. Or maybe we've "thrown the baby out with the bath water" after a few scalding-oil baths in rigid, cruel theology.

That's too bad, because there *is* more – so much more. Travel and true growth aren't just about Landscapes. True Travel, like our True Essence, is multidimensional and also includes Mindscapes and Soulscapes.

Chapter Twenty-Three

The Dragonfly Winks

Thump…Thump…Thump…

✦✦✦ A drum thuds monotonously as we slowly make our way clockwise around the ceremonial stones. Flute notes hang in the air, full but sad, as flitting river birds chime in with their whimsical chorus. Late winter resists the advances of an impatient spring and a detached hazy sun provides just enough warmth to counter the chill in our hearts this March day.

We're a quickly assembled rag-tag group, gathered on the banks of Idaho's Snake River to celebrate Clifton's life and honor his great transition.

Clifton defied convenient profiling. Layer after layer of paradox jumped off his résumé: surfer bum, seminarian, bus driver, Reiki Master, construction superintendent, video game fanatic, and detached sage. He was a hybrid of Grizzly Adams and Thomas Merton, with a little bit of Mikey the cynical cereal-cruncher lurking around the edges. An encounter with Clifton might start with a giant bear hug and proceed into a marathon debate about the Enneagram, that nine-pointed road map of personality dynamics. A coffee break could begin with a dissertation about why the roof leaked and the sewer line was plugged, moving quickly into a graphic description of an ethereal light in the sky that no one else (but Clifton) had seen…

He may not have suffered fools gladly, but he *did* disarm them with an affable knee-slapping belly laugh that was usually predicated by some anecdote of his own foibles, laying them out as if to say, "Come join the parade of banal, perplexing, beautifully irrational humans." He had a penchant for absurdity that never betrayed the spontaneous combustion of a child at play – not a Sartre-like "who cares, we're all gonna die" existential cynicism; rather, the gleeful acceptance of an existence guided by hidden puppeteers. He certainly wasn't perfect – he'd fume for hours from some slight, and he'd drag himself into near-despondency from the latest media torrent of bad news or purported abuses of the rich and powerful. In addition, household chores often had to settle for second place if competing against Star Trek reruns or Madison Avenue's latest eye-candy (electronic gadgetry, in particular).

But he was loved and respected. A rising talent with his commercial construction employer, he had advanced from carpenter to foreman to supervisor to superintendent in just four years. He had the handyman's gift combined with unbridled enthusiasm for making anything out of brick, steel, concrete, wood, glass, nails, screws and glue. Although his politics and beliefs were more than odd to his rough and tumble fraternity of blue-collar brethren, he nonetheless fit in. More than one co-worker feigning work-related needs would slip by Clifton's desk to hear about how many dimensions there were in hyperspace. He entertained, enlightened and was followed. I had often thought if the meek were to inherit the Earth, it would be Clifton at the vanguard – but only after he'd built the commencement podium, delivered a few choice words, videotaped the whole damn thing for good measure, then laughed uproariously over his oratory *faux-pas* while downing a third bowl of popcorn.

* * * * * *

In the cadence of the contemplative, our steps are filled with memories, love, thanks and grief; perhaps, even in a few cases, with regret. There are 33 of us, coincidentally – a propitious number to those intrigued by the gray science of numerology.

The stark, undulating prairie hills of the Snake River Plateau, bereft of trees but dotted with sage brush, shelter our ceremony while the namesake river slithers through the volcanic walls like a silent artery. High above, petroglyphs dating back 7,000 years stare down on us stoically. How many times have they witnessed this scene, I wonder – what could they tell us? The artists' descendants, an amalgam of Shoshone, Bannock and Paiute tribes teamed with enterprising Boy Scouts and receptive park authorities to construct and dedicate this "Medicine Wheel" several years ago. They made a good call – it's hard to conceive of a better place to pay respects to the seasons of the soul than this riverbank at the edge of the Birds of Prey National Conservation Area. Thirty miles away lay Boise, separated by a checkerboard of alfalfa fields, homesteads and quaint community stores. But for all practical purposes, we could have been in Timbuktu or Mongolia.

* * * * * *

Clifton had a curious fascination about dragonflies. He loved them. His house was cluttered with dragonfly memorabilia – mobiles, posters, jewelry, trinkets, tee shirts and literature. The dragonfly was his adopted totem. When he was a boy, the story goes, once he had supposedly been surrounded by a swarm of them while on a family camping outing, an episode he later referred to as "absolutely terrifying." But rather than subsequently shunning dragonflies, eventually he became enamored of them.

In some native mythologies, dragonflies are said to symbolize the power of illusion and light. In the Oriental view, they represent all the temporal fickleness of a passing summer day: fleeting, a whirlwind of frenetic energy, swirling, darting and disappearing – so majestic, so fragile – the human diary rolled into a few passing days. Still others attach it to happiness, strength, courage and success. The northern plains Indians, strangely enough, have often linked the dragonfly with snakes. That irony wasn't lost on me, here on the banks of the Snake River. In any case, dragonflies had a lasting impact on Clifton. He'd been hooked for life – as temporal and frenetic as it was.

* * * * * *

Earlier that day I'd strolled along the greenbelt of the Boise River, a tributary of the Snake, lost in reverie about a life well-lived and contemplating the koan of Clifton's sudden departure. Friends say they'd never seen him so buoyant as in those last few weeks.

"Stephen, the shame of it all is that he was really coming into his own," his wife Patricia had remarked. "The job, our house; ya know, he was getting mobilized and productive after all the downtime we'd gone through after our bookstore in Coeur d'Alene went under. I'd just seen him some 20 minutes earlier. He came by to drop off a belated paycheck, and he was beaming like a big, happy 49-year old kid."

This was 20 minutes before Clifton had apparently slumped over the wheel of his red '91 Chevy, crossed the center lane on a six-percent downgrade, and left us with more questions than answers.

But Patricia also admitted she'd been getting a feeling recently that he might be flirting with some kind of accident.

"He'd been running ragged at work, then he went down to Florida to play with his ol' childhood buddy Steve. When those guys get together they go crazy like teenagers. Only they're not teenagers anymore, I told 'em. I was so worried about him being exhausted, I figured he might be getting set up for something bad. I even had him promise to call me several times en route."

Clifton had honored that plea with all the humility and good judgment of a man who understands a woman's superior instincts. Still, after flight delays had shortchanged his sleep the night of his return from Florida, he had nonetheless woken Monday morning with the satisfaction of a man climbing the ascendancy of career, family and community. So, tired or not, he charged off to work, happy to be back. Clifton wasn't the type to ponder if it was "just too good'" – he accepted the bliss and reveled in it.

As my walk slackened, my reverie of his last days gave way to self-absorption and I reflected on how Life can go through our plans like a twister through a trailer park. I remembered the wry joke: "Wanna give the Almighty a good side-splitter? Tell'm your goals!" I chided myself for all the supercilious garbage that I thought was important. All the brain's bugaboos continued to come home to roost – money (need more), time (is passing us by...), responsibility (scary), dharma (I should be out saving the world). On the battleground of my mind the forecast has been fair to partly cloudy, the willpower fair to middlin.'

My rational overseer slowly retreated and the empty enigmatic moment played 52-card pickup with my senses and feelings:

Pettiness. Perspective. Pain. Perplexity. What to do – how to be – and the whole why, where, and when of it all. A time to reap, a time to sow, a time to live, a time to…screw you, Ecclesiastes (you, too, McGuinn). Turn, turn, turn. Yada, yada, yada.

OK Clifton, I hope you're now officially an expert on this whole post-life thing. It'd be a drag later to find out no one's there (providing of course, there's an "I" to be disappointed). Please gimme a sign that you're on the other end of this S.O.S. Better yet, lemme know that you're dancing the big celestial jitterbug right now. Smoke and lightening aren't necessary, just a whisper "bro," or some kinda poignant symbol, even a swift kick in the ass will do. Just some entreaty that there's more legacy to our little cameo/soliloquy down here than scrapbooks and worm food…Some token that justifies keeping around a Bible, Torah, Koran, Bhagavad-Gita or tattered copy of The Prophet *for some purpose other than a backup supply of toilet paper.*

In the spur of the moment, I knew what I had to do: on to the liquor store.

* * * * * *

Clifton was of Portuguese ethnic heritage and no stranger to the conviviality of food and drink. I reckoned a well-hoisted *saludos* of Iberian vintage, shared among friends, would be a fitting send-off. Not a Port with its syrupy dessert leanings, but a robust, full-bodied, blood-red workin' man's table wine.

"Can I help you find something?" the smiley grocer-turned-sommelier chimed in.

"Portuguese. Cheap. But not Port," I responded.

"Hmmm…let's have a look."

Minutes later, after combing shelves and stock rooms and other nooks and crannies, we found our quarry. There, on a remote shelf, was the *only* bottle left of the *only* (non-Port) Portuguese brand carried by the store. A 1999 Altano Douro, at a humble $7.95 but with an inviting presentation. So be it. *In vino veritas* ("In wine there is truth") said the sage, but he never said anything about price. I took it home and gently uncorked the bottle, careful not to spill a drop. I then put the cork back in the bottle for safe transport to the ceremony.

* * * * * *

Medicine Wheels are utilized by indigenous peoples across the Northern Plains and Northwest. Comprised of basically rocks and soil, they represent the circle of life, the four directions and union of sky and earth. They are templates or models for the interrelationship of life. How they are entered and what the visitor does, reflects the seasons of one's soul: to the east, *Illumination*; to the south, *Innocence and Trust*; to the west, *Introspection*; to the north; *Deep Wisdom*. In turn, different tribes associated different animals with key positions, as totems or guardian spirits. But at the center was always *You* – a Universe of One – everything and nothing. "Mankind has not created the web of life; He is but one strand in it; All things connect," said Chief Seattle in perhaps the greatest environmental speech ever given: poignant words and an implicit warning so callously disregarded in this day and age of helter-skelter, quarterly profit pursuit.

* * * * * *

The third time around the Medicine Wheel's 50-foot diameter, we stopped at our original positions. The last drum echoes rolled away; the breeze carried off the fleeting notes from the flutes. Even the birds seem muted. In the center of the Wheel, accessed through the eastern entrance (the gateway of the rising sun), an altar of rocks was piled high with firewood and tribute: flowers, amulets, tokens, tobacco, and a bottle of Portuguese wine. Next to the altar was the small box with Clifton's ashes.

Patricia, his wife of 10 years, was conducting from the Wheel's southern point – the place of the heart. She choreographed us with grace, dignity and humor, never betraying her obvious sorrow.

"I'm no stranger to grief," she had told me the previous night at her house.

"After Jeff's crash (her youngest son, a regrouping prodigal, had also been killed on the road a few years before), I didn't think it could get any tougher than that. Ya know, I slept pregnant on park benches, in my early twenties, without a clue where my next meal was coming from. I did "body piles" and all that Free Love stuff back in the Sixties, secretly hating it the whole time. And I've now seen four marriages end in either disillusion or heartbreak. But it has been such a wonderful experience with Clifton. It's all been worth it.

"Know what the amazing thing is?" She shook her head, her eyes growing moist. "We just had our tenth anniversary – and by four days, I'm eligible to receive his Social Security benefits. I know enough to know I'm in shock right now; I guess that's how Spirit eases the pain. All I know is that The Guys must have some pretty big plans for Clifton – I guess it's his graduation day. And I hafta believe they're looking after me, too."

In the 18 years of our acquaintance, Patricia had blossomed into the strongest person I'd ever known. The nervous, timid medical transcriber somehow had found the fortitude to embrace life's gauntlet; emerging as a commercial entrepreneur, a grassroots animal rights and environmental organizer, four-time published author, and now a spiritual Den Mother for dozens. Every venture was funded by nothing but pennies and prayers, her indomitable will and quixotic vision galvanizing resources and allies around her like steel ingots pulled to a magnet.

Although sappy nostalgia would be completely understandable under the circumstances, instead Patricia chose just a few simple words, spoken softly but firmly in her usual style. She praised and sobbed, directed and exhorted. She also received the collective heart and awe of our little group, and crafted a fitting epitaph that extolled Clifton's many virtues, giving deference to his inner brat, acknowledging his unfulfilled dreams and projects, and then thanking us for our attendance.

(I conjured up an image of Sacagawea and dressed it in freckles and a red fop of hair. I vowed to share this with her later, knowing she'd probably tell me to "go get a lobotomy").

It was time for the offerings, and everyone had their say. We wished Clifton God-speed, related a few favorite stories and told him to "be good or be good at it." One by one, contributors walked around the Medicine Wheel's periphery, entered the eastern opening and proceeded to the altar to make their consecration.

I took the bottle of Altano Douro, eased the cork back out a second time and handed it to Patricia. She drank with great reverence. Then it was my turn, followed by 31 others, all toasting the Hero's journey as we imbibed the imported fruits of Clifton's forefathers and contemporary kinfolk. Hints of clay, pepper, cherry, plum and currants tweaked our taste buds as the vintage ran down our chins in bloody rivulets. Full bodied, not too many tannins. Just like Clifton.

Three times the bottle went around, for 99 swigs. A final splash on the ground acknowledged the keepers of the Medicine Wheel, and bestowed our respects for its tradition.

As Patricia hoisted up the bottle for a final inspection, suddenly her eyes widened and she eyed me incredulously. "Stephen, did you look closely at the label when you bought this bottle?"

I had not, I replied. On the left hand side of the label, about the size of a dime was the object of her fascination: *a dragonfly*.

* * * * * *

Clifton had earned his day at the head of the class. It seemed I had received an answer to my earlier petition within minutes of the request. But the greeting had eluded me until now, when all could share in the joke. Humility and humor always did run through that boy in alternating currents...

Soon after, his ashes were released into the river, where they would eventually roll past the confluence of the Salmon, merge with the mighty Columbia and rest in the Pacific – the great calm. A final garland of flowers saw him off, blanketing the Snake like sparkling dew on a serpentine Ganges. We drove away, exiting the valley floor to the rim of the canyon. The sun, now brilliant crimson, bid adieu and eased itself onto the horizon, flanked by two "Sun Dog" rainbows at the 10:00 and 2:00 positions.

On the opposite horizon, the moon was rising in a hue of pink and lavender. Looking over our shoulder, we could see the Snake glistening one last time as it slowly rounded a volcanic outcropping: like the gleeful winking of an eye.

For life and death are One, even as the river and sea are One.
–Kahlil Gibran

Chapter Twenty-Four

Mucking About on the Ethereal Bridge

The wave waved to the particle, and said "Which one of you am I?"
– Author unknown

The mournful dirge of an Irish fiddle faded behind me as I walked out of the tavern into the cold Utah night, strolling to my car, about 100 yards down the canyon road. All was serene: no traffic, no quarrelsome teenagers, no airplanes overhead. The only sounds were the faintest murmur of a roadside brook and some fir branches groaning from snow and ice that had overextended their stay. It had been a fine evening – the intimate folk music, rustic setting and best hamburger in town. I was healthfully balanced on the fulcrum between melancholia and the countenance of a life richly lived.

I looked up at the sky, half-consciously mapping the constellations I'd learned in my youth. They were all there holding court, shepherded by Vega, Rigel, Betelgeuse, Sirius, Procyon, Deneb, Regulus, Altair and a host of other red, white and blue caretakers. They looked pretty much the same now as they did when I was eleven – never mind that over the last three decades they were hurling through space and had separated themselves by billions of more miles. Relatively, they hadn't moved at all. It was I who had been traveling.

My old friends now seemed neither distant nor timeless, no longer gaseous giants in a far-away sky, but intelligent and intimate; personal and in my face. The tapestry of the sky behind them was blacker than a witch's soul and the Milky Way spun like a gossamer veil across the gap between the woods. I sighed in thoughtless reverie. Object and subject blurred.

First I felt it, and then I heard it:

"Don't you know that you will never be alone?"

For what may have only been a moment, I was "Home," merged with some tribe, or family.

I can't determine the origin of the voice, although I knew it was mine, carrying such conviction and warmth and speaking from some timeless void that sent lightning bolts through every limb and tissue in my body.

It rang in my head, in my cells and wherever else consciousness lurks and dreams go to play. My feet may have been on terra firma, but I momentarily floated in some kind of primordial soup that only knew eternity, infinity and being. It was knowledge, not dogma; Truth, not faith or hope; and it wasn't me, but it *was Me*.

From all ages, through all ages.

The moment didn't last, of course – my brain tried to analyze the sound and convince myself I had conjured up an errant thought, my feet complained they were cold, and my internal pragmatist reminded me of tomorrow's shopping list. But I knew something – not a fact-based snippet of trivia, but an experiential knowledge of a grander Self, connected to all. Separate, but same.

* * * * * *

That wasn't the first or last time I'd mucked about on the ethereal bridge that spans the pylons of presumed reality and assumed fantasy. But it was perhaps the most poignant, and left an indelible impression. If I'm not alone, who, or what, is with me? More precisely, *who* is "Me"?

I've found that these transcendental two-by-fours come in different packages, and like Hermes, flash unexpectedly onto the psychic big-screen with the temerity of quicksilver.

Dreams are maybe the most common, but I'll be damned if I can figure them out. There's something just a little too fuzzy with suspension of all the faculties that detracts from whatever validity they may actually possess: think *Mr. Toad's Wild Run* tag-team wrestling with *The Brothers Grimm*. Maybe on the margins there's some truth to Carl Jung's ideas about "archetypes" and universal harbingers, but still that doesn't cover all the territories of weirdness. Throw in the fact that common signs, symbols and critters signify varying themes to different cultures, and one is left dangling from the horns of an interpretational dilemma.

To me, dreams are like LSD – one can get caught up in the high drama or just sit back and watch the show: the danger is in assigning values, morals, context, or even meaning.

Not that dreams can't be spot-on, even monumental. The story is told of a young Corporal Hitler in the trenches of World War I having a horrendous nightmare that his bunker had just been hit, obliterating the company. Upon waking in a cold sweat and instinctively running outside before he realized it was a dream, he looked back just in time to witness the bunker being blown to pieces by a well-lobbed mortar. He was the only survivor. Thus it can rightfully be said that Herr Hitler's dream affected history, enabling him to live so that others may soon die. Many others. Without this freaky dream, it's possible that Europe of the 1930s and '40s might have been a far jollier place.

The problem with taking everything so literally is that the world is full of kooks, narcissists and megalomaniacs. For every Florence Nightingale beckoned to higher calling, there's the neighbor moving to the North Pole to await Santa Claus' imminent return (harmless enough), or the vigilante compelled by a 100- foot-tall Jesus to blow up everything east of the Urals and north of Singapore (not so harmless). Dreams can be cute, but they can also be dangerous tar pits for the traditionalist insisting on reading the bones their own way.

Do they truly signify anything other than the brain playing twister with its weaving waves of alphas, betas, deltas and thetas? Entire tribes in the Amazon and in Africa base group decisions on their members' dreams. Talk about betting the farm – literally. Like, what if they're wrong? Is there a shaman's guild to appeal to, in case say, the village burns down or a crop is decimated as a result of an errant deciphering? I've generally considered dreams a cheap way of going to the movies, and place about as much significance in them.

On the other hand…

Out-of-Body Experiences (OBEs)

"Lucid dreams" – or more to the point, Out-of-Body Experiences (OBEs) – are a different matter. OBEs are the Big Leagues, and unlike their dopier cousins, are sharp, refined, vivid – and conscious. As conscious as the writer who types this line, or the eyes that read it. Oh, they're just as wily and unpredictable. But they *seem* so damn real, and are usually accompanied by a rush of psychic adrenalin so rich, the buzz endures for hours, even days after, in waking consciousness.

It is believed that about 25% of people have at least one OBE in their life. My first OBE was in my early thirties, and they've occurred probably 25-30 times over the last 15 years. One thing's for sure – unlike the elusive dream memory, one doesn't forget an OBE unless one is also prone to forgetting their wedding day, a game-winning basketball shot, or falling out of a five-story window.

Anyone who has seen the movies *2001: A Space Odyssey* or *Contact* has received – or rather viewed – a glimpse of the sensation. In *2001*, astronaut Bowman enters the domino-shaped monolith exclaiming, "My God, it's full of stars!" and is sucked through it at warp speed on his way to Star Child immortality. Jodie Foster's character (Dr. Arroway) in *Contact*, to the chagrin of NASA, has the ride of her life through a cosmic "Worm Hole," a shifting network of inter-dimensional Slinkies with instantaneous access to the star system of Vega, a mere 26 light years away. OK, so that's only 156 *trillion* miles from us.

I must admit that from personal experience – Hollywood sensationalism notwithstanding – although these films are faithful in their representations, they cannot begin to deliver the euphoric rush that really accompanies the ride. It is more thrilling than any Earth-bound sensation I've ever had. From somewhere deep in sleep, I'm suddenly very aware – not awake, but totally conscious. The "setting" could be any number of venues, the same backdrop as a dream; yet I know I'm "asleep" and not bound to anything. Soon enough, I'm soaring up through the skies, through buildings and other solid objects (look Ma, no kryptonite!), up into the heavens, the night sky, the curve of the Earth, and on beyond. There's a *whoosh* of acceleration as frequencies rise, cells tingle (ah, I am in a "body") and every square inch of this invisible body feels like a Caligulan cocktail of Viagra and amphetamines. Faster and faster, through Bowman's Star Gate and Foster's Worm Hole, finally just morphing into a blur.

And how wonderful it is – not one iota of fear, no sense of isolation or getting lost – only an insatiable curiosity to keep going, the urge-to-merge (with *what?*) and the absolute most euphoric, gasket-blowing, mind-blasting, soul-shaking spirit ride that can possibly be imagined.

One flight in particular gradually decelerated to a standstill in whatever framework of space and time supported me. There in front of me, galaxy after galaxy spun out into infinity, silken arms of inconceivable light and beauty. I was Everything – love, being and eternity – without a single thought: certainly without a trace of guilt, anger, jealousy or shame. Staring – through what "eyes" I don't know – into the center of this cluster, I was aware that I was at an impasse and was being gently prodded by Something that related to making a decision. Tangible, analytical thought wasn't in order. Good thing; I would've soiled my jammies. But from some deep place within my essence came a voice again – not me, but Me.

It said:

"I am committed."

WHOOOOOSH. Like a Star Wars cruiser making the jump to light speed – or more like Cupid's arrow into the heart of the All That Is – I was sucked into the middle of a blinding light. I guess my circuits blew, because there I was again in my bed, fully awake in the 3-D carnival we call Earth: gob-smacked, bliss-whacked, and very much in love with Something. And very, very alive.

Most times I can just keep going. I've woken myself up a time or two; regrettably, just to make sure I can "get back." I no longer will have such little faith.

Some of the forays involve more terrestrial explorations. One in particular took me around the pastoral setting of what, from past physical visits, I instinctively knew was New Zealand. On the side of a hill was a tremendous tree, the tallest I've ever seen; I hovered around it inspecting every leaf. It was hundreds of feet tall, standing all by itself. I knew I was in La-La-land; but once again my faculties and discernment were greater than the reality of waking life. Months later the grandeur endured; the colors just right, a vivid 360-degree absorption.

What brings on an OBE? Hard to say, but I've noticed a tendency for them to cluster around the turning points in my life – hence, the 25-30 occurrences of the last 15 years. Decisions such as "to work, or not to work," "to move, or not to move" ...flip-flop points that usually revolve around wallet, vocation/*dharma*, *l'amour*, or general antsy-ness.

I can only hope – *I choose to believe* – they are meant to comfort, like the soul's *modus operandi* of handing Linus a blanket, a celestial lifebuoy for the treading capsize-ee.

"I am committed."

(To What? Who is responsible for having shown me that commitment?)

Why don't these OBEs happen to everyone? Maybe they would, if people believed in them and cultivated the experience. I've also considered that they're related to my wanderlust...the curiosity to go everywhere, meet people of all cultures, experience everything life has to offer. Why not include Out-of-Body experiences in this list of timeless travel? And so I did – unwittingly!

Some books claim that one can learn to induce OBEs. I don't know if I want to let that genie out of the bottle. Be careful what you ask for. As they say on Wall Street, "Pigs get fat, hogs get slaughtered." On the other hand, it might make for some fun water cooler chitchat:

Me: "Whadju do last night?"

Colleague: "Watched Leno and crashed – whadju do?"

Me: "Went to Patagonia, Venus and Alpha Centauri. First class."

Colleague: "Show-off."

OBEs are celebrations of joy and unity. They are a homecoming – to *Something* – that allows and encourages total freedom and exhilaration. The OBE drills a laser into your cerebellum and downloads the experience into your mind bank.

Somewhere, a scientist snickers. New Age fluff, this is. Never mind the guy on the operating table who takes a little "stroll" and later, reunited in body and consciousness, proceeds to describe the Fruit-of-the-Looms on some orderly working on a *completely* different floor of the hospital…at the *exact* moment as his operation.

Coincidence? Hallucination? *Right*…If OBEs are indeed a phantasmagoric hallucination, then bring 'em on: the real somnolence lies in a species that wars on itself and craps in its own bed. If the fleeting pinnacle of an OBE brings perspective to the cultural insanity we call "Waking Life," then it's a boon well-earned. *Bon voyage*, sweet dreamer.

Balancing on the Fulcrum

Visions, particularly those of animals, seem to inherit the landscape of my meditations. In 1983 I took up Transcendental Meditation (TM), which simultaneously is the easiest and hardest thing one can ever do. Easiest, because all you have to do is just let yourself go and turn off the brain through some diversionary chanting and rhythmic breathing. Hardest, 'cause you have to turn off the brain.

We identify with our brains, particularly those of us matriculating in Western Civilization. Although brains can be particularly handy, say trying to figure out your IRS 1040 or designing the longer lasting light bulb, it could easily be argued – and has been for thousands of years by a host of mystics, swamis, monks and soothsayers of many faiths big and small – that the brain is encompassed in a greater field of consciousness, and the Steve/Ego and I/Me have only a loose, temporal, fraternal bond. Christian mystics, Islamic Sufis, Jewish Kabbalists, Native American Shamans and counterparts from Buddhism and Hinduism can all attest to this – the veil of duality merges into the Sea of the One. Forget deity, dress or P.O. Box – it's the same shtick and has long been a thorn in the side of their organized brethren, the latter generally preferring pre-packed "truths," slick advertising and a wallop of fear (AKA: punishment) to those who wander too far from the fold. Oliver Cromwell, spearheading the usurpation of the Irish and then, temporarily, the British throne, borrowed from Milton to claim, "Better to rule in hell than serve in heaven." He's had three incendiary centuries now to test that theory, I guess. If there's one thing control freaks hate, it's losing control. But as Gandhi said, "I seek truth, not consistency."

TM researchers dating back nearly 40 years have claimed that the metabolic state induced therein is a state much deeper than the deepest sleep – accompanied, ironically, by an almost hyper-consciousness: maximum brain waves for minimum burn rate. Once again my empirical experience supports this. Meditation can clear the mind like a breeze on a spring afternoon, or the surreal bliss that follows a lazy Sunday's nap when you're fully recharged and jettisoned of stress. Not that all sittings are blissful. Some seem to derive a sadistic pleasure from uncorking suppressed tensions, pressures, thoughts – thoughts, always thoughts – and it's easy to spin oneself into an agitated frenzy and chuck the whole session in about 10 minutes. Hard as it is, I'm thankful for the surfacing jetsam and flotsam – crap that would otherwise *abracadabra* itself into an ulcer, obsession, cancer, etc. Discipline's the game. Staying with the mantra, watching the thought-clouds go by but not identifying with them, more often than not produces a greatly relaxed state. No mind: "Me," but not me; aware but impersonal. The Emperor may not be wearing any clothes – *but he doesn't need any.*

I lost another girlfriend (not to the Himalayas, this one) over my refusal to accept that the feelings, voices, images and released stresses were indeed "devils." In my humble opinion, it doesn't take much to see how that kind of neurotic opinion can devolve into war and separation: separation of peoples, a schism of one's own heart, alienating everything and anything "suspect." We and They – "with us, or against us" – the mantra of fear-mongers and political-Pinocchio's everywhere. More to the point – if the jostled thought-forms really *are* devils, then how can letting them sit around and stew under one's noggin' be considered healthy? Get 'em outta here! (Furthermore, who was the linguistic joker who decided the word "devil" should be the inverted flip-flop of the word "lived?" – or "evil" for "live?")

Meditation is simply the flip-sided coin of Prayer. As a four-year old might euphemistically sum it up, the latter is "You talking to God;" the former is "God talking to you." It seems to me we all have the modems, including free broadband. Curiously, few use them – or they simply insist on asynchronous conversations, like presenting Santa with a Christmas wish list, or begging for indulgence when life takes a left turn.

Bring on the Beasts...

It's in this realm that the visitors have often dropped by, unpredictably and especially when not expected. For about a year in the early '90s, I played host to bears. Bears of all sizes, shapes and colors. Sometimes they just appeared in the "third-eye" spot of my meditative projector screen and stared at me. Or, I was walking, playing or even wrestling with them. Sometimes they were in outlandish costumes, or appeared as a *decoupage* in some bizarre piece of artwork. Grizzlies, Kodiaks, Polars, Browns, even cute little cubbies. Ursas Gordas, Ursas Horribles, Ursas Comedias – but always my friends.

I felt like Yogi Bear at the Jellystone Reunion. At least 15 scenarios occurred that year. Also during this time, while browsing through a jewelry store, I unexpectedly came across a pendant of onyx circled by seven bears; "7," coincidentally, has always been my favorite number. The pendant's been mine ever since, and I've never seen another like it.

There have also been cats. Not cute little Fluffies or a buffoonish Sylvester from the Tweety show – but big cats, and a different sort of visitor from the amiable bears.

One was a mountain lion (cougar? panther?) that just walked right up through the astral cobwebs and stared at me from about 18 inches away. I snapped out of my session and almost jumped through the wall. In another episode I was lying on the bed, watching a jaguar stroll by a window ledge. Remembering their penchant for ferocity, I tried to yell out, but as in a dream, I couldn't articulate. Detecting me, he turned around with great interest in the object of his distraction. He could have come through the window screen like a buzz saw through paper. This one just faded away, but I remember thinking we probably wouldn't be together on Letterman's *Stupid Pet Tricks* any time soon.

Some meditative encounters have been simply auditory and not always sensory. I can always tell the difference between a sound track from today's activities replaying itself, versus the unusual whisper/flash through the inner ear.

One time I got the message "Vesta" – neon lights in the Third Eye. I supposed that was related to vestal virgins, which most assuredly weren't on my mind. The handy Webster's informed me that Vesta was the Roman goddess of Home and Hearth. So, who cares? Some months later I abandoned home and hearth (and employer and girlfriend) traveling halfway around the world with a backpack. Returning to town months later, I had neither home, hearth, employer nor girlfriend. I may or may not have been wiser. I was definitely shorter of funds.

Should I have stayed – "Home and Hearth?" I still don't think so. Karma laid waiting and roads were untrodden.

"I Am Committed."

Here's an insight I want to share with you. As Frank Zappa might say, it's the "Crux of the biscuit." I get messages, or signals, and it's as if I have to follow those whisperings or bread crumbs to where they want to take me…that time, it was to the other side of the planet, for yet another journey. Sometimes it's a career change. Sometimes it's an admonition to sit tight, shut up, and wait – to "not change," be grounded, run the gauntlet, and feel the thorns.

What could this be all about?

Years later, I decided this is the secret or core of "Gulliver" and its meaning: to be able to pay attention to what is *intended* for us to hear, and then act upon it. Apparently the job and relationship as well as the home atmosphere were not benefiting me in the way the cosmic "Gulliver" (or my "Highest Self," as some would call it) desired. I have come to treasure and be grateful for these messages. I've also come to learn that the "commitment" referred to is commitment to the Voices and the Messages. Commitment to Me, my Highest Self – that grail of integrity, consciousness and awareness that, while perhaps never totally achievable in light of our human foibles, nonetheless serves as an inspiring beacon or roadmap. It is our true essence, the unchanging "Home Port."

This was my big "Ah-ha," the revelation/insight, the final piece I mentioned at the outset of writing this journey/journal. It is the underlying message that I want to share with you, the core of my renewed inner joy and zest for life.

Commitment.

Each of us has a Gulliver or "Higher Self" that is guiding us on our life journey. My commitment to Gulliver and thus to the Universe, was to explain the nature of this journey to others, and to inspire them – you – to befriend their/your own Gulliver...instead of getting stuck in the ruts of complacency, fear, regret, dissatisfaction...all the life-sucking elements of our Ego-self that pull us back from experiencing our highest freedom, growth and joy.

* * * * * *

Here's an example of what I mean by befriending your Gulliver. While in Africa, in meditation one day I received the flash "Trust Life." Sweet and simple. A few days later, at a bus station in Moshi, Tanzania while waiting for a ride to the Indian Ocean coast, I was daydreaming about what to do when this sojourn ended. I looked up at a billboard erected by some Pentecostal organization. It said: "Trust Life."

And so it goes.

Sometimes the specters take on quasi-religious themes. I was living in Santiago, Chile, bereft of direction (this was the "trust" that had followed the African tour) and dissatisfied with my unfettered bearings. I loved Chile and its people, but employment, other than teaching English, seemed untenable. Since I had been out of the professional rat race for a long time, my left-brain muscles were aching for some heavy lifting. I also desired an income.

The vision found me on a peninsula in the middle of a jungle. I saw big cats – Lions – approaching (*Felinis Curiosis* again) and sensed they meant business.

I was totally alone, but on the other side of the isthmus, a flock of sheep was strolling by. One of them approached me – the lone white sheep in a sea of black. Maybe I've been programmed by too much catechism, but the thought form that shot through my psyche (once again "Me" but not "me") was "Lamb of God." I surfaced into total peace and comfort.

I must admit, I love the flash & dash, the bullet rides through the heavens, the Grand Bazaar of psychic sleight-of-hand. But truthfully, what thrills me most is when grace filters into the realm of the 3-D and twirls its cape in front of my waking eyes. *Here* – where tears are spilled, jobs cursed, bones atrophied and torches passed on to future generations wondering how in the hell they'll survive the madness they've inherited.

Here – where nature is harnessed, environments sanitized, food sterilized, and a veneer called "Civilization" programs us unconsciously into believing we've created order and structure.

How the Gods laugh!

As some ancient Greek or Roman poet once said, "The Gods actually *envy* us." Blissfully strumming their harps on Mt. Olympus, they'll never know the excitement and thrill that mortality offers: those actions noble and grandiose that propel the Life Force headlong into walls of uncertainty – or even the passions woven into literature, art and music. Here, in the midst of all this chaos and sadness is where I most cherish the Out-of-the-Ordinary. If we just pay attention, we soon realize there is no "Ordinary."

We are mesmerized by Hollywood Blockbuster sagas and epics: an *Iliad and Odyssey*, a crusade for a Holy Grail, a tear from a statue of the Virgin, a separation of the Red Sea, Mel Gibson and Bruce Willis beating back the bad guys, and other saintly visages and brain-twisting coincidences that betray statistics.

Much or all of this could be "real." But what is most sacred to me is the deeply personal event. It's like our own little joke with the hidden puppeteer. It doesn't have to necessarily be profound as long as it's something magical that strikes us deeply and takes us out of space and time.

Trigger Points

The bells of Notre Dame did it for me. It was after lunch one day, when the tourists of Gay París had miraculously deserted the cathedral and I had the bell tower to myself for a good five minutes. There, almost leaning out over the guardian gargoyle, I heard – and felt – successive peals of that ancient bell rolling out into infinity and coalescing into a standing wave pattern. I felt – and saw in my "Third Eye" – a simultaneous portrait of the city: armies departing for crusades, mobs pouring into the Bastille, troops from Napoleon and the Third Reich pompously parading through the Arc de' Triumph to the west; drunk GI's puking in Latin Quarter gutters to the swinging tunes of Glenn Miller; Le Notre's great gardens and museums forming an architectural jigsaw across the Seine; Voltaire, Descartes and Sartre holding court at a seditious café; great festivals and celebrations; horrendous plagues; misery, and anguish and gnashing of teeth (if I were a gargoyle, I'd steer clear of the fray, too). My mind wandered in and out of this so easily; I was in two worlds at once – the world of flesh and the world of thought-sensation.

Water, too, does it for me; especially the ocean's rolling waves moving majestically across vast distances before colliding abruptly with landfall. For example, the Cliffs of Moher on the northwest coast of Ireland: at a height of 700 feet, undulating for miles along the jagged coastline, the sound is barely audible but the hypnotic rhythm of "Something" moving through the great rolling waves below struck me as the heralding of timelessness and distant origins.

Likewise, peering off the Cape Point of South Africa at the collision of two mighty oceans, the sight of hundreds of waves like scalloped scythes, simultaneously delivering tidings from somewhere in India and somewhere in the frozen wastelands of Antarctica's underbelly. So peaceful, so synchronized, so choreographed. *And never alone…*

Perhaps it's a harkening back to a time when the amniotic fluid of the womb represented our Universe. Maybe these are unconscious memories of an infant's baptism, or even a cellular, hereditary memory of life billions of years ago. Is there anything more lovely yet forlorn than a rolling wave, sculpted by mysteries and doomed to a fatal crash? It's the human experience in a nutshell: *Carpe Wave – and Hang Ten.*

Sometimes the awe is sparked by brick and mortar colliding in strange permutations. These are easy to explain but invoke incredulity because they seem to defy mathematical possibility. They're Magic,

Juju and Medicine all rolled into one.

Once while sitting with my parents in a cozy lodge at Lake Louise, Alberta, we watched for nearly 20 minutes the fine point of a crescent moon bounce down the side of a mountain. Perfectly. The sharp illusory point just barely "touched" the mountain's contour, and kept "sliding." Considering the Earth's rotation, the mountain's slope, the moon's shape, and our juxtaposition in the room (coincidence?), what were the odds of that – minute after minute? Heaven and earth in perfect choreography – not enough to make the papers, not enough to start a lunar cult, but amazing to behold.

Then there are those experiences which, although not necessarily stretching the statistician's curve, still are too weird and fantastic to explain. Once while driving home from work along the Wasatch Front of northern Utah, I noticed a flotilla of pink and purple mushroom clouds hovering over Mt. Olympus (there's that name again) and surrounding peaks. Catching the setting sun just right from the opposite horizon, they were perfectly shaped – absolutely symmetrical, like harmless aftermaths of imagined 100-megaton hydrogen bomb blasts; as smooth and rounded as a baby's tush, about seven or eight flawlessly shaped mushrooms.

For 10, maybe 15 minutes I gawked in wonder as I continued to drive along at 65 miles per hour. Later I looked for stories or news photos in the media: nothing. I asked people at work, some who commuted that road every day at the same time I did, if they had seen it: nothing. I described it to friends, who looked at me with gaping jaws and then excused themselves for a root canal appointment they had forgotten.

To me, these personal encounters are the holiest, and the richest. They speak just to me, as your encounters presumably speak just to you. Since we are all unique beings, citizenship and Costco cards notwithstanding, so do our interpretational filters respond differently to whatever cosmic or terrestrial stimuli are buzzing around in our sphere of perception. Teilhard de Chardin, the Jesuit-turned-scientist, called it the "Noosphere" (a term he borrowed from Goethe): an ethereal "fluid" of collective consciousness – the Group Mind – that surrounds the Earth, accounting for synchronicity, serendipity and the acoustic insults of AM Radio.

DNA – Downloadable Network for Advancement?

Of even greater mystery to me than "encounters" are the underlying props for our human existence. DNA, thanks to the sweat equity of contemporary Russian scientists, is now hypothesized to be more than just a genetic storehouse. It is described as a *communicative medium* as well – possessing a type of vibration mathematics, which if hypothesized correctly, accounts for the evolution of our language. This means perhaps, that our propensity as a species toward more sophisticated vocabulary (excepting Hip-Hop music) is *hardwired* and not merely a result of millions of years of grunts coalescing in random error to a by-default, agreed-upon-"meaning."

Moreover, though the scientific evidence is still being bandied about, it appears we can *influence* this DNA wiring with thought /words/music, etc. – what the Great Masters were saying long before they were syndicated. They just didn't call it "DNA" – they used allegories; i.e., Jacob wrestling an angel on a ladder (perhaps denoting our cosmic "ascent" of the twin-strand helix of DNA; the rungs of adenine, cytosine, guanine, and thymine?).

Maybe the creationists are on to something after all, if they could just s-t-r-e-t-c-h their world view to consider the *mechanisms* that a creative force might use to produce its effects. "Conscious Evolution" would seem a workable term for both camps, AKA, a "Creative Intelligence" using the clay and bricks of "Evolution" at its own pace. But please, leave the textbooks and name-calling out of it...

Humankind contributes its own sleight-of-hand to the mystery...or does it? Take numbers, the genius creation of the first abacus counter. A strange but beautiful number known to mathematicians as the *Fibonacci Constant* – 1.6180339887 – describes the underlying symmetry of much of the observable universe. If one were to add together increasing strings of consecutive numbers (1+2 = 3; 2+3 =5; 3+5 = 8; 5+8 = 13, etc.) and examine the ratio between any two successive sums (5/3 = 1.67; 8/5 = 1.6; 13/8 = 1.625, etc.) what *eventually converges* is a "Golden Mean" – 1.6 blah-blah-blah.

Here's where it gets strange: by "squaring" it (multiplying it by itself) and subtracting the number 1, you get: *It*. Conversely, by taking its reciprocal (dividing the number 1 by it) and adding the number 1, you once more get: *It*. Now that's impressive – really impressive, if one considers those are *mutually exclusive* (in mathematical jargon) calculations – yeah, coincidence.

But Fibonacci's Golden Mean is much more than mental masturbation for geeks. That special number happens to describe the ratio of human anatomy (limb/trunk proportions), seashell formation (i.e., the swirl patterns of the Nautilus), flower petal arrangements, ripple patterns in a pond – and the sweeping arms of galaxies. So the question must be asked: did humans "invent" numbers, just happening to choose the right digits, which when added together, made Signore Fibonacci of 13th century Pisa a famous man – or decipher them, abstractly (but correctly) interpreting an underlying *harmonic pattern* of nature – including our very bodies? (In *Whose image* were we created?) Implications are that it was either dumb luck, or we were intuitively honing in on the Creator's calculator: mess with the Big 1.6xyz, and London Bridge comes crashing down.

Let's not forget Zero, the brainchild of those clever Arabs in the Eighth Century (who, to be fair, had stolen it from Brahmagupta, an Indian). Of course, 0 / Zero isn't really a number *because it doesn't exist*. But without this oval placeholder, higher mathematics would forever evade our grasp; meaning that our ability to manipulate the building blocks of the Universe (and balance our checkbooks) is totally dependent on "non-reality."

Did the Indians/Arabs truly invent the concept of Zero – or, discover it? Perhaps the Romans' inability to hold their Empire intact had less to do with licentious living (good wine, bad orgies) than it did with their inability to add X, L, C, M, V, and I without getting a migraine or mouthful of alphabet soup. Multiplication, division, differential equations? Forget about it. But by embracing 0 / Zero – *nothing* – we now stare, calculate and analyze into the farthest reaches of space and finest microcosms of the infinitesimal.

Out of the Void – *Nothingness* – came the Word. And flesh, rocks, and thoughts. 0, *Om*, the primordial grunt of the Cosmos, the very shape of its symbol representing eternity looping back on itself – making all things possible.

Statisticians, those High Priests of "Cartesian" thinking (named for Descartes, the father of X and Y graphs) and lackeys of every political pollster say that with 6 ½ billion people on Earth, each with tens of thousands of "experiences," it's inevitable that the juxtaposition of all that stew stock would produce probability collisions much higher than we lay persons would think. We always seemed amazed that at some party we find a significant chunk of the crowd has birthdays in the same month – not just the random one-twelfth.

Leaving the mathematics to those with too much time on their hands, just take it as fact that statistics do indeed explain a lot of our presumed miracles. But as some wisecracker once said, we need to remember that "statistics are like bikinis: What they reveal is suggestive; what they *conceal* is vital."

We could just as easily say that with 6 ½ billion people, each receiving approximately 4 billion perceptual "inputs" *a second* and only able to process a few hundred (relegating the rest to that moldy cellar called the Subconscious), the idea of a society operating as a truly collective norm is akin to the odds of two hyperactive electrons coincidentally circling the same pimple on the same ass of the same tsetse fly on the same head of a pin.

In other words, once more (to quote author Dan Millman): there is no "Ordinary" – *only the veneer of convention.* But more to the point – all seems to be a continuous, changing miracle. Thus, it strikes me as imperative to spend time learning about other cultures, other individuals…and learning to understand and accept them, just as they are.

The Revolving Door of Truth

The challenge presented by OBEs, visions, dreams, earthly substances, spooky visitors and bizarre synchronistic experiences – chucking absolutism out the window – is: What/whom can we believe…hold onto…*live and die for?*

These phenomena turn our senses inside out and generally obliterate force of reason. Combined with the never-ending discoveries of honest scientists constantly poking around in Pandora's Box, we're left with trying to not only interpret "The Truth," but what appears to be a *constantly changing* Truth. No wonder the perpetrators of the Inquisition got a little hot under the collar, and the Imams of the Middle East still equate intellectual scholarship (or worse, spirituality) with the parroting ability of a five-year-old. After all, who needs a Galileo or a Copernicus hanging around and spoiling the party? Imagine, the earth rotating around the sun! Ha! Bring out the stakes and lighter fluid. If you've got a great racket going, the last thing you want is a few nay-sayers questioning the official party line of the One True Faith – a faith that has a vast closet full of robes, beads, yarmulkes, totems, turbans and business suits alike…

History reeks of world-models – "paradigms," an overused, but appropriate word – being splintered by timely sledge hammers. Unfortunately, the swinger of the hammer is usually derided, boiled in oil or crucified (though being worshipped later might be an okay consolation).

As a paradigm/world model, "Absolutism" is absolutely flawed. Even death and taxes are not so sure – you can avoid paying taxes (providing you're OK with three square meals in a small locked room), and according to more than one soothsayer (and a few magicians), death can be transcended, if not avoided. Space and time surely aren't absolutes, either. Einstein's and Heisenberg's scientific formulae validated what mystics and shamans have been saying ever since their early forefathers stumbled out of the cave and chewed their first hallucinogenic herbs.

If the concept of Infinity hurts the brain, consider the alternative: you buzz to the edge of the Universe in your protective suit and Energizer-Bunny battery pack, stop at the edge – and put your hand across – into *what*? Is it not more space? In other words, as difficult as Infinity is to fathom, "Finity" (finite-ness) is a more perplexing conundrum.

Same thing with Time – try doing the chicken and egg thing, back ad-nauseum. Big Bang? Maybe – but just so many snorts of

Brahman's breath, say the gurus of the Ganges – the endless circle-dance of "inhale/exhale." Is there any reason to believe this "exhale" (Big Bang) was not preceded by a previous "inhale"...and so on? Try applying the same approach to yourself. Did consciousness appear out of nothing? *"In the beginning was the Word."* How do we know that, unless there was someone, some thing, some *consciousness* to hear it (the resonating "Om," the first *Allee-Allee-In-Come-Free!*)?

Even basic physics contains its own logic-twister. For example, it is inherent in the mechanics of solids that chaos, or instability, is additive. This is intuitive and easily demonstrable. When combining two objects of such-and-such measurement tolerance (think meshing gears, or planks in a house, etc.) the overall design must default to the combined tolerances of the two. If not, things don't work. A 1970s Ford Pinto and its gas tank come to mind. This principle even extends to social systems: just witness a soccer game between Brazil and Argentina, or a Boy Scout camporee... the destructive capability of the population is geometric to the number of participants.

Yet...in "Natural" systems, according to Nobel prize winning physicist Ilya Prigogine (and recapped by Fritjof Capra in *The Turning Point*) a principle known as "Dissipative Structure" exists which displays the opposite behavior: the resulting "structure" is more stable than the constituent masses. To wit, a cell has a longer lasting life than any of its RNA, DNA, mitochondria, wall tissue, etc.

Certainly, a bottle of 1989 Marques de Caceres Gran Reserva tastes yummier than a sixteen-year old grape or an old packet of yeast. Or on a more personal level, since every cell in my body is replaced within any rolling seven-year time frame, who's that man behind the curtain pretending to be Me?

But to really take things to the point of absurdity, how can a galaxy – say, bigger than a breadbox – be more stable than the countless number of infinitesimal electrons, quarks and mesons swirling around like mad honey bees after a bear raid? How do patterns of randomness so mysterious, they can only be measured in probability patterns at the subatomic level (e.g., is the electron a wave, particle, both, or neither?) *combine together* to form a round planet, a star-centric solar system, a galaxy itself, and even clusters of galaxies rotating around each other in measured choreography – *each more predictable than its constituent building blocks?*

In the words of physics, how does throwing together more entropy (e.g., the tendency of something to "break down") result in greater homeostasis (harmony, stability)? Why can Nature do this – and not Man? And more important: how can one patent this really cool technology?

Here We Come, There We Went

It gets even weirder. Thanks to the Kirlian camera and hypersensitive electron microscopes – an item can be "seen" *in two different places at the same time.* How about inducing "spins" in one member of a particle pair and observing its Siamese twin react simultaneously – in time and distance frames that defy the speed of light (e.g., certainly there must be measurable "time" for the message to get through, even at "short distance")? Or, on a very *non*-subatomic level, experiments with human fluids (blood, saliva, and semen) have shown non-random, measurable agitation (frequency, wavelength, and temperature changes) when the experimental donor thinks certain thoughts – *sometimes from miles away.* Now there's a wet dream to be proud of. $E=MC^2$? Sorry Albert, only up to a point. Then we're down Lewis Carroll's rabbit hole…

Yes, it's time for an Advil – or maybe a shot of something stronger.

Yet, as uncomfortable as are the concepts of Infinity and Eternity, the alternatives seem ludicrous. It certainly increases the size of the chalkboard for creativity, much to the chagrin of the popes, ayatollahs, TV ministers, our political parties and more than a few parents. But it *does* give you and me room to roam, if we care to saunter out of the box. And that's where the pyrotechnics start.

All those who spawned the Great Books knew this. Jesus certainly did, even if he was a bit of a ham with all that water-walking, wine-switching and laying-on-of-hands stuff. But I'll give him the benefit of the doubt – what better way to liberate human consciousness from its "demons" – *the shackles of self-limitation* – than to exhibit and proclaim, "As I have done these things, so shall you do even greater things." Or how about, "Know ye not that ye are Gods?" (Old English always brings out the "oomph" in religiosity).

The prolific Arthur C. Clarke wrote another book called *The Nine Billion Names of God.* I've got news for Sir Arthur; there are a lot more names than that. Point is, I don't recall too much about J.C. demanding worship from star-struck followers. And talk about putting your money where your mouth is – that whole thing with the thorns and nails would've left anyone cross. But not the Man from Galilee.

Buddha, too, knew the powers of the Unseen and potential of every lotus as yet unopened. But he milled his grist differently. Once, he chastised a follower who'd spent 20 years learning to levitate so he could cross a river – "Why didn't you just row a damn boat?" – and presumably use those two decades to serve humanity better while also having some fun.

So indeed, if the Kingdom truly lies inside each of us, and we are "gods" (or at least well-mannered pixies) – then *what, and who, are we to believe?* If we should not kill (uh, which Commandment is that?), then why do we sanction society to demonstrate our revulsion to killing by killing the killer? And if indeed we are a "Brotherhood of Man" (and "Sisterhood of Woman") isn't it time for the nation-state to put its medals, cannons, flags and oom-pah-pahs back in the toy box and grow up? *"When I was a child, I played like a child…"*

To the degree that convention – or tradition and ritual – is based on some sharing of ideas or values that allow us to live and breathe without killing one another, I wholeheartedly salute the Ten Commandments, the Upanishads, the Code of Hammurabi, the Boy Scout oath or even the Mickey Mouse jingle. After all, we live in a society that settles disputes with a Luger 9mm and drives our freeways like a kid at a bumper-car arcade. But these are powders for the lowest common denominator, not tonics for consciously taking our place in the cosmic soup. (Gandhi again – "The problem with an Eye-for-an-Eye is that we both go blind.")

Unfortunately, the scribblers of the Great Books watered things down a bit, out of necessity and/or ignorance, and like a game of Chinese Whispers mouthed for a hundred generations, we're left with a mangled mash of profound truths, gross distortions (intentional and accidental), blatant lies, and most insidiously – edits and deletions.

Infallible? Only if you believe the same deity that promotes the turning of (other) cheeks also peddles slaves, plunders neighbors, rapes women, fondles little boys and hanky-pankies with animals; all the while despising those who aren't "Chosen." To paraphrase a theological discussion I saw once: "What perfect, eternal, omnipotent, loving deity would create a being 'in its image,' curse it with 'original sin' and proceed to set the bar so high, its creation could never be good enough; with the punishment for the failed probate being an eternity of suffering?" It seems a grotesque, barbaric theology, and actually kind of funny, until you stop and realize that a lot of our world's institutions dance to this tune. Ouch.

WWJD and Other Anagrams

"Love thy neighbor" …no – wait: "Vengeance is mine, sayeth the Lord." Now there's a seriously schizophrenic deity. Does the great Alpha & Omega, the Creator / Sustainer / Destroyer, really have an *ego?* (As those cute little rings inscribe, WWJD – What Would Jesus Do?) Somehow I believe the problem lies not with Him/Her/It but *elsewhere.* To paraphrase an old adage: God created Man in his image, and Man has been returning the favor ever since."

Faith and trust are valuable, yes, even *vital* for navigating the vicissitudes of our earth-bound pilgrimage. But faith and trust in what, in whom – *someone else's* words, *their* books, *their* rules? *Their* judgment? Methinks judgment is a man-made contraption. That intangible Something, the Great All That Is, seems to be neutral on the subject, at least from my observations. What spiritual arrogance (and what disempowerment!) to believe we were given discerning faculties – including brains – but aren't supposed to use them. Faith without Reason usually means you're a meal ticket for a huckster. And there's no lack of carneys in glittering, sanctimonious booths, waiting to punch your ticket. As the sagacious Trappist monk Thomas Merton warned:

The most dangerous man in the world is the contemplative who is guided by nobody. He trusts his own visions. He obeys the attractions of an inner voice, but will not listen to other men. He identifies the will of God with his own heart...And if the sheer force of his own self-confidence communicates itself to other people and gives them the impression that he really is a saint, such a man can wreck a whole city or a religious order or even a nation. The world is covered with scars that have been left in its flesh by visionaries like these.

Yet...yet...sometimes, due to circumstance, faith is all we have to go on. So, again – what/whom to believe? I turn to the OBE flights, the meditations, the visitors, the murmurs, and yes, even those mischievous dreams. There's also a prized place for logic, providing I don't paint myself into a corner. I listen to others, or at least I *try* to. I read the Great Books dedicated to and supposedly quoted from, all those mysterious Masters. I seek forgiveness, from myself and others, for all the bad things I've done and all the bad things I'm going to do. I'll even forgive you, most of the time. Longfellow said, *"If we could read the secret history of our enemies, we would find in each person's life sorrow and suffering enough to disarm all hostility."*

But mostly I turn to the miracle of the Here and Now. I have no idea if any of these things really represent "The Truth" or if there even is such a thing. But those experiences are mine, and as that Voice once reassured me – absolutely –

Don't you know that you will never be alone?

Sometimes naked, sometimes mad,
Now the scholar, now the fool,
Thus they appear on earth: the free men.

– The Bhagavad-Gita

Do not believe on the strength of traditions,
Even if they have been held in honor
For many generations
And in many places;

Do not believe anything
Just because many speak of it;

Do not believe that which
You have yourselves imagined,
Thinking that a god has inspired you;

Believe nothing which depends
Only on the authority
Of your master, or of priests.

After investigation,
Believe only that
Which you have yourselves tested
And found reasonable,
And is for your highest good
And that of all others.

– Gautama Buddha

PART V
THE GRAND "BIZARRE": MAYHEM
IN THE MARKET

Life isn't fair. Don't take it personally. And never, ever, cut yourself out of the budget.
  – Bill's Corollary

The Market is an open door to the world at large. Like a huge raffle cage basket that shakes everything and everyone up in quirky permutations, one can expect to find almost anything or expect almost anything to happen in The Market. With the right synergy, it's the perfect way to do business: supply and demand, bartering of goods and services with good will toward all, and much room for gamesmanship prowess. Most of all, The Market is a lot of fun, and after all, it is in many ways, a mirror of our lives, as we move through our own marketplace meeting people, creating relationships and placing values on each of our talents and abilities in order to offer them to others and share in the wealth of every outcome.

Following suit with Heisenberg's Law that the only Certainty is Uncertainty, in The Market there is never a shortage of surprises, as my own experiences attest.

Chapter Twenty-Five

A Birds'-Eye View of The Market

The old *abuela* was on the horns of a dilemma: she could take my offering, which in addition to providing her with both capital and gifts for the grandkids, would get the pestilent gringo off her back; or, she could refuse to budge, which would deny her those boons and leave me pestering her in her shop for hours to come. But I wanted that poncho, damn it, and she must have sensed that resistance was futile.

"*¿Por favor, senora? Es muy bonito, muy guapo*" ("It's very pretty, very handsome.")

"*Gracias, señor.*" Half-hearted smile, shuffling of feet, turning of head, back to work...

There was something about the poncho that I couldn't quite finger. It was nothing extraordinary; in fact, it was a dull beige/brown. It surely wasn't smooth like those shiny alpaca sweaters on Rodeo Drive or the Champs-Elysées; the ones that would never see hard work; the ones that cost a Third World nation's GDP and then spend eternity in some socialite's cedar chest. Nope, this poncho smelled of the Earth and of its Peruvian donor. Made from alpaca wool, it was elegant in its simplicity: coarse but refined, with no distracting geometric symbols or frilly colors and embellishments to detract from its core essence. It displayed its several handsome flaws without a hint of humility and it would be quite the gift for a special friend who would wear it until its threadbare skeleton just slid off one day and shirked back to the earth – wool to dirt.

It almost seemed that the dear *abuelita* didn't *want* to part with the poncho. There was a pensive, hesitant furrow to her graying brow that hinted money wasn't the issue (Did I have B.O.? Was it the haggard beard, the mangy-mongrel look? My overly-flattering impetuousness, perhaps?) In fact, she never even gave back a price. I threw down my final salvo (ah, but would it have been, had she refused?), a Miami Dolphins visor, onto the makeshift table in the back of her humble all-purpose shop. The visor landed softly on my first two volleys, the Sun Valley tee shirt and green note sporting the stern mug of Mssr. Hamilton sandwiched between two number "Tens" in each corner.

I gave her a peck on the cheek – *besos y abrazos* – and she feigned a smile. She was either satisfied with the deal, or respectful of my persistence. Maybe she was just glad to be rid of me. She then eyed my bulging shirt pocket – *"Propina,"* she half-suggested, half-demanded a tip, a reward. "OK, granny, you've earned it." Out came the pack of Dentyne, out came her wider smile, and out went I into the encroaching dusk, navigating the dimly-lit alleys of Cusco with my new prize.

* * * * * *

Maybe we in the West put too much stock in our baubles from exotic places. Some of it really *is* crap; cheaply made stuff that even most Big Lots wouldn't touch (and that's saying a big lot). There's certainly an allure to items such as the cool Gunga Din jammy-looking trousers in Kathmandu, or wild-colored shirts from deepest, darkest Africa. But other than the occasional Halloween party, many items are destined for a moldy drawer until they're liberated for fifty cents at a garage sale years later. The Ironwood elephant and Happy Buddha just don't *look* right, sandwiched between the hand-me-down Remington prints and rabbit-ear telly in the backroom. Nor is that Lladro peasant lady happy guarding a sink of dirty dishes from her station on the window sill.

I've come to believe it's the "Imprint Factor" that so beguiles us. We had a good time on our journey. The artifacts and trinkets, of which some truly *are* pieces of art, are indeed different and not everyday items – not in our culture, at least. They say that we the owner, are unique, worldly and different. They represent a time and contact that removed us from the ordinary and opened us up, thrust us into something truly different. Sure, we may have gotten sick, had a lumpy bed or missed a train, but the glitz and glamour overwhelm all that. Simply put, traveling and schmoozing in The Market are cheap and non-threatening forms of heroin, and we relish the rush. So, we occasionally scan the room and the house, letting our trappings uplift us and take us away.

* * * * * *

One day I was daydreaming in my cozy little carriage house in Boise. Outside, spring was at play and all the lilacs and plum and cherry trees surrounding my sandstone bungalow were blooming and filling the neighborhood with aromatic ambrosia. My temperament mirrored the change in the air; I was restless and itchy, ready to go somewhere and do something. My current job didn't help, since it was more oriented toward "straightjacket and stiff upper lip" than "wanton abandon for the sake of growth and curiosity."

Leaning back in my dilapidated thrift-store chair, I did a 360° scan. Included in my "junk" were framed tapestries from Peru of mischievous gods (prompting me to a bigger expression of myself?), Australian boomerangs hanging on the wall – what, a masochistic reminder that I had ended up back in the throes of corpor-mania once more? – and a Viking ship dominated the mantle. Perhaps a voyage to new places? There were also Caribbean motifs resembling voodoo dolls, surely a reminder about the consequences of forgetting one's good manners. I'd collected Native (North) American trinkets as well, many of them reminding me of the sanctity of my home turf, seen through others who had a far greater appreciation of its essence.

At that moment I knew I was hooked on collecting "stuff" from the wide world. Also, I now realized I was hooked on the *exchange*, "The Market…" because connecting with all those people – the merchants, artists, teachers – even the bloody custom agents – was what it was all about for me. The stuff was just a conduit.

* * * * * *

"Every deal a good deal; every day, my friend. Make me a good offer. I can never say 'No.'"

I sure wanted that curving scimitar "sword." It had ornate features and a handsome sheath of fine carved wood. Never mind that the sword was blunt (a cheap metal alloy), the "jewels" on the scabbard, bogus sea shells...Furthermore, it was probably thrown together in 30 minutes down the road in Kuşadasi.

"I'll bet you *can* refuse my low offer," I grinned like the Cheshire cat.

"Ah, but if I don't say 'no,' that does not mean I say 'yes,'" he grinned in return. "But you look like an honest chap. I guarantee you lowest price in all of the Grand Bazaar. My name is José."

"Well, thanks, José." His real name was probably Mehmet or Hasad (or Kemal or Ahmet or Jemal), but he probably figured to tweak my subconscious sympathies for his knowledge of my culture and our frequent forays to our neighbors to the south. He just wanted to connect with his quarry. José /Hasad was well dressed and in his late twenties. Possibly college educated, he spoke the requisite 6-8 languages of Turkish merchants, including clichés and colloquialisms. He could sip tea with Arabs, uttering such prosaic nonsense about "birds of paradise" or "a thousand pardons"; he could match the Germans, fact for voluminous fact, without a trace of embellishment or emotion; he could gesticulate wildly with Italians, raising and dropping his voice like a rollercoaster; and he could slam vodka with Russkies and utter fashionable grunts to Manhood & Motherland. All of these, of course, were his stories, but if his knowledge of those other cultures was as good as it was of mine, he was a bonafide U.N. jack-of-all-trades. I also have no doubt he knew French and Spanish – I'd seen his type in action for weeks, and their competencies are legendary. Of course, most of the English he learned was from reruns of *Columbo* and *Monty Python's Flying Circus* on the tiny black and white TV in the corner. We all have our teachers, and they come in unusual packages.

When I returned the next morning, he gobbled up my offer of $10 U.S. (the original asking price was $50). "See, always lowest price!" José beamed, leaving me to wonder how much I had left on the table. But, like anyone driving off the lot of a used car dealer, I had to believe I "got a good deal."

There were many Josés in the Grand Bazaar, Istanbul's version of an ancient crossroads welded onto a K-Mart Blue Light Special. It has over 50 streets, and houses somewhere between 3,000 and 4,000 shops. Graceful colored archways with Ottoman mosaics separate entire corridors, which are surprisingly clean. Nearly 300,000 people a day – say, the population of Boise's greater valley when first we met – carouse those hallowed halls, shopping, gawking and flirting. Did I mention that it's all covered?

The Grand Bazaar is an unwieldy Sociology thesis, a giant Petri dish for human behavior in all of its variants of greed, pleasure, cunning, humor, civility, remorse, confusion and complete befuddlement. Savvy buyers could find goods of equal-to-superior quality a few blocks away at much cheaper prices, but what the Grand Bazaar lacked in bang-for-the-buck it made up for in variety, intrigue, odor, noise and entertainment. One could literally get lost – maps were scarce at that time, and the three-score "streets" resembled what I imagine an M.C. Escher print might have looked like, had the gifted genius dipped into one of Aldous Huxley's goody bags. It was an "orderly chaos," even fairly hygienic; and, thankfully, it lacked the explosive, enraged shopkeeper buffoonery caricatured by a Cecil B. DeMille movie – Turks take great pride in distancing themselves from the histrionics of Arab merchants. Also, the bazaar was safe – relatively – despite being Ground Point Zero for Istanbul pickpockets. Besides, why steal illegally when you can "steal" legally? But mostly, it was fun. That's The Market: it is madness and mayhem, and it can truly be "bizarre."

One can find everything and anything in this amazing complex of buildings: jewelry; beautiful ceramics emblazoned with Koran or Sufi quotes and sacred geometry; replica "weapons" like my sword; intricate carpets and *kilims* (needled impressively at 60-70 stitches to the square centimeter); every type of food and drink; entertainers of every shape, size, and color; huge, four-foot hookah pipes, ideal for filtering and cooling harsh tobacco (and other products); intricate wood carvings, in the form of game-boards (backgammon and chess); exquisite furniture, including entire beds; and silks, gorgeous scarves and shawls – homegrown, at that, despite Turkey's legacy of being near the end of the ancient silk routes through Cathay and Persia. The Grand Bazaar is a flea market with flair; it is Halloween, Harrods and Hollywood all thrown into one stewing polyglot. And everywhere, ubiquitous and omnipresent, is Allah's "Evil Eye" – the little blue amulet engraved, embossed, or imprinted on countless mediums for warding away evil – *not* projecting it, contrary to the ideas of many westerners. Like the Christian gargoyle, whose assigned charge was to protect churches from insidious intruders, the Evil Eye is much maligned and misunderstood...which is a shame, 'cuz it's really cute.

Bartering is not only normal here; it is expected. Only a fool or misplaced philanthropist (one and the same) would offer full price. It is the opposite of an auction, where the price only goes up. This price comes down, often in tumbling cascades, and sometimes in the slow-drip of Chinese water torture. But it's all in the game; the stone-walled face, slow retreat, shrugging pirouette that turns slowly and waits for one last "*señor – madam – capitán – hey buddy – please to consider*"...or not. Sometimes you just gotta know when to fold 'em, as Kenny Rogers said. Or, you can just pay them the damn money, if you think it's worth it. Trust me, these vendors will never embarrass you in front of your friends at home...though the latter may do that for you themselves.

For thousands of years, markets have been the heartbeat of cultures; the nucleus of daily life for millions – billions – of people. Not even churches or festivals hold a candle to them; the former, too solemn and the latter too infrequent. Only The Market provides that delicate chemistry of "win & lose," hope and disappointment. Only The Market can rivet our attention and intention on such concentrated material assets, those *de facto* icons of a culture's relative values. Only The Market allures such spirited exchange; such insights into the beneficence, magnificence and treachery of the human soul.

It's an ancient debate as to the relative degree one is enriched by a church service, and a conundrum worth debating. But there is absolutely *no* question that if The Market doesn't work, then people go hungry, children go un-shoed, and tourist bureaus board up their offices. Is it any wonder markets are high on the list of places most likely to be bombed? After all, they're just another version of the World Trade Center, only instead of reaching into the sky like moneychangers in the temple, these bazaars reach out horizontally: tentacles ensnaring and coaxing, tempting and annoying, and connecting us to each other – whether or not we like it.

The Market is the human experience in one clamorous microcosm. Hence the violence of a terrorist bomb, say, is more than just the disruption of commerce; it is the severing of an artery of the human body; a schism in the psyche of our primary channels of interaction, communication, exchange – and, yes, even knowledge.

The Market seems insane precisely *because* such an array of human experience is on the table. Sure, one can get ripped off, but isn't *Caveat Emptor*, or "Buyer beware" the Eleventh Commandment? There is also *Honor* in the market. I once had a merchant track me halfway across Kathmandu's Thamel Market, Abe Lincoln-style, to return less than a buck of change (I let the gracious courier keep it, all praise on his family, and even threw in more Dentyne). At the market, one can also be *blessed* with gifts…by meeting incredible, interesting individuals and even getting invited to their home. (Advice: never turn down this offer unless you feel you're getting hustled into "sponsoring" a loved one to your country; an uncomfortable dilemma I've encountered in Thailand, Fiji, Kenya, and Wyoming. Besides, what if that little piece of wood really *was* from the "True Cross?" Never mind that enough True Crosses have been sold to replace the denuded cedar forests of Lebanon – sometimes we must suspend reason.)

The Market is the ultimate power game. Instead of winning or losing money – which is simply "packaged energy" in the words of mythologist Joseph Campbell – we exchange an actual item – "kinetic energy," sort of – food, art, clothing, a neighbor's wife. Was it worth it? Who knows? But we do know how it makes us *feel*; unlike money, it has an intrinsic beauty, a different aesthetic, essence and vibration. The classic test of our discernment is to not confuse the message (the goods) with the medium (money). Not that it's bad to have either, even *a lot* of both, in fact – as long as said goods don't transmogrify into a ball and chain around one's heart.

The Market tests our fortitude: not just the physical and mental energy to stay centered in the clamoring maelstrom of a dozen simultaneously shouting touts, but, also, it tests our emotional and spiritual energy to deal with the desperate pleas of some who really are hungry, and need your capital. Do you ignore them? Take their product at full price, without bartering, even if you don't want it? Screw them to the wall because you know they'll blink? ($10 U.S. – black market, of course – buys a month of maize for a Zimbabwe family.) Make an offering and leave the product (caution, that one, if you're in a public place)? Make apologies, and then walk away? All are possible paths, all have unique circumstances; and your choice is beyond my judgment. But I do guarantee that you'll never *forget* these encounters...

The Market mesmerizes and intrigues us; it also nauseates, mystifies and spellbinds, such as at The Witch Doctor's Market in La Paz, Bolivia. Let's just say it'll never make the Vatican's recommended tour list. This market is a *Who's Who* of shamanism-run-amok, with shrunken, shriveled reptiles; aborted fetuses; amulets, icons, totems; strange instruments to call on capricious gods and detour prankster spirits; every kind of potion, lotion, elixir, powder, balm, remedy and cure known to the greater Altiplano or Amazon. *"Eye of newt, toe of frog, wool of bat and tongue of dog...*this joint has it all..."Lovely and scary," just like the chant. It doesn't hurt that the ramshackle cubbyhole-shops, high up on the winding streets of La Paz, have that certain *Macbeth* look to lend an eerie, spooky quiescence. The Witch Doctor's Market is a definite peek into an alternate reality, or at least an alternate *perception*. But then, what's the difference? Everything has power in it; often we just don't notice. The Aymaran natives had no problem co-opting the rich symbology of Christianity, already laden with centuries of absorbed paganism, into their own myth and folklore. They reckoned the more gods one knows, the better. Sadly, the new guys didn't see it that way, rounding up the heathens by the hundreds of thousands and sending them to the tin and copper mines.

Then there's the floating market of Bangkok – *Damnoen Saduak* – a Venice-esque maze of canals and all-purpose sewer, race track, stock market, produce stand and gossip fence. Little old ladies commandeering sleek boats barrage you at your beckon, or preemptively, with every imaginable type of Southeast Asian produce and matchbox trinket. It's a Gatlin-Gun compared to the ordered chaos of the Grand Bazaar, or the brooding somnolence of the

Witch Doctor's Market. There's no time for chitty-chatty with these peripatetic grannies or for getting to know names and nationalities. But if Damnoen Saduak is indeed a shooting gallery and you are a duck, is this any different from standing in line like cattle at a sleek, sanitized Western retail store, while some proudly unionized, highly overpaid, yawning clerk ("I don't wanna be here" say the mascara-smeared eyes) processes you like one more check stub; spouting out a monotone, perfunctory "Have a nice day" with not even one blink of eye contact?

Gimme "Grandma Banzai" *anytime.*

* * * * * *

It behooves us as well to remember that every medium of commercial exchange, not just those cute little Kasbahs in Marrakesh and Bali, is part of The Market. Who says it is only for the arcane and bizarre, or the exotic and provocative?

In every major city the world over are gargantuan, intimidating, markets: New York, London, Frankfurt, Zurich, Tokyo, Singapore… where a push of a button props up an empire or tears it down; or buys that second house; or pisses away the kids' college fund in a moment of whimsy. These markets may appear to be cold and impersonal, like a boring computer game, but there's definitely someone behind the curtain, and they definitely care if they win or lose. Any snapshot of a trading pit, with sweating, screaming, tennis-shoed "buy and sell" monkeys, sleeves rolled and fingers waving, should dispel the notion of detached abstraction. And these imposing pits of Wall Street are every bit as intriguing to me as the perfume factories of Grasse, France (did you know that a mediocre "Noser" can detect at least 300 unique odors, and some can discern more than *1,000?*); the back alley silk shops of Bangkok (handed down for 20+ generations); or the steaming spice markets of Zanzibar…which were a former commercial crossroads of three continents. They breathe and exude passion – sometimes with a cold, calculated burst, other times with a soft and gentle sigh. But however they are expressed, the bottom line is the same: they move the wheels of commerce, feed (or deplete) our retirement accounts and refrigerators, aid the afflicted, and jump-start the intrepid into the throes of entrepreneurialism. Just because some of them are selfish, heartless bastards doesn't exclude them from their right to participate in the madness and mayhem of The Market.

The Market also resides among the sleek and subtle, luring and alluring, ritzy and refined. Rome wasn't built in a day, nor were New York's 5th Avenue, Palm Beach's Worth Avenue, Paris' Champs-Elysées, Toronto's Bloor Street, Barcelona's Las Ramblas, Mayfair's Bond Street or any other boulevards prowled by jaguars, paparazzi and wide-eyed tourists. These markets will be glad to valet park your rented steed, take your plastic, gift wrap your purchase and ship it anywhere in the world – for the right fee, of course. But the only uniqueness these markets can claim is their circumstances. Some merchants and shopkeepers are lucky, others are plucky; some went to the right college or knew the right family or investor. Some, to be totally fair, worked their butts off and followed their bliss. But just because the vast majority are no shrewder or saintlier than a kiosk carney in Cairo doesn't mean they are deserving of our contempt or disapproval – they, too, have their story (best to *Listen Carefully*), their angle (recommend *Question Endlessly*), and their hook (definitely *Think Deeply*).

Ultimately, The Market is balance: Yin-Yang; the glass half-empty and half-full from the giving and the taking; with the heart open, brain full, wallet clutched and solar plexus riveted…as with the protracted negotiation I once had in Malawi for the wooden basket that so beguiled me.

It was – is – the most delicately crafted, ornate piece of hand carving I've ever seen. Constructed from the native Mukwa tree (or "bloodwood") it is two feet high, about 1-½ feet in diameter at its maximum bulge, with an additional lid adding four or five more inches. Lions, elephants, rhinos, leopards and water buffalos – the African "Big Five" – roam its exterior, intricately "interwoven" by primitive tools into a transparent matrix. A fine coating of oil from some plant or root gave it a shining luster, not unlike the handsome shield of Lemon Pledge that augments your mahogany coffee table.

In a bleak, humble, dusty stall, really just a meager footprint of dirt, our negotiation took nearly three hours. This included numerous "side trips" to visit or confer with family members, grab tools and dies or exchange pleasantries with each other about weather and health. No tea was served – this was a far more spartan operation than the Mediterranean hospitality of the Turks or Egyptians; my poor host probably didn't even have any such luxury. We danced with our bids and rejections and conjured numbers like puppeteers pulling on hidden strings. With a fine, tired waltz the offers and counteroffers flew.

[*Bid – reject...*] "When will the rains start?"

"Soon; very soon, we hope." [*Counter-offer...*]

"That's good, the roads are really dusty, and I know your crops could use the water." [*Refuse counter...*]

"Have you lived here all your life?" [*Test new waters; raise bar, small upward drift...*]

"Yes, other than one year in Lilongwe (the capitol) to try art school." [*New bid too low; won't buy maize; doesn't represent the two months' manual labor...*]

A pair of three-year-olds trundle by; the bulging bellies (from malnutrition) belie the transient joy sparkling in their eyes.

"I will consider X an excellent price ..."

[*Not so fast, a lot of slack left in that rope...*] "Perhaps, papa, but it is *too* excellent a price for me. I am already committed to buying a soapstone family from your neighbor *there* (a finger across the courtyard) and a backgammon board from your friend *there* (two clicks to the left; adjust sextant)."

So it went, as flies buzzed, babies cried, dogs barked and a half-dozen hearty tourists ran the gauntlet. Every vendor had a shtick; a stage name gleaned from god-knows-where, considering this entire village had neither television nor subscription to *People* magazine. I met Elvis Presley, Kokomo Johnny, Bob Marley (whose namesake was an unofficial patron saint in Malawi, along with David Livingstone) and a number of other jokers. In another time and place, they'd have made great DJs or Hip-Hop artists. Their shuck may have been jive, but it was the real thing: the person and persona (their masks) were one. Hunger stalked them, capital lured them, desperation drove them...but they played their parts well.

My price rose like a lake filling up, from 5 to 10 to 20 and beyond (dollars, mind you, as the Malawi *kwacha* is more valuable as toilet paper – which, come to think about it, has considerable value if you're a First World tourist). My host's price dropped from 225 to 100 to 50 to below...We met at the fine apex of $25; he validating his labors and the virtue of his artistry; I, validating the basket's relative market worth (never mind the $400 it could fetch in Soho – *getting it there,* not considered by most casual shoppers, is 95% of the battle.) We respected each other. We were exhausted, and vindicated. We passed and enjoined spirit as it morphed between us, irrespective of language, culture or status. It was the magic carpet, and that afternoon we both flew it.

Lessons Learned from the "Grand Bizarre"

* Don't assume that "Win-Win" negotiations make the world go 'round. It's a great concept invented by the gentility of western nations, and one worthy of integrity. Just realize a lot of the world's merchants don't dance to that tune. Not that others are necessarily trying to "beat you" – although some say the Chinese, in particular, and some Arabs, are taught to do *precisely* that – it's just that they know what they want; and other than taking pride in their handiwork and wanting you to like it, you're just a catalyst for reaching their goal. They could give a tinker's damn whether you "get a good deal" or not. Those who respect the Eleventh Commandment – *Caveat Emptor* – will never go thirsty in paradise.

* Never confuse your host's education level or environment with their business acumen. Market experience *always* trumps schooling, style and appearance. Some of these babushkas and papa-sans in their rickety kiosks have 100 generations behind them – or more – in their respective trade: 12 hours a day, 6-7 days a week, every week, month and year of their straining lives. Really think you're gonna get the hustle on 'em?

✳ Don't get carried away. You'll likely see the same stuff, maybe even better, a few blocks away; or perhaps down the road a few clicks. Also, will you *really* wear, or display, the item? Will your fickle friend, who doesn't know Albania and Zanzibar from a Dr. Seuss book, really be thrilled (other than being nice to you) about that magic amulet or relic? The "exotica" of an item, which may look so apropos in the buying environment, often looks dorky and downright misplaced at home. Remember that "one man's treasure is another man's rubbish" and one woman's "rare find" is another gal's "kitsch."

✳ In Third World markets, carry small bills, if you're dealing in dollars, pounds, euros or Swiss francs. It's an utter drag to negotiate your *pièce de résistance* down to £10 from £20 and find out the proprietor can't (or secretly, won't) change it. Cabbies are the worst, though some shopkeepers give 'em a run for your money (pun intended).

✳ They all know each other (in a given market) – some competitors are even family! Like the ancient shell-game, using planted proxies ("naïve" buyers) as bait, there's only one winner in a battle of egos – and it ain't gonna be you. If the item is common, one man's low price is likely to be the same as another. Trick is, can you figure out what that is? The exception – which is definitely not for the queasy – are the markets run by the truly disenfranchised; the *real* hungry (e.g., mostly in Africa and parts of India). The stomach trumps the laws of supply and demand every time. This is doubly true if the customer is carrying hard tradable currency, which is usually a hedge against spiraling inflation. For example, that buck will buy twice as much millet or maize next month as now.

My only rule of thumb is, if I'm truly interested in the item, I'll be "quick" (or risk being encircled in a cloud of locusts from the competition) and generous. Within reason. I'm already bound to get a "good deal" by the very nature of the circumstances: they're desperate. To squeeze the vendor to their last kwacha, dinar, baht or peso is cruel, sadistic and inhumane. If one's willing to enter these places and buy the goods in the first place, please consider that a few more bucks can literally be saving (or prolonging) lives. Your heart will enjoy the "gain" more than your ego will suffer the "loss."

* Do your math before employing your yap, because those complex currency conversions can be tricky. Lowering a previously offered price, out of confusion – as a friend of mine once did – not only humors and/or irritates the vendor, it will embarrass you; and well, the whole thing only gets ugly after that...

One might ponder a million other tips, such as packing small wads of cash in various (zipped) pockets throughout your clothed body; but traveler's security is not the thesis here. Suffice it to say that you'll be fine and have fun if you 1) use common sense; 2) do a little bit of research by browsing around; 3) never confuse "wants" versus "needs"; and 3) don't forget The Golden Rule – *even if others might*. Anything else, and you're a prime candidate for P.T. Barnum's boot camp for suckers. But don't take it personally – anyone who has "skipped the light Fandango" of The Grand Bizarre has battle scars and stories of woe. If not, they're either lying or suffering from advanced Alzheimer's disease.

* * * * * *

Great labor, passion and precision can manifest in a truly quality product. But ultimately, does that object really *mean* anything hanging on our walls, around our necks, on our shelves? I say, it only has significance to the degree that we relate it to the hidden essence that reminds us of who we are (*or would aspire to be*); that we connect to the artist's passion and awareness as they chiseled that stone, brushed that canvas or penned those notes; and that we recognize the inherent perfection and flaws in all – even in a Mona Lisa or a David. I say that the thought behind the intentionally-botched stitch in the quilt of American pioneer women is a form of salvation: a recognition that *all* will succumb, dust to dust – every mansion, every Louvre, Hope Diamond, Bayeaux Tapestry...every Shroud of Turin, Great Wall, sarcophagus and stupa...all of Aunt Betty's heirloom broaches, our Sixth Grade swimming ribbons, every golden chalice, and even every piece of the True Cross. All will decay into the dust and one day vaporize when our sun goes "Nova" (which ironically means "No go" in Latin)...freeing us from the "pull" of gravity and object alike, and allowing us to enjoy the ride and each other without taking it all too seriously.

* * * * * *

Just as "All the world's a stage and all the men and women merely players," so is The Market our mighty mirror, and the players our shadows, saviors, sorcerers and sirens. But we must remember, as author and psychotherapist Sheldon Kopp said, "If you meet the Buddha on the road (e.g., *outside of one's self*) – kill him!"

PART VI
S-T-R-E-T-C-H-ING BEYOND OUR OWN BORDERS

Join the Army. Travel to strange, exotic lands. Meet exciting, unusual people. And kill them.
– 18th Century British military satire

The use of traveling is to regulate imagination by reality.
– Samuel Johnson

Chapter Twenty-Six

The Gulliver Project™: Creating Your Trans-Cultural Connection

In early 2003, I did a lot of staring out of my apartment window in Santiago, Chile. It was a grand view – a bustling skyline, fueled by a decade of nearly ten percent annualized economic growth; embassies and consulates beneath me, waving their flags of many colors, and the Virgin Mary (well, in statue form) towering over the adjacent hillside of Cerro San Cristobal, the latter sloping down to the funky bohemian barrio of Bellavista. On clear days, the towering 20,000-foot wall of the Andes, just a cab ride away and forming the backbone of this 2,700 mile long millipede of a country, lorded over the city of six million like a snowy, silent sentinel.

It wasn't always a perfect view, of course – what in life is? Santiago is prone to horrible air pollution, courtesy of that same gargantuan wall. In addition, considering its location on the southeastern loop of the Pacific's "Rim of Fire," possessing over 100 volcanoes and home of "a 9.5," the world's largest recorded earthquake (or "terremoto)," Chile is a seismic jumping bean. More than once we shook, rattled and rolled in our 12-story crow's nest, praying that Chilean architectural engineering competency was as good as touted. It was the strangest thing, looking down on the embassy of an Eastern European nation and watching its swimming pool still sloshing around long after a 6.9 quake had finished its gyrations.

However, these were small things, and we endured. It had been a fun respite away from the U.S. and was only six months removed from our African sojourn. Alexis and I loved the Chileans. For the most part, they're a friendly, quiet (by Latin standards) and gracious people, somewhere in between the gregarious-but-temperamental Brazilians and proud-but-brooding Argentineans (stereotypes notwithstanding). So we had taken it in, exploring some major chunks of Chile and Argentina, mostly the Lake District ("Little Bavaria") of northern Patagonia, and the valleys and coasts of the Mediterranean-like Central wine country. We had earned our TEFL (Teaching of English as a Foreign Language) certificates in Santiago while simultaneously student teaching.

All the while, I felt like one foot was still out the door – or heading back out the door, to be exact. It was a gnawing restlessness that I call "the Sagittarian Blues." Part of it, I know, was a smoldering desire to go back to work – it had been 15 months since my left-brain had done any heavy lifting; and, as mentioned in a previous chapter, the bank account sure could have used a few doses of whatever health supplement Barry Bonds was taking to chase Hank Aaron's home run record.

The greater part of my ennui, however, was far more difficult to pin down, because this part wasn't just about personal dissatisfaction, boredom or self-centered avarice. Or even fear. A feeling had been brewing for some time, that all of my travels and observations and interactions were merging into some vocational destiny – that I had something to do, something to say, someone to "Be." This wasn't an ego thing – narcissism, status, etc. – rather, it was something with a will of its own that wanted *out* of me by going *through* me and *to* others.

For years, I had pondered ideas that could connect me with global commerce, and directly with other cultures in a manner that wasn't predatory or boring. I had even been a partner in a company in the Natural Foods industry, importing some successful, unique products; we had launched one of our partners' products, "Swedish Oat Milk," so well in North America, it won one of six special prizes handed out by the National Natural Foods Association at the 1996 annual convention in Baltimore. (Not bad, considering that approximately 1,500 new items were launched in that industry each year). But that enterprise eventually succumbed to cash-flow hiccoughs and the politics of international arm-wrestling, and went by the wayside. Altruism notwithstanding, it had never really scratched my itch, anyway.

One morning, sitting on my Chilean couch and sipping coffee in silent reverie, the thought hit me that I wanted to create something that connected people. Not just another NGO (non-governmental organization); not another bureaucracy-riddled U.N. "do-good" placebo or run-of-the-mill pen pal or exchange program; but something that would compel folks to increase our capacity to *understand* each other better. The net result of all of my travels had convinced me that failure to understand each other was the source of many of our global problems and challenges – as well as our national and personal ones.

Those were the seed-thoughts that grew into the roots, trunk, and branches of The Gulliver Project™.

* * * * * *

The Gulliver Project™ owes its name to Lemuel Gulliver, the fanciful 18th Century creation of Jonathan Swift in his classic, *Gulliver's Travels*. Over the course of four voyages, set mythically in the East Indies and Asia, Doctor (and Mariner) Gulliver has a series of frightening, humorous, and intriguing encounters with a variety of beings. As observer, participant, scribe, victim and catalyst, Gulliver deadpans the reader through a satirical parody of humanity, particularly the European customs of his time.

It's all there: the buffoonery of politicians and bumbling bureaucrats; zeal of religious righteousness; legal obfuscation of those wishing to entrench their power by bamboozling the uneducated; class discrimination against those who simply look or act different; military aggrandizement against real-or-imagined enemies; empty (and often callous) sophistry of heartless theoreticians; obstreperous clamor of the mob; and preoccupation with preserving life, beauty, fame and wealth to the detriment of putting meaning *into* life. Like all good epics, *Gulliver's Travels* transcends its time period: The story is eternal.

The Gulliver Project™ is a forum of ideas and approaches, with the specific aim of motivating people to launch experiential-based activities that stimulate trans-cultural awareness, interest, and sensitivity. The core idea is that people, institutions and nations can lead richer lives and have better relations through increased understanding, and celebration of our many cultural differences – and that fun, interactive activities, are the best ways to promote both of these opportunities. To the degree that we become aware of others and cognizant of each other's fears, insecurities and misperceptions, the greater shall be our capacity for positively impacting the world through more enlightened decision making. (Note: "Sensitivity" as mentioned above does not refer to "being nice," e.g., disempowering ourselves to real threats. It refers to the degree to which we become aware of what drives "others" – in the same way that a chief negotiator would want the run-down on the other party.)

The Gulliver Project™ recognizes that we live in a wildly diverse world: religions, philosophies, attitudes, myths and folklore, architecture, food, music and geography. We therefore seek not to find the "best" way, but rather to empower ourselves *with a broader context* for making informed decisions which are ultimately for our highest good and that of others.

The goal: true strength, fueled by compassion and bolstered by knowledge. The Gulliver Project™ is committed to preparing tomorrow's leaders – corporate, civic, religious, institutional and family – for a greater understanding of the world we live in. There will always be disagreements and conflict, but expanded awareness achieves three monumental accomplishments:
1) The ability to defuse potential conflict through greater empathy and understanding;
2) The synergy that is derived from combining the best attributes of each culture, institution, or nation into a greater composite; and
3) The benefits of joy and inspiration that we humans crave when free to experience and explore our inherent desires.

The Gulliver Project™ is all about *positive* intentions and actions. Individuals have an innate curiosity, which when freed from misperceptions or fear and stimulated by fun and adventure, can spark monumental changes.

The Gulliver Project™ is dedicated to the belief that this world *can and will* be a better place if we commit ourselves to a spirit of cooperation and compassion that provides for all people the affordability and easy access to explore, and embrace each other's cultures – and differences.

* * * * * *

Central to The Gulliver Project™ is the belief that *awareness, inclusiveness and involvement are more beneficial in the long run than fear, naiveté and misperceptions; and that activities promoting this "reaching out" can yield untold benefits for humanity.* To that end, The Gulliver Project™'s commitment is to provide stimulating and enriching programs that foster a transpersonal, trans-cultural and transnational infusion of new and shared ideas.

The world is witnessing the paradox of expanding economic coalitions side-by-side with splintering ethnicity, each phenomenon having its own advantages and disadvantages. The tribal / family / clan network is the greatest place where values can be instilled, the first place to give and receive love, and the cultural form where identity takes root; yet, it is also the most vulnerable to exclusivity, isolationism, naïveté and "fear of outsiders" (xenophobia). On the other hand, a "New World Order" based upon conformity to homogeneity at the expense of personal, tribal or cultural identity, is prone to large-scale manipulation by unscrupulous interests. It is also not workable.

Thus we face the central question of our time:

How do we retain the rich identity and colorful customs of our individuality – as unique beings, tribesmen, or nationalities – while learning to appreciate and cooperate with those who are different?

How, in a sense, do we achieve "Unity through Diversity?" That is the crux of The Gulliver Project™: to expand our capacity to make informed decisions, trusting in our innate humanity that our actions – some seemingly opposed to others – can and will provide optimal solutions to quicken our individual predilections, while also developing the strength and solidarity that comes from an expanded sense of humanity.

Awareness alone isn't sufficient. Even a program based on expanded awareness, in the form of "intelligence," does not guarantee peace or beneficial solutions. For example, approximately 70% of Hitler's senior SS officers supposedly possessed doctorate degrees (PhDs) – but other than making the trains run on time, manipulating the egos of a downtrodden people and constructing a highly efficient killing machine, their talents didn't add one iota to the cause of humanity. An effective program must stress cooperation, compromise and synergistic problem-solving through active participation.

We must also nurture compassion for others, seeing ourselves through the eyes of others and asking at all times, "What if I were that person who is dealing with poverty, hardship, suffering, illness? In reversed circumstances, it could indeed be me...*let me feel what it must be like, and honor that person's courage!*"

We do not have to be enlightened, rich, or born under the right astrological sign. But we do have to be willing to WAKE UP, and that's what The Gulliver Project™ is all about. We must truly rub shoulders with others, and reach out – nothing compels as much as curiosity merged with fun, in the form of experience, discovery, and "reward."

The Gulliver Project™ embraces the idea that impassioned individuals, acting in the interest of inclusiveness, can have a critical-mass effect upon humanity. Call it the Hundredth Monkey Principle (named by author Ken Keyes), Critical Mass, or the Ripple Effect. Indeed, our most enduring religious and government models, imperfect as they may be practiced, were sparked by individuals with the highest ideals and spiritual principles rooted in another version of The Golden Rule: "Love thy Neighbor as Thyself..." Consider the current program of *Doctors Without Borders* as an example of inclusiveness... or the universal love of a Mother Teresa, neither a shrinking violet nor naïve do-gooder...or even the single and courageous act of Rosa Parks, refusing to give up her seat at the front of the bus, regardless of the rules about "blacks going to the back." She was a human being also, was she not? We can no longer ignore our "Globalism," nor can we afford to pretend that we are incapable of loving all people as our brothers and sisters.

One of the biggest mistakes people make is in not recognizing their own inherent abilities, or gifts. We all have choices, or "roles" in which our individual creativity and inner genius can flourish. And, through the power of geometric influence, it can explode. "All things connect," said Chief Seattle. "As you believe, so shall it be" said Jesus. I contend those are not cutesy metaphysical ponderings, but the hidden strings that construct the web of humanity and carry the pulses of the Universe – *the reality behind the perceptions*.

The Gulliver Project™ is about waking people up to a wonderful world, even one fraught with dangers. It embraces affirmation of the positive, as accentuated by empowered individuals making constructive contributions to their community, nation and world through a broader understanding of the dynamics of relationship. It is about fostering a greater appreciation of our beautiful gem of a planet, coupled with a respect for the inherent brilliance of our brothers and sisters in all their shapes and forms.

Appendix

What Can *You* Do?

If you've read this far, chances are you want to know more about Trans-Cultural Communication – even, perhaps, how you can get "involved." In the following pages, I've provided a rough systematic way of creating your own Gulliver experience. Think of these suggestions simply as a "jumpstart," or catalyst.

TRAVEL
Student Exchange or Study Abroad
These may be in one's own country, or another one, and often consist of longer term stays, such as for a semester or year. It's one of the best ways to see through the lenses of another culture's perspective – and to test the validity of one's own culture. Many fine institutions offer student exchange programs to kids ages 15-18, including the American Field Service (AFS), Rotary International, AYUSA International, the National Student Exchange (NSE), and others. An excellent list of organizations in North America, the UK, and Australia and a handful of other countries can be found at Yahoo!'s educational directory http://dir.yahoo.com/Education/Programs/Student_Exchange/

One can find a large number of university exchange programs as well. The International Student Exchange Program (ISEP – www.isep.org) is an example.

The *Transitions Abroad* magazine is a great source for finding out more about these experiences: *www.transitionsabroad.com*

Group/club trips
These are a great way to be with peers and still get a healthy dose of another country's culture. For youth, this may include band

and choir trips, Scouts, and other organizations with international chapters. One of my favorite memories is the 1975 World Scout Jamboree in Lillehammer, Norway. Before and after the main event, my group stayed with host families throughout Scandinavia. One of the subtle advantages of this type of program is that when we associate with colleagues (in the host country) who have similar interests, it becomes easier to accept, or at least acknowledge customs we might otherwise reject. The "human factor" of bonding with them allows us freedom to observe a wider variety of human behavior, in many cases, leading to positive experiences. It's well known in the world of sales and marketing that the chances of a "sale" are increased when a common bond is established, such as a hobby, or growing up in the same part of the country, even if it has nothing to do with the product or service being exchanged.

For adults, likewise, it may include professional or recreational groups, photographers, musicians, artists, teachers, bikers/hikers and many more. (Note: There are countless interests, such as ski groups, for example, that by nature of their activity, can serve to insulate one from the real sinew of society. St. Moritz isn't Switzerland, nor is Queenstown representative of New Zealand, nor Portillo of Chile, just as Aspen is only one small slice of America. Definitely go – and have a great time! At least you'll run into other "foreigners," albeit on a chairlift or in a restaurant. But do try and get out in the countryside or in the bohemian part of town, where the *real* stories happen...)

Student Travel

This is a hybrid of Student Exchange and Group/Club trips. Of relatively short duration, for example, during a school break or in the summer, ranging from 8-18 days, often they involve an academic topic (literature, history, language, etc.), even for credit. Some of the better known programs are the National Educational Travel Council (NETC), Passports, Explorica, EF Educational Travel, Global Vistas, and CHA Educational Tours. (A good portal to find these and more is www.schoolcatalogs.net/travel.htm)

A fantastic way for kids to get immersed in the world is through programs that combine travel with educational programs, language, and volunteer work. A great example of this is an organization named The Experiment in International Living, www.usexperiment. org. "Fun-Knowledge-Adventure-Service": it doesn't get any better than that.

Vacations

There are a hundred reasons I could give to spend more time in one's own country – after all, if we're going to be *de facto* ambassadors for our own culture when we go abroad (whether we intend to be or not), shouldn't we get to know "ourselves" better? This is particularly true in large countries, such as the U.S. and Canada, Australia, Russia, China, India, Brazil, etc.

Staying within one's boundaries is particularly compelling for the budget conscious. Nevertheless, international travel doesn't have to be expensive, depending on where, when and how one travels. Furthermore, no matter how vast the differences we may have with subgroups of our own cultural polyglots, the intrepid seeker will *usually* find greater differences once they cross their national boundaries. And no matter how many awe-inspiring mountain ranges, deserts, forests, shorelines and glistening cities we have in our own little slice of paradise, there's always something different "out yonder."

Travel off-season, or at least "shoulder" season. Much of Europe and North America are surprisingly affordable during our "non-tourist" times. Airfares as well as hotels are often greatly reduced; lines are shorter and reservations not as mandatory; the natives more engaging and not as likely to bite. Although Asian economies are growing impressively and their hospitality industry prices are rapidly closing the gap with the West, their countries are affordable year round (Japan is definitely an exception). Most of Latin America and Africa are so inexpensive it's ridiculous (e.g., a bushel of oranges in Morocco for $1USD...Throw in some $2 Russian vodka, and you could make screwdrivers for the entire entourage.)

There are scores of budget travel books (such as *Rough Guides, Frommer's, Fodor's, Lonely Planet, Let's Go!, Rick Steve's Guides, and Moon Handbooks*) with creative ways – and ample listings – to find nutritious food; quiet, safe, and well-situated lodging; and affordable transportation. If you really want to see a place, please don't let price be your final excuse.

Adventure travel. If you hanker to be a modern-day Lawrence of Arabia, Edmund Hillary, David Livingstone or Jacques Cousteau, there's a seemingly unending list of choices for all disciplines. Some are brutal and for masochistic diehards only. Others surround you with modern amenities and 5-star meals (well, maybe 3.5 stars!). Camel trekking across the Outback? Parachuting over the surreal Martian orange of Namibia? Source-to-ocean on the Amazon? Scuba-diving? Sailing? Dogsled racing? Mountaineering? Rafting? Biking? Sailing?

Those with a little time on their hands, desiring a ground-level view of the flora and fauna, should look into "Overlanding" (see reference in *Nyaminyami Throws a Tantrum*). Rugged trucks take guests on extended journeys. Some organizations even operate in all six inhabited continents. In the process, guests mix it up with the locals, participate in numerous "activities" (though usually not strenuous), and take in a copious amount of national parks, cultural/ heritage sites, and of course, pubs and trinkets. Most Overland companies provide trip legs (segments) which can be strategically accessed at different points, so travelers may get on or off at certain locations depending on the desired length and content of their journey. For example, it's possible to go from London to Cape Town (with a little bit of creative ferrying) via multiple routes; all the way across Europe and Asia; and even from northern Alaska to Tierra del Fuego. One can do the entire junket – impressive indeed! – or perhaps just join up for a week or two or four. Not including airfare, travel insurance, or personal curios, the daily cost of these junkets is surprisingly cheap. Most Overland organizations are headquartered out of the UK, and have seen a steady, growing business for the last 20-25 years. Some of the more well-known include Acacia, Go Nomad, Exodus, and Dragoman.

Homestays. A great way to meet the natives is to stay in their homes. They'll feed ya, do your laundry, provide you with valuable inside scoops not found in the best guide books, and show ya where the key is if you want to go out on the town. You can also pick up some of the language in an intimate setting.

A subset of the Homestay category, "Farmstay," enables those boarding with a family to earn their keep. Although this is popular with the backpacking crowd, it generally is not strenuous and any relatively healthy person can participate, if you don't mind pulling fruit off a tree or squeezing udders for a few hours each day. A search of the Internet or travel guides will show that these exist in a surprising number of places, not just in the West, but also in numerous countries in Asia, Africa, and South America as well.

Travel with kids. A surprising number of organizations offer off-the-beaten path trips for families to far-flung places. Rascals in Paradise (U.S.-based) is one such organization

Avoid resorts. What's so bad about kidney-shaped swimming pools, manicured golf courses, swaying palm frocks and smiling attendants? Why, it's all the amenities of home! That's great – if all you care about is insulating yourself from your host country and chilling out for a week. But you'll never feel the pulse and soul of the natives, not even the ones who come to the resort nightly at 7:00 to conduct their fine structured dances or walk on coals to the praise of your "oohs" and "ahs."

Stay in small, funky hotels or family-run *pensions*. One doesn't have to go claptrap – many are quite charming and rustic. So what if you have to walk a few more blocks to get to the Plaza de Armas (central square)? You'll probably benefit from the walk, and it's quiet, if you research well. So what if the privy is shared by several rooms? Just get up early – there's a heckuva lot you've come to see anyway! This may not be quite as intimate as the Homestay (although many are), but the primary reason for staying in this mode (besides being cheaper) is that you'll meet some interesting folks – not just the natives, but fellow travelers. It's easier to chit-chat with that Japanese woman or Dutchman or Argentinean couple when you're sitting at a shared breakfast table with them. You simply get a Deluxe package of cultural immersion for the price of the Basic one. Furthermore, the best "inside" info I've ever received – advice, tips, etc. – has come from the owners of these small family-establishments.

Hostels: These are either privately-run or standards-based associations (such as the International Youth Hostel Federation

—www.yha.org.uk, with a modest 4,000+ hostels in 80 countries). Contrary to popular belief, most of these are not age-limited (some even offer senior discounts), although many do require membership for a modest fee. They provide a glorified dormitory (think two bunk-beds, ergo four people, in an adequate room), or a larger gymnasium-type room with rows of beds. Toilet and shower options run from "shared by room" to locker-room type facilities. They also usually provide some central kitchen facility for those wishing to cook. Some divide visitors by gender; some don't care. Such establishments *can* be very inexpensive (not always), say $6-10 USD per night. But the best feature of hostels is that they are a fabulous way to meet people. I've maintained friendships for years with international Gullivers I've met in hostels. I've also traveled for long stretches with these new acquaintances, or made arrangements to meet them a few weeks hence at a designated spot "up the road."

Sabbaticals (or "Leave of Absence")

These are great if you can get 'em – especially if you get a *paid* leave. But even for those not so fortunate, try to find a way. I guarantee you that with few exceptions (there are always going to be the spoilers of the statistician's curve!) you'd be hard-pressed to find anyone who has ever taken a travel-oriented sabbatical or leave-of-absence that regrets it. In fact *most will say that the experience instigated either a minor or major life-changing perspective*, and upon discovering that, will further tell you to be creative, find the funds and take the time if you really want to enrich your life.

Think it's not practical or affordable? I have never had a paid sabbatical, a guaranteed job waiting for me (other than my cross-country move out of college), or a guaranteed spot reserved for my "leave of absence." I also have never received a severance package, the golden parachute cord of the Midas Age. Nor am I a "Trust-afarian" (a Trust-Fund baby), that small-but-growing subculture that lives off the willed proceeds of a family or other benefactor – darn good work if you can get it!

I'm not saying everyone could or should do it my way…again, it sure helps being a Sagittarian! Furthermore, the compelling will to seek the open road clashed at such fractious angles that (as several stories in this book attest to) I often felt dispossessed, even "depressed." Regardless, I'm convinced that it's entirely possible for a vast majority of middle class citizens (yes, even those with families, though obviously at strategic break points) in most Western countries to immerse themselves in a "Leave" – if they're up to it. To those who would like to do so if only they could muster the courage, I'd recommend Marsha Sinetar's book *Do What You Love, and the Money Will Follow*. Although the book refers to seeking "vocation" as opposed to "vacation," it nonetheless speaks to following one's heart – and travel, for many, is one hell of a way to do it.

In Fiji I once met a South African couple who had most recently lived in London. They'd quit their jobs and with their seven-year old son were taking a year off to see the world. They had bought "Round-the-World" air-passes (see www.airbrokers.com for a good web portal), some of which are surprisingly cheap. The passes may allow prolonged stop-offs at more than 10 locations, which in turn can act as central hubs for travels to outlying regions or even other countries via boat, ship, bus or train. The family was staying in simple hotels or pensions and eating cheaply. Every time they landed somewhere new, it was all the parents could do to stop their youngster from running pell-mell into the nearest village to start playing with the native kids – *after* he had finished his homework, that is! Seems like Mom and Dad had received a year's worth of school assignments from his approving teachers and were enforcing his disciplines to the letter. But what an education! No offense to the London School of Economics, or Dale Carnegie sales classes, or Survivor/Reality TV shows – but no school, employer or organization for the rest of his life will ever be able to provide the depth and breadth of that year's experiences. I'd like to meet him when he's in his thirties or forties – he'll sure be an interesting fellow, and probably doing something very worthwhile for the world.

Volunteering

Volunteer opportunities exist in many capacities, for short or long durations, in and out of one's own country. By definition, volunteering can fit into any of the above "vacation" modes. Numerous roles are available for both trained professionals and those wishing to just donate their brawn and good cheer.

Professional: Healthcare workers; math / science / language / computer science teachers; business professionals (sales / marketing / economics / finance); agronomists; civil engineers; mechanics / craftsman; and many others are always high in demand. For example, Doctors Without Borders ("Médecins Sans Frontières") has volunteer emergency medical personnel in over 80 countries. State-sponsored organizations, such as the (American) Peace Corps, exist in all countries in the Western World and many developing countries as well. NGOs (Non-Governmental Organizations) are also plentiful.

Other organizations such as Habitat for Humanity, WorldTeach, the Earthwatch Institute, Health Volunteers Overseas, and Cross-Cultural Solutions have a wide variety of short (1-2 week) to long (1-2 year assignments) throughout the world. Many of these roles don't require professional degrees or experience, as long as one has done some basic training or low-level certification within the organization (though often some type of college degree is preferred, even if not pertinent to the designated volunteer position).

Remember – you don't have to leave your own country! For example, Habitat for Humanity (a non-proselytizing Christian organization) operates in over 1,500 locations in the U.S. alone. In the U.S., thousands of volunteer roles are available to people 17+ under the auspices of the federally funded Corporation on National and Community Service (AmeriCorps and Senior Corps are two examples). You will definitely be exposed – immersed – in working with individuals of different ethnic and economic classes.

Some great sources for information on international volunteer opportunities can be found in International Living (www.internationalliving.com) and Transitions Abroad (www.transitionsabroad.com) magazines, and The International Directory of Volunteer Work (Louise Whetter). An impressive collection of volunteer (and ex-pat, exchange, etc.) organizations is chronicled in *The Global Citizen* (and www.the-global-citizin.com) by Elizabeth Kruempelmann. Another excellent book is Stephen Wearing's

Volunteer Tourism: Experiences That Make a Difference. [A wonderful all-purpose travel and sightseeing book for vacationers and adventurers is Patricia Schultz' *1,000 Places to See Before You Die.*]

CONTESTS / GAMES / COLLABORATIONS

One of the best ways to stimulate Trans-cultural Communication is through competition and/or collaboration. These activities can entertain, inform, and spark involvement, or at least interest. Games and contests are great for this, as are all the Arts. Many venues don't require travel or don't necessarily involve competing or collaborating with participants outside their own countries. However, all may involve subject matter from outside one's own country or culture.

Some extremely valuable themes could be conveyed through venues that stress:

* Fact-finding about other countries and cultures, presented vicariously around a plot or specific subject matter. Entertainment, and ideally interactive involvement can make this experience fun; the "learning" becomes incidental.

* Conflict and resolution – or not. Conflict (e.g., culture clash) can be presented humorously, satirically (bittersweet humor, with subtle messages), such as *Gulliver's Travels*; or seriously (Helen DeWitt's *The Last Samurai*). Paradox, and/or the arbitrary nature of cultural "truths," is a great theme.

* Beauty! Conveying the awesome grandeur of this world is always uplifting. Mother Gaia is a compelling subject when one considers that, other than telescopes, space craft transmissions and the occasional Out-of-Body experience, all we know of "existence" is right here on Earth!

* Brotherhood & Sisterhood: These modes would emphasize, or at least subtly suggest that our commonalities dwarf our differences. (To paraphrase Crocodile Dundee, the clashing of rigid belief systems is like "fleas fighting over who owns the dog.")

* Adventure! Plots that entertain us with physical, mental, emotional or spiritual challenge and entertainment. "Movement" is the key.

Note to educators and commercial entrepreneurs: A great many of the categories listed above lend themselves to practical implementation in the classroom. Many of these can be done inexpensively; others may require capital and complex logistics. There is almost no end to the possibilities for constructive "contests." It is the hope of The Gulliver Project™ that the lessons and experiences received by younger people, say, junior high through college, will bear fruit in future generations through more enlightened decisions, as they take their place as civic, corporate, clerical leaders.

Enterprising, creative (and in some cases, well financed) folks might consider a few of these modes:

Software games

* These could be for kids/students or adults. Factual, or fictitious. Some could be highly entertaining. Consider that *Where in the World is Carmen Sandiego?* with its array of chases and clues across different countries, was the most highly *adult-watched* kids' television show of all time in the U.S. (A great game out now is Strategy First's "Europa Universalis," a multi-dimensional, intense version of the old board game Risk, complete with diplomats, armies and navies, terrains, rebellions and insurrections, and other variables depicting real-life power struggles between nations and cultures. A bit predatory, for sure, but a very good "teacher" of what has driven world politics for centuries. Good or bad – it helps to know.)

* Points can be tracked online to display achievement. Wrapping this into well-promoted contests could result in grand prizes of educational trips, products "toys" from corporate co-sponsors, or even cash.

Board games

Yes, there's still a great market for games not requiring "joy sticks." Moreover, these can attract parents or others who currently shun or spend minimal time at the computer. The classic *Risk* games from Parker Brothers, though a bit predatory, involving "conquest" by cleverly mustering and allocating military assets throughout global regions, are a great example. Some peaceful themes might include:

∗ Successful navigation of geographical features – think a Marco Polo expedition, or Speek and Burton seeking the headwaters of the Nile, Shackleton wandering in Antarctica. What are points being awarded or subtracted for – avoiding (or not!) obstacles, confrontation (peace vs. war), and natural disasters; finding food; making discoveries; acquiring riches or creating a trade pact, etc.? These so-called "expeditions" also could be races, challenges, etc. A favorite book, *Road Fever*, by Tim Cahill, humorously chronicles the journey of the author and his buddy who beat the overland speed record from Barrow, Alaska, to Tierra del Fuego (23 days, officially). It requires all of their wit, skill and a fair amount of luck to avoid disasters, stay out of jail, bribe border guards, acquire help, etc.

∗ Trading/transacting currencies and commodities across regions: what affects positive vs. negative points – weather, supply distributions, labor strikes, government policies, currency devaluations, war, competitors or substitute products, unemployment, new technologies, joint ventures – collaboration, "co-opetition?" Outsourcing vs. "Insourcing?"

∗ "Good works" having measurable impact upon communities or individuals. This could involve the best way to deploy precious assets – money, land, teachers/ideas, infrastructure, etc. Philanthropy, NGO organizations, and "non-proselytizing" missionary efforts would be good examples. A good role model for this, which could be greatly expanded upon, is the movie *Pay it Forward* (Warner Bros.) where people repay favors they've anonymously received by doing more good works – also anonymously – for others.

∗ "Negotiations" to achieve goals with calibrated point rewards. Ideally, but not necessarily trying to achieve one's goals without causing the other to "lose honor." For example, contestants must employ a variety of different cultural norms: consider that for the Chinese, "there is no absolute truth," for the Italians, "truth is relative," for Americans and Germans, "truth (contracts) is absolute," etc. Consider that for Japanese, silence is strength and for Americans it's deemed weakness; consider that certain cultures see the "Win-Win" approach as honorable and others see it as naïve; some see table positioning (who sits where) as irrelevant while to others it's critical.

* Adventure / Chase / Investigation / "Race with the clock" thrillers – such as *Where in the World is Carmen Sandiego?* (mentioned above, and now a game by The Learning Company). How about a global version of *Clue*, where contestants have to learn certain phrases, recognize certain dress codes, identify certain foods, get acquainted with certain monuments or markers (manmade or natural), seek certain benefactors and avoid bad guys, etc.?

Dozens of genres could be explored – and in truth, there's a lot out there already. But I'm convinced there's tremendous latitude for market success with the right product package and the right marketing.

"Scavenger Hunts"

This is a loose term for international contests requiring geo-physical involvement by a team. This team could be all from one country/culture; or better yet, an international team. The latter could be generated through people signing up through a web portal – it wouldn't take a lot of creativity or cost for the right website and promotion to make this vehicle known internationally.

What would this look like? One (team) might have to track down, find, and/or collect actual icons or artifacts from somewhere – perhaps something unique, or something in a particular category that's represented by all. Like some of the games or movies mentioned above, this could be a global version of Hasbro's *Dungeons and Dragons*, although not necessarily focused on the "macabre." In fact, myths and legends are great teachers of a culture's background and mores.

As with software games, educational versions of this could be created (say, ages 12- 18; even collegiate versions) that could result in paid educational trips, prizes, cash, etc., that may even bring together a team at some international cultural festivals.

Artistic Collaborations

Many artistic outlets exist, either competitive or collaborative, for exploring Trans-cultural Communication. As with several of the other genres, these can be structured via contests with attractive rewards, gifts, etc.

* *Independent Film*: Conflict/resolution of cultural clashes, either humorously or seriously. What about a contest for high school and college kids? Rewards can be trips to other countries; honorariums at independent film festivals; introduction to celebrities or industry spokespersons; or commercial backing (if you're a philanthropist or investor) for presentation to distributors. Think a more "organic version" of the Sundance Film Festival aimed specifically at schools/youth.

* *Music*: Same as above, in its respective genre. If you're a musician or singer, learn how to play/sing instruments and/or songs from other cultures; play/sing with musicians from those cultures if possible. If you're an entrepreneur, sponsor collaborations, ethnic music events, tours, etc.

As with film, a large number of international festivals provide quality exposure to new, interesting talent. A key advantage of the technology age is that both genres, film and music, allow for production and "mixing" without the logistical rigors of old-fashioned recording; e.g., having to travel to centralized production studios.

* *Literature / Writing* projects with Trans-cultural themes: How about developing a cultural conflict and resolution theme (a "brand") that can be replicated (think of the.... *for Dummies* series by Wiley and Sons) by other authors, including other countries. For example, a theme could be a mythical family from Country A that goes to Country B – what happens to them, independently and/or separately? These stories could be fictional or factual; e.g., based on the author's real experiences. And they don't have to be your mom and dad's *Bobbsey Twins*, either! The stories could be racy, satirical, risqué, frightening, unsettling, provocative, hilarious, etc. Or the theme could be much broader – simply any character either visiting another culture, or entertaining/encountering visitors – think Jonathan Swift's *Gulliver's Travels*, or Mark Twain's *The Innocents Abroad*.

An entrepreneur along these lines could "contract" out work, even through contests, to prospective international authors – and receive valuable inroads into widespread distribution (not to mention receiving royalties through the use of their trademark/brand).

* *Photography*: As with music or film, this genre lends itself to contests, awards, recognition, etc. This doesn't have to be a rehash of the last hundred years of *National Geographic*. Innovative themes could be developed and presented as a "side-by-side" collage: smiles from around the world; an international fashion show; dances; foods; skylines; churches and temples; athletics; a gauntlet of emotions (joy, rage, anger, pride, sloth, etc.) across a rainbow of ages and cultures. The list of topics seems endless.

TRANS-CULTURAL (and/or "Trans-belief") EVENTS
Attend Ethnic Festivals

Most mid-size and all large cities in the Western World have ethnic festivals. It's a great way to have a first hand experience: wonderful food, clothing, dance, arts & crafts, folklore, music, and more. If you're a member of an ethnic-community (American-Czech, or British-Indian) definitely participate: you'll be doing your fellow citizens an inestimable favor by exposing them to your culture/ethnic roots in a fun, non-threatening way. Think of yourself as a playful teacher. Consider launching such an event if it doesn't already exist in your community. You'll probably find resources at your disposal that you didn't know about.

These events do not have to occur in metropolitan areas of the country. Consider North American Indian Pow Wows, Aboriginal Didgeridoo ceremonies, or the Maori Matariki (kites!) festivals in New Zealand.

Attend Foreign Movies

These are found in most mid-to-large Western World cities, and many other venues in both developed and developing countries. Just like home, not all are good but a disproportionate number of foreign flicks coming to your town have probably won some international film awards, so generally the quality will tend to be respectable, and you're guaranteed to learn something you didn't know before. The important thing, of course, is to note that all people, cultures and nations have their fair share of problems and joys; they're human, just like us.

Attend A(nother) Church Service

Even if theology isn't your goblet of wine – but especially if it is – drop in on your neighbor's friendly service. Whether you're from one of the main franchises, or a Wiccan, Rastafarian, Rosicrucian or Zoroastrian, you don't have to buy the party line, or pad the collection basket…but it might be beneficial to experience some of the different ways that others s-t-r-e-t-c-h (or sadly, contract), for a sense of higher meaning in life. We're all struggling humans (cats excepted) and as Jim Morrison said, "No one here gets out alive." Best to give the tribe the benefit of the doubt, even when they say their way is the "only way." If you don't like it or if you're indifferent, don't go back. Now, was that so difficult?

Attend Trans-cultural Speeches

Here in my latest Port O'Call of Scottsdale, Arizona, the city government sponsors a wonderful series of events called "Diversity and Dialogue." Interesting speakers, some known and some not, talk about a variety of racial, ethnic, and religious issues facing us as a society. These talks are free and they even serve you dinner if you pre-register! As you might expect, the speakers are "insiders" – e.g., a holocaust victim, a civil rights crusader, a successful entrepreneur within a challenged community, etc. – and have some compelling personal stories to relate.

Likewise, most universities feature a variety of modestly priced symposiums with well-known speakers representing a cadre of foreign affairs, cultural exchanges, etc. Keep your eyes open, especially for the ones where the speakers themselves are from that "foreign" country or culture.

Pen Pal Networks

These have been around for decades, but they no longer have to be the old-fashioned airmail letter slowly going back and forth. The Internet and video streaming have opened up a whole other realm with applications in the classroom. Imagine entire classes regularly corresponding with counterparts; say respective geography (or language) classes of British and Chileans; or Australian and Swedes. All kinds of contests and/or projects could easily emerge from this, collectively or between individual pairings of students.

Go to your local bookstore, library or Internet terminal.

Access stories and current events from locales that intrigue you.

CURRENT MEDIA

Often we don't realize how affected we are by the bombardment of media that hits our eyes and ears daily. If you gravitate toward one selected medium, ask yourself if it's because a) you agree with it the most; b) have "always" followed it; c) you learn the most from it; or d) they have the least-offensive commercials.

Just as "You are what you eat," I'd suggest you are also "what you see, hear, and think." Considering how much of our media is controlled by corporate sponsors or special interest groups, the best that can be said is that we receive "selective truth." (We won't talk about the *worst* that can be said). If for no other reason than to try to make that net a little wider, try changing and possibly adding to the agenda.

TV / Radio / Newspaper / Internet:

A mainstream person in the U.S. (e.g., one who follows ABC, CBS, NBC, CNN, Fox, MSN, etc.) could give PBS or NPR a whirl. If you're a Brit committed to *The Economist* (great stats) or *The Sun* (great stacks!), try out the *Red Pepper* or *Spiked*. If you're tired of hearing/reading Michael Moore, Al Franken, Rush Limbaugh and Anne Coulter mud-wrestle each other across their respective polarized camps, follow some centrists for a while. For those who are committed followers of any of the preceding, see if you can read, listen (to), or watch their adversary's book/show "objectively." It's possible some of your views may get altered, if you're brave and industrious enough to check the veracity of the comments. Truths, half-truths, and half-non-truths can be found in all forms of media. (And don't forget to check into who's paying their bills and depositing their proceeds.)

WORK / VOCATION

The capability of professionals to positively impact others about our wide world is tremendous. People who travel internationally, work ex-pat assignments or just intermingle with "foreigners" have a lot to say to us about the challenges and rewards of "getting along." They've got some pretty good tales to tell, as well. If you happen to be one of these folks, consider the following mediums:

Public Speaking (about your Trans-cultural experience)

Venues may include: Rotary International groups in your town; churches, schools, camps, career days, etc. Bring slides, digital pictures, and cool memorabilia.

Conversely, inquire with the consulates (or divisions of foreign companies) of other countries if they would send some of *their* staff out to speak to your function.

Seek ex-pat assignments

Many large companies and some mid-sized ones who have international dealings, have ex-pat assignments available for employees who don't mind trading some of the comforts of home for the excitement and rewards of working abroad. The pay is usually good and benefits can be exceptional, although the conditions and cultural challenges (languages, customs, etc.) might be a little testy. Not for the faint-hearted, but very rewarding. A great source of practical information can be found in Robert Kohl's *Survival Kit for Overseas Living*. There are even books for children of ex-pat families, such as *Where in the World Are You Going?* By Judith Blohm.

Retirement or self-driven "exile"

The days when the wealthy trundled off to paradise and hung out on golf courses and hammocks haven't completely disappeared. But look closer and you'll find a whole new world of vibrant and engaged retirees of modest means having meaningful and productive lives in other countries.

Considering the cost of land in many countries (relative to the richer societies of the West), and an emerging paradigm of more active, inquisitive retirees, there are tremendous opportunities to rub shoulders with new cultures – and to bring your experiences back to your country to share with friends, family and colleagues.

A couple of great sources of information can be found at www. escapeartist.com and www.internationalliving.com. These web portals are gold mines for retirees or self-proscribed ex-pats, with excellent contacts for real estate and investment information, employment opportunities, health care, government contacts, local associations, volunteer roles, moving and adjusting information, hobbies/networks, other people's stories (what you're getting into!), and a wealth of demographic information.

ADVOCACY (of Trans-cultural, or commonly shared topics)

This can be *for* something, or *against* something. The objective is not to take sides; rather, to remind folks that this is a privilege of a free democracy. One can participate usually without having to worry about the government or shadowy special interests interrogating, shooting or incarcerating you. Usually. Besides, they might even like your idea.

Industry/Trade interests (cross-border)

Do you have empathetic colleagues in other countries? Contact them (find their websites, get commercial affiliations from their consulate's commercial/trade arm or Chamber of Commerce affiliate). Start a website; advertise. Take advantage of whatever government programs may aid your cause. Lead a boycott if it seems appropriate. Or, just the opposite – speak out *for* something (organic food products, alternative energy sources, the longer-lasting light bulb.) Speak to officials, industry counterparts, media, politicians, vendors, customers. Many will share your interest, or inadvertently show you to someone who does. As stated before, a common cause is a great way to witness humanity stretching across all cultural and ethnic borders.

Students

Find international peers who share your concerns and interests. Are there common issues with environmental regulations? Sex education? Food safety? Drug laws? Juvenile Crime? You're not too young to get involved if one can grasp a subject, talk, and/or push the "send" button. Ideas and approaches used elsewhere may have a profound impact upon someone halfway around the globe.

Write your congressman, MP, emir, countess or chief. Get signatures. "Lobby" (emails, phone calls, petition drives, etc.) the embassies and consulates of affiliated countries – ideally, with your counterparts within those countries. Start grassroots media show'n'tell in your home town, and don't forget to share the digital pix or streaming video with your counterparts. Create clever ways to contact and get endorsement and participation from celebrities – they love to be affiliated with "causes" (think Bono and African AIDS, or Sting and the Amazon Rainforest). Absorb and enforce the idea that *we are all connected.*

Peace-Exchange Initiatives: There are a growing number of "special project" organizations popping up around the world committed to bridging cultures that have been (recently, or historically) at odds with one another. Many of these are a combination of advocacy, volunteering, and student exchange. Seeds of Peace (promoting Arab-Israeli exchanges and camps) and The Ulster Project (likewise, promoting Catholic and Protestant harmony in Northern Ireland) are two examples.

READ & WATCH THE "GREAT WORKS"

All of the following represent, to me, great "travelers" of geography, mind, and/or soul/spirit/heart. These examples are only intended to be navigational points, like buoys. Obviously, many significant works are not included in this list; it's just a starter or launching pad, and I invite you to add the many other qualified works that have enriched your life and provided great inspiration.

I have intentionally omitted the names of works that have only vaguely crossed over the travel theme. For example, the works of Hemingway – exotic locations but dwelling more on personal *angst* than cultural interchange – don't necessarily focus on the inclusiveness aspects of Trans-cultural Communication. No disrespect intended – just that the author had different fish to fry. Certainly trying to list great thinkers or travelers of the Mind would be as futile as counting the grains of sand at the seashore: And let's not forget that many of these mental giants were anything but inclusive or magnanimous.

Cinema/Theater – where to start? Many of us are familiar with contemporary works of a Steven Spielberg, or the works of a George Bernard Shaw, Samuel Beckett, Fellini or Bergmann, who are all masters of Trans-cultural Communication collisions – but what about the scores of culture clash (conflict/resolution/paradox) streaming out of Japan, Argentina, India, South Africa, Romania, et al? I'd suggest keeping your eyes on the play list of your local Import/Alternative flick houses.

As long as the overarching topic of Trans-cultural Communication is covered, nothing is sacred. Thus examples are found from many different slants: Geo-politics and Economics, Ecology, Spirituality, Quantum Physics, Fiction (including Science Fiction and Poetry), Human Potential, Adventure, etc. Some of these represent schools of thought deemed heretical by some, but I feel the subject matter demands honest inquiry. Hence, I might condone a work not necessarily for the opinions expressed but for the richness of the subject covered. For example, despite the love affair modern romanticists have with Che Guevara's *The Motorcycle Diaries*, we conveniently forget that he feverishly urged Castro to launch Soviet nukes into the U.S. during the 1962 Cuban Missile Crisis, which would have essentially started World War III and ruined Che's future T-shirt market.

GREAT TRAVELS

* *Anything/Everything by*: National Geographic / Royal Geographic Society (and equivalents in all countries); James Michener, Rudyard Kipling, Jack London, Thomas Costain; Alexander Dumas; Herodotus and Pliny (travel historians of antiquity); EM Forster; D.H. Lawrence

* *Traveler's Tales*: a series of publications by Larry Habegger and Sean, James, and Tim O'Reilly; "Publishers of Stories, Wit and Wisdom from Travelers Around the World"; *A Book of Traveler's Tales*: Assemblage by Eric Newby from famous, infamous, and anonymous personages throughout world history; *The Travels of Marco Polo*: (autobiography) 24 years, 15,000 miles, and a "Who's Who" of The Silk Road; *The Long Walk* (Slavomir Rawicz) an unbelievable survival trek (which some critics believe is a hoax); *Undaunted Courage* (Stephen Ambrose's account of the Lewis and Clark saga, which required Native American assistance for its very survival)

* Misc. Epics: *The Arabian Nights*; *The Iliad and Odyssey*; *The Gilgamesh*; *Milton's Paradise Lost*; *Dante's Divine Comedy*, *Goethe's Faust*; *King Arthur Legends*; *The Lord of the Rings*, etc.

THE SATIRISTS (the Classics)
* Jonathan Swift (*Gulliver's Travels*); Geoffrey Chaucer (*The Canterbury Tales*); Miguel Cervantes (*Don Quixote*); Francois Voltaire (*Candide*); Lewis Carroll (*Alice in Wonderland*); Mark Twain (*A Connecticut Yankee in King Arthur's Court*, *The Innocents Abroad*); Boccaccio (*The Decameron*); James Joyce (*Gulliver's Travels*)

THE DHARMA SEEKERS
* Herman Hesse (*Siddhartha, Magister Ludi*); Peter Matthiessen (*The Snow Leopard*); Dante Alighieri (*The Inferno*); Somerset Maugham (*The Razor's Edge*); Scott Peck (*The Road Less Traveled*); William Least Heat Moon (*Blue Highways, Riverhorse*); Robert Pirsig (*Zen and the Art of Motorcycle Maintenance*); Ernesto Guevara (*The Motorcycle Diaries*), Antoine Marie Roger de Saint Exupéry (*Wind, Sand, and Stars*), Roger Housden (*Sacred Journeys in a Modern World*), Joseph Dispenza (*The Way of the Traveler*), Rosemary Mahoney (*The Singular Pilgrim*)

THE BIG BOOKS
* *The Bible* (ah, but which one? There are 200+ versions, not including language translations); *The Koran/Quoran*; *The Bhagavad-Gita / Mahabharata / Vedas / Upanishads*; *The Torah*, *The Tao Te Ching*;

The *Kabbalah*; the *Avesta* (Zorastrian); the *Tipitaka* (Buddhist); the *Sri Guru Granth Sahib* (Sikh); the *Book of Mormon, The Kalevala* (Rosicrucian)…and guess what? There's a whole bunch more…(there are estimated to be between 2,500 and 9,000 religions – at last count)

THE MUSES (WORKS OF)

٭ Shakespeare! Jalaluddin Rumi (Sufi poet); Kahlil Gibran (*The Prophet*); Francis Assisi; the "Antiquity" plays of Sophocles, Euripides, and Aeschylus; Meister Eckhart (medieval mystic); Aesop's Fables; Lao Tzu & Confucius; Thomas Merton (*Contemplation in a World of Action*; and *No Man is an Island*); the Dalai Lama (Tenzin Gyatso)

"TERRA GNOSIS" – (World Knowledge) – works by *or about*:

٭ Gurdjieff ("multimodal" teachings corresponding to mind, emotions, and body); Tielhard de Chardin (Jesuit-turned scientist: *The Phenomenan of Man*; Carlos Castaneda (*A Separate Reality*); Fritjof Capra (*The Tao of Physics*; and *The Turning Point*); Ken Wilbur (a modern day hybrid of Gurdjieff and Chardin); Barbara Marx Hubbard (futurist or change agent?: see *Conscious Evolution*); Joseph Campbell (*The Power of Myth*); Jose Arguelles (*The Mayan Factor* and other time/space trips); Thich Nhat Hanh; Paramahansa Yogananda (*The Autobiography of a Yogi*); Krishnamurti; Jack Kornfield (*A Path With a Heart*); Shunryu Suzuki (*The Three Pillars of Zen*); Martin Luther King; Mahatma Gandhi; Hildegard of Bingen (visionary/ mystic, musician, scholar, diplomat, and sexual libertine – quite the hat-trick for a 12th Century nun!); Wayne Dyer (*The Power of Intention*; *Your Erroneous Zones*, etc.); Arthur C. Clarke (*2001: A Space Odyssey*; *Childhood's End*)

THE TRANSCENDENTALISTS

٭ William Blake, Walt Whitman (*Leaves of Grass*), Henry David Thoreau (*Walden*), Ralph Waldo Emerson, Frederick Douglas, Nathanial Hawthorne, Emily Dickenson, and a cast of thousands

CONTEMPORARY CULTURAL COLLISION-ISTS: GEO-POLITICS, SATIRE, ENVIRONMENT, AND "ALL THAT IS"

* Tom Robbins (Everything is sacred – and nothing is sacred; with scores of far-flung exploits poking us that "life is too mysterious to be taken serious"); Barbara Kingsolver (*The Poisonwood Bible, Pigs in Heaven*, etc.); Tim Cahill (*Road Fever* and other madcap, zany escapades to the four corners of nowhere); Paul Theroux (regarded by some as "The greatest living travel writer"); Pico Iyer (everything!); Isabel Allende (*My Invented Country*); Salman Rushdie (uh, is it blasphemy just to *recommend* him?); Alice Walker (*The Black Woman's Book of Travel and Adventure*); Thomas Friedman (*The World is Flat*, and *Longitudes and Attitudes*); Václav Havel (diverse poetry and stories); Alexander Solzhenitsyn (*The Gulag Archipelago*); Paul Hawken (*Natural Capitalism* – a recipe for a new, ecologically-sound "industrial revolution"); Jimmy Carter (lots); Desmond Tutu (tons); Richard Lewis (*When Cultures Collide* and *The Cultural Imperative: Global Trends in the 21ˢᵗ Century*); Bill Bryson (*A Short History of Nearly Everything* and *Notes from a Small Island*)

> *But real adventures, I reflected, do not happen to people who remain at home: they must be sought abroad.*
> – James Joyce